AEPA®

Early Childhood Education Practice Questions

Mometrix
TEST PREPARATION

DEAR FUTURE EXAM SUCCESS STORY

First of all, **THANK YOU** for purchasing Mometrix study materials!

Second, congratulations! You are one of the few determined test-takers who are committed to doing whatever it takes to excel on your exam. **You have come to the right place.** We developed these practice tests with one goal in mind: to deliver you the best possible approximation of the questions you will see on test day.

Standardized testing is one of the biggest obstacles on your road to success, which only increases the importance of doing well in the high-pressure, high-stakes environment of test day. Your results on this test could have a significant impact on your future, and these practice tests will give you the repetitions you need to build your familiarity and confidence with the test content and format to help you achieve your full potential on test day.

Your success is our success

We would love to hear from you! If you would like to share the story of your exam success or if you have any questions or comments in regard to our products, please contact us at **800-673-8175** or **support@mometrix.com**.

Thanks again for your business and we wish you continued success!

Sincerely,
The Mometrix Test Preparation Team

Printed in the United States of America

TABLE OF CONTENTS

PRACTICE TEST #1 1
ANSWER KEY AND EXPLANATIONS FOR TEST #1 20
PRACTICE TEST #2 38
ANSWER KEY AND EXPLANATIONS FOR TEST #2 56

Practice Test #1

1. Of the following, which is correct regarding arts education in early childhood?

a. EC teachers should focus on assigning separate art activities so children realize art's importance.
b. EC teachers enhance learning and comprehension by integrating art into the overall curriculum.
c. EC teachers are told by many state standards to integrate art into units but not whole curricula.
d. EC teachers who assign art process activities should be giving children any rules or steps in advance.

2. Piaget described children as "little scientists" interacting and experimenting with the environment to learn about it and actively build their own knowledge. This reflects which type of philosophy and psychology?

a. Scaffolding
b. Cognitivism
c. Constructivism
d. Zone of Proximal Development

3. After a reading fluency check, a first-grade teacher has noticed that a student is struggling to distinguish between open and closed syllables when reading aloud. Which of the following interventions would likely best support the student's development of this skill?

a. Reviewing how to blend and segment syllables
b. Having the student sound out words letter by letter
c. Providing direct instruction on the beginning, middle, and final phonemes in words
d. Having the student practice forming words with letter tiles and reading them aloud

4. For a lesson on basic multiplication facts, a third-grade teacher provides each student with an individual whiteboard and manipulatives. During the lesson, the teacher shows several problems on the board for students to solve using their manipulatives, and asks them to write their answers on the whiteboards to hold up when they're finished. This activity is an example of which of the following formative assessment approaches?

a. Total participation techniques
b. Informal observation
c. Think-pair-share
d. Student self-assessment

5. A third-grade teacher is planning a unit on identifying and writing compound sentences. Which of the following instructional strategies would best support students' understanding of this concept?

a. Creating a word wall with a list of common conjunctions
b. Asking students to identify compound sentences in grade-level reading passages
c. Implementing sentence-dictation exercises
d. Having students practice the concept using sentence-building strips

6. A fourth-grade teacher is planning a multi-day unit in which students will write a short research essay on a topic of their choosing. Students will first brainstorm topics using a graphic organizer, and, after a demonstration, will gather relevant supporting evidence for their topics using color-coded notecards. Students will then create an outline of their essay and begin a rough draft, which will be peer-edited prior to writing the final version. By incorporating these activities into the unit, the teacher is planning to guide students through which of the following?

a. Strategies for editing writing using language conventions
b. A formative assessment of students' writing skills
c. Foundational steps of the research process
d. How to use transitional words and phrases to manage the sequence of events

7. After completing a unit on continuity and change over time, a second-grade teacher wants to evaluate students' ability to use timelines for recording events. Which of the following assessment approaches would be most effective in achieving this goal with students of this age group?

a. Observing students as they sequence events from a fictional story
b. Assigning students to write a biographical essay about a prominent historical figure
c. Having students create an autobiographical timeline
d. Having students identify past, present, and future events on a classroom calendar

8. Which of the following activities is most focused on children's *identifying* patterns?

a. Stringing beads with different colors in a certain order to make a necklace design
b. Counting the number of blue dots before a green dot appears in a printed fabric
c. Arranging alternating pieces of different sizes and gluing them to paper or board
d. Hopping two times on one foot, then the other; then three times each; four; etc.

9. Print awareness skills typically demonstrated independently by preschoolers include:

a. Recognizing printed letters, but not necessarily also printed words.
b. Reciting the alphabet, but not identifying single letters in isolation.
c. Recognizing printed words, but not using these for communicating.
d. Reciting ABCs; recognizing letters and words; print communication.

10. Which of the following statements is NOT true about the Gilded Age in America?

a. The Gilded Age was the era of the "robber barons" in the business world.
b. The Gilded Age got its name from the excesses of the wealthy upper class.
c. The Gilded Age had philanthropy Carnegie called the "Gospel of Wealth".
d. The Gilded Age is a term whose origins have not been identified clearly.

11. A first-grade teacher works with a beginner-level ELL student who has minimal previous experience with the English language. After reading an illustrated book aloud to the class, the teacher asks the student to sort events from the story using pictures and a graphic organizer. The student is then asked to describe his favorite character to his table partner. These activities demonstrate the teacher's understanding of which of the following in regard to implications for teaching ELL students?

a. Beginner-level ELLs can understand general language related to the content area and can produce short, simple sentences.
b. It is important to incorporate linguistic aids to help beginner-level ELLs.
c. Social language is developed in collaborative settings for beginner-level ELLs
d. Academic language is typically more difficult for ELLs to acquire

12. Of the four parenting styles identified by psychologists, which one is found most likely to result in children who have problems with authority figures, poor school performance, and poor self-regulation?

a. Authoritarian
b. Permissive
c. Authoritative
d. Uninvolved

13. For developmentally appropriate instruction of young children, which essential aspects should educators consider?

a. The child's age is more important than individual child growth patterns.
b. The child's individual growth patterns supersede any cultural influences.
c. Cultural influences are more significant than age or growth patterns.
d. Age, individual growth patterns, and cultural influences are all essential.

14. A prekindergarten teacher has decorated the classroom with brightly colored posters, signs, and charts, and frequently refers to them throughout the school day. This strategy supports the development of which of the following emergent literacy skills?

a. Letter recognition
b. Word association
c. Print awareness
d. Phonological awareness

15. A first-grade teacher has noticed that one student struggles to recall stories in the correct sequence. The student often mixes up events from the beginning, middle, and end of the story, and confuses important connecting details. Which of the following strategies would likely best support this student's language skill development in this area?

a. Fostering personal connections between the student's life and events from stories
b. Providing the student aids such as graphic organizers, story maps, and pictures that correspond with events from stories
c. Exposing the student to a variety of texts relevant to her personal interests
d. Reading aloud to the student individually and asking open-ended questions about the story

16. In early childhood, which of these strategies that support cognitive development is useful for teaching children cause-and-effect relationships?

a. Playing the "peekaboo" game
b. Books about leaving and returning
c. Books with pictures hidden behind flaps
d. Busy boxes/toys registering different actions

17. When reading aloud to students, a kindergarten teacher makes sure to speak expressively by pausing at the end of each sentence, changing intonation, and correlating inflection with differences in punctuation within the text. In doing so, the teacher models which of the following?

a. The correct usage of academic language
b. Differences in writing styles of literary and informational texts
c. Interest and enthusiasm for reading
d. The relationship between English grammatical conventions in written and spoken language

18. Which behavior indicates a child has attained understanding of symbolic representation?

a. Seeking unseen things
b. Playing "make-believe"
c. Enjoying "peek-a-boo"
d. Addition using pennies

19. An adult places a sticker on a small child's face and then introduces a mirror. When the child sees the sticker in the mirror, she reaches toward her face to remove it rather than toward the mirror. Which level of self-awareness does this demonstrate?

a. Permanence
b. Differentiation
c. Situation
d. Identification

20. Which of the following would likely be the LEAST effective technique for early childhood teachers to promote oral language and vocabulary development using shared reading?

a. Pointing to book illustrations of new words
b. Relating new words to words children know
c. Giving many varied examples of new words
d. Having children read on their own without teacher intervention

21. To effectively design and deliver instruction that is responsive to all students' needs, teachers must recognize and understand the influence that which of the following factors has on learning and development?

a. The degree to which instruction aligns with state academic standards
b. Students' prior knowledge and experiences
c. Attitudes, behaviors, and values modeled by the teacher
d. Students' overall attitudes toward learning

22. In the Directed Reading Activity (DRA) approach to reading instruction using basal readers, the first of five steps is the teacher's preparing and motivating students to read, and introducing new concepts and vocabulary words. Which of the following shows the correct sequence of the other four steps?

a. Guided silent reading; comprehension discussion; reading aloud; workbook activities
b. Reading aloud; comprehension discussion; workbook activities; guided silent reading
c. Comprehension discussion; workbook activities; guided silent reading; reading aloud
d. Workbook activities; reading aloud; guided silent reading, comprehension discussion

23. Which geographic features were most conducive to the development of early civilizations?

a. Rivers
b. Deserts
c. Forests
d. Mountains

24. It is snack time in your kindergarten class, and you pour two children equal amounts of water; however, one child's cup is bigger. The child with the bigger cup complains that he has less water. In terms of cognitive development, what can you determine by this complaint?

a. The child has a developmental delay because he does not understand conservation.
b. The child has not reached the concrete operational stage and does not understand conservation; this is normal for a child of this age.
c. The child is displaying a delay in intuitive processes commonly acquired during the preoperational stage of cognitive development.
d. The child is displaying a preconceptual process that is common among this age group.

25. Which of the following exemplifies the multiplier effect of large cities?

a. The presence of specialized equipment for an industry attracts even more business.
b. The large population lowers the price of goods.
c. Public transportation means more people can commute to work.
d. A local newspaper can afford to give away the Sunday edition.

26. A third-grade teacher wants to develop a community of readers by fostering connections between the literacy curriculum and students' lives. Which of the following strategies would best achieve this goal?

a. Offering students a choice in activities related to literacy instruction
b. Providing daily opportunities for self-selected reading
c. Immersing students in a print-rich environment
d. Incorporating literacy materials that reflect students' diversities into the curriculum

27. A class of second-grade students is working in small groups to investigate whether music affects plant growth. Each group will be given four basil plants, and will expose two of them to music. As students begin the experiment, the teacher reminds each group to make sure that all plants receive equal amounts of sunlight and water. In doing so, this teacher reinforces which of the following concepts related to scientific learning?

a. The importance of verifiable evidence
b. How to properly follow the steps of the scientific method
c. How to accurately and consistently record observations during a scientific investigation
d. The importance of following directions when conducting an experiment

28. A first-grade teacher reviews high-frequency sight words with students each day by having them recite the words aloud from the class word wall, trace them on dotted lines, and practice writing the words independently. These strategies are likely intended to develop which of the following skills?

a. Phonemic awareness
b. Text comprehension
c. Orthographic processing
d. Phonological processing

29. Which of the following is true regarding development in early childhood?

a. Young children tend to use speech more than physical aggression during conflict.
b. Young children develop and apply motor skills before verbal skills.
c. Young children often know constructive management of strong emotion.
d. Young children learn social skills directly rather than with puppets.

30. A class of second-grade students is learning about the organ structures of various plants. Which scientific learning tool would best support their learning and development of this concept?

a. A scale
b. A microscope
c. A reference guide on the structure of plants
d. An observation log

31. Students in a first-grade class are participating in an activity in which they go outside and trace one another's shadows on the sidewalk in the morning, at lunchtime, and at the end of the school day. This investigation is most likely intended to develop students' fundamental understanding of which of the following concepts?

a. Living things require sunlight for survival.
b. Sunlight is a form of energy.
c. All planets rotate around the Sun.
d. Earth rotates on its axis every 24 hours.

32. To create a culturally inclusive learning environment that promotes acceptance and respect for student diversity, it is important that teachers do what?

a. Establish and maintain frequent communication with students' families.
b. Hold all students to the same high academic expectations.
c. Emphasize positive communication skills to promote healthy interpersonal relationships.
d. Teach lessons focused on holidays and traditions from different cultures around the world.

33. Concerning motivating young children to engage in writing activities, which is true?

a. Children should learn to write their own critiques of authors and books before evaluating them.
b. Children are motivated to write up classmate interviews by teacher modeling and guidance.
c. Teachers should never deliberately commit errors when transcribing the children's dictation.
d. Teachers can bring in samples of their own writing, but asking children to do so will backfire.

34. Erikson designated his stage of psychosocial development focused on the conflict of initiative vs. guilt as a period characterized by:

a. Friends
b. Hope
c. Trust
d. Play

35. According to Kohlberg, at which developmental level do children understand that good behavior is expected?

a. Post-conventional
b. Conventional
c. Pre-conventional
d. Adolescent

36. An EC teacher has written down a lesson plan for an art activity step by step. Which of the following steps should the teacher and students do last?

a. Have a preliminary discussion about the activity.
b. Look at activity-related artworks and photos.
c. Set up the necessary materials and instruments.
d. Share and read books related to the art activity.

37. A second-grade teacher is planning a project in which students will plant seeds in containers and then cover some of them with plastic bottles that have been cut in half. This activity is likely intended to begin developing students' understanding of which concept related to agriculture?

a. Plants and animals need food to survive.
b. Recycling materials for agricultural purposes helps reduce waste.
c. There is a relationship between the greenhouse effect and food production.
d. Agricultural practices vary depending on the crop.

38. Which of the following graphs represents the inequality $-2 < x \leq 4$?

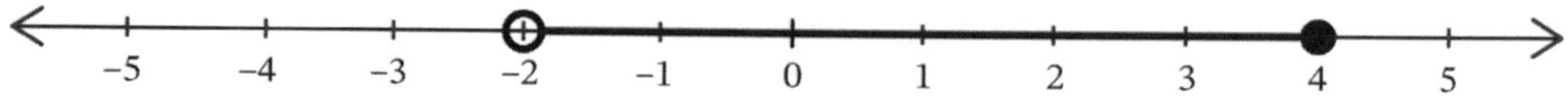

a.

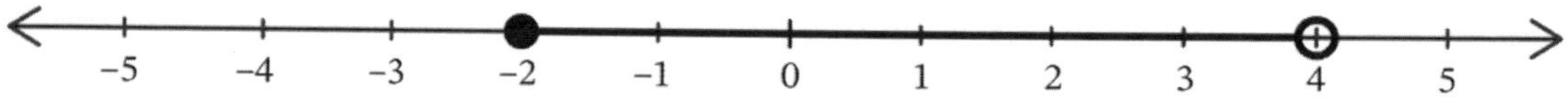

b.

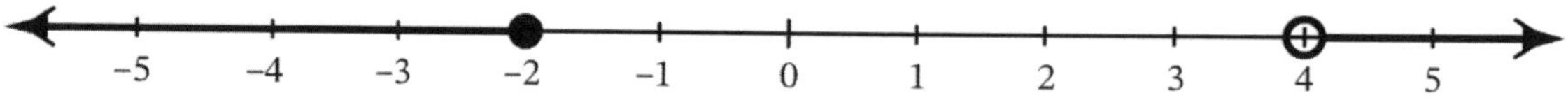

c.

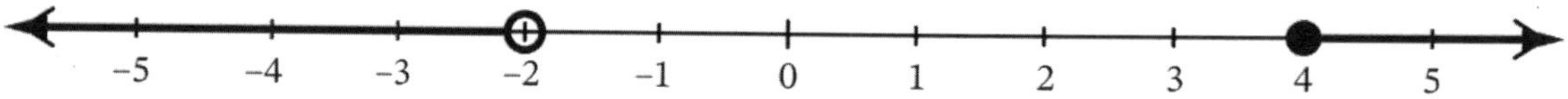

d.

39. A first-grade teacher is planning a lesson focused on recalling the main idea and key details from informational texts. Which of the following strategies should this teacher use to align learning with students' zone of proximal development as they learn this new concept?

a. Flexible grouping
b. Formative assessments
c. Differentiated instruction
d. Scaffolding

40. One of the most important factors influencing the quality of learning and development among young children is:

a. Background knowledge and experiences
b. Adequate health and nutrition
c. Intrinsic motivation
d. Parental involvement in the education program

41. After conducting a survey on students' favorite seasons, a first-grade teacher tallies up responses on the board. Then, the teacher provides students with a bar graph template and instructs them to color in the appropriate number of spaces to correspond with how many students prefer each season. This strategy is likely intended to develop students' understanding of which of the following?

a. When to use estimation versus calculation
b. The fact that changing an object's appearance does not alter the quantity
c. The idea that data can be represented in multiple ways
d. How to make reasonable predictions in math

42. Of the following preschool activities involving texture in art, which is most closely related to developing their skills of symbolic representation?

a. Identifying textures by touch without seeing them
b. Identifying different textures used in a work of art
c. Producing different textures in their own artworks
d. Exploring various ways of visually showing textures

43. A prekindergarten teacher is planning instruction to develop students' foundational understanding of the properties of matter. Which of the following strategies would likely best promote curiosity and inquiry related to this concept?

a. Demonstrating the changes that occur when substances are heated or cooled
b. Providing a sensory bin that incorporates various types of matter
c. Leading a class discussion in which students compare and contrast the characteristics of different types of matter
d. Incorporating music and movement into instruction to promote student engagement

44. Which of the following is NOT true about democracy and the formation of the United States?

a. The founding fathers stated in the Constitution that the United States would be a democracy.
b. The Declaration of Independence did not dictate democracy but stated its principles.
c. The United States Constitution stipulated that government be elected by the people.
d. The United States Constitution had terms to protect some, but not all, of the people.

45. A first-grade teacher has just completed a lesson on cardinal directions. Which of the following instructional activities would be most appropriate for allowing students of this age group to practice using this skill?

a. Using written directions to draw landmarks on a town map
b. Placing pictures of household items in the correct location on a floor plan template
c. Using an online satellite map to locate various physical and man-made landmarks
d. Comparing and contrasting the features of different types of maps

46. Being read to in early childhood helps develop metalinguistic abilities. Young children can tell stories in books through the pictures. Eventually, they understand that the words printed in the books are connected to spoken words. This is an example of which of these four metalinguistic abilities?

a. Word consciousness
b. Conventions of print
c. The functions of print
d. Reading with fluency

47. A fourth-grade teacher has assigned an art project in which students will apply their knowledge of acute, right, and obtuse angles to create a realistic drawing of a city. This strategy promotes students' understanding of which of the following concepts?

a. The importance of accuracy when creating artistic representations
b. The connection between mathematics and the arts
c. How to properly scale a drawing to size
d. The relationship between basic elements of the visual arts

48. Which statement is most accurate regarding young students' reading comprehension?

a. Students missing main ideas while noticing details are more likely to have comprehension issues.
b. Missing either the main ideas or the details of the text signifies comprehension problems.
c. Students who cannot repeat any details but get the main idea have good comprehension.
d. If a student gets the main ideas, the ability to retell logical event sequences is immaterial.

49. A fourth-grade student has difficulty distinguishing between homophones, particularly during writing activities. For example, when writing, she often mixes up such words as "they're," "there," and "their"; "here" and "hear"; and "eight" and "ate." Which of the following interventions would likely best address this issue?

a. Assigning vocabulary lists that include frequently confused homophones and administering weekly spelling tests
b. Implementing sentence dictation exercises, providing visual aids, and reviewing the morphology of frequently confused homophones
c. Having the student practice reading aloud from a variety of texts that incorporate homophones
d. Asking the student to practice segmenting complex multisyllabic words

50. Which of the following would be most effective to help young children learn geometry?

a. Giving them hands-on activities manipulating concrete objects
b. Giving them the earliest geometric theorems to memorize
c. Giving them everyday life activities only after they learn basics
d. Giving them instructions for drawing geometric shape diagrams

51. Of the following, which is a principle wherein Albert Bandura's theory *agrees with* behaviorist learning theory?

a. Consequences reinforce or punish behaviors.
b. Learning always results in a change in behavior.
c. Internal cognitive processes must be examined.
d. Social interactions are very important in learning.

52. Some basic elements of music that an early childhood educator should know include:

a. Bass, treble, alto, and soprano
b. Common instruments and how to read music
c. Rhythm, melody, harmony, timbre, texture, and form
d. Strings, percussion, woodwinds, and bass

53. A kindergarten teacher is reviewing CVC words with students using letter tiles. After students read each word aloud, the teacher removes the first letter and asks them to recite the remaining sound. This activity is an example of which of the following instructional strategies to promote phonemic awareness?

a. Phoneme substitution
b. Phoneme isolation
c. Decoding
d. Phoneme deletion

54. According to Piaget's theory of cognitive development, how do very young children approach the ideas of part-whole and fractions?

a. They typically think several pieces of an apple equal more fruit than one whole apple.
b. They typically understand that pieces are parts of a whole even at the youngest ages.
c. They typically recognize fractions as parts of a whole if they can use concrete objects.
d. They typically see wholes as more than parts, but not how many parts make a whole.

55. The physical geography of a region most directly affects which of the following?

a. The religious beliefs of the native population
b. The family structure of the native population
c. The dietary preferences of the native population
d. The language spoken by the native population

56. Which of the following statements is true of vocal changes in developing adolescents?

a. It is largely a myth and can be kept in check by teaching proper technique.
b. Girls' singing voices do not change, although boys' singing voices do change.
c. Because their voices change in unpredictable ways, boys should stop singing during the middle school years and then resume in high school.
d. Girls' singing voices change just as boys' voices do.

57. Which of the following statements is NOT an accurate statement about the Puritans in England?

a. The Puritans unconditionally gave all their support to the English Reformation.
b. The Puritans saw the Church of England as too much like the Catholic Church.
c. The Puritans became a chief political power because of the English Civil War.
d. The Puritans' clergy mainly departed from the Church of England after 1662.

58. Which of the following instructional strategies likely best promotes development of phonemic awareness in early childhood students?

a. Providing multiple opportunities for students to engage in writing activities
b. Asking students to sequence the events of a story using pictures
c. Incorporating activities such as rhymes, songs, and alphabet games
d. Creating a print-rich environment using labels, word walls, posters, and bulletin boards

59. A second-grade teacher has decorated the classroom with a word wall, labels, a bulletin board, and a class calendar. This teacher has also created a classroom library that includes several leveled texts of varying genres for students to utilize. This is an example of which of the following strategies for promoting the learning and development of language and literacy skills for all students?

a. Providing opportunities for student choice in learning
b. Modifying instruction to align with varying abilities
c. Creating a print-rich environment
d. Scaffolding learning activities

60. A prekindergarten teacher uses daily circle time for reading aloud to students. When introducing new vocabulary words from a text, the teacher pauses to explain their meaning, and adds them to the class word wall with corresponding pictures. After each read-aloud, the teacher also asks students to discuss their favorite parts of the story. By implementing these strategies, the teacher demonstrates understanding of which of the following?

a. Individual differences in developmental levels among young children
b. The role of receptive and expressive language in literacy development
c. Interventions for supporting literacy development in struggling students
d. The importance of differentiating instruction to align with individual students' needs

61. In addition to building content knowledge, a kindergarten teacher wants to design instruction that promotes academic language acquisition among the ELLs in her classroom. Which of the following instructional approaches would be most effective in achieving this goal?

a. Scaffolding the linguistic complexity of instructional activities
b. Providing a print-rich environment
c. Implementing thematic units
d. Reviewing new vocabulary using flash cards

62. A first-grade teacher works with a group of students that have varying skills, abilities, and learning needs. During English language arts lessons, she groups students based upon literacy abilities and English language proficiency levels, and she adapts texts to vary in complexity. This is an example of which of the following instructional strategies?

a. Inquiry-based learning
b. Total participation techniques
c. Scaffolding
d. Student-led learning

63. Which of the following is accurate regarding the 3N instructional strategy for EC literacy development?

a. The Notice step involves having the student observe his or her own literacy strategies.
b. The Nudge step involves teachers' providing scaffolding to raise student literacy levels.
c. The Narrate step involves having the student verbally describe his or her literacy activity.
d. The Narrate step involves having the student verbally reflect on the literacy activity.

64. According to Lev Vygotsky's sociocultural theory, which of the following best describes why a student's culture impacts his or her learning and development?

a. Learning and cognitive development are intrinsic
b. Learning and development occur primarily through interactions with individuals in one's immediate environment
c. Different cultures place varying degrees of emphasis on education
d. Language barriers may impact the rate at which students learn

65. What is most accurate regarding the basal reader series used in today's classrooms?

a. Texts used are by subjects, not reading levels.
b. Texts used are expository, not narrative work.
c. Texts used are the children's literature genre.
d. Texts used are thematically organized by unit.

66. According to Scarborough's reading rope, skilled reading is developed by a combination of factors related to:

a. Frequent exposure to literacy materials
b. Orthographic processing skills
c. Expressive and receptive language
d. Word recognition and language comprehension

67. During a math lesson, a second-grade teacher writes and solves an addition problem on the board in the following two ways:

$$34 + 58 = 92$$

$$30 + 50 = 80 \qquad 8 + 4 = 12 \qquad 80 + 12 = 92$$

By demonstrating that numbers can be added in different ways, this teacher promotes students' learning and development of which of the following skills?

a. Algebraic thinking
b. Estimation and rounding numbers to the nearest ten
c. Cardinality and sequencing
d. Data analysis and representation

68. A third-grade teacher is preparing to introduce an informational text to students. As a prereading strategy, the teacher reads a portion of the text aloud to the class and pauses at unfamiliar vocabulary. The teacher then asks students to identify surrounding words that may indicate examples, synonyms, antonyms, or definitions of the new words. This strategy is likely intended to develop which of the following skills?

a. Contextual analysis
b. Structural analysis
c. Phonological processing
d. Decoding and encoding

69. Which of the following should adults include in their conversations with young children to help them build strong oral language skills?

a. Simple vocabulary and simple sentence structures
b. Primarily telling things rather than asking questions
c. Doing the majority of the talking to model for them
d. Questions requiring them to express abstract ideas

70. A fourth-grade class is reading an informational text about the role of local, state, and national government in daily life. As they read, the teacher instructs students to highlight unfamiliar vocabulary words, circle important information, and write down questions about parts they do not understand. Which of the following skills does this promote?

a. Phonological processing
b. Structural analysis
c. Critical analysis
d. Contextual analysis

71. During a field trip to a local recycling center, a group of kindergarten students learned that mixing recyclable materials prevents some items from getting recycled. To reinforce this concept in the classroom, the teacher should:

a. Have students conduct an experiment to demonstrate the impacts of litter on the environment.
b. Show examples of recyclable and nonrecyclable materials.
c. Assign an art project that incorporates recyclable materials.
d. Place labeled recycle bins in the classroom.

72. During Piaget's second stage of cognitive development, adults should realize that children's thinking is primarily:

a. Logical
b. Intuitive
c. Sensory
d. Motoric

73. Among instructional strategies that aid in student comprehension of nonfictional text, which of these is most useful for promoting critical thinking?

a. Answering open-ended questions about texts
b. Skimming the text for features that give signs
c. Establishing connections between text and life
d. Establishing connections between text and self

74. Which statement about the impact of chemistry on society is NOT true?

a. The fluoridation of water has had no effect on the rate of cavities as compared to unfluoridated water.
b. Chemical fertilizers have tremendously increased food production per acre in the US.
c. Chemistry played a central role in the development of nuclear weapons.
d. The use of catalytic converters in automobiles has greatly reduced exhaust products that contribute to acid rain.

75. A second-grade teacher has noticed that one student consistently struggles to focus in class. The student often fidgets, speaks out of turn, and has difficulty staying in her seat. The student also has difficulty with reading comprehension, and is not developing at a grade-level-appropriate pace. This may be indicative of which of the following?

a. The student's family does not reinforce learning at home
b. A potential behavioral disorder that impedes effective learning
c. A learning disability that impacts literacy skills
d. Inadequate classroom management procedures

76. A typically developing child is shown a TV with live video of herself. Additionally, she is shown adult researchers who are imitating her behaviors. The child can tell the difference between the video and the imitators. This child is most likely:

a. A newborn
b. 2 years old
c. 4–7 months old
d. 1–3 months old

77. Which statement is most accurate regarding children who have good reading comprehension?

a. They read material which is familiar within their existing knowledge.
b. They are skilled at decoding, so they do not need good vocabularies.
c. They can summarize what they read and predict what will come next.
d. They comprehend text without needing to use the sentence structure.

78. Which of the following most accurately reflects expert recommendations for indoor learning environments to accommodate planned curriculum activities for toddlers and preschoolers?

a. Furniture should be lightweight and easy to move around.
b. Art and cooking activities should be separated from water.
c. Dramatic play, blocks, reading, and music can be combined.
d. Separate areas should be provided for school-age children.

79. Which of the following can preschool children learn in lessons about the element of color in art?

a. The names of different colors
b. Skills of sensory discrimination
c. Children can learn all of these
d. Skills for making classifications

80. A child in a preschool learning center likes to sort rocks by their colors. Which of the following teacher practices best represents an emphasis on building the child's problem-solving skills?

a. The teacher asks afterward how else he or she could sort the rocks.
b. The teacher explains to the child that he or she is classifying the rocks.
c. The teacher asks the child which way he or she is sorting rocks.
d. The teacher leaves the students to sorting without intervening.

81. When reading grade-level texts, a third-grade student struggles to recognize both new and familiar vocabulary words. The student reads slowly, and often has trouble deriving meaning from what he has read. Based upon this information, this student appears to have difficulty with which of the following skills?

a. Irregular sight word recognition
b. Prosody
c. Phonemic awareness
d. Automaticity

82. What is the correct definition of the alphabetic principle?

a. The knowledge of all alphabet letters in order
b. The idea that letters represent speech sounds
c. The recognition and naming of alphabet letters
d. The ability to identify letter names and shapes

83. A fourth-grade teacher asks her students an open-ended question about the author's purpose relating to a novel they are reading. She gives students a few minutes to think about their personal responses before discussing them with partners for a few additional minutes. Finally, she asks students to discuss their responses as a class. Which instructional strategy is the teacher using?

a. Think-pair-share
b. Jigsaw
c. Close reading
d. Cloze reading

84. A second-grade teacher is planning a project in which students will design and construct a suitable habitat for a frog. Prior to beginning the project, the teacher should ensure students have a solid foundational understanding of which of the following concepts?

a. All living things are made up of matter.
b. Ecosystems are composed of several components that work together to function.
c. Living things require food, water, shelter, and space for survival.
d. Differences between the needs of plants and animals

85. A second-grade teacher gives each student a list of familiar vocabulary words and asks them to circle the ones that are misspelled. In doing so, this teacher is assessing which of the following skills?

a. Word association
b. Phonological processing
c. Phonemic awareness
d. Orthographic processing

86. Of the following, which is true of teaching preschool children about the visual art element of color?

a. Teachers cannot use stories or songs to teach children about colors.
b. Children can learn color names, discrimination, and classification.
c. There are no art museums that offer lessons for preschool ages.
d. Preschool children cannot appreciate viewing works of fine art.

87. How are instructional objectives that apply Bloom's Taxonomy also influenced by a major principle of behaviorist learning theory?

a. They use Bloom's Taxonomy terms requiring students to remember and understand.
b. They use only action verbs to describe how students must demonstrate their learning.
c. They use only behaviorist methods of changing behavior for teaching new information.
d. They use only behaviors that can be externally observed, whether measurable or not.

88. A first-grade teacher is planning instruction focused on the structural analysis of words to promote vocabulary acquisition and decoding skills. Which of the following strategies would be most effective in achieving this?

a. Using rhymes and songs to promote phonemic awareness
b. Having the class participate in a choral reading of a familiar text
c. Creating a word-building game in which students construct vocabulary from a set of root words and affixes
d. Holding a reader's theater in which students act out dialogue from a story

89. Which teaching strategy for developing written communication skills can also be used to develop spoken communication skills?

a. Written Responses, Varying Answers
b. Written Responses, Same Answers
c. None of these work for both
d. Think-Pair-Share activities

90. A prekindergarten teacher has brought in several costumes for students to use for dressing up, as well as props to represent a restaurant, bank, doctor's office, and kitchen. This teacher demonstrates understanding of which of the following?

a. Strategies for developing gross and fine motor skills in early childhood students
b. The importance of dramatic play for early childhood development
c. Activities for supporting cross-curricular learning
d. Effective assessment approaches in arts and humanities

91. To help young children learn about geometric shapes, figures, and angles, adults can first tell them the names of these while they look at them together. Thereafter, in which sequence should adults do the following exercises with young children?

a. Have them name shapes; describe them; trace drawings of them; finger-draw them in air; and draw them.
b. Have them describe shapes; name them; trace drawings of them; draw them; and finger-draw them in air.
c. Have them trace drawings of shapes; finger-draw them in air; draw them; describe them; and name them.
d. Have them draw shapes; trace drawings of them; finger-draw them in air; name them; and describe them.

92. Which of the following is NOT an example of an oxidation-reduction reaction?

a. A volcano eruption can be modeled using vinegar and baking soda.
b. Steel cans are electroplated with tin to produce grocery store food cans.
c. Blood catalyzes the decomposition of hydrogen peroxide on a cut.
d. Bread dough rises from the production of carbon dioxide gas by yeast.
e. Rust forms on a steel fence that is exposed to wind and rain.

93. To promote young children's developing abstract thinking, which teacher technique to use during and after shared readings is best suited for use with children in the younger, rather than older, ages of early childhood?

a. Asking children to predict what they think will happen next in the story
b. Asking children to imagine beyond the story: "What would you do if...?"
c. Asking children to identify vocabulary words and describe story details
d. Asking them to make conclusions about why characters do/feel things

94. Regarding young children's early comprehension of fractions, which of these is accurate?

a. Children must know how many parts a unit is divided into, but not what comprises the unit.
b. Children must know what makes a whole unit, but not into how many pieces it was divided.
c. Children must know how many pieces a unit is divided into, but not if they are of equal size.
d. Children must know what a whole unit is, how many parts there are, and if part sizes match.

95. A third-grade student is having difficulty with the notion that fractions represent parts of a whole. Which of the following learning materials would best support the student's understanding of this concept?

a. A geoboard
b. Base-ten blocks
c. Unit cubes
d. Pattern blocks

96. A second-grade teacher is planning a unit focused on markets and economic systems. After a field trip to the grocery store, students will participate in a classroom market with a limited number of available items. Each student will be given pretend money to spend, and will plan a budget, as well as a list of items they intend to purchase. By implementing these strategies, the teacher demonstrates knowledge of which of the following?

a. Techniques for selecting appropriate activities to support children's development and fostering connections between social studies and other content areas
b. Criteria for designing and adapting tools and technologies to differentiate instruction
c. Understanding of how to use formative assessment throughout instruction to evaluate student understanding and engagement
d. Strategies for supporting children's learning of major concepts related to government

97. To learn the sounds spelled by printed or written letters and recognize printed words, children must:

a. Know the order of the alphabet.
b. Know the names of the letters.
c. Know how to write the letters.
d. Know letter shapes, not names.

98. Which of the following is correct regarding the benefits of direct instruction in phonological and phonemic awareness (PPA) for young children?

a. Preschool-aged children benefit from PPA instruction, but first-grade students do not.
b. Preschool children with delays in language development benefit from PPA instruction.
c. Preschool-aged children with articulation disorders are not helped by PPA instruction.
d. School-aged children with spelling disorders reap no benefits from instruction in PPA.

99. In a kindergarten classroom, the teacher has included several learning stations, such as a dramatic play area, sensory bin, science center, music area, and art center. In doing so, the teacher supports students' learning and development by providing multiple opportunities for:

a. Direct instruction
b. Formative assessment
c. Hands-on learning experiences
d. Individualized instruction

100. A third-grade teacher is planning a unit on forces of motion in which students will work in pairs to investigate the speed at which marbles of varying sizes and weights roll down a ramp. Prior to introducing the unit, the teacher administered a diagnostic exam and identified a few students that will likely need additional support. Which of the following strategies should this teacher implement during the investigation portion of the unit to ensure these students can learn effectively?

a. Provide these students with a graphic organizer to fill out during the investigation.
b. Strategically pair these students with others that can provide scaffolding.
c. Check frequently for understanding throughout the investigation.
d. Have these students complete self-reflection activities at the end of each lesson during the unit.

Answer Key and Explanations for Test #1

1. B: EC teachers are advised to teach art not only in isolated lessons (A), but moreover to integrate art into the entire curriculum, which is now included in many state standards (C) for early learning and is found to improve children's understanding of many concepts and enhance their learning. Such state standards recommend integrating art projects into both individual learning units and entire curricula (C). When EC teacher assign process activities in art, they should always provide the children in advance with rules and steps (D) for proceeding, and also explain these to the children beforehand.

2. C: The philosophy and psychology of actively constructing one's own knowledge of the world is known as constructivism. Scaffolding (A) is temporary needed support teachers provide for student learning and gradually withdraw as students acquire higher skill levels. Cognitivism (B) is the type of psychology Piaget's theory involves as a theory of cognitive development; however, the description of actively building one's own knowledge refers specifically to constructivism. The Zone of Proximal Development (D) was Vygotsky's term for the distance between what a learner can do independently and what that learner can do with help or guidance.

3. D: Distinguishing between syllable types is essential to developing the decoding skills necessary to facilitate reading comprehension, spelling, and writing abilities. Closed syllables are ones that include the short vowel sound followed by a consonant, whereas open syllables end with a long vowel sound. Students that struggle to recognize the difference will likely require additional support to ensure proper literacy development. Having these students practice forming words with letter tiles and reading them aloud provides a multisensory approach to develop this skill. This activity allows students to visualize, verbalize, and physically manipulate letters to strengthen their understanding of the different sounds produced by these two syllable types.

4. A: Total participation techniques are whole-class activities in which students are prompted to actively participate in the learning experience. Such activities are intended to promote student engagement, strengthen understanding, and serve as a valuable formative assessment tool for teachers. By having students hold up their answers to multiplication problems on individual whiteboards, this teacher can quickly and formatively evaluate students' understanding. This strategy will provide the teacher with the feedback necessary to make adjustments throughout instruction, implement supports, and identify areas that may need reteaching to better meet students' learning needs.

5. D: Compound sentences occur when two independent clauses are joined by a conjunction, such as "and" or "but." This concept builds on students' knowledge of simple sentences, which consist of only one independent clause. Teaching the components and formation of compound sentences is important in developing students' ability to write on a more complex level, as well as their understanding of the characteristics and functions of the English language. Introducing compound sentences using kinesthetic materials, such as sentence-building strips, allows students to explore this concept in a hands-on learning setting. This strategy allows students to physically construct sentences using independent clauses and conjunctions, strengthening their understanding.

6. C: Guiding students through the foundational steps of the research process should begin in early elementary school. Doing so promotes writing skill development while establishing a foundation for success across content areas. In this situation, the teacher plans to guide students through the steps of the research process with each activity. Having students brainstorm topics will help them narrow their essay's focus. Demonstrating how to gather evidence shows students how to effectively support their writing topics with relevant information. Assigning students to create outlines prior to beginning rough drafts will help them organize their writing, while peer-editing will help them refine it. These activities for each stage of the research process will help students produce clear, coherent, and organized essays while promoting writing skill development.

7. C: Authentic summative assessments provide students with relevant and meaningful opportunities to demonstrate what they have learned. This assessment approach places learning in a familiar and real-world context, fostering students' personal connections for greater understanding. By second grade, students can reasonably be expected to create and use simple timelines to record events, including from their own lives. An autobiographical timeline project provides students with a personalized, engaging, and grade-level-appropriate learning opportunity to demonstrate their knowledge of how to sequence events chronologically.

8. B: When a child counts how many dots of one color there are in a fabric print before a different color is used, this activity is focused on identifying the pattern(s) in the print. Stringing beads with different colors in a pre-selected order (A), arranging and gluing down pieces of alternating sizes (C), and hopping on each foot for pre-determined different numbers of times (D) are all activities that are focused on *creating,* rather than *identifying,* patterns.

9. D: Normally developing preschoolers typically develop print awareness skills that include all of these: reciting the alphabet; recognizing both printed letters and printed words; and using print as a vehicle for communication.

10. D: It is not true that the Gilded Age is a term whose origins have not been identified clearly. In 1873, Mark Twain and Charles Dudley Warner co-authored a book entitled *The Gilded Age: A Tale of Today*. Twain and Warner first coined this term to describe the extravagance and excesses of America's wealthy upper class, who became richer than ever due to industrialization. Furthermore, the Gilded Age was the era of the "robber barons" such as John D. Rockefeller, Cornelius Vanderbilt, J.P. Morgan, and others. Because they accumulated enormous wealth through extremely aggressive and occasionally unethical monetary manipulations, critics dubbed them "robber barons" because they seemed to be elite lords of robbery. While these business tycoons grasped huge fortunes, some of them—such as Andrew Carnegie and Andrew Mellon—were also philanthropists, using their wealth to support and further worthy causes such as literacy, education, health care, charities, and the arts. They donated millions of dollars to fund social improvements. Carnegie himself dubbed this large philanthropic movement the "Gospel of Wealth." Another characteristic of the Gilded Age was the Beaux Arts architectural style, a neo-Renaissance style modeled after the great architectural designs of the European Renaissance. The Panic of 1893 ended the Gilded Age and began a severe four-year economic depression. The Progressive Era followed these events.

11. A: According to English Language Proficiency Standards (ELPS), beginner-level ELL students are expected to understand general language related to the content area and produce common phrases or short sentences in oral communication. In asking the student to sort events from the story using pictures and a graphic organizer, the teacher recognizes the ability level of beginner ELLs by asking him to demonstrate comprehension using visual aids as linguistic supports. Further, by asking the student to describe a favorite character to a table partner, the teacher demonstrates awareness that beginner-level ELLs can typically produce short, simple sentences related to the content area.

12. B: Permissive parents are nurturing, responsive, and communicative with their children; however, they avoid confronting and/or disciplining children and do not expect them to demonstrate much self-control or maturity. Consequently, their children tend to have problems with authority figures, poor school performance, and deficits in self-regulation. The children of unresponsive, overly strict, demanding, harshly punitive authoritarian parents tend to develop proficient technical and school performance and obedience, but they lack social skills, self-esteem, and happiness. The children of authoritative parents, who have the ideal parenting style, tend to develop competence, success, and happiness. Uninvolved parents, who are undemanding but also unresponsive, uncommunicative, detached, and maybe even neglectful, tend to produce children lacking competence, self-esteem, and self-control.

13. D: Experts in early childhood education identify child age (a), individual child growth patterns (b), and cultural influences (c) as three main, essential aspects for educators to consider in the assessment methods, classrooms, and instructional techniques they use in order to establish developmentally appropriate instructional practices.

14. C: Print awareness is the understanding of the prevalence of printed language in everyday life, as well as the recognition that printed words and letters convey meaning. Understanding this basic concept of print is foundational in emergent literacy skill development, so it must be emphasized in the early childhood classroom. Surrounding young children with multiple examples of environmental print, such as posters, signs, and charts, demonstrates the existence and purpose of printed language to begin building print awareness.

15. B: Sequencing in language arts is a reading comprehension skill that refers to one's ability to recall and arrange events from a text. If a student struggles with sequencing, the teacher must implement appropriate interventions, as development of this language skill is necessary for success in learning across content areas. For example, sequencing also applies to one's ability to follow a set of directions or steps in the correct order to solve problems; recognize cause and effect; and recall major events from history. In this situation, providing visual aids—such as graphic organizers, story maps, and pictures that correspond with events from stories—supports the student in developing this language skill. The teacher must continuously monitor this student's progress to determine if additional interventions are necessary.

16. D: Busy boxes and other toys that provide different reactions to different actions are useful for teaching cause-and-effect relationships to young children. Playing "peekaboo" (a), books about leaving and returning (b), and books with pictures hidden behind flaps (c) are all useful strategies for teaching young children the concept of object permanence (i.e., that things and people still exist even when they are out of the child's sight or presence).

17. D: Recognizing the characteristics and functions of English grammatical conventions is important for reading comprehension development. Further, modeling to students how these patterns apply to spoken language is necessary for fostering reading fluency and expressive language skills. By pausing between sentences, changing intonation, and correlating inflection with variances in punctuation within the text, the teacher effectively models the relationship between English grammatical patterns in written and spoken language.

18. B: When children engage in "pretend" or "make-believe" playing, as when they play "house" and pretend to be parents; pretend to be fantasy characters; or use toys to represent real persons, animals, machines, etc., they understand one thing can be used as a symbol to stand for something else, i.e., symbolic representation. When babies look for things they saw that were then hidden so they can no longer see them (A), they have attained object permanence. The emergence of this understanding that things out of sight still exist is also indicated by their enjoying playing "peek-a-boo" (C). (Infants without object permanence are truly surprised to see a hidden face reappear;

those developing object permanence laugh with delight to see the face reappear; and those with fully developed object permanence may eventually lose interest in the game.) When children can add or subtract using pennies (D) or other concrete objects, this shows they have attained concrete operations, i.e., mental operations using concrete objects.

19. D: Identification is the third of five progressive levels of self-awareness that children develop. In differentiation (the first level), children can distinguish their mirrored images from other people and realize that their reflection's movements correspond to their own movements. In situation (the second level), children realize their mirror images are unique to themselves and that their bodies and selves are situated in space. In identification (the third level), children identify their reflections as "me." When they see something on their reflected faces, they know to touch their faces rather than the mirror to touch or remove the object. In permanence (the fourth level), children realize their self is permanent over time and space, recognizing themselves in photos and videos regardless of their ages, clothing, location, etc. The fifth level is self-consciousness or "meta"-self-awareness (i.e., seeing oneself from others' as well as one's own perspective).

20. D: To enhance their shared reading to promote young children's development of vocabulary and oral language, teachers can explain the meanings of new words to them; point at illustrations in books depicting new vocabulary words; connect new vocabulary words to words the children already know; and give children multiple and various examples to teach new vocabulary words. Young children are unlikely to be able to effectively develop their vocabulary and oral language on their own.

21. B: All students will arrive in the classroom with varying experiences and levels of prior knowledge. Understanding that these factors will inevitably influence learning and development is essential to designing and delivering instruction that is responsive to all students' needs. By learning about individual backgrounds, strengths, skills, and interests, teachers can meet students where they are in terms of development while providing engaging, challenging, and relevant instruction that builds upon their abilities. Doing so creates meaningful and responsive learning experiences that align with students' individual needs and fosters personal connections for greater understanding.

22. A: In the DRA approach, after teacher preparation and motivation of students and introduction of new concepts and vocabulary words, in the second step, students read silently with questions and statements from the teacher guiding their reading. In the third step, teacher and students discuss what they have read to develop student reading comprehension. In the fourth step, students read aloud. They also read answers aloud to questions the teacher has asked; this is called "purposeful rereading." The fifth step involves follow-up activities and practicing that students do using the companion workbooks to the basal readers. In some cases, there may also be enrichment activities that relate the reading to writing, art, drama, or music experiences.

23. A: Rivers promoted the development of the ancient river valley civilizations of the world, including in the Middle East, India, and China. Rivers not only supply water for drinking and crop irrigation, but also provide fertile soil, vegetation for shade cover, food, building materials, and animal life. They additionally allow water travel to other locations. Although some peoples have settled and lived in deserts, they are among the most inhospitable climates. Forests also provide plenty of flora and fauna and exist in areas receiving enough rainfall, but rivers have been historically superior in attracting human societies. Mountains near living areas provide protective barriers; however, though some peoples live there, as in deserts, living in the mountains is difficult due to high altitudes, harsh climates, poor soil for planting, and rough terrain.

24. B: The child is developing normally; typical of his age group, he is in the preoperational stage of development and has not yet mastered conservation. Conservation is the ability to use logical reasoning to determine quantity. In this case, the child thinks one glass has more water simply because the glass is smaller. As this child enters into the concrete operational stage of development, he will understand that two amounts can be equal despite the size or shape of the container they are in. However, since this skill is not yet developed, the child will continue to believe one has more. If the teacher pours the water from the bigger glass into a glass that equals the size of his classmate's, the child will have a different reaction and possibly think the two are now equal.

25. A: One example of the multiplier effect of large cities would be if the presence of specialized equipment for an industry attracted even more business. Large cities tend to grow even larger for a number of reasons: they have more skilled workers, they have greater concentrations of specialized equipment, and they have already-functioning markets. These factors all make it easier for a business to begin operations in a large city than elsewhere. Thus, the populations and economic productivity of large cities tend to grow quickly. Some governments have sought to mitigate this trend by clustering groups of similar industries in smaller cities.

26. D: Students achieve more when they are able to make personal connections to the curriculum through relevant, meaningful learning experiences. For literacy instruction specifically, this includes incorporating materials into the curriculum that reflect students' diverse backgrounds, cultures, and experiences. Doing so helps to create an inclusive learning environment that contributes to developing a community of readers. When students can see themselves represented in literacy materials, they are able to establish personal connections, fostering positive attitudes and encouraging active participation in learning.

27. A: Teaching young children to rely on verifiable evidence is a foundational skill for scientific learning, as it emphasizes the importance of supporting one's own claims using valid data, as well as determining the credibility of other investigations. By reminding students to ensure that all plants receive equal amounts of sunlight and water, this teacher reinforces the concept of establishing a control variable to produce verifiable evidence from their investigation. Developing this skill ultimately strengthens students' ability to explain the results of investigations and apply logical reasoning skills, both to scientific learning and across content areas.

28. C: Orthographic processing skills are the ability to recognize and recall written words. These skills are necessary for the development of reading and writing fluency, as they are foundational for decoding both familiar and unfamiliar words, as well as using proper spelling and punctuation conventions. Activities to promote orthographic processing skills should include multiple opportunities for students to use and visualize words in written form, such as by tracing and writing sight words and reciting them aloud from a word wall. Such activities help students internalize the spelling, pronunciation, and meaning of new vocabulary, thus building writing and reading comprehension skills.

29. B: Children's motor skills typically develop sooner than their verbal skills. During conflict, young children are more likely to use physical aggression like kicking, biting, hitting, and pushing/shoving to get what they want rather than using speech (A). Young children also often have trouble self-regulation emotion, so teachers must help them learn how to manage their strong emotions constructively (C). Young children do not learn social skills only directly; teachers can help develop their social skills by demonstrating aggressive vs. proactive behaviors using puppets (D), which preschoolers find entertaining as well as concrete representations of emotions they can understand.

30. B: Scientific learning and development are best supported when young children are provided with opportunities that allow for active exploration. This includes incorporating realistic and developmentally appropriate scientific tools for students to use when investigating a new concept. Doing so creates a learning environment that fosters students' natural curiosity and inquiry, and reinforces the notion that in science, specific tools are used for gathering information. In addition, this strategy increases the relevancy of learning by placing it in a real-world context, as students have the opportunity to work with the same tools as scientists. Letting second-grade students investigate the organ structure of plants using microscopes provides such a hands-on learning experience, promoting engagement, exploration, and deeper understanding.

31. D: Activities that demonstrate abstract scientific concepts through concrete learning experiences are beneficial in building students' foundational knowledge for continuous development. Such activities demonstrate the prevalence of seemingly complex scientific ideas in daily life, thus making learning relevant and accessible for greater overall understanding. The notion that Earth rotates on its axis every 24 hours, for example, may be initially difficult for young children to grasp. Having students trace one another's shadows at varying times throughout the day is an effective strategy for placing this concept in an age-appropriate and immediately applicable context. In doing so, students are prompted to notice the changing location of their shadows, thus fostering further inquiry and promoting a fundamental understanding that the position of Earth in relation to the Sun changes as the day progresses.

32. D: A culturally inclusive classroom is one that accurately and respectfully reflects the diversity of its students. Such an environment promotes positive self-identify as well as social and emotional skill development by encouraging students to value their own uniqueness while instilling acceptance and appreciation for others' differences. Teachers can create such an environment by incorporating lessons focused on holidays and traditions from different cultures around the world into the curriculum. Specifically, these lessons should reflect the cultures of the students within the classroom. Doing so would promote inclusivity by allowing students to see themselves reflected in daily learning experiences while providing the opportunity to learn more about their classmates' backgrounds and experiences.

33. B: When teachers model for children and guide them in writing questions, reading them to ask classmates in "interviewing" them, and writing up their responses, this promotes children's motivation to write by connecting writing to familiar people and topics and by providing an activity they find exciting or interesting. To motivate young children to write, teachers should also provide them with opportunities to practice evaluating authors and books first until they eventually learn to write their own critiques—not vice versa (A). Experts advise teachers to make some deliberate errors when transcribing children's dictation (C) to give children opportunities to identify and correct the errors. They also recommend that teachers both bring in samples of their own writing and also invite children to do the same (D).

34. D: Erikson's nuclear conflict and stage he termed as initiative vs. guilt is associated with preschool ages (i.e., 3–5 years old). Erikson called this stage the "play age." At this age, children have developed the ability to use symbols, such as using toys or objects to represent other objects or using people (like children) to represent other people (like adults), and engage in "make-believe" or pretend play, which was a development also noted by Piaget in his theory. Children take initiative to plan and enact pretend roles and scenarios. Erikson's stage of industry vs. inferiority, coinciding with elementary school ages, focuses on friends (A) and school. Erikson identified hope (B) as a positive outcome of resolving the conflict of basic trust (C) vs. mistrust in his first stage during infancy.

35. B: There is actually a hint to this answer in its name. According to Kohlberg, the stage of development during which children learn conventional behavior—e.g., good behavior—is the conventional stage.

36. C: A good first step in the EC art activity lesson plan is to engage the children in a preliminary discussion about the activity (A), so they understand its purpose, nature, and some of its procedures; can ask questions and contribute their ideas and experiences; and feel more prepared for the activity. A good second step is for the teacher and students to share or read books about the art activity (D), which gives them more information about it, represents some primarily nonverbal procedures in verbal description, and integrates art with literacy. Then, the teacher can provide photos, reproductions, and actual artworks related to the planned activity (B), giving the children concrete examples for modeling and visual demonstrations of what they have verbally discussed and read. The last step they should take is for the teacher to dispense the needed materials and instruments (C), having the children help to assemble these in preparation for executing the hands-on activity/project.

37. C: As young children begin learning about agricultural systems, food production, and its relationship to the environment, it is important that they also learn about the implications of the greenhouse effect. The greenhouse effect is a phenomenon in which certain gases in the atmosphere, including carbon dioxide, water vapor, methane, and nitrous oxide, trap heat and humidity. While an excess of these gases is harmful, the greenhouse effect is necessary for the growth of plants, so it can be beneficial for agriculture and food production. The greenhouse effect can be created by forming an enclosure in which plants can harness sunlight, but gases are not released into the atmosphere. This allows for plant growth throughout the year in a variety of climates and locations. Providing active, hands-on learning experiences is most effective in developing students' understanding of this concept in the early childhood classroom. By having students plant seeds and cover only some of them with a plastic bottle that has been cut in half, students can observe and compare how greenhouse gases affect plant growth. This will ultimately establish a foundation for understanding the relationship between the greenhouse effect and food production.

38. A: When graphing an inequality, a solid circle at an endpoint means that the number at that endpoint is included in the range, while a hollow circle means it is not. Since the inequality says that x is strictly greater than −2, the circle at −2 should be hollow. Since the inequality says that x is less than or equal to 4, the circle at 4 should be solid. $-2 < x \leq 4$ indicates that x is between −2 and 4, so the area between the circles should be shaded.

39. D: The zone of proximal development (ZPD) is a concept developed by Lev Vygotsky to refer to one's ability to perform a given task with the assistance of a more experienced or knowledgeable individual. This is the second of three stages of learning outlined by Vygotsky, with the first referring to that which one cannot achieve even with assistance, and the ultimate being what one can do independently. Vygotsky proposed that if individuals are provided with adequate support while in the ZPD, they will ultimately be able to perform new tasks independently. This theory helps teachers understand how to appropriately scaffold instruction to align with students' abilities and provide necessary guidance as they learn new concepts. In this situation, scaffolds such as graphic organizers, visual aids, or chunked reading passages would be effective in supporting students in their ZPD as they learn to recall the main idea and key details of informational texts.

40. B: The quality of health and nutrition significantly impacts nearly all aspects of learning and development among young children. These factors contribute to students' energy levels, ability to focus and sustain attention in class, working memory, and emotional regulation. Further, adequate health and nutrition are necessary for proper long-term cognitive, physical, social, and emotional development. Teaching young children about the importance of nutrition and maintaining a healthy lifestyle establishes a foundation for encouraging healthy choices throughout life. In addition, teachers must know how to recognize when students' health and nutritional needs are not being met so as to provide the appropriate support and resources.

41. C: Teaching students to analyze and interpret data is essential in fostering their ability to identify patterns and relationships, compare information, and make informed predictions. This includes demonstrating that data results can be represented in multiple ways, such as bar graphs, pictographs, line plots, pie charts, or tally marks. Developing students' understanding of this concept is necessary to help them learn to analyze and interpret data in various formats, as well as determine when each one is most applicable. By having students create a bar graph based on tally marks to represent students' favorite seasons, this teacher demonstrates two ways that the same data can be presented.

42. D: Preschool children can develop their tactile discrimination through identifying textures by touch without seeing them. They develop both visual and tactile discrimination and judgment skills through identifying textures in a work of art (B). They develop their creative thinking skills, imaginations, fine-motor skills, and application skills through producing different textures in their own artworks (C). They develop verbal skills as well as visual and tactile discrimination through discussing the feels and looks of different textures. Through exploring various ways of visually representing different-feeling textures, they develop their skills of symbolic representation.

43. B: Sensory play activities are highly valuable in providing young children with hands-on learning experiences. Such activities promote students' natural sense of inquiry and curiosity for scientific learning, as they encourage the exploration of new concepts through the physical senses. Further, sensory play experiences often lend themselves to unstructured learning opportunities that allow young children to investigate, manipulate, observe, and test out ideas in a natural setting. A sensory bin with varying types of materials fosters inquiry among prekindergarten students when introducing the physical properties of matter. Students can actively explore different shapes, colors, sizes, and textures of materials, thus establishing a foundation for understanding that matter exists in multiple forms.

44. A: It is not true that the founding fathers specifically stated in the Constitution that the United States would be a democracy. The founding fathers wanted the new United States to be founded on principles of liberty and equality, but they did not specifically describe these principles with the term *democracy*. Thus, the Declaration of Independence, like the Constitution after it, did not stipulate a democracy, although both did state the principles of equality and freedom. The Constitution also provided for the election of the new government, and for protection of the rights of some, but not all, of the people. Notable exceptions at the time were black people and women. Only later were laws passed to protect their rights over the years.

45. A: Providing young children with hands-on experiences to practice skills related to social studies strengthens their internalization of foundational concepts necessary for continued success in learning. Doing so helps establish a framework for reference that students can apply when learning increasingly complex topics in the content area. The ability to use cardinal directions, for example, is necessary for describing the locations of places and regions, as well as understanding more complex ideas related to geographic literacy, such as spatial awareness, latitude, longitude, and time zones. In this situation, having students use written directions to physically draw landmarks on a town map allows them to visualize cardinal directions in a hands-on, developmentally appropriate learning setting.

46. A: This is a description of the metalinguistic ability of word consciousness. The metalinguistic ability of print conventions involves learning how to hold a book properly, where to start reading it, the directionality of print, and line-to-line continuity. The metalinguistic ability of print functions involves learning that print can be applied for different functions and purposes, like conveying information or providing entertainment. The metalinguistic ability of reading fluency involves learning, via being read to by adults, how to use intonation correctly and how to read in phrases rather than single words.

47. B: Integrating the arts and humanities into other disciplines strengthens students' content knowledge while promoting creative development. Further, providing such cross-curricular learning activities illustrates the connection between the arts and other subject areas, increasing relevance by demonstrating their prevalence in everyday life. By having students apply their knowledge of acute, obtuse, and right angles to draw a realistic impression of a city, this teacher facilitates students' ability to make connections between art and mathematics. In doing so, this teacher fosters greater understanding of both disciplines by demonstrating how concepts learned in each content area can be applied to one another.

48. B: Reading comprehension problems can be indicated by either or both: focusing on details to the exclusion of main concepts, i.e., "missing the forest for the trees," (A) can signal inadequate comprehension; but even when understanding the main ideas, being unable to relate any details (C) like a story's setting, characters' appearances, etc., can equally signify comprehension problems. Good comprehension enables both understanding the main points and also noticing and retaining supporting details. In addition, even if a student gets the main ideas, an inability to retell logical sequences of events in the reading (D) is a sign that the student's reading comprehension is deficient.

49. B: Homophones are words that sound the same when spoken aloud, but are spelled differently and have different meanings. Since homophones sound the same in spoken language, discerning between them often proves difficult for young students, particularly during reading and writing activities. However, the ability to correctly identify and use homophones is necessary for vocabulary acquisition, as well as the development of spelling, reading comprehension, and writing skills. Intervention is therefore necessary when a student is experiencing difficulty with this concept. Strategies that provide repetition, visual aids, and deeper understanding of word meanings promote students' ability to distinguish between commonly confused homophones. For example, sentence dictation exercises provide students the opportunity to practice writing homophones while reinforcing the concept through repetition. Visual aids, such as pictures to correspond with vocabulary words, promote students' ability to recognize and differentiate homophones. Teaching the morphology of vocabulary words also strengthens students' understanding of how parts of words are constructed, thus supporting their ability to distinguish between frequently confused homophones.

50. A: Young children need concrete objects to manipulate to learn geometry concepts. In early childhood, they think concretely and thus need to see, touch, and manipulate real things to help them understand abstract concepts; therefore, their memorizing theorems (B) at this age, when most children cannot even read let alone understand them, would be ineffective. Children should be given everyday life activities that teach geometric concepts—e.g., cutting their sandwiches into different geometric shapes, naming these for them, and letting them assemble and/or rearrange the pieces—*before* rather than after (C) they learn formal geometry basics, as activities that are part of daily life are relevant to young children and an effective way to teach concepts. Instructions to draw geometric diagrams (D) are more appropriate when children are older and have learned geometry concepts from interacting with solid objects and also have better-developed fine motor skills. Certainly, adults can help them draw shapes, but this should not be a first and/or isolated exercise.

51. A: Whereas behaviorist learning theorists believe that learning always results in some change in behavior, Bandura disagrees, finding children could learn something new without necessarily producing new or different behaviors. Bandura agrees with the behaviorist concept that consequences (events immediately following behaviors) either reward them, reinforcing and increasing their probable recurrence, or punish them, decreasing their probable recurrence. Unlike behaviorists who insist only externally observable, measurable behaviors can be changed, Bandura emphasizes the importance of internal cognitive processes in learning and thus of examining their roles (C), as well as social interactions in learning (D).

52. C: Music education offers significant benefits for early childhood development across domains. It is important that daily music instruction is incorporated into the curriculum, both as its own subject and throughout content areas. To effectively integrate music into the classroom, early childhood educators must be able to recognize some basic musical elements. Doing so is necessary for designing and implementing instructional strategies, activities, and learning experiences that foster students' understanding of musical concepts and promote whole-child development. Some examples of basic musical elements include, but are not limited to:

Rhythm: the pattern of sounds or beats that make up a piece of music
Melody: the progression of rhythmic sounds or beats that form a tune
Harmony: the sound created when multiple notes are played simultaneously
Timbre: the tone quality of an individual musical note
Texture: how individual components of a musical piece work together to create a whole composition
Form: the overall structure of a piece of music

53. D: Phoneme deletion is an instructional activity in which students practice sounding out parts of words after one phoneme, or sound, has been removed. This strategy develops students' sense of phonemic awareness, or the ability to distinguish individual sounds in spoken words or parts of words. Building phonemic awareness is foundational for emergent literacy skill development, as it contributes to phonological awareness, which is the ability to differentiate and understand words and sounds in spoken language as a whole.

54. A: Piaget demonstrated through experiments with very young children that they cannot yet perform logical or mathematical mental operations like dividing a whole into parts. They focus on only one aspect or property of an object rather than multiple properties; Piaget named this *centration.* When children in Piaget's Preoperational stage see several pieces of an apple, they see the total number of pieces rather than their sizes and assume several pieces equal more than one whole apple. Therefore they do not yet understand the part-whole concept {(B), (D)}, even if they can use concrete objects (C). Children in Piaget's Concrete Operations stage, around elementary school age, can understand these concepts as long as they are accompanied by concrete objects. They cannot understand them abstractly without concrete examples until Piaget's stage of Formal Operations, around the preteen to teen ages.

55. C: Physical geography focuses on processes and patterns in the natural environment. What people eat in any given geographic region is largely dependent on such environmental factors as climate and the availability of arable land. Religion, family, and language may all be affected by geographical factors, but they are not as immediately affected as dietary preferences.

56. D: Girls' singing voices change just as boys' do. While the change may begin earlier—as is the case with most of a girl's adolescent development—and is subtler, it does indeed take place. Girls who wish to sing through early adolescence and beyond will need the coaching of a good, patient instructor. Because girls' voices change, (A) and (B) are incorrect. Also incorrect is (C). Boys, like girls, can make good music in elementary and middle school, regardless of the changes taking place in their voices.

57. A: The inaccurate statement is the Puritans unconditionally supported the English Reformation. While they agreed with the Reformation in principle, they felt that it had not pursued those principles far enough and should make greater reforms. Similarly, they felt that the Church of England (or Anglican Church), though it had separated from the Catholic Church in the Protestant Reformation, still allowed many practices they found too much like Catholicism. The Puritans did become a chief political power in England because of the first English Civil War between Royalists and Parliamentarians. The Royalists had a profound suspicion of the radical Puritans. Among the Parliament's elements of resistance, the strongest was that of the Puritans. They joined in the battle initially for ostensibly political reasons as others had, but soon they brought more attention to religious issues. Following the Restoration in 1660 and the Uniformity Act of 1662, thereby restoring the Church of England to its pre-English Civil War status, the great majority of Puritan clergy defected from the Church of England. It is also accurate that the Puritans in England disagreed about separating from the Church of England. Some Puritans desired complete separation; they were known first as Separatists and after the Restoration as Dissenters. Others did not want complete separation but instead desired further reform in the Church of England. While they remained part of the Church of England, they were called Non-Separating Puritans, and after the Restoration, they were called Nonconformists.

58. C: Phonemic awareness refers to one's ability to decipher, identify, and manipulate individual sounds within spoken words. Developing this skill in young children is integral to building phonological awareness, which is the ability to differentiate and understand words and sounds within spoken language as a whole. Activities focused on developing students' phonemic awareness, such as rhymes, songs, and alphabet games, emphasize individual sounds within words. Implementing such activities helps establish the foundation of understanding necessary for literacy skill development.

59. C: Print-rich environments promote language and literacy skill development among young children of all proficiency levels, including English language learners and students with learning disabilities. Such an environment exposes students to and encourages them to interact with a variety of print materials, promoting acquisition and retention while demonstrating the applications of literacy in daily life. Further, a print-rich environment aligns learning with students' individual needs, as teachers can provide materials to accommodate a wide range of skill levels. By incorporating a word wall, labels, bulletin board, and calendar, as well as a classroom library with leveled texts, this teacher effectively creates a print-rich environment that is accessible and enriching for all students.

60. B: Receptive and expressive language skills are fundamental to literacy development among young children. Receptive language skills (the ability to understand and internalize language) are necessary for developing expressive language skills (the ability to accurately produce language). Both are necessary for building the background knowledge and vocabulary necessary for effective skill development in all areas of literacy, and therefore must be emphasized in the early childhood classroom. By reading aloud to students and providing explanations and visual examples, the teacher conscientiously promotes receptive language skill development. Further, in asking an open-ended question after the read-aloud, the teacher encourages expressive language skill development by prompting students to use expanded vocabulary to describe their favorite parts of the story.

61. C: When working with English language learners at all stages of proficiency development, it is important for teachers to recognize that the complexity and content-specific nature of academic language is often more difficult for these students to acquire. To promote retention, teachers should design learning experiences that demonstrate the use of new academic vocabulary in multiple contexts while allowing students several opportunities to practice interacting with the language. Thematic units are an effective strategy for promoting academic language acquisition in the early childhood classroom. This instructional approach implements activities across content areas that center upon a specific topic, thus providing multiple exposures to new academic vocabulary while simultaneously developing content knowledge. Further, thematic units often incorporate all areas of language development, thus promoting English acquisition across domains.

62. C: Early childhood educators must understand the general cognitive, physical, social, and emotional developmental levels of their students while recognizing and adapting instruction to accommodate individual learning differences. In scaffolding instruction to align with varying abilities and needs, teachers provide the necessary support to promote learning and development for all students in a developmentally appropriate setting.

63. B: In the 3N strategy, the Notice step does NOT involve having the student observe his or her own literacy strategies (A); it involves the teacher's observing the student's current literacy level. The Nudge step does involve the teacher's providing temporary support, i.e., scaffolding, to help the student achieve literacy tasks he or she could not yet accomplish independently. This scaffolding is gradually decreased as student proficiency levels increase. The Narrate step does NOT involve having the student verbally describe (C) or reflect on (D) his or her literacy activity; it involves the teacher verbally describing and reflecting on what the student did and accomplished during the activity.

64. B: Lev Vygotsky proposed that learning and development occur through interactions with individuals in one's immediate environment. For young children, therefore, most early learning experiences take place within the family and community setting prior to beginning school. As values, behaviors, beliefs, and interactions vary among cultures, the nature of learning and development among children will also differ. Teachers must be aware of these differences, as well as the role of family and culture in learning and development, so as to design cross-culturally competent instruction.

65. D: Basal reader series feature texts that are graded by reading levels (A), include both expository and narrative writing (B), and in children's literature and various other writing genres (C) are thematically organized by unit (D).

66. D: The reading rope was created by Dr. Hollis Scarborough to demonstrate the intricacies of building fluent reading skills. According to this model, the ability to read is developed through an interdependent combination of factors related to language comprehension and word recognition. Language comprehension becomes strategic in nature over time and consists of the learner's background knowledge, vocabulary, literacy knowledge, verbal reasoning, and understanding of language structures. Word recognition becomes primarily automatic with proper development and refers to the learner's phonological awareness, decoding and spelling skills, and sight recognition. Both components must be developed through effective instructional practices in order to work together in building reading fluency. When planning language and literacy instruction, the reading rope can be utilized as a framework for reference to ensure all components necessary are incorporated for reading fluency development.

67. A: Understanding algebraic concepts requires abstract thinking skills that must be developed in early childhood. Doing so provides students with a foundation of understanding that can be expanded and applied to more advanced mathematical concepts. Such development includes teaching young children to identify patterns and relationships among numbers, as well as different ways in which numbers and equations can be represented. By showing students how to solve the same addition problem in both standard and expanded form, this teacher demonstrates that numbers can be added in different ways by recognizing relationships between them, thus promoting algebraic thinking skills.

68. A: Contextual analysis skills, or the ability to look for clues within a text to decipher the meaning of unfamiliar words, are essential to vocabulary acquisition and reading comprehension. Examples of context clues include synonyms, antonyms, examples, or definitions that are embedded throughout the text and indicate the meaning of the new word. Teaching students to locate and use these clues helps them learn to make educated guesses regarding the meaning of unfamiliar terms, which increases vocabulary and improves reading comprehension skills.

69. D: To help them build strong oral language skills, adults should include questions in their conversations with young children that require them to form and express abstract concepts to answer. They should use rich vocabulary and complex sentence structures rather than simple ones. They should not just tell young children things but also ask them questions. Adults should not do most of the talking but engage young children in interactive conversations where both contribute equally.

70. C: Critical analysis skills are necessary for effectively reading, analyzing, and interpreting texts across genres and content areas. The ability to read critically enhances students' overall connection to and comprehension of a text, so it must be taught explicitly. In this situation, the teacher is asking students to engage in a close reading of an informational text by marking it with various symbols as they read. This strategy helps students focus intently on the text, promoting their ability to think critically about it and ultimately strengthening their understanding of the information presented.

71. D: Placing new concepts in a relevant, meaningful context promotes scientific learning and development among young children. Doing so lets students recognize the real-world implications of their learning as it applies to their own lives, fostering personal connections for greater understanding. In this situation, placing labeled recycling bins in the classroom demonstrates to students how they can use concepts learned on the field trip in everyday situations. This strategy encourages students to incorporate recycling into their daily routines while simultaneously prompting them to classify recyclables by material to promote appropriate recycling practices.

72. B: During Piaget's second stage—the preoperational stage—toddlers' and preschoolers' thinking is primarily intuitive as opposed to logical (A); logic does not develop until later. Primarily, sensory (C) and motoric (D) bases of thought are more closely associated with Piaget's first stage—the sensorimotor stage—during infancy.

73. A: Among instructional strategies defined by a master teacher (Robb, 2002), asking students open-ended questions about the texts they read is the most useful for helping students to read critically. Teaching students how to skim text for headings, subheadings, boldface, illustrations, captions, sidebars, the index, and other text features that give signs (B) of pertinent material is most useful for helping students locate information. Guiding students to make connections between text and their own personal experiences (D), everyday life (C), world events, and other texts is most useful for helping students understand the relevance of learning materials.

74. A: Communities around the world who drink fluoridated water have shown dramatic decreases in the number of dental cavities formed per citizen versus those communities that do not drink fluoridated water.

75. B: The symptoms exhibited by the student are characteristic of attention deficit hyperactivity disorder (ADHD), a behavioral disorder that impacts one's ability to focus, sustain attention, and control impulses. ADHD also frequently impacts the development of reading comprehension skills, because in addition to impeding focus, it often affects language processing skills. According to the Individuals with Disabilities Education Act (IDEA), if a teacher suspects a student has a disability that impedes their ability to learn effectively must refer the student for an initial evaluation to determine the need for special education services.

76. C: Babies typically develop the self-awareness ability to differentiate between live video of themselves and people imitating their behaviors around 4–7 months of age. Newborns (A) demonstrate the self-awareness ability of differentiating their bodies from the environment and internal/self from external/other stimulation from birth. At 2 years old (B), most children demonstrate awareness of symbolic representation, understanding that mirror images and photos represent themselves. Around 1–3 months of age (D), babies are typically able to smile in response to stimuli and have some ability to lift their head when in the prone position.

77. C: Research finds that children with good reading comprehension are able to summarize the text they have read and make predictions based on it. Rather than only reading text familiar within their existing knowledge (A), they are able to make connections or associations of new material to the knowledge they already have that is pertinent to the text. They are not only skilled at decoding words, but they also have good vocabularies, which *is* necessary (B) because it is exceedingly hard for readers to comprehend text if they are unable to define many of the words in it. Readers with good comprehension also do show skills in using the sentence structure (D) in the text they read to aid their reading comprehension. Many cues in sentence syntax and grammar help them rule out some meanings and confirm others.

78. D: School-age children are likely to be working on ongoing projects which toddlers and preschoolers will not; and other activities that are age-appropriate for older children are not for younger ones, so the school-age children should have separate areas provided for their activities. Furniture should NOT be lightweight and easy to move around (A): while this would facilitate rearrangements in other cases, for infants and toddlers to pull up, balance, and cruise, the furniture must be heavy, sturdy, and bolted in place. Art and cooking activities should be near sinks or other water sources (B) to enable easier cleanup. There should be separate areas for dramatic play, block-building, book-reading, and music activities (C).

79. C: In lessons about color as one element of visual arts, preschool children can learn the names of different colors (A); skills of sensory discrimination (B) in telling different colors apart from each other; and skills of classification (D) by separating different colors and experimenting with mixing colors to see what other colors they produce.

80. A: By asking the child to come up with alternative criteria for sorting (e.g., by size, shape, or weight instead of by color), the teacher is helping the child to develop problem-solving skills in thinking of a variety of alternative solutions/answers. Telling the child that he or she is performing classification (B) is a better example of teaching formal math vocabulary by connecting it with informal math activity rather than promoting problem solving. Asking the child how he or she is sorting the rocks (C) is a better example of promoting math communication through explaining the sorting criterion rather than promoting problem solving.

81. D: Automaticity refers to one's ability to quickly recognize and understand written words. This skill is fundamental to the development of reading fluency, and is cultivated by frequent exposure to new vocabulary, printed words, and patterns of phonics. Students that struggle with automaticity typically have trouble recognizing written words, reading at a grade-level-appropriate pace, and comprehending what they have read. Difficulty with automaticity in reading may result from numerous factors, such as limited phonics knowledge or exposure to printed language, weak decoding skills, or a learning disability. As this skill is integral to language and literacy development, struggling students must receive necessary interventions and support.

82. B: The alphabetic principle is the concept that written/printed letters are symbols that represent the speech sounds that make up words. Civilizations develop writing systems after spoken language. Hence written letters reflect spoken sounds. Children must not only know the entire alphabet in sequence (A), but also recognize and be able to name all letters in the alphabet (C) and identify their shapes as well as their names (D) as parts of understanding the alphabetic principle.

83. A: This example describes the think-pair-share strategy, where a teacher poses a question, gives students time to think about their responses independently, and then puts them in pairs to discuss their responses together. Next, students discuss the responses as a whole class. In the jigsaw approach, students are put into small groups, and each student is assigned one portion of the content that he or she is responsible for learning and presenting to the group. Close reading involves multiple readings of the same text, exploring deeper layers each time. Cloze reading involves giving students a brief passage with some omitted words, which students fill in using clues or background knowledge.

84. C: Building students' foundational understanding of basic scientific principles is essential to ensuring they have the tools necessary for approaching increasingly advanced concepts. Doing so provides students with a framework of reference from which to apply knowledge for continuous scientific learning and development. In this situation, implementing a project in which students construct a suitable habitat for a frog is an effective strategy for demonstrating that living things must have their needs met to survive. To be successful in this project, students must first have a fundamental awareness that all living things require food, water, shelter, and space. With this information in mind, students can begin to brainstorm what to include in the frog habitat, calculate the appropriate amount of space, and effectively plan the necessary steps for creating a suitable, functioning habitat that meets its survival needs.

85. D: Orthographic processing skills encompass the ability to recognize and recall written words, as well as implement conventions related to writing, including spelling, punctuation, and capitalization. Students with strong orthographic processing skills are able to visually identify when a word is spelled incorrectly because of their understanding of the parts of words. In this situation, by asking students to circle misspelled words from a list of familiar vocabulary, the teacher is assessing students' orthographic processing skills in relation to writing conventions.

86. B: In instruction about color as an element of visual art, preschool teachers can help children learn color names, sensory discrimination, and classification skills. Teachers can read children a story about colors, or sing/play a song about colors to introduce a lesson (A). Some art museums do offer pre-designed lessons in visual art elements for preschool ages (C), which teachers can use as models. After a story or song, teachers can present a painting or other artwork, which young children can appreciate (D) on their own levels.

87. B: Instructional objectives are influenced by the major behaviorist learning theory principle that only behaviors that other people can observe and measure can be modified. Hence, in applying Bloom's Taxonomy, such objectives avoid vague internal terms like 'Remember' and 'Understand' (choice A) and instead use only action verbs to describe how students must demonstrate learning (choice B). Choice D is incorrect because it suggests measurability is optional, whereas behaviorism emphasizes observable and measurable behavior.

88. C: The ability to analyze the structure of words is necessary for vocabulary acquisition, decoding, and ultimately, reading comprehension. This skill becomes increasingly important as older students are exposed to more complex vocabulary, as it allows them to more effectively examine the parts of unfamiliar terms to derive meaning. Hands-on learning opportunities, such as word-building games, are beneficial in allowing students to physically manipulate the components of multisyllabic words, thus strengthening structural analysis skills.

89. D: Think-Pair-Share activities involve students' discussing assigned subjects with partners, giving each other constructive feedback, and then applying this feedback in sharing with the whole class. Teachers can use this for both spoken and written student responses. Written Responses, Varying Answers (A) involves students' checking written responses with partners, revising as needed, and reading them when teachers call on them. Written Responses, Same Answers (B) involves students' writing answers to teacher questions on boards and then holding them up upon teacher signaling. Since answer choice D is correct, answer choice C is incorrect.

90. B: Allowing multiple opportunities for both structured and unstructured dramatic play offers significant benefits for whole-child development, so it must be incorporated in the early childhood classroom. Doing so promotes creative development and self-expression as students assume and act out various roles. In addition, through dramatic play, students can explore, process, and organize new information to strengthen their understanding of the world around them. Dramatic play also supports development of young children's linguistic and interpersonal skills, as it provides opportunities to communicate with one another, work together, as well as develop problem-solving and conflict-resolution skills. By providing students with various costumes and props, this teacher demonstrates understanding of the importance and benefits of incorporating dramatic play into the classroom at this developmental stage.

91. A: After adults tell young children the names of geometric shapes they are looking at, adults should thereafter ask children to tell them these names the next time. Then, they should ask children to describe different shapes. They can then ask children to use their fingers to trace existing drawings of shapes and draw different shapes in the air with their fingers. Finally, they can ask children to make their own drawings of the shapes.

92. A: A model volcano eruption using vinegar and baking soda is an acid-base reaction, not an oxidation-reduction reaction. Tin cans are steel cans with a tin coating. Applying this coating involves an oxidation-reduction reaction. Decomposition of hydrogen peroxide and dough rising through the production of CO2 by yeast are both redox reactions. Rust formation is a redox reaction of iron, oxygen, and water. While the wind and rain are physical factors, rust formation is a chemical process.

93. C: Teachers can ask children at younger ages of early childhood to identify vocabulary words used in shared readings, e.g. "What was this called?"; and describe story details, e.g. "How did they do that?" Asking children to predict coming events in a story (A), to imagine applications of story situations beyond the story (B), and to conclude why story characters act/feel as they do (D) are all appropriate techniques to use during and after shared readings with children at older ages of early childhood. These elements of literature may be too abstract with the younger ages of early childhood.

94. D: To understand fractions, children must know all of these things: what makes up a particular whole unit; how many pieces that unit is divided into; and whether the pieces are all of the same size or not. Knowing the number of parts but not what makes up the unit (A); knowing what comprises the whole unit, but not how many pieces into which it has been divided (B); or knowing both what makes up the whole unit and how many pieces it has been divided into, but not knowing whether the pieces are equal in size or not (C) will not allow children to comprehend the concept of fractions. For example, a child will not understand the idea of thirds if something is divided into three parts of *unequal* size, because each piece is not equal to one-third of the whole.

95. D: The idea that fractions represent parts of a whole can be difficult for young children to grasp initially, as it requires a degree of abstract thinking. Incorporating manipulatives, such as pattern blocks, can help promote understanding for struggling students by adding a concrete element to learning. Pattern block sets are typically composed of squares, equilateral triangles, hexagons, rhombuses, and trapezoids, and are often used to demonstrate that shapes can be divided into equal parts. This resource allows students to visualize and physically manipulate shapes into equal parts, strengthening their understanding that fractions represent parts of a whole.

96. A: Young children internalize new concepts most effectively when provided with a variety of hands-on, relevant, and interactive learning opportunities. The teacher's awareness of this notion is evident throughout the activities selected for a unit on markets and economic systems. By following a field trip to the grocery store with a classroom market activity, the teacher provides varied and active learning experiences to foster engagement and exploration of how the concept being taught applies to daily life. Further, by incorporating such activities as planning a budget and using pretend money, the teacher establishes cross-curricular connections between social studies and math for strengthened overall understanding.

97. B: Children cannot learn the sounds represented by printed/written letters, and cannot recognize printed words, without knowing the letters' names. Knowing letter names is closely correlated with being able to see words as combinations of letters and to remember printed words. Knowing the alphabet sequence helps students remember all the letters but is not as important to learn letter-sound correspondences as being able to identify and name them. They must be able to write letters to write words, sentences, and beyond but not to learn sound-letter relationships or read words. They must learn both letter shapes and letter names to recognize letters, learn letter sounds, and identify words.

98. B: Research finds that preschool-aged children exhibiting delayed language development are more likely to receive diagnoses of reading disorders when they begin school, and that instruction in PPA helps them. PPA instruction is also found to help preschoolers with articulation (pronunciation) disorders (C) and school-aged children with spelling disorders (D). In fact, all children who are learning to read, including not just preschoolers but also kindergarteners and first-graders (A), benefit from instruction in PPA.

99. C: Young children learn by interacting with their environment in a hands-on setting. Learning stations provide multiple opportunities to do so, as students are encouraged to observe, explore, and engage with the world around them. This allows young children to formulate questions, test new ideas, and solve problems within their physical environment, thus developing learning experiences they can build upon. In addition, learning stations provide opportunities for structured and unstructured learning, both of which are integral in supporting the cognitive, physical, social, and emotional development of young children.

100. B: Scaffolding science instruction helps to ensure that students of varying needs, skill levels, and abilities receive the support necessary to succeed in all stages of the learning process. Scaffolds can be implemented in a number of ways to accommodate a variety of learning situations. Many science activities incorporate hands-on, collaborative investigations, so strategic pairing scaffolds learning to facilitate all students' participation in the process. This strategy allows students who may need extra help to build upon the knowledge, skills, and understanding of their partners to promote their own learning and development in science.

Practice Test #2

1. A third-grade teacher is planning a unit in which students will independently read a work of fictional literature. Which of the following prereading strategies would likely be most effective in enhancing students' overall comprehension of the text?

a. Administering a diagnostic exam to determine students' level of literacy development
b. Providing students with a word bank of unfamiliar vocabulary from the text
c. Scaffolding the text by chunking it into smaller parts
d. Having students complete an anticipation guide prior to reading the text

2. What is correct about the role of telling stories in young children's language development?

a. Storytelling does not generally provide much benefit besides entertainment.
b. When listening to children's storytelling, teachers should generally refrain from asking questions.
c. Storytelling permits young children to exercise their powers of imagination.
d. Teachers should let children express their ideas without building onto them.

3. A third-grade teacher is planning a unit on the characteristics of different freshwater and saltwater bodies. Which of the following accompanying activities would best connect this topic to social studies?

a. Leading a class discussion on how hurricanes, tsunamis, and floods impact the environment and human activities
b. Having students complete a research project on how proximity to water bodies influenced human settlement patterns
c. Creating a Venn diagram to compare and contrast the characteristics of saltwater and freshwater bodies
d. Instructing students to identify rural, suburban, and urban locations on a map

4. Which of the following instructional strategies is the most practical technique to modify music instruction when teaching classical guitar in a general music classroom?

a. Separate high achievers from low achievers
b. Eliminate individual formative assessments
c. Provide each student with short personal lessons
d. Design group projects based upon mutual interests

5. The price of oil drops dramatically, saving soda pop manufacturers great amounts of money spent on making soda pop and delivering their product to market. Prices for soda pop, however, stay the same. This is an example of what?

a. Sticky prices
b. Indiscriminate costs
c. Stable demand
d. Aggregate expenditure

6. What is the correct meaning of cognitive dissonance?

a. A cognitive processing disorder affecting understanding
b. A disruption of cognition caused by a sensory overload
c. A feeling of discomfort due to contradictory information
d. A lack of compatibility between instruction and learning

7. Which of the following strategies would best incorporate students' cultural and linguistic diversities into instruction?

a. Establishing and maintaining frequent communication with students' families
b. Collaborating with grade-level colleagues to host a culture day for students
c. Selecting instructional materials and resources that reflect students' backgrounds
d. Teaching about the customs, traditions, and values of different cultures around the world

8. In addition to artistic functions, art within its context can serve physical, personal, and/or social functions. Which of the following examples has an artistic function but no physical function?

a. An elegant raku bowl used in a Japanese tea ceremony
b. A Dada artist's cup, saucer, and spoon covered with hair
c. An exquisitely crafted tribal war club to beat the enemy
d. Any and all of these examples serve a physical function

9. During a lesson on two- and three-dimensional shapes, a second-grade teacher leads students around the school and asks them to identify triangles, quadrilaterals, pentagons, cubes, and hexagons within the architecture of the building. In doing so, this teacher demonstrates to students which of the following concepts?

a. How to develop mathematical communication skills
b. Connections between mathematics and other content areas
c. Applications of mathematics in real-world contexts
d. Problem-solving strategies

10. During an unstructured play activity, a second-grade teacher notices two students disagreeing about whose turn it is to use a particular toy. Based upon the typical characteristics related to social and emotional development for students of this age group, the most appropriate response would be to do what?

a. Contact the students' families to inform them of the conflict.
b. Separate the students to avoid further disagreement.
c. Suggest that one student play with a different toy.
d. Allow the students to resolve the conflict among themselves.

11. Paper strips and Cuisenaire rods are manipulatives used to teach

a. Place value
b. Fractions
c. Addition of whole numbers
d. Percentages

12. After completing a unit on the characteristics and processes of the water cycle, a fourth-grade teacher wants to evaluate students' understanding of the concept. Which of the following summative assessment approaches would be most developmentally appropriate for this age group?

a. Having students complete a self-reflection activity once the unit is complete
b. Administering a vocabulary quiz on key terms related to the water cycle
c. Having students work collaboratively to create a model of the water cycle
d. Assigning students to participate in a virtual field trip to various bodies of water

13. A kindergarten teacher shows students a jar of red, green, and blue beads. The teacher asks students to predict which color of bead is most prevalent in the jar, and records their responses on a bar graph. Which of the following developmental concepts is this strategy likely intended to support?

a. Estimation and measurement
b. Operations and algebraic thinking
c. Number sense and ordering
d. Data analysis and probability

14. Which of the following strategies would likely be most effective in developing and implementing culturally competent learning experiences that meet the needs of all students?

a. Incorporating opportunities for student choice in learning
b. Attending back-to-school night to meet students' families
c. Supplementing instruction with appropriate accommodations and modifications
d. Diversifying instruction to accurately and respectfully reflect differences within the classroom

15. Which of the following correctly sequences the steps in research to teach to students for research-based writing?

a. Generate subtopics; establish and triangulate topics; read, think, and select information; identify sources; take notes; write from notes plus previous knowledge; sort notes
b. Identify sources; read, think, and select information; take notes; sort notes; establish and triangulate topics; generate subtopics; write from notes plus previous knowledge
c. Read, think, and select information; identify sources; take notes; sort notes; write from notes plus previous knowledge; generate subtopics; establish and triangulate topics
d. Establish and triangulate topics; generate subtopics; identify sources; take notes; sort notes; write from notes plus previous knowledge; read, think, and select information

16. Mrs. Cranston, a seventh grade science teacher, tries to provide her students with several options when assigning projects. This approach is useful because it fosters emotional development in which of the following areas?

a. Development of a variety of learning approaches
b. Development of self-concept
c. Developing a sense of autonomy
d. Developing identification with peer groups

17. A third-grade teacher is preparing a unit on integrated pest management. To strengthen students' understanding of what constitutes a pest and why it must be controlled, this teacher should be sure to cover which of the following topics during instruction?

a. Common plants and animals found on farms
b. The difference between living and nonliving things
c. The habitats and survival needs of animals
d. Examples of ecological relationships found in nature

18. During which stage of spelling development do children typically first start to understand correspondences of alphabet letters to speech sounds?

a. In the Transitional stage
b. During the Correct stage
c. During the Phonetic stage
d. In the Semiphonetic stage

19. A man's lawn grass is 3 inches high. He mows the lawn and cuts off 30% of its height. How tall will the grass be after the lawn is mowed?

a. 0.9 inches
b. 2.1 inches
c. 2.7 inches
d. 2.9 inches

20. In EC development in the area of interpersonal interactions, which do children typically develop first?

a. Autonomy/independence
b. Trusting/mistrusting others
c. A sense of initiative or guilt
d. Make-believe/pretending

21. Of the following, which is the most accurate statement regarding stereotyping in early childhood?

a. Preschoolers naturally form stereotyped cognitions about other people.
b. Preschoolers are not cognitively developed enough to form stereotypes.
c. Preschoolers do not naturally stereotype others but can be taught to do so.
d. Preschoolers do not understand stereotyping as it is an abstract concept.

22. EC teachers can use puppet shows to help preschoolers develop their social skills through an entertaining medium. What is true about puppet show content and guiding children's discussion of it?

a. Teachers should not encourage being judgmental by asking if puppets are good or bad.
b. It would be irrelevant to ask children which puppets they liked and which they disliked.
c. This is a good way to demonstrate it is preferable to use words over aggressive action.
d. Children should be allowed to say what occurred but not predict what may occur next or offer alternative behaviors.

23. A fourth-grade teacher uses a classroom token economy in which students can redeem tickets earned for positive behavior in exchange for various prizes. The most sought-after prizes require more tickets, whereas less desired items cost less. This strategy promotes students' understanding of which of the following concepts?

a. Supply and demand
b. Scarcity and choice
c. Limited resources
d. Profits and losses

24. What is true about the sequence that teachers should use for phonics instruction with young children?

a. Teachers should introduce letters with similar sounds in separate lessons.
b. Teachers should introduce stop consonants before continuous consonants.
c. Teachers should introduce letters that look similar during the same lesson.
d. Teachers should introduce low-utility before high-utility letters and sounds.

25. Each week, a kindergarten teacher introduces a new short-vowel sound. To practice, the teacher implements letter games that incorporate movement, chooses books to read aloud that focus on the new sound, and has students recite it along with corresponding CVC words. These activities are beneficial in building which of the following emergent literacy skills?

a. Phonics
b. Receptive language
c. Reading comprehension
d. Orthographic processing

26. At the beginning of each school day, a kindergarten teacher reviews the monthly calendar with students. The teacher labels days of the week as "yesterday," "today," and "tomorrow," and asks students to identify important events throughout the month. This strategy is beneficial in developing students' sense of which foundational concept related to social studies?

a. How to differentiate between fact and opinion about important events
b. Personal responsibility when working with a group
c. Time, continuity, and change
d. The importance of structure and routine to the function of an organization

27. Which of the following elements is NOT audiated by students?

a. Intervals
b. Melodic contour
c. Time signatures
d. Harmonic functions

28. A prekindergarten teacher leads the class in singing a song that incorporates movement and dance. Throughout the song, students can run in place, jump, wave their arms, and kick their legs. The teacher likely selected this song to promote students' development of which of the following?

a. Phonological awareness
b. Fine motor skills
c. Gross motor skills
d. Auditory discrimination

29. To apply Bandura's theory, educators must realize that he emphasized ______ as the most important influence on learning.

a. nuclear conflicts
b. erogenous zones
c. cognitive abilities
d. social interactions

30. A second-grade teacher is planning a unit on adding and subtracting numbers up to 1,000. Prior to beginning the unit, the teacher administers a diagnostic assessment focused on content and skills from the upcoming unit. Which of the following foundational concepts should this teacher include on the assessment?

a. Comparing three-digit numbers
b. Order of operations
c. Place value
d. Creating and extending patterns

31. When applying the following identified motivational factors specifically to student motivation to write, which one applies more to overall writing skills than to specific writing tasks?

a. Students' beliefs about their self-efficacy
b. Students' goals for performance/mastery
c. Students' interest/value for writing tasks
d. Students' attributions for failure/success

32. A third-grade teacher works with students of varying needs and learning abilities, including English language learners. For an upcoming math unit on fractions, which of the following instructional approaches would be most effective in making learning accessible to all students?

a. Incorporating digital resources to promote engagement
b. Beginning the new unit by reviewing previously learned material
c. Presenting new information through a variety of mediums
d. Aligning instructional activities with grade-level district academic standards

33. In which of the following stages of spelling development do children use letters to represent speech sounds in a systematic and understandable way?

a. Correct
b. Transitional
c. Semiphonetic
d. Phonetic

34. Which learning theory is based on the idea that students are actively involved in constructing their own meaning, and that teachers should guide students through scaffolding rather than using instructor-led teaching techniques?

a. Behaviorism
b. Cognitivism
c. Constructivism
d. Social learning theory

35. A second-grade teacher is planning a lesson on the life cycle of plants. Which of the following strategies would best incorporate arts and humanities into this lesson?

a. Having students participate in a class nature walk to observe and record various types of plants
b. Allowing students to observe the details of various plants using a microscope
c. Leading a class discussion on the similarities and differences between the life cycles of plants and animals
d. Having students create paintings or drawings to depict each stage of the plant life cycle, and incorporating a song focused on the topic

36. After having students read an informational text on the life cycle of plants, a third-grade teacher noticed that some individuals struggled to understand key vocabulary in the passage. Which of the following strategies would likely best help these students improve their comprehension?

a. Assigning comprehension questions corresponding to the text
b. Having students complete a KWL chart
c. Demonstrating how to look up unfamiliar vocabulary in the dictionary
d. Having students create a semantic map

37. Of the following, which is true about providing affective learning experiences for preschoolers?

a. Affective learning activities are more time-efficient and easier to facilitate in large classes.
b. Learning to understand their feelings will not help children with self-regulation.
c. Affective activities cannot inform teachers of children's feelings or preferences.
d. Children's social development and interactions require emotional development.

38. Of the following theories of cognitive development, which proposes discrete developmental changes?

a. Skinner's
b. Vygotsky's
c. Bandura's
d. Piaget's

39. To strengthen beginning preschoolers' alphabetic knowledge, teachers should:

a. Focus on cumulative reviews of letter-sound matches children have learned.
b. Focus on creating occasions for children to practice new letter-sound matches.
c. Balance knowledge reviews with learning practice, including phonetic spellings.
d. Avoid supplying children with incorrect phonetic spellings of words they know.

40. Which of these is NOT one of the major personality structures proposed by Sigmund Freud in his psychoanalytic theory of development?

a. Id
b. Ego
c. Libido
d. Superego

41. Which part of a hurricane features the strongest winds and greatest rainfall?

a. Eye wall
b. Front
c. Eye
d. Outward spiral

42. A fourth-grade student with medically diagnosed attention deficit hyperactivity disorder (ADHD) often becomes overwhelmed and struggles to focus on lengthy reading passages. Which of the following accommodations would best support the student's ability to fully engage in reading assignments?

a. Preferential seating toward the front of the room
b. Providing audio recordings of reading passages
c. Reducing the length of reading assignments and providing enlarged font
d. Chunking the texts and providing extra time for processing

43. Labeling items throughout the classroom with words and corresponding images is an effective strategy for promoting prekindergarten students' ability to:

a. Understand the purpose of written language
b. Read written text from left to right
c. Describe the connections between pictures and words
d. Identify and name objects

44. What is true about general behavior management principles for early childhood?

a. Adults need to make rules, but they do not always need to follow them.
b. Adults need only repeat rules that they made a few times for young children.
c. Adults must always consistently enforce whichever rules they establish.
d. Adults should only reward children for good behaviors some of the time.

45. Which of the following is NOT correct regarding assumptions of mercantilism?

a. The money and the wealth of a nation are identical properties.
b. In order to prosper, a nation should try to increase its imports.
c. In order to prosper, a nation should try to increase its exports.
d. Economic protectionism by national governments is advisable.

46. Each day during music time, a first-grade teacher leads the class in singing songs that incorporate group movement and dance. Which of the following additional learning materials would promote students' sense of spatial and kinesthetic awareness?

a. A variety of musical instruments
b. Props such as hula hoops, ribbons, and sticks
c. A metronome for keeping time
d. Visual examples of various dance movements

47. A second-grade teacher is planning a unit on the basic needs of plants and animals in aquatic ecosystems. The teacher wants to incorporate a hands-on learning experience that allows students to interact with and compare different aquatic habitats, but due to their location, a field trip is not feasible. In which of the following ways could the teacher use technology to create a similar active learning experience?

a. Have students conduct online research about different aquatic habitats.
b. Create a slideshow presentation on the basic needs of plants and animals in aquatic ecosystems.
c. Have students participate in a virtual field trip in which they explore various aquatic habitats.
d. Show a documentary on the characteristics of aquatic ecosystems.

48. A third-grade teacher has noticed that a student often skips words or guesses them incorrectly when reading aloud. When writing, the student often uses inventive spelling, particularly for complex words. The student would likely benefit from intervention to develop which of the following skills?

a. Listening responsively to spoken language
b. Initiating and responding appropriately in conversations
c. Irregular sight word recognition
d. Decoding and encoding

49. A first-grade teacher has organized a food drive in which students are encouraged to bring in cans of nonperishable food for donation. Which of the following best describes the benefit of such a project?

a. Achieving academic benchmarks related to civic rights and responsibilities
b. Developing students' civic values through public service
c. Providing hands-on learning experiences that incorporate student choice
d. Instilling a sense of personal responsibility among students

Refer to the following for question 50:

An EC teacher gives children an art activity of illustrating and labeling plants or animals by name that they learned about in a science unit. However, one student in the classroom has difficulty focusing on her project and is often found wandering away from her desk, distracting other students.

50. This activity best exemplifies which learning application of art?

a. Using art to build their language skills and vocabularies
b. Developing skills of color recognition and discrimination
c. Developing awareness of line, shape, color, and texture
d. Using art to express feelings and thoughts, and tell stories

51. A third-grade student has a physical health impairment that makes lengthy writing assignments time-consuming and painful. Which of the following accommodations would best support this student's ability to participate in writing activities?

a. Reducing the length requirement of writing assignments
b. Preferential seating in the front of the classroom
c. The option to complete an alternative assignment
d. Speech-to-text technology

52. A kindergarten teacher is planning to introduce students to word families. A beneficial concept to teach first would be:

a. Automaticity
b. Semantics analysis
c. Onset and rime
d. Prosody

53. A fourth-grade teacher is planning a unit in which students will write narrative essays, and wants to focus on developing students' ability to establish a clear beginning, middle, and end. Which of the following prewriting strategies would be most effective?

a. Having students complete a story map
b. Demonstrating how to gather supporting evidence
c. Asking students to brainstorm topics for their narratives
d. Conducting a lesson on transitional words and phrases

54. A kindergarten teacher uses color-coded letter cards to spell a word and asks students to read it aloud. The teacher then replaces one letter card with a different one, and asks students to identify the new word. For example, after spelling the word "cat," the teacher replaces the letter "c" with "b" and asks students to read the new word. This strategy is likely intended to teach which of the following skills?

a. Phoneme substitution
b. Alliteration
c. Identification of rhyming words
d. The alphabetic principle

55. A kindergarten teacher reads a series of vocabulary words aloud and asks students to identify which sound they hear at the beginning of each one. In doing so, this teacher is assessing which of the following skills?

a. Expressive language
b. Students' ability to identify high-frequency words
c. Phonemic isolation
d. Reading comprehension

56. According to Jean Piaget's theory of cognitive development in children, prekindergarten students are most likely to engage in:

a. Circular reactions
b. Logical problem-solving
c. Symbolic play
d. Abstract reasoning

57. While reading a work of fictional literature, a third-grade teacher asks students to circle words that describe the main character in order to determine the character's motives throughout the story. This strategy is likely intended to develop which of the following skills?

a. Literal reading comprehension
b. Inferential reading comprehension
c. Critical reading comprehension
d. Evaluative reading comprehension

58. A first-grade teacher has included some non-decodable words on students' weekly vocabulary list. Each day, the teacher reviews these words using flashcards as a whole-class activity. During class circle time, the teacher reads aloud a story that incorporates these vocabulary words. Students also practice tracing and writing the new words, as well as using them in sentences. These strategies are likely intended to promote the development of which of the following skills?

a. Recognizing consonant-vowel-consonant (CVC) words as individual units
b. Morpheme division in multisyllabic words
c. Irregular sight word recognition
d. Distinguishing between digraphs and blends

59. A first-grade teacher wants to monitor individual students' progress in developing several artistic skills throughout the school year. Which of the following assessment approaches would best achieve this goal?

a. Collecting samples of students' artwork to create individual portfolios
b. Periodically observing students using a checklist to assess skill development
c. Grading students based on participation in art projects
d. A multiple-choice quiz to determine students' knowledge of key vocabulary related to various forms of art

60. The Seven Years' War, called the French and Indian War by the Colonists:

a. Was the precursor to the American Revolution
b. Was a conflict related to European colonization
c. Primarily took place in Canada
d. Ended European conquests

61. A third-grade teacher is planning a unit in which students will be assigned to write fictional narratives. Prior to engaging in writing, the teacher wants to develop students' ability to gather and coherently organize ideas. Which of the following strategies would likely be most effective in achieving this?

a. Demonstrating and having students practice the steps of the research process
b. Providing students with a graphic organizer as a pre-writing activity
c. Incorporating peer-editing opportunities throughout the writing process
d. Conferencing individually with students to provide feedback on their narratives

62. Social and behavioral theories of learning stress the importance of:

a. Good behavior on the part of students
b. The social interactions of students that aid or inhibit learning
c. A reward system for good behavior or growth in skills
d. The direct connection between thoughts and speech

63. The idea that the purpose of the American colonies was to provide Great Britain with raw materials and a market for its goods is an expression of:

a. Free trade
b. Most favored nation status
c. Mercantilism
d. Laissez-faire capitalism

64. If a child who is 9–10 years old does not correctly pronounce the phonemes /s/ and /r/, what does this most likely represent?

a. A definite sign of hearing loss
b. A kind of intellectual disability
c. Normal language development
d. A possible articulation disorder

65. A first-grade teacher is planning a lesson in which students will identify and compare the features of different earth materials, including soil, rock, pebbles, and clay. Which of the following activities would best promote students' sense of inquiry about this concept?

a. Showing students pictures of different types of earth materials
b. Having students conduct online research about the characteristics of different earth materials
c. Asking open-ended questions about why earth materials take different forms
d. Having students search for and identify different earth materials on the school campus

66. During a lesson on seasonal changes, a fourth-grade student asks the teacher why there is less sunlight during the winter months. Which of the following activities could this teacher implement to best help the student investigate and understand this concept?

a. Creating a three-dimensional model of the Earth's revolution around the Sun
b. Building a diorama of the Earth's position in relation to other planets
c. Constructing an outdoor sundial using recycled materials
d. Having the student keep a daily log of sunrise and sunset times

67. A second-grade teacher is planning a unit on renewable versus nonrenewable energy sources. To best promote students' understanding of the difference between the two, it would be helpful for this teacher to first review which of the following?

a. The morphology of the words "renewable" and "nonrenewable"
b. Each form of energy and ways in which it is used
c. The process through which fossils are formed
d. Ways in which different living things use sunlight for energy

68. A child who understands that the word *books* means two or more while *book* means one is demonstrating an understanding of:

a. Phonology
b. Morphology
c. Syntax
d. Semantics

69. A second-grade teacher is planning a unit on English grammatical conventions to ultimately develop students' writing skills. Before beginning the unit, the teacher administers a pretest that includes questions about capitalization, punctuation, and spelling. Which of the following best describes how the data from this pretest will improve instructional effectiveness?

a. Providing students with context regarding what they will be learning
b. Determining students' areas of strengths and needs to inform instructional planning
c. Exposing students to material that will appear on the summative assessment
d. Promoting students' curiosity and interest in the upcoming unit

70. According to Piaget's theory of cognitive development, ______ and ______ are processes included in the overall process of ______.

a. assimilation; accommodation; adaptation
b. adaptation; assimilation; accommodation
c. accommodation; adaptation; assimilation
d. adaptation; accommodation; equilibrium

71. Which map describes the movement of people, trends, or materials across a physical area?

a. Political Map
b. Cartogram
c. Qualitative Map
d. Flow-line Map

72. A preschool teacher has children lie down on butcher paper in whatever body positions they choose. The teacher outlines the children's body contours with a marker and has the children personalize them using various drawing tools. This activity best illustrates instruction in which element of visual art?

a. Color
b. Shape
c. Light
d. Line

73. The whole language approach is best suited to which kind of literacy instructional activity?

a. Teachers reading books aloud to children
b. Small reading groups guided by teachers
c. It is equally well suited to any/all these.
d. Children reading books independently

74. What is the most appropriate principle for EC teachers to follow for children's science inquiry and discovery learning?

a. Teachers should teach only things that the children enjoy the most.
b. Teachers should teach things that they know and enjoy themselves.
c. Teachers should direct children to standard use of learning materials.
d. Teachers should assign structured activities with new materials first.

75. A young child in Piaget's Preoperational stage of cognitive development is most likely to draw which of the following conclusions?

a. That one whole cookie and another cookie the same size cut into four pieces are the same amount
b. That one whole cookie is a larger amount than another cookie the same size cut up into four pieces
c. That one whole cookie is the same amount as one piece of the same size cookie cut into four pieces
d. That one whole cookie is not as much as another cookie the same size that is cut up into four pieces

76. A first-grade teacher works with a group of primarily native Spanish-speaking students, many of whom are identified as English language learners. In the classroom, this teacher incorporates students' native language into instruction by labeling items in both English and Spanish, including Spanish texts in the class library, and teaching Spanish vocabulary words that correspond to daily lessons. Which of the following best describes the benefit of this strategy?

a. Promoting bilingual immersion for all students
b. Creating an inclusive environment that recognizes the importance of students' primary language in English language acquisition
c. Providing English language learners with the opportunity to learn in their preferred language
d. Scaffolding instruction to align with varying levels of English language proficiency

77. A first-grade student often leaves out the ending sounds when reading regular high-frequency sight words aloud. Which of the following strategies would best help this student improve her decoding skills?

a. Having the student practice sounding out words using letter tiles
b. Incorporating rhyming games and songs into instruction
c. Giving the student a list of spelling words to practice each week
d. Having the student trace and practice writing high-frequency sight words

78. Power divided between local and central branches of government is a definition of what term?

a. Bicameralism
b. Checks and balances
c. Legislative oversight
d. Federalism

79. A class of third-grade students is working in small groups to investigate the differences in pitch produced by striking glass bottles filled with varying amounts of water. In addition to scientific learning and development, such an activity is beneficial in demonstrating which of the following concepts?

a. The characteristics of scientific inquiry
b. The connection between scientific concepts and music
c. The benefits of collaborative learning in strengthening concept knowledge
d. The importance of following the scientific method when conducting an investigation

80. A prekindergarten teacher places two groups of eight one-unit cubes on a table. In one group, the cubes are arranged neatly into two small rows of four. In the other group, the cubes are spread far apart. When asked which group has more cubes, students chose the pile in which the cubes were spread apart. Which of the following best explains the reason for the students' answer?

a. The teacher did not ask students to count the unit cubes individually.
b. Students have not yet learned one-to-one correspondence.
c. Prekindergarten students have not yet developed an understanding of conservation.
d. Students did not have the opportunity to physically manipulate the unit cubes.

81. Which of the following strategies would best demonstrate to prekindergarten students the purpose and use of a printed book?

a. Taking a class trip to the school library
b. Asking students to bring in their favorite book from home
c. Modeling how to hold a book, turn pages, read from left to right, and pointing out key characteristics
d. Incorporating time for reading aloud into the school day

82. Which of the following strategies for teaching new vocabulary best demonstrates knowledge of the Four-Part Processing Model for word recognition?

a. Reading new vocabulary words aloud and having students clap out syllables
b. Displaying sentence strips that include new vocabulary and corresponding images and reading them aloud to the class
c. Using sentence dictation exercises to develop students' receptive and expressive language skills
d. Having students create semantics features maps to learn new vocabulary and create word families

83. According to Erikson's theory of psychosocial development, which ability must be achieved during the period of adolescence?

a. Identity
b. Intimacy
c. Industry
d. Autonomy

84. What does the 10th Amendment establish?

a. Any power not given to the federal government belongs to the states or the people.
b. The president is responsible for executing and enforcing laws created by Congress.
c. Congress has the authority to declare war.
d. The Supreme Court has the authority to interpret the Constitution.

85. What is a purpose and characteristic of thematic instruction?

a. Teaching cognitive skills in the context of academic subjects
b. Teaching broadly enough to enable creative exploration
c. Teaching specifically enough for practical applications
d. Teaching both (b) and (c) rather than only (a)

86. Which of the following instructional strategies best demonstrates a way to prevent letter confusion in kindergarten students?

a. Introducing the letters in alphabetical order
b. Teaching visually similar letters, such as *b* and *d*, separately
c. Requiring students to master each letter before introducing the next letter
d. Focusing more on letter sounds than on letter names

Refer to the following for question 87:

Ms. Franklin is teaching a second-grade class a lesson on ceramics. While students are engaged in creating their own pieces, Ms. Franklin shows them other students' work.

87. Which of the following would be the most appropriate activity for students at this grade level?

a. Making pinch pots and coil pots
b. Throwing pots using a pottery wheel
c. Making and attaching handles to pots
d. Glazing pots using a kiln

88. A first-grade teacher works with students of varying levels of literacy skill development. Which of the following strategies would likely best address these students' individual learning needs to build fluency and promote reading comprehension skills?

a. Homogenous flexible grouping with leveled texts
b. Scheduling daily class read-aloud time
c. Creating a print-rich environment
d. Providing struggling students with individualized instruction

89. Which of the following is NOT true about the whole language approach to literacy instruction?

a. The whole language approach is effective for children with language processing disorders.
b. The whole language approach is effective for supporting constructivist learning of literacy.
c. The whole language approach is effective for integrating literacy across content domains.
d. The whole language approach is effective for emphasizing cultural diversity in instruction.

90. Which of the following is true about preschool activities to teach scientific inquiry and discovery?

a. Exploring the solubility in water of various substances is not a scientific activity.
b. Seeing what colors result from mixing other colors is strictly an art class activity.
c. Comparing similarities and contrasting differences in objects are good activities.
d. Creating a science center as a preschool teacher is typically always expensive.

91. A second-grade teacher is planning a reader's theater in which students will act out the story of a familiar text. Students will practice in small groups throughout the week, and will be encouraged to focus on expression, inflection, and intonation as they read the story's dialogue. This activity is most likely intended to promote the development of which of the following skills?

a. Prosody
b. Automaticity
c. Sight word recognition
d. Phonological awareness

92. A second-grade teacher works with a group of students that have varying skills, abilities, and needs, including individuals with learning disabilities and English language learners. During a math lesson on adding and subtracting three-digit numbers, the teacher groups students based upon ability level to work on a series of task cards that include solving word problems. Which of the following additional strategies would be beneficial in modifying instruction to support these students' learning and development?

a. Leveling the complexity of the task cards and incorporating visuals
b. Providing multiple examples of how to add and subtract three-digit numbers
c. Monitoring each group and checking frequently for understanding
d. Strategically grouping students with others that can provide scaffolding

93. To practice decoding skills, a first-grade teacher has students clap out each sound of multisyllabic words. Which of the following additional strategies would best promote the development of this skill for children in this age group?

a. Exposing students to new multisyllabic words in a variety of contexts
b. Having students cut and paste letters to form multisyllabic words
c. Using a semantic map to demonstrate the features of new multisyllabic words
d. Having students identify the prefixes and suffixes of multisyllabic words

94. The youngest children in Piaget's stage of concrete operations are typically in:

a. Toddlerhood
b. Preschool
c. Elementary school
d. Middle school

95. Clay's rating scale for assessing children's emerging writing skills rates three areas of composition. Of these, which one includes identifying whether the child understands the concept of symbolic representation?

a. The language level
b. Directional principles
c. The message quality
d. Fluency

96. After reading an informational text, a third-grade teacher has students write a short opinion piece using sentence frames to guide their responses. This strategy is likely intended to develop students' understanding and use of:

a. Nonverbal communication
b. Context clues
c. Academic language
d. High-frequency sight words

97. A teacher uses a mixture of whole-group and small-group reading instruction. Which of the following activities would be the best choice for a whole-group lesson rather than small-group or individualized instruction?

a. Practice applying specific phonics skills
b. Independent reading of unfamiliar texts
c. Analyzing character development after the teacher reads a novel aloud
d. Spelling patterns

98. Which of the following is an example of EC student difficulty with word decoding and phonics?

a. A child matches up the letters he or she sees with corresponding sounds.
b. A child matches up the sounds he or she hears with corresponding letters.
c. A child includes letter sounds he or she has learned in his or her written work.
d. A child looks at the first one or two letters of a word to guess what it is.

99. What is the most accurate statement about developmentally appropriate teaching practices for students in early childhood?

a. Products and accomplishments should be rewarded more than effort or persistence.
b. Feedback teachers give to young children should be generalized rather than specific.
c. Teachers should combine modeling/demonstrating behaviors with verbal directions.
d. To promote language development, teachers must verbalize approaches/behaviors.

100. In a prekindergarten classroom, students are creating bird feeders using recycled materials and seeds. The teacher plans to hang the feeders outside and allow students to observe as birds come to eat the seeds. This activity is likely intended to introduce which of the following scientific concepts?

a. The life cycle of animals
b. The difference between living and nonliving things
c. The basic needs of animals
d. The fact that animals grow and change over time

Answer Key and Explanations for Test #2

1. D: Prereading strategies enhance overall student engagement and comprehension. Activities such as anticipation guides serve to provide context, establish purpose for reading, and elicit prior knowledge to strengthen understanding, evoke interest, and make the learning experience meaningful and relevant for students. These guides typically ask students to agree or disagree with a series of statements related to the reading, and to make predictions about the text. This encourages students to actively engage with the text as they determine whether their predictions were correct, or whether their original opinions remained the same during and after reading, which promotes comprehension.

2. C: One benefit of children's storytelling is that it allows them to engage and exercise their imaginations. Teachers should also ask children questions about their storytelling to model correct sentence structure and get children to elaborate on what they say. Teachers should not only let children express their ideas through storytelling; they should also build further upon these ideas by asking them guiding questions to elicit more information.

3. B: Cross-curricular opportunities enrich instruction by demonstrating the relevance of learning in various contexts to strengthen students' understanding across content areas. When social studies is incorporated into other subject areas, students can explore its prevalence and application in daily life. In this situation, incorporating elements of social studies into a science unit on saltwater and freshwater bodies helps students understand the characteristics of different water resources, as well as how physical geography impacts human life. With exploratory activities such as a research project, students can learn how proximity to different bodies of water influenced human settlement patterns, and ultimately, other aspects of civilization, such as agriculture, diet, and commerce.

4. D: Option D is the correct answer because teachers can group by student preferences when offering choices of tunes or songs that students want to learn, learning about the history and use of the guitar in different cultural settings or genres, and then having the different groups of students present their findings and perform to the rest of the class, etc. Option A is incorrect because high and low achievers learn from one another (often more than they do from the teacher), even when differentiating instruction, such as progressing with tonal and rhythm patterns through Gordon's skill learning sequence, or when assigning students different tunes or songs to learn as homework in order to play for the class, etc. Option B is incorrect because formative assessment assists the teacher in deciding how to differentiate instruction based upon achievement and preferences. Option C is incorrect because it is impractical to provide individual lessons to each student. A better option is to pair high achievers with low achievers for peer coaching.

5. A: The phenomenon of "sticky prices" refers to prices that stay the same even though it seems they should change (either increasing or decreasing).

6. C: Cognitive dissonance is a term coined by psychologist Leon Festinger to describe the discomfort we feel when considering contradictory information. We resolve this discomfort by rejecting certain information, or forming new schemata or changing existing ones to accommodate some information. This term is not related to a disorder (A), sensory overload (B), or incompatible instructional and learning (D) processes.

7. C: Selecting instructional materials that reflect students' cultural and linguistic backgrounds helps create an inclusive learning environment in which all students feel respected, welcomed, and appreciated in their diversities. For English language learners, this strategy communicates that their primary language is valued as an asset for English language literacy development. Examples include incorporating texts in the students' primary language, teaching lessons that accurately portray their cultural and linguistic backgrounds, and integrating these diversities into the classroom environment, such as through posters, labels in the primary language, and decorations.

8. B: Meret Oppenheim, an artist of the Dada movement, created a (1936) work with a teacup, saucer, and spoon all covered with hair. This work has an artistic function as it can be viewed, makes a statement, and evokes various reactions in its viewers, and a social function in the artist's protest of the war and other social issues, but no physical function as it cannot be used for any physical purpose. The raku pottery (A) has both an artistic function in its elegance and a physical function in its use of holding and drinking tea during the traditional Japanese tea ceremony. The tribal war club (C) serves an artistic function in its exquisite craftsmanship and a physical function in its use to bludgeon enemies. Therefore (D) is incorrect, as not all of these have physical functions.

9. C: Learning becomes more relevant and meaningful when students are aware of its applications in real-world contexts, as this demonstrates how concepts learned in class can be used in daily life. This strengthens students' connections to learning, fostering deeper understanding of concept knowledge. By leading students around the school building to identify shapes learned during a geometry lesson, this teacher effectively demonstrates the applications of mathematics in real-world contexts by showing students where they appear in a familiar environment.

10. D: Healthy social and emotional skills are developed through positive interactions with others and one's environment. As such, it is important to emphasize developmentally appropriate strategies for productive communication, self-regulation, and conflict resolution in the early childhood classroom. By second grade, most students with typical patterns related to social and emotional development are able to verbally resolve simple conflicts among themselves. Therefore, in this situation, the most appropriate response to noticing a disagreement between two students would be to allow them to work through it independently. Doing so promotes the development of problem-solving and communication skills and positive interpersonal relationships.

11. B: Students can manipulate the different lengths of materials like paper strips and Cuisenaire rods, in order to determine that one rod is one-half the length of the other, for example.

12. C: Summative assessments are assessments that take place at the end of a unit to assess mastery of concepts. These are distinct from formative assessments, which take place alongside instruction and can be used to modify the curriculum while students are still learning. Effective summative assessments allow students to demonstrate understanding of a concept in a manner that aligns with their developmental levels, characteristics, and capabilities. When summative assessments are developmentally appropriate, teachers can more accurately assess students' mastery of learning targets as they progress through the curriculum, and identify any potential need for remediation. Fourth-grade students are in the concrete operational stage of development, so summative assessments that incorporate logical reasoning skills, physical manipulation and exploration, and collaborative learning, are most effective. A collaborative project-based summative assessment, such as creating a physical model of the water cycle, is therefore most appropriate in letting students of this age group demonstrate their understanding.

13. D: Teaching young children to make predictions is an effective strategy for supporting their learning and development related to probability, as it encourages students to consider the likelihood of potential outcomes. This establishes a foundation of understanding that can later be applied to more advanced mathematical situations that involve determining probability. Further, representing students' predictions using a bar graph promotes the understanding that information can be quantified and represented in visual form, which supports learning and development in data analysis.

14. D: A culturally competent classroom is one in which the teacher recognizes the diversities among their individual students, and incorporates these differences accurately and respectfully throughout instruction. Reflecting students' diversities through developmentally appropriate instructional materials strengthens personal connections to make learning meaningful, relevant, and engaging for all students. This serves to deepen overall understanding, promote positive attitudes toward learning, and foster greater academic achievement.

15. D: The first step in research for writing is establishing topics that appeal to students, are challenging yet feasible, and support grade-level standards to align research with classwork, along with triangulating to confirm three kinds of sources available on the topics. The second step is generating subtopics based on what students want to learn as guidelines for topic study. The third step is identifying at least three sources. The fourth step is reading sources and identifying information that supports subtopics. The fifth step is taking notes on source information. The sixth step is sorting the notes taken, and writing using the notes plus previous knowledge. The seventh step is to read, think, and select information and it refers to a revision phase of the process in which you review your own notes and ensure the final selection of material makes sense and contributes to the overall goal of the writing.

16. C: Providing learning options is very useful in the middle grades because students are developing a sense of autonomy, and this allows them to exercise it. While the choices students make may reflect their self-concept or choice of peer group in some way, this is not the main area of development that such an exercise fosters. This exercise also reflects the fact that students have different learning styles, but this is not a developmental characteristic unique to middle school students.

17. C: Incorporating a unit on integrated pest management techniques into the early childhood science curriculum is beneficial in deepening students' understanding of the environment, ecological systems, and the ways in which both can be negatively impacted. This includes teaching young children that plants, animals, insects, and other organisms are considered pests when they exist in unwanted areas and have the potential to cause harm, and that when this occurs, their population must be controlled. Teachers can strengthen students' knowledge of these concepts first by teaching them what causes an organism to be classified as a pest, namely, how harmful and prevalent it is in the ecosystem in question. Pests are generally pervasive and harmful to the environment or other organisms in the area. After teaching how to identify an organism as a pest, it would subsequently be helpful to educate them on the habitats and survival needs of pests during such a unit. Doing so would help students build an understanding of the role of pests in their natural environment and the conditions that make certain locations hospitable. It would also help students brainstorm effective strategies for controlling pests in unwanted areas.

18. D: Gentry (1982) identified five stages of spelling development. Children can use letters of the alphabet during the Precommunicative stage, but they do not yet understand letter-to-sound correspondence. In the second, Semiphonetic stage, children first begin to understand that certain letters stand for certain sounds. In the third, Phonetic stage (C), children represent every speech sound they hear with letters—logically and systematically, albeit not always correctly (e.g., "wuz" for "was"). In the fourth, Transitional stage (A), children progress from their phonetic spellings to the conventionally correct spellings of words—though they are still apt to make mistakes as they learn. During the fifth, final Correct stage (B), children generally use accurate spelling.

19. B: First, calculate 30% of 3 inches.

$$3 \times 0.3 = 0.9$$

Then, subtract this value from the original height.

$$3 - 0.9 = 2.1$$

The grass is now 2.1 inches tall.

20. B: According to Erikson's theory of psychosocial development, the earliest stage in a child's first year of life is when he or she develops a basic sense of trust or mistrust in parents and the environment. Having needs met sufficiently and consistently engenders trust, while having needs met inadequately and/or irregularly spawns mistrust. The second stage, in toddlerhood, involves developing a sense of autonomy or independence (A) versus one of shame and self-doubt. According to Piaget's theory of cognitive development, it is during this time period that children also develop an understanding of symbolic representation, evidenced by their engaging in make-believe or pretend play (D). According to Erikson, preschool children aged around three to five years develop a sense of initiative through exploring and exercising power over their environment, or they develop a sense of guilt (C) if they garner disapproval for exerting excessive power.

21. A: Preschoolers do naturally form stereotypes about others. According to Piaget, children aged 3–6 years are in the Preoperational stage and do not think logically yet. Thus, they tend to base opinions about others on aspects they can see, like people's appearances, the material things they own, or what things they like or dislike. This is natural during their stage of cognitive development; thus (B) is inaccurate. While preschoolers may be taught to stereotype by those around them, stereotyping is considered a natural process for children this age, as they have a natural tendency to categrorize (C). It is also inaccurate to say preschoolers do not understand stereotyping as an abstract concept (D). Preoperational children are cognitively able to categorize people as well as things, and stereotyping or typecasting other people is a form of categorization. Parents and EC educators can reduce stereotyping through modeling, discussion, answering children's questions honestly, promoting tolerance and respect, and confronting biased and intolerant actions.

22. C: Puppet shows are not only entertaining but are also concrete ways to engage young children in viewing and then discussing demonstrations of desirable/undesirable social behaviors. Since motor skills develop before verbal skills, many preschoolers use physical aggression to get what they want instead of expressing themselves verbally. A puppet show depicting the failures of aggressive actions and successes of verbal communication can couch instructive content in a fun format. For preschool ages, teachers should ask children which puppets were good and which were bad; this does not encourage being judgmental but simply helps children define socially acceptable and unacceptable behaviors. For the same reason, it is not irrelevant to ask children which puppets they liked and disliked. Young children can not only summarize what happened during the show, they also can and should be encouraged to predict what could happen next and how puppet characters could behave differently to exercise and enhance their social understanding and interactions.

23. A: Understanding the concept of supply and demand—the notion that the availability of and desire for a product influences its price—is important for developing economic literacy. This skill is necessary for grasping increasingly complex topics, such as economic interdependence, price determination, and market competition. Students learn this foundational concept most effectively when provided with opportunities to interact with it in a relevant and meaningful way. By requiring more tickets for sought-after prizes, this teacher incorporates supply and demand into the classroom token economy in a real-world, applicable context to promote student understanding.

24. A: Teachers should keep from confusing young children by introducing letters to them that have similar sounds in separate lessons. They should introduce continuous consonant sounds (f, r, s, m, n), which are easier to produce in isolation with less distortion, before they teach consonant sounds that are stops (p, b, t, d, k, g), which are more difficult for young children to produce, not vice versa (B). Letters with similar appearances should be presented during separate lessons, not the same one (C), also to prevent confusion. Teachers should introduce high-utility letters/sounds first, not low-utility (D), as the high-utility ones are those they will hear, see, and use most often.

25. A: Explicit phonics instruction is essential for developing foundational reading and writing literacy skills among young children. Phonics is the ability to recognize which sounds are made by individual letters or groups of letters, and is therefore necessary to decode, comprehend, and produce entire written words. Many beginner-level sight words, such as consonant-vowel-consonant (CVC) words, are easy to spell and include short-vowel sounds, so using them to introduce phonics promotes word recognition and retention. Further, reviewing short-vowel sounds through varied repetition and kinesthetic activities helps young children internalize the concept of phonics to build literacy skills.

26. C: Teaching young children the notion of time, continuity, and change is necessary to develop their understanding of foundational concepts related to social studies, such as cause and effect, as well as how to accurately situate, recall, and make connections between historical events. Doing so should take placc in a developmentally appropriate, familiar, and applicable context to ensure understanding. In this situation, labeling the days of the week as "yesterday," "today," and "tomorrow," as well has having students locate various events on a monthly calendar, shows how time functions in their daily lives. This strategy helps students begin to understand that time is linear and events happen chronologically, developing their sense of time, continuity, and change.

27. C: Students audiate musical meter and tonality—they internally hear and feel patterns of beat, tonal center, scale degrees, intervals in context, melodic contour, and harmonic functions (e.g., tonic vs. dominant). Time signatures, however, are notation symbols that label meter on the page; they are not perceived directly in inner hearing. Thus, time signatures are not audiated, while the other options are.

28. C: Gross motor skills refer to the ability to engage in movements that require the coordinated use of large muscle groups. Such movements include running, jumping, kicking, and waving one's arms. By prekindergarten, most young children have developed a variety of gross motor skills. Teachers can enhance this development by incorporating activities that promote students' sense of coordination between their bodies and actions. For example, integrating movement and dance into musical activities encourages young children to engage in large-muscle movements, promoting the development of gross motor skills.

29. D: Bandura's social learning theory places emphasis on social interactions as the most important context of, and influence on, learning. Bandura says children learn by observing and then imitating others' behaviors. Nuclear conflicts (A) were Erikson's term for the central crisis to be resolved in each of his psychosocial stages of development. Erogenous zones (B) were Freud's term for areas of the body where children's attention focused in each of his psychosexual stages of development. Cognitive abilities (C) were the focus of each of Piaget's stages of cognitive development.

30. C: Before introducing a new concept in mathematics, it is important to determine whether students have developed a solid understanding of related fundamental concepts. Doing so ensures that students have the foundation of knowledge necessary to grasp increasingly complex concepts, problems, and methods. Administering diagnostic exams before a new unit of instruction gives teachers insight on students' level of background knowledge related to new material. The feedback provided from such assessments allows teachers to address areas of student need, clarify misconceptions, and identify any potential need for remediation to facilitate all students' ability to learn effectively. In this situation, students must have mastered the concept of place value in order to properly understand how to add and subtract numbers up to 1,000. This skill serves as an important framework for reference on how to set up addition and subtraction problems with two- and three-digit numbers, work within the appropriate columns, and regroup as necessary. Including this concept on a diagnostic test will help ensure students are fully prepared for success in learning when the new unit begins.

31. A: Research finds that among the motivational factors of self-efficacy—students' goal orientation for task performance and/or skills mastery (B); their interest and the value they perceive in a writing task (C); and to what causes they attribute their failures and/or successes in writing (D)—students' perceived competence, i.e., their sense of self-efficacy, for overall writing skills influences their motivation to write more than their respective self-efficacy for individual writing tasks.

32. C: Applying universal design principles to instruction helps ensure that learning opportunities are equitable and accessible to all students, including those with learning disabilities and those who are English language learners. This approach emphasizes the importance of implementing various methods for engagement, representation, action, and expression of information to meet students' diverse needs in the classroom. In this situation, the teacher could incorporate universal design principles by introducing the new unit on fractions through a variety of mediums. This could be achieved by incorporating such accommodations as visual representations, audio and video clips, and assistive technology as necessary. Doing so would create an inclusive classroom environment in which all student needs are met to promote success in learning.

33. D: Five stages of spelling identified (Gentry, 1982) are: Precommunicative; Semiphonetic; Phonetic; Transitional; and Correct. In the Phonetic stage, children represent all the speech sounds they hear in words with written letters. While their spelling in this stage is not always correct, it is nonetheless applied systematically and understandable to others. Children in the fifth, Correct (A) stage usually spell words accurately and recognize misspellings. In the fourth, Transitional (B) stage, children begin moving from using phonetic spellings to conventional ones. In the second, Semiphonetic (C) stage, children are just beginning to represent sounds with corresponding letters. (In the first, Precommunicative stage, children may use alphabet letters, but do not yet show understanding of letter-sound correspondences.)

34. C: Constructivism is a learning theory based on the idea that people are actively involved in the learning process, rather than being passive receivers of knowledge. Constructivism suggests that children learn best by solving real-world problems, gathering information, testing ideas, and other active processes, with teachers guiding and scaffolding them along the way.

35. D: Cross-curricular activities enhance students' understanding of new information. Specifically, by integrating arts and humanities across content areas, teachers can strengthen students' connections to learning and promote creative development while demonstrating how the arts and humanities are applicable in all aspects of life. In a scientific lesson about the life cycle of plants, providing opportunities for students to engage in music and artistic expression is an effective strategy for incorporating arts and humanities into cross-curricular learning.

36. D: Vocabulary acquisition is a necessary component in the development of reading comprehension skills. When engaging with a new text, students may struggle to understand unfamiliar terms, impeding their ability to comprehend the text as a whole. Semantic mapping is an analysis strategy intended to help students develop word-learning skills by having them categorize the features of new vocabulary using a graphic organizer. This activity allows students to visualize the characteristics of and relationship between new words associated with a particular concept, thus strengthening overall understanding, and ultimately, reading comprehension. In this situation, having students complete a semantic map of words associated with the life cycle of plants would be beneficial in improving their comprehension of the informational text.

37. D: Not only is emotional development necessary in itself, but it is also a prerequisite and a support for children's development of social interactions and social skills. Affective learning activities help children to express their emotions and understand them. Understanding them will in turn help children develop emotional self-regulation. In addition, affective learning activities can inform teachers about how children feel and which activities most interest them. These activities can be more time-consuming, however, and more difficult to implement in larger classes.

38. D: Piaget's theory posits four distinct stages of cognitive development, each with specific distinguishing characteristics and corresponding to approximate age ranges. Skinner's (A) theory of cognitive development is behavioral. It does not include stages but focuses on the premise that changes in behaviors over time represent learning and that this learning occurs through the antecedent and consequent events immediately before and after a behavior, which increase or decrease the probability of the individual's repeating the behavior. Vygotsky's (B) theory also has no stages and focuses on sociocultural influences as sources of learning. Bandura's (C) social learning theory has no stages either; it focuses on learning through observation, imitation of models, and vicarious learning.

39. C: To strengthen beginning preschoolers' alphabetic knowledge, teachers should not only review what children have learned cumulatively about letter-sound correspondences (A), and not only provide opportunities to practice letter-sound relationships they are newly learning (B), but should do both. One good way to provide occasions for children to apply their emerging alphabetic knowledge early and often is to give them phonetic spellings of words familiar to them so they can read these.

40. C: The libido is part of the id according to Freud. It represents psychic energy as well as sex drive. Freud's three major personality structures are the id (A), which generates unconscious impulses; the ego (B), which realistically regulates acting on id impulses; and the superego (C), which pursues morality and perfection.

41. A: The eye wall of a hurricane has the strongest winds and the greatest rainfall. The eye wall is the tower-like rim of the eye. It is from this wall that clouds extend out, which are seen from above as the classic outward spiral pattern. A hurricane front is the outermost edge of its influence; although there will be heavy winds and rain in this area, the intensity will be relatively small. The eye of a hurricane is actually a place of surprising peace. In this area, dry and cool air rushes down to the ground or sea. Once there, the air is caught up in the winds of the eye wall and is driven outward at a furious pace.

42. D: Students with learning disabilities often require special accommodations to support their individual needs. Accommodations typically do not alter what the student is expected to learn, but facilitate their ability to do so effectively in an equitable environment. Students diagnosed with attention deficit hyperactivity disorder (ADHD) often struggle to focus in class, and may easily become overwhelmed by lengthy assignments. Chunking long reading passages into smaller, more manageable parts, and giving extra time for processing, would help this student sustain attention while reducing feelings of being overwhelmed. These accommodations would ensure that the student is provided with the support necessary to fully engage in learning without reducing academic expectations.

43. D: Learning to name and identify objects is an essential component of speech and language development. This concept should be integrated throughout all areas of the early childhood curriculum. Strategies that promote receptive language skills, such as labeling items in the classroom with words and corresponding images, help young children learn the names of objects around them. This provides consistent exposure to vocabulary in a variety of contexts to reinforce understanding and increase retention.

44. C: Consistency and repetition are key in early childhood behavior management. Whatever rules adults make, they must always follow them (A); they must repeat them to children many times (B) to make them work; and they must always enforce them consistently (C). Likewise, adults should provide positive reinforcement for good behaviors consistently every time they observe them, not some of the time (D).

45. B: In order to prosper, a nation should not try to increase its imports. Mercantilism is an economic theory including the idea that prosperity comes from a positive balance of international trade. For any one nation to prosper, that nation should increase its exports but decrease its imports. Exporting more to other countries while importing less from them will give a country a positive trade balance. This theory assumes that money and wealth are identical assets of a nation. In addition, this theory also assumes that the volume of global trade is an unchangeable quantity. Mercantilism dictates that a nation's government should apply a policy of economic protectionism by stimulating more exports and suppressing imports. Some ways to accomplish this task have included granting subsidies for exports and imposing tariffs on imports. Mercantilism can be regarded as essentially the opposite of the free trade policies that have been encouraged in more recent years.

46. B: Incorporating music into daily learning experiences promotes development across domains, including students' ability to express themselves creatively. Further, incorporating group movement and dance activities into music instruction develops students' sense of spatial and kinesthetic awareness. Kinesthetic awareness is the understanding of how one's body moves, whereas spatial awareness is the awareness of one's body in relation to other individuals or objects. Through group movement and dance, students develop a greater understanding of how their bodies move, both individually and in relation to their environment, ultimately promoting the development of purposeful, coordinated movements. Providing students with physical props during these activities, such as hula hoops, ribbons, or sticks, enhances the development of these skills, as it encourages students to physically manipulate objects with purposeful awareness as they move within the group.

47. C: Conducting field trips to reinforce classroom instruction gives students hands-on opportunities to interact with and explore scientific concepts in a natural setting. This increases the relevancy of learning while fostering students' natural sense of inquiry. However, physical field trips may not always be possible, and can sometimes be limited in scope. Virtual field trips can provide similar interactive learning experiences. For this unit specifically, leading students in a virtual field trip allows them to explore and compare the characteristics of aquatic ecosystems in various locations, thus providing an active learning experience that expands their understanding of the concept.

48. D: In phonics, decoding refers to one's ability to recognize and correctly pronounce sounds produced by written letters and words. Encoding refers to one's ability to identify and produce written letters and words to correspond to the sounds of spoken language. These skills are reciprocal, and both are imperative for literacy development across domains, as they directly contribute to students' reading comprehension, writing, and oral language abilities. In this situation, the student shows deficiencies with both decoding and encoding, and therefore would benefit from more support to develop these skills.

49. B: Actively engaging students in public service projects is an effective strategy for promoting the development of civic values, as well as an understanding of their roles and responsibilities in the community. Doing so should begin in early childhood, and should provide hands-on opportunities to serve others in a meaningful way, establishing a foundation for increased awareness of how individuals in a community work together to support one another. By organizing a class food drive, this teacher provides such an opportunity. By encouraging students to participate in a project that will directly benefit members of the community, the project promotes values that contribute to the development of civic competence.

50. A: In addition to integrating art into the science unit and the curriculum, this activity applies artwork to build children's language skills by having them illustrate plants or animals whose names and characteristics they have learned in words; it also builds their vocabularies by having them both represent the word names and concepts of plants or animals visually, and label their pictures with the correct word names. Activities like correctly identifying, comparing, and contrasting word names for different colors of paints, paper, and other art materials are examples of (B). Activities wherein children explore basic visual art elements by viewing and discussing artworks, and experimenting with creating their own lines, shapes, colors, and textures, are examples of (C). Activities wherein teachers ask children to make artworks showing how they feel, representing an idea, or illustrating a story are examples of (D).

51. D: Applying universal design for learning principles includes allowing multiple outlets for students to express and communicate information. In this situation, physical writing is time-consuming and painful for the student. By providing assistive speech-to-text technology, the teacher accommodates the student's individual learning need by providing an alternative means of expression and communication, ensuring their ability to fully participate in writing assignments.

52. C: Word families are words that are spelled and pronounced similarly. For example, the words "brain," "rain," "stain," and "train" all share the "-ain" ending, and therefore belong to the same word family. Introducing word families using the concept of onset and rime—the beginning and ending sounds of a syllable—familiarizes students with the different parts of words. The onset is the initial consonant that begins the syllable, and the rime consists of the remaining vowels and consonants. Teaching this concept first contributes to developing the phonological awareness skills necessary for decoding written language. Doing so helps students identify words in the same word family while promoting vocabulary acquisition, word recognition, and ultimately, reading comprehension skills.

53. A: Effective writing includes a clear beginning, middle, and end. Teaching students this important skill is essential to developing their ability to write clearly and for a variety of purposes.

As young children learn to express themselves in writing, particularly in narrative form, they may find it difficult to organize their thoughts in such a way. Story maps are a versatile form of graphic organizer that can be used as a prewriting activity to help students organize the events of their narrative pieces. This resource provides students with a visual aid to better arrange their ideas into a distinct beginning, middle, and end, improving the clarity and organization of their writing.

54. A: Phonemic substitution is a phonological awareness skill that refers to the ability to recognize the creation of a new word when one sound is replaced with another. Understanding this concept is necessary for the development of reading comprehension and spelling skills, so it must be taught explicitly. By using color-coded letter cards to spell vocabulary words and replace individual sounds, the teacher shows students how phonemic substitution is used to create new words. This strategy also supports students' recognition of the relationship between phonemic awareness and phonics, as it allows them to visualize the substitution of individual letters to produce new sounds and words.

55. C: Phonemic awareness refers to one's ability to decipher, identify, and manipulate individual sounds within spoken words. This skill consists of several components, including phonemic isolation, which is the ability to distinguish individual phonemes, or sounds, within words. By asking students to identify the sound they hear at the beginning of each vocabulary word, the teacher evaluates students' phonemic awareness by asking them to demonstrate their understanding of phonemic isolation.

56. C: Jean Piaget believed that children pass through four distinct developmental stages, with each characterized by increasingly complex skills, abilities, and processes. According to his theory, prekindergarten students are in the preoperational stage of cognitive development. In this stage, young children typically engage in symbolic play as a means of organizing, representing, and understanding both their own thoughts and the world around them. Symbolic play is integral to promoting cognitive, social, emotional, physical, and behavioral development in preoperational children.

57. B: Reading comprehension refers to one's ability to read and understand a text. This skill can be categorized into three levels with increasing degrees of complexity. Literal reading comprehension refers to the ability to read and understand the basic meaning of words and sentences in a text. Inferential reading comprehension requires individuals to employ higher-order thinking skills by using contextual clues to determine what is implied by the author's use of literary techniques. Evaluative, or critical, reading comprehension occurs when readers connect a text to their own background knowledge and experiences to formulate personal thoughts and opinions on what they have read. In this situation, the teacher asks students to circle descriptive language that may indicate the motives of the main character. Students are tasked with using evidence from the text to support their thoughts and ideas about this topic, promoting the development of inferential reading comprehension skills.

58. C: The term "irregular sight words" refers to high-frequency vocabulary words that are not spelled phonetically. Recognition and understanding of these words are necessary for vocabulary acquisition, as well as the development of reading comprehension, spelling, and writing skills. However, since these words cannot be sounded out using conventional rules of phonics, students must memorize them. Therefore, repetition through a variety of instructional strategies is most effective when teaching high-frequency irregular sight words. In this situation, the teacher reviews irregular sight words daily with students using multiple activities. Doing so fosters students' recognition, understanding, and retention of such words, thus promoting reading fluency as well as the development of other necessary literacy skills.

59. A: Artistic expression is personal to each individual, so teachers should typically refrain from formal evaluation of ability, especially in the early childhood classroom. Doing so allows students the freedom and flexibility to fully engage in the artistic process in a way that is relevant to their interests, promoting confidence for further exploration and creative development. It is possible, however, to monitor individual progress in artistic ability over time by collecting samples of students' artwork to create personalized portfolios. This approach would allow the teacher to monitor each student's progress in the arts throughout the school year while avoiding a formal assessment of skill.

60. B: The Seven Years' War was a global military conflict. In the Americas, the conflict was largely between Western European countries, particularly Great Britain and France.

61. B: Graphic organizers are highly beneficial in providing students with a visual aid when gathering and organizing ideas prior to beginning a writing assignment. These resources are versatile, as they can be differentiated to accommodate a range of purposes and student needs. In this situation, a graphic organizer such as a story map would allow students to more effectively establish a situation, introduce a narrator and characters, as well as arrange their narratives with a sequence of events that has a definite beginning, middle, and end. Using graphic organizers as a pre-writing activity ultimately promotes the development of students' writing skills, as it allows for more organized and coherent fictional narratives.

62. B: Social and behavioral theories of learning stress the importance of social interactions between students, as they can aid or inhibit learning. According to these theories, students do not just learn in isolation or in a one-on-one relationship with a teacher. They also learn attitudes toward education from their peers, sometimes positive and sometimes negative.

63. C: Mercantilism is the economic theory that nations advance the goal of accumulating capital by maintaining a balance of trade such that the value of exports exceeds that of imports. Great Britain maintained colonies to provide an inexpensive source of raw materials while creating markets for the goods manufactured in England. Under free trade, governments refrain from hindering the international exchange of goods and services. Nations that are granted most favored nation status are assured of enjoying equal advantages in international trade. A laissez-faire capitalist economy would theoretically be completely free of government regulation.

64. D: The age norm for correctly pronouncing /s/ and /r/, the two most difficult phonemes for children to articulate, is around 7–8 years of age. Therefore, if a child who is 5–6 years old cannot correctly pronounce these sounds, it would be considered normal language development (C) as many children's speech mechanisms are not yet mature enough to produce them perfectly. However, in a child 9–10 years old, such misarticulations could indicate a possible articulation problem, which is often corrected fairly easily with speech therapy. Although hearing loss (A) and intellectual disability (B) are two possible sources of articulation disorders, there are many other causes. Hence, it cannot be assumed that either one is the reason for the misarticulation.

65. D: Scientific learning and development are best supported when young children are provided with opportunities that facilitate their natural inclination to observe and interact with the world around them. Such activities foster students' inherent sense of inquiry, as they are encouraged to use their physical senses to actively explore, investigate, and make discoveries as they build understanding of new concepts. In this situation, having students search for and identify different earth materials around the school campus would promote such inquiry by prompting students to physically interact with their immediate environment. In doing so, students would learn where these materials can be found in a natural setting, and would have the opportunity to observe, touch, and compare differences between them, thus strengthening their overall connection to learning.

66. A: Developing students' understanding of the causes of seasonal changes requires them to have a foundational awareness that the Earth revolves around the Sun on a tilted axis. This understanding helps students recognize that as the Earth revolves around the Sun over the course of a year, its axis points either toward or away from the Sun, causing varying degrees of sunlight. When learning about the causes of seasonal changes, young children may have difficulty comprehending how the Earth's position relative to the Sun affects the amount of sunlight they experience throughout the year. Young children build connections to learning through hands-on, project-based experiences, so having this student create a three-dimensional model of the Earth's revolution around the Sun would let the student investigate and gain clarification about this concept.

67. A: Students that have a strong foundational knowledge of the morphology of words are more effectively able to understand and acquire academic language. For science instruction specifically, this skill enables students to break down complex terms by identifying affixes and root words to determine their definitions. In this example, reviewing the morphology of the words "renewable" and "nonrenewable" would be helpful in promoting students' ability to comprehend the meaning of and distinguish between the two types of resources. Showing students that the words "renewable" and "nonrenewable" share the root word "new" and the suffix "-able," meaning "capable of," but that the prefixes "re-" and "non-" mean "again" and "not," respectively, helps them grasp that renewable resources can be replenished whereas nonrenewable resources cannot. Ensuring students can differentiate between these definitions at the beginning of the unit will be beneficial in establishing a framework of reference for building greater understanding of the concept.

68. B: Morphology is the smallest structural units that determine grammatical differences in meaning, like the *–s* ending differentiating the singular noun *book* from the plural *books*. Phonology (A) is the rules for combining a language's phonemes or speech sounds into syllables and words. Syntax (C) is the ordering of words and structuring of word combinations to make grammatical sentences. Semantics (D) is the meanings of the words in a language.

69. B: Diagnostic assessments are administered prior to beginning a new unit of instruction, and can take several forms, such as pretests, anticipation guides, or surveys. These assessments contain new material from the upcoming unit, and provide teachers with valuable information on students' background knowledge and level of understanding prior to beginning instruction. Teachers can use this feedback to guide the planning process, as it allows them to identify areas of whole-class and individual strength and need to implement the most effective strategies, supports, and accommodations for promoting student success. Diagnostic assessments are also beneficial in allowing teachers to identify areas of misconception to clarify prior to instruction, avoiding the need for later remediation.

70. A: Assimilation is fitting a new experience into an existing schema. Accommodation is altering an existing schema or forming a new schema to accommodate a new experience. These two processes are part of the overall process of adaptation, i.e., adjusting one's thinking to the environment via interacting with it. This adaptation process helps the individual to maintain equilibrium, or balance.

71. D: A flow-line map describes the movement of people, trends, or materials across a physical area. The movements depicted on a flow-line map are typically represented by arrows. In more advanced flow-line maps, the width of the arrow corresponds to the quantity of the motion. Flow-line maps usually declare the span of time that is being represented. A political map depicts the man-made aspects of geography, such as borders and cities. A cartogram adjusts the size of the areas represented according to some variable. For instance, a cartogram of wheat production would depict Iowa as being much larger than Alaska. A qualitative map uses lines, dots, and other symbols to illustrate a particular point. For example, a qualitative map might be used to demonstrate the greatest expansion of the Persian Empire.

72. D: This activity best illustrates instruction in the visual art element of line, as the children are working with outlines and experimenting with drawing lines. An activity in color could involve identifying different colors in a work of art and mixing paint colors. An activity in shape might involve identifying different shapes in an artwork and arranging shapes to make pictures. An activity with light could entail identifying light and dark areas of artworks and selecting similar pieces to create contrasts.

73. C: The whole language approach can be applied when teachers read books aloud to young children (A) who are not reading on their own yet. This approach can also be used when teachers divide beginning or more advanced readers into small groups for guided reading sessions (B). The whole language approach additionally offers many opportunities for children to read independently on their own (D).

74. B: Experts advise EC teachers to teach what they themselves know and enjoy best. They can appeal to children's natural interests while selecting activities related to their own interests, e.g., plants, flowers, or animals. They should not limit their lessons to only things the children enjoy most (A), particularly if they are not things with which the teacher is most familiar. Teachers can learn from new discoveries young children make, so they should not direct children to make only standard use of learning materials (C): unusual/non-standard uses of materials by children can indicate new inquiry and result in such new discoveries, so teachers must use their observational skills during activities. Teachers are also advised to let children play with materials before using them in structured activities (D) so children can explore them and understand their uses, purposes, and care.

75. D: Piaget demonstrated that young children are not yet able to perform and reverse abstract mental operations, including the logic of understanding fractions, e.g., pieces of a cookie vs. a whole cookie. Preoperational children focus on one rather than all properties of an object. Therefore, when they see four pieces compared to one whole cookie, they "centrate" and focus on the number of pieces rather than the total amount, commonly concluding that four pieces equal more cookie than the same amount in one piece. They do not recognize that, whether whole or cut up, both cookies are equal amounts (A). They typically do not see the single cookie as equaling more than the four pieces (B). Though they do not think logically, they do base intuitive decisions on appearance, and hence do not conclude that a quarter-piece of cookie is as much as the whole cookie (C).

76. B: Incorporating students' cultural and linguistic diversities into instruction is an important part of creating an inclusive environment in which all students feel safe and supported to engage in learning. For ELL students specifically, this strategy also fosters positive attitudes toward learning English, as it communicates that their primary language is valued and respected in the classroom. Further, incorporating students' native language into instruction promotes English language acquisition, as many foundational literacy skills from one's first language are often transferable to subsequent languages.

77. A: The ability to isolate individual phonemes is essential to building the degree of phonemic awareness necessary for oral language and reading comprehension development. While activities such as rhyming games, chants, and songs help young children acquire this skill, such activities often present new words in their entirety, which proves difficult for some students. When decoding regular high-frequency sight words, students may recognize and correctly pronounce the root of the word, but often ignore modifiers such as prefixes or suffixes, leading to errors in pronunciation. Having struggling students practice sounding out words using letter tiles lets them visualize and physically manipulate each letter, strengthening their understanding of letter-sound relationships.

78. D: Federalists who helped frame the Constitution believed the central government needed to be stronger than what was established under the Articles of Confederation. Anti-federalists were against this and feared a strong federal government. A system of checks and balances was established to prevent the central government from taking too much power.

79. B: Students' learning and development are enhanced across content areas when they know how concepts from one subject area apply to another. Demonstrating cross-curricular relationships increases the relevancy of scientific instruction, fostering students' connections and understanding of how science is present in everyday life. In this situation, students are investigating differences in pitch when glass bottles are filled with varying amounts of water. Such an experiment demonstrates the factors that influence sound while promoting students' ability to recognize the connection between science and music, strengthening their knowledge in both content areas.

80. C: When teaching foundational mathematical skills to early childhood students, it is important to recognize the characteristics and abilities of their cognitive developmental levels. Prekindergarten students are in the preoperational stage of cognitive development and have not yet acquired concrete thinking skills. The ability to understand conservation—the idea that altering the appearance of something does not change the quantity—does not develop until the concrete operational stage of development. Therefore, when asked which group of unit cubes contained more, students were unable to recognize that both groups consisted of eight cubes. Rather, they selected the group that visually appeared larger.

81. C: Understanding basic concepts of print is a fundamental skill for emergent literacy development in young children. While most prekindergarten students have not yet learned to read fluently, it is still important to demonstrate the prevalence and application of printed language in daily life. This includes teaching young children about the purpose and use of printed books. Modeling how to hold a book, turn pages, read from left to right, and pointing out key characteristics, such as a book's title, cover, and author's name, develops print awareness in prekindergarten students. Doing so promotes students' understanding that books contain printed words that convey meaning, establishing a foundation for emergent literacy development.

82. B: The Four-Part Processing Model for word recognition provides a framework for understanding how individuals acquire reading skills. According to this model, word recognition, and eventually, automaticity, occurs when four processors within the brain work together simultaneously. The phonological processor is responsible for differentiating, understanding, and attaching meaning to words and sounds in spoken language. Further, the orthographic processor works with the phonological processor to recognize and recall the meaning of written words as well as the sounds produced by written language. Through the context processor, individuals recall background knowledge and construct meaning using clues such as visual representations and surrounding words in a sentence. The meaning processor refers to one's knowledge of vocabulary, multiple meanings of words, and semantics. Helping young children become skilled readers requires that instruction incorporate all four components in the processing model. In this situation, displaying new vocabulary in a written sentence strip with corresponding images simultaneously stimulates the orthographic, context, and meaning processors. By reading the sentence aloud to the class, the teacher addresses the phonological processor, thus incorporating all components of the Four-Part Processing Model for word recognition.

83. A: Erikson identified a nuclear conflict to be resolved in each stage of psychosocial development. Babies confront basic trust versus mistrust, toddlers autonomy (D) versus shame and self-doubt, preschoolers initiative versus guilt, school-aged children industry (C) versus inferiority, adolescents identity (A) versus role confusion, young adults intimacy (B) versus isolation, middle adults generativity versus stagnation, and older adults integrity versus despair.

84. A: The 10th Amendment establishes that any power not given to the federal government in the Constitution belongs to the states or the people. The federal and local governments share many responsibilities.

85. D: Thematic instruction emphasizes holistic learning across curriculum subjects within real-life, coherent, whole experiences with overarching themes. Cognitive skills are taught in the context of real-world topics, rather than only of academic subjects (a). Its purposes and characteristics also include teaching both broadly enough to enable students to explore subjects creatively (b), and also specifically enough to enable them to apply learned skills in practical use (c).

86. B: Children tend to confuse letters that are visually similar, such as *b* and *d*. Introducing them separately helps to prevent confusion between them. While there are differing theories on which order to use when introducing letters, generally alphabetical order is not the most effective. Letters are sometimes grouped for instruction by the difficulty of their sounds, their formation, or relevance to the students (such as introducing letters in their names first). Letters may be introduced in small groups to allow students to practice them in context, and both letter sounds and letter names are important for students to learn.

87. A: The most appropriate activity for students at this grade level would be making pinch pots and coil pots. Pinch pots are formed by creating a depression in the center of a ball of clay and smoothing the sides. Coil pots are formed by creating a long, thin length of clay and coiling it to form a pot. Unlike making and attaching handles to pots or throwing pots using a pottery wheel, creating this type of object with clay is appropriate given the fine motor skills and technical sophistication of second graders. The art teacher could model glazing pots using a kiln, but this activity would be too dangerous for young students to attempt on their own.

88. A: Flexible grouping refers to the temporary and strategic grouping of students to address specific needs or develop particular skills in a given area. This strategy is beneficial in differentiating instruction to accommodate variances in abilities, learning styles, and developmental levels. Flexible groupings can be either homogenous, in which students are grouped with others of the same or similar abilities, or heterogenous, in which students of varying skill levels work together. In this situation, homogenous flexible groupings would help with scaffolding instruction to align with students' individual needs. This would allow the teacher to provide leveled texts according to students' levels of literacy skill development to effectively promote fluency and support reading comprehension.

89. A: The whole language approach, as its name implies, is holistic in nature and founded on constructivist principles; it supports children in constructing their own knowledge and meaning through interacting with their environments (B). This approach does emphasize the integration of literacy instruction across the various subject content domains (C). It also emphasizes cultural diversity in learners, instruction, and learning (D). However, because it is holistic rather than analytical like phonics, the whole language approach is NOT as effective for children who have language processing disorders and/or reading disorders because they require explicit instruction to learn the decoding skills and strategies that other children learn incidentally as they learn to read and write.

90. C: One way to engage preschoolers in scientific inquiry and discovery is to have them compare similarities and contrast differences among various objects because observation and classification are scientific principles and process skills for children to develop. Exploring the solubility in water of various substances *is* a scientific activity (A), as it involves inquiring and discovering the properties of different forms of matter. Mixing colors is not strictly an art activity (B); it can be used equally well for scientific inquiry and discovery. Preschool teachers can create science centers inexpensively (D) by using common objects like magnets, mirrors, scales, magnifying glasses, prisms; by selecting books, games, puzzles, etc. related to various science themes; and using models, puppets, and other inexpensive, preschool-friendly objects and materials.

91. A: Prosody in reading refers to tone, pace, and stress placed on spoken words. Prosody does not refer to *which* individual phonemes are used in spoken words, but *how* the phonemes are used by changing the pitch, speed, and stress. This skill is a distinct measure of students' progress in reading fluency development, as it indicates their ability to recognize the relationship between written and spoken language. Reader's theaters offer an engaging learning opportunity for developing prosody in reading among young students. This activity allows them to assume the roles and act out the dialogue of characters from stories, thus encouraging them to read with increased expression while also promoting reading comprehension and fluency skills.

92. A: Adapting instructional practices, activities, and assessments to align with differences in individual ability and need is necessary to provide equitable and engaging learning opportunities that promote learning and development for all students. This includes modifying instruction as necessary for students that require additional support to make learning accessible as they build upon their skills and concept knowledge. In this situation, implementing flexible grouping strategies allows the teacher to differentiate the math lesson on adding and subtracting three-digit numbers according to students' ability level. The teacher could further support students, including ELLs and those with learning disabilities, by modifying the complexity of the task cards for each group and supplementing the word problems with visual aids. Doing so would be effective in scaffolding instruction to meet students' learning needs and providing clarification while implementing the appropriate amount of challenge for each group.

93. B: Decoding is the ability to recognize and pronounce written language by correctly sounding out the letters within words. Selecting age-appropriate learning materials is important in designing instruction that builds this emergent literacy skill to ultimately promote reading comprehension and fluency. Young children learn best through active, hands-on learning experiences, implementing kinesthetic activities in literacy instruction helps to strengthen connections and increase retention. In this situation, having students cut and paste letters to create multisyllabic words allows them to physically interact with learning materials, promoting their understanding of letter-sound relationships to build decoding skills.

94. C: It is not a coincidence that children in Piaget's concrete operations stage of cognitive development are around elementary-school age. In this stage, they are first able to perform mental operations with logical sequences when associated with concrete events, enabling them to learn basic arithmetic and conjugate verbs. Toddlers (A) and preschoolers (B) are typically in Piaget's preoperational stage and cannot yet think logically. Middle school-aged children (D), ages 11–14, typically progress from Piaget's stage of concrete operations into his formal operations stage, wherein they can perform logical mental operations abstractly without concrete events.

95. C: Clay's (1993) rating scale for emergent writing skills in children assesses three areas: language level, message quality, and directional principles. Language level includes progressing from letters, to words, to phrases, to sentences, to punctuated stories, and then to stories including two themes and more than one paragraph. Message quality includes understanding the concepts of signs or symbols and message communication, copying messages, repeating sentence patterns, writing one's own ideas, and successful composition. Directional principles includes learning the correct directionality and spacing in writing text. Fluency is not one of Clay's areas.

96. C: Academic language is language used primarily in the realm of education. Its complexity and content-specific nature often make it difficult for young children to acquire, comprehend, and use correctly. However, academic language is a necessary component to literacy skill development and achievement across content areas. Sentence frames are an effective tool for guiding students as they learn to use this unfamiliar vocabulary. This strategy contextualizes and scaffolds learning by prompting students to fill in blanks as they craft written responses, supporting their understanding of how to use academic language.

97. C: One of the challenges of large-group instruction is meeting the needs of diverse learners. Reading a novel aloud helps to make the content accessible to all learners. If students were to read it independently, as in choice B, the text would likely not be challenging enough for some readers and too difficult for others. Therefore, basing a comprehension lesson on a book that was read aloud assists all students with participating. While teachers sometimes introduce and practice phonics skills in large groups, students are likely to have differing skill levels in this area. Proficient first-grade readers, for example, may read consonant blends and digraphs with ease, which struggling readers may still be learning the alphabetic principle. Students in a classroom are also likely to have vastly different spelling skills, making the need for differentiation important.

98. D: If a child only looks at the first letter or two of a word and tries to guess at the word from this limited information, this is a sign that he or she could have difficulty with phonics, and with decoding words by their correspondence with the speech sounds they represent and vice versa (A and B). After the teacher instructs the class in several letter sounds, if a student then incorporates these in his or her writing (C), this is a sign that the student has mastered and is applying these, not having difficulty with them.

99. C: According to early childhood education experts, teachers should reward young children's efforts and persistence, not just their products or accomplishments (a); provide them with specific rather than generalized feedback (b) on their performance; and pair modeling or demonstrations with clear verbal directions (c) rather than only verbalizing approaches or behaviors (d), because showing AND telling children how to do something is more effective than only telling them.

100. C: Introducing new concepts in science using active learning opportunities to promote exploration, creativity, and observation fosters students' natural sense of curiosity in the early childhood classroom. Doing so strengthens students' connections to learning by encouraging them to ask questions and test ideas, and helping them process new information. By having students create bird feeders to hang outside and observe, this teacher uses a hands-on learning approach to introduce the concept that animals have basic needs. This strategy will encourage students to watch as birds come to eat from the feeders they created, establishing a real-world foundation for understanding that living animals require food for survival.

Mometrix
TEST PREPARATION

TExES

Social Studies 4-8 (118) Secrets Study Guide

Dear Future Exam Success Story

First of all, **THANK YOU** for purchasing Mometrix study materials!

Second, congratulations! You are one of the few determined test-takers who are committed to doing whatever it takes to excel on your exam. **You have come to the right place.** We developed these study materials with one goal in mind: to deliver you the information you need in a format that's concise and easy to use.

In addition to optimizing your guide for the content of the test, we've outlined our recommended steps for breaking down the preparation process into small, attainable goals so you can make sure you stay on track.

We've also analyzed the entire test-taking process, identifying the most common pitfalls and showing how you can overcome them and be ready for any curveball the test throws you.

Standardized testing is one of the biggest obstacles on your road to success, which only increases the importance of doing well in the high-pressure, high-stakes environment of test day. Your results on this test could have a significant impact on your future, and this guide provides the information and practical advice to help you achieve your full potential on test day.

Your success is our success

We would love to hear from you! If you would like to share the story of your exam success or if you have any questions or comments in regard to our products, please contact us at **800-673-8175** or **support@mometrix.com**.

Thanks again for your business and we wish you continued success!

Sincerely,
The Mometrix Test Preparation Team

Need more help? Check out our flashcards at:
http://MometrixFlashcards.com/TExES

TABLE OF CONTENTS

INTRODUCTION 1
SECRET KEY #1 – PLAN BIG, STUDY SMALL 2
SECRET KEY #2 – MAKE YOUR STUDYING COUNT 3
SECRET KEY #3 – PRACTICE THE RIGHT WAY 4
SECRET KEY #4 – PACE YOURSELF 6
SECRET KEY #5 – HAVE A PLAN FOR GUESSING 7
TEST-TAKING STRATEGIES 10
HISTORY 15
- WORLD HISTORY PRE-1400 15
- WORLD HISTORY 1400 TO 1914 24
- WORLD HISTORY 1914 TO PRESENT 30
- AMERICAN HISTORY PRE-COLUMBIAN TO 1789 38
- AMERICAN HISTORY 1790 TO 1898 46
- AMERICAN HISTORY 1899 TO PRESENT 61
- TEXAS HISTORY 78
- HISTORIOGRAPHY 81
- CHAPTER QUIZ 84

GEOGRAPHY 85
- GEOGRAPHY 85
- TEXAS GEOGRAPHY 98
- CHAPTER QUIZ 99

ECONOMICS 100
- CHAPTER QUIZ 112

GOVERNMENT AND CITIZENSHIP 113
- US GOVERNMENT AND CITIZENSHIP 113
- TEXAS GOVERNMENT 125
- CHAPTER QUIZ 128

CULTURE, SCIENCE, TECHNOLOGY, AND SOCIETY 129
- ANTHROPOLOGY, SOCIOLOGY, AND PSYCHOLOGY 129
- TEXAS CULTURE 137
- CHAPTER QUIZ 140

SOCIAL STUDIES FOUNDATIONS AND SKILLS 141
- SOCIAL STUDIES SKILLS 141
- CHAPTER QUIZ 147

SOCIAL STUDIES INSTRUCTION AND ASSESSMENT 148
- SOCIAL SCIENCE CLASSROOM MANAGEMENT 148
- CHAPTER QUIZ 156

TEXES PRACTICE TEST 157

ANSWER KEY AND EXPLANATIONS 173
ONLINE RESOURCES 186

Introduction

Thank you for purchasing this resource! You have made the choice to prepare yourself for a test that could have a huge impact on your future, and this guide is designed to help you be fully ready for test day. Obviously, it's important to have a solid understanding of the test material, but you also need to be prepared for the unique environment and stressors of the test, so that you can perform to the best of your abilities.

For this purpose, the first section that appears in this guide is the **Secret Keys**. We've devoted countless hours to meticulously researching what works and what doesn't, and we've boiled down our findings to the five most impactful steps you can take to improve your performance on the test. We start at the beginning with study planning and move through the preparation process, all the way to the testing strategies that will help you get the most out of what you know when you're finally sitting in front of the test.

We recommend that you start preparing for your test as far in advance as possible. However, if you've bought this guide as a last-minute study resource and only have a few days before your test, we recommend that you skip over the first two Secret Keys since they address a long-term study plan.

If you struggle with **test anxiety**, we strongly encourage you to check out our recommendations for how you can overcome it. Test anxiety is a formidable foe, but it can be beaten, and we want to make sure you have the tools you need to defeat it.

Secret Key #1 – Plan Big, Study Small

There's a lot riding on your performance. If you want to ace this test, you're going to need to keep your skills sharp and the material fresh in your mind. You need a plan that lets you review everything you need to know while still fitting in your schedule. We'll break this strategy down into three categories.

Information Organization

Start with the information you already have: the official test outline. From this, you can make a complete list of all the concepts you need to cover before the test. Organize these concepts into groups that can be studied together, and create a list of any related vocabulary you need to learn so you can brush up on any difficult terms. You'll want to keep this vocabulary list handy once you actually start studying since you may need to add to it along the way.

Time Management

Once you have your set of study concepts, decide how to spread them out over the time you have left before the test. Break your study plan into small, clear goals so you have a manageable task for each day and know exactly what you're doing. Then just focus on one small step at a time. When you manage your time this way, you don't need to spend hours at a time studying. Studying a small block of content for a short period each day helps you retain information better and avoid stressing over how much you have left to do. You can relax knowing that you have a plan to cover everything in time. In order for this strategy to be effective though, you have to start studying early and stick to your schedule. Avoid the exhaustion and futility that comes from last-minute cramming!

Study Environment

The environment you study in has a big impact on your learning. Studying in a coffee shop, while probably more enjoyable, is not likely to be as fruitful as studying in a quiet room. It's important to keep distractions to a minimum. You're only planning to study for a short block of time, so make the most of it. Don't pause to check your phone or get up to find a snack. It's also important to **avoid multitasking**. Research has consistently shown that multitasking will make your studying dramatically less effective. Your study area should also be comfortable and well-lit so you don't have the distraction of straining your eyes or sitting on an uncomfortable chair.

The time of day you study is also important. You want to be rested and alert. Don't wait until just before bedtime. Study when you'll be most likely to comprehend and remember. Even better, if you know what time of day your test will be, set that time aside for study. That way your brain will be used to working on that subject at that specific time and you'll have a better chance of recalling information.

Finally, it can be helpful to team up with others who are studying for the same test. Your actual studying should be done in as isolated an environment as possible, but the work of organizing the information and setting up the study plan can be divided up. In between study sessions, you can discuss with your teammates the concepts that you're all studying and quiz each other on the details. Just be sure that your teammates are as serious about the test as you are. If you find that your study time is being replaced with social time, you might need to find a new team.

Secret Key #2 – Make Your Studying Count

You're devoting a lot of time and effort to preparing for this test, so you want to be absolutely certain it will pay off. This means doing more than just reading the content and hoping you can remember it on test day. It's important to make every minute of study count. There are two main areas you can focus on to make your studying count.

Retention

It doesn't matter how much time you study if you can't remember the material. You need to make sure you are retaining the concepts. To check your retention of the information you're learning, try recalling it at later times with minimal prompting. Try carrying around flashcards and glance at one or two from time to time or ask a friend who's also studying for the test to quiz you.

To enhance your retention, look for ways to put the information into practice so that you can apply it rather than simply recalling it. If you're using the information in practical ways, it will be much easier to remember. Similarly, it helps to solidify a concept in your mind if you're not only reading it to yourself but also explaining it to someone else. Ask a friend to let you teach them about a concept you're a little shaky on (or speak aloud to an imaginary audience if necessary). As you try to summarize, define, give examples, and answer your friend's questions, you'll understand the concepts better and they will stay with you longer. Finally, step back for a big picture view and ask yourself how each piece of information fits with the whole subject. When you link the different concepts together and see them working together as a whole, it's easier to remember the individual components.

Finally, practice showing your work on any multi-step problems, even if you're just studying. Writing out each step you take to solve a problem will help solidify the process in your mind, and you'll be more likely to remember it during the test.

Modality

Modality simply refers to the means or method by which you study. Choosing a study modality that fits your own individual learning style is crucial. No two people learn best in exactly the same way, so it's important to know your strengths and use them to your advantage.

For example, if you learn best by visualization, focus on visualizing a concept in your mind and draw an image or a diagram. Try color-coding your notes, illustrating them, or creating symbols that will trigger your mind to recall a learned concept. If you learn best by hearing or discussing information, find a study partner who learns the same way or read aloud to yourself. Think about how to put the information in your own words. Imagine that you are giving a lecture on the topic and record yourself so you can listen to it later.

For any learning style, flashcards can be helpful. Organize the information so you can take advantage of spare moments to review. Underline key words or phrases. Use different colors for different categories. Mnemonic devices (such as creating a short list in which every item starts with the same letter) can also help with retention. Find what works best for you and use it to store the information in your mind most effectively and easily.

Secret Key #3 – Practice the Right Way

Your success on test day depends not only on how many hours you put into preparing, but also on whether you prepared the right way. It's good to check along the way to see if your studying is paying off. One of the most effective ways to do this is by taking practice tests to evaluate your progress. Practice tests are useful because they show exactly where you need to improve. Every time you take a practice test, pay special attention to these three groups of questions:

- The questions you got wrong
- The questions you had to guess on, even if you guessed right
- The questions you found difficult or slow to work through

This will show you exactly what your weak areas are, and where you need to devote more study time. Ask yourself why each of these questions gave you trouble. Was it because you didn't understand the material? Was it because you didn't remember the vocabulary? Do you need more repetitions on this type of question to build speed and confidence? Dig into those questions and figure out how you can strengthen your weak areas as you go back to review the material.

Additionally, many practice tests have a section explaining the answer choices. It can be tempting to read the explanation and think that you now have a good understanding of the concept. However, an explanation likely only covers part of the question's broader context. Even if the explanation makes perfect sense, **go back and investigate** every concept related to the question until you're positive you have a thorough understanding.

As you go along, keep in mind that the practice test is just that: practice. Memorizing these questions and answers will not be very helpful on the actual test because it is unlikely to have any of the same exact questions. If you only know the right answers to the sample questions, you won't be prepared for the real thing. **Study the concepts** until you understand them fully, and then you'll be able to answer any question that shows up on the test.

It's important to wait on the practice tests until you're ready. If you take a test on your first day of study, you may be overwhelmed by the amount of material covered and how much you need to learn. Work up to it gradually.

On test day, you'll need to be prepared for answering questions, managing your time, and using the test-taking strategies you've learned. It's a lot to balance, like a mental marathon that will have a big impact on your future. Like training for a marathon, you'll need to start slowly and work your way up. When test day arrives, you'll be ready.

Start with the strategies you've read in the first two Secret Keys—plan your course and study in the way that works best for you. If you have time, consider using multiple study resources to get different approaches to the same concepts. It can be helpful to see difficult concepts from more than one angle. Then find a good source for practice tests. Many times, the test website will suggest potential study resources or provide sample tests.

Practice Test Strategy

If you're able to find at least three practice tests, we recommend this strategy:

Untimed and Open-Book Practice

Take the first test with no time constraints and with your notes and study guide handy. Take your time and focus on applying the strategies you've learned.

Timed and Open-Book Practice

Take the second practice test open-book as well, but set a timer and practice pacing yourself to finish in time.

Timed and Closed-Book Practice

Take any other practice tests as if it were test day. Set a timer and put away your study materials. Sit at a table or desk in a quiet room, imagine yourself at the testing center, and answer questions as quickly and accurately as possible.

Keep repeating timed and closed-book tests on a regular basis until you run out of practice tests or it's time for the actual test. Your mind will be ready for the schedule and stress of test day, and you'll be able to focus on recalling the material you've learned.

Secret Key #4 – Pace Yourself

Once you're fully prepared for the material on the test, your biggest challenge on test day will be managing your time. Just knowing that the clock is ticking can make you panic even if you have plenty of time left. Work on pacing yourself so you can build confidence against the time constraints of the exam. Pacing is a difficult skill to master, especially in a high-pressure environment, so **practice is vital**.

Set time expectations for your pace based on how much time is available. For example, if a section has 60 questions and the time limit is 30 minutes, you know you have to average 30 seconds or less per question in order to answer them all. Although 30 seconds is the hard limit, set 25 seconds per question as your goal, so you reserve extra time to spend on harder questions. When you budget extra time for the harder questions, you no longer have any reason to stress when those questions take longer to answer.

Don't let this time expectation distract you from working through the test at a calm, steady pace, but keep it in mind so you don't spend too much time on any one question. Recognize that taking extra time on one question you don't understand may keep you from answering two that you do understand later in the test. If your time limit for a question is up and you're still not sure of the answer, mark it and move on, and come back to it later if the time and the test format allow. If the testing format doesn't allow you to return to earlier questions, just make an educated guess; then put it out of your mind and move on.

On the easier questions, be careful not to rush. It may seem wise to hurry through them so you have more time for the challenging ones, but it's not worth missing one if you know the concept and just didn't take the time to read the question fully. Work efficiently but make sure you understand the question and have looked at all of the answer choices, since more than one may seem right at first.

Even if you're paying attention to the time, you may find yourself a little behind at some point. You should speed up to get back on track, but do so wisely. Don't panic; just take a few seconds less on each question until you're caught up. Don't guess without thinking, but do look through the answer choices and eliminate any you know are wrong. If you can get down to two choices, it is often worthwhile to guess from those. Once you've chosen an answer, move on and don't dwell on any that you skipped or had to hurry through. If a question was taking too long, chances are it was one of the harder ones, so you weren't as likely to get it right anyway.

On the other hand, if you find yourself getting ahead of schedule, it may be beneficial to slow down a little. The more quickly you work, the more likely you are to make a careless mistake that will affect your score. You've budgeted time for each question, so don't be afraid to spend that time. Practice an efficient but careful pace to get the most out of the time you have.

Secret Key #5 – Have a Plan for Guessing

When you're taking the test, you may find yourself stuck on a question. Some of the answer choices seem better than others, but you don't see the one answer choice that is obviously correct. What do you do?

The scenario described above is very common, yet most test takers have not effectively prepared for it. Developing and practicing a plan for guessing may be one of the single most effective uses of your time as you get ready for the exam.

In developing your plan for guessing, there are three questions to address:

- When should you start the guessing process?
- How should you narrow down the choices?
- Which answer should you choose?

When to Start the Guessing Process

Unless your plan for guessing is to select C every time (which, despite its merits, is not what we recommend), you need to leave yourself enough time to apply your answer elimination strategies. Since you have a limited amount of time for each question, that means that if you're going to give yourself the best shot at guessing correctly, you have to decide quickly whether or not you will guess.

Of course, the best-case scenario is that you don't have to guess at all, so first, see if you can answer the question based on your knowledge of the subject and basic reasoning skills. Focus on the key words in the question and try to jog your memory of related topics. Give yourself a chance to bring the knowledge to mind, but once you realize that you don't have (or you can't access) the knowledge you need to answer the question, it's time to start the guessing process.

It's almost always better to start the guessing process too early than too late. It only takes a few seconds to remember something and answer the question from knowledge. Carefully eliminating wrong answer choices takes longer. Plus, going through the process of eliminating answer choices can actually help jog your memory.

Summary: Start the guessing process as soon as you decide that you can't answer the question based on your knowledge.

How to Narrow Down the Choices

The next chapter in this book (**Test-Taking Strategies**) includes a wide range of strategies for how to approach questions and how to look for answer choices to eliminate. You will definitely want to read those carefully, practice them, and figure out which ones work best for you. Here though, we're going to address a mindset rather than a particular strategy.

Your odds of guessing an answer correctly depend on how many options you are choosing from.

Number of options left	5	4	3	2	1
Odds of guessing correctly	20%	25%	33%	50%	100%

You can see from this chart just how valuable it is to be able to eliminate incorrect answers and make an educated guess, but there are two things that many test takers do that cause them to miss out on the benefits of guessing:

- Accidentally eliminating the correct answer
- Selecting an answer based on an impression

We'll look at the first one here, and the second one in the next section.

To avoid accidentally eliminating the correct answer, we recommend a thought exercise called **the $5 challenge**. In this challenge, you only eliminate an answer choice from contention if you are willing to bet $5 on it being wrong. Why $5? Five dollars is a small but not insignificant amount of money. It's an amount you could afford to lose but wouldn't want to throw away. And while losing $5 once might not hurt too much, doing it twenty times will set you back $100. In the same way, each small decision you make—eliminating a choice here, guessing on a question there—won't by itself impact your score very much, but when you put them all together, they can make a big difference. By holding each answer choice elimination decision to a higher standard, you can reduce the risk of accidentally eliminating the correct answer.

The $5 challenge can also be applied in a positive sense: If you are willing to bet $5 that an answer choice *is* correct, go ahead and mark it as correct.

Summary: Only eliminate an answer choice if you are willing to bet $5 that it is wrong.

Which Answer to Choose

You're taking the test. You've run into a hard question and decided you'll have to guess. You've eliminated all the answer choices you're willing to bet $5 on. Now you have to pick an answer. Why do we even need to talk about this? Why can't you just pick whichever one you feel like when the time comes?

The answer to these questions is that if you don't come into the test with a plan, you'll rely on your impression to select an answer choice, and if you do that, you risk falling into a trap. The test writers know that everyone who takes their test will be guessing on some of the questions, so they intentionally write wrong answer choices to seem plausible. You still have to pick an answer though, and if the wrong answer choices are designed to look right, how can you ever be sure that you're not falling for their trap? The best solution we've found to this dilemma is to take the decision out of your hands entirely. Here is the process we recommend:

Once you've eliminated any choices that you are confident (willing to bet $5) are wrong, select the first remaining choice as your answer.

Whether you choose to select the first remaining choice, the second, or the last, the important thing is that you use some preselected standard. Using this approach guarantees that you will not be enticed into selecting an answer choice that looks right, because you are not basing your decision on how the answer choices look.

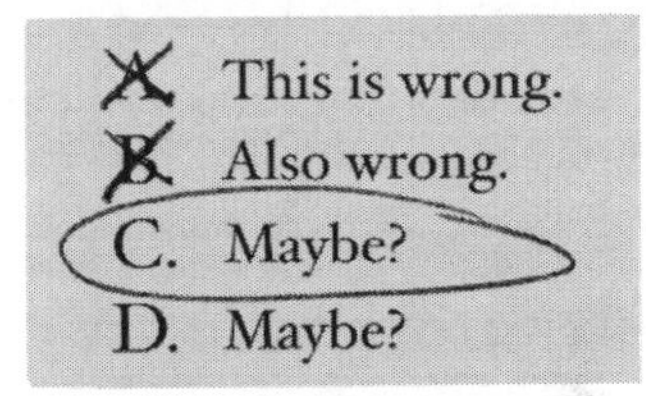

This is not meant to make you question your knowledge. Instead, it is to help you recognize the difference between your knowledge and your impressions. There's a huge difference between thinking an answer is right because of what you know, and thinking an answer is right because it looks or sounds like it should be right.

Summary: To ensure that your selection is appropriately random, make a predetermined selection from among all answer choices you have not eliminated.

Test-Taking Strategies

This section contains a list of test-taking strategies that you may find helpful as you work through the test. By taking what you know and applying logical thought, you can maximize your chances of answering any question correctly!

It is very important to realize that every question is different and every person is different: no single strategy will work on every question, and no single strategy will work for every person. That's why we've included all of them here, so you can try them out and determine which ones work best for different types of questions and which ones work best for you.

Question Strategies

READ CAREFULLY

Read the question and the answer choices carefully. Don't miss the question because you misread the terms. You have plenty of time to read each question thoroughly and make sure you understand what is being asked. Yet a happy medium must be attained, so don't waste too much time. You must read carefully and efficiently.

CONTEXTUAL CLUES

Look for contextual clues. If the question includes a word you are not familiar with, look at the immediate context for some indication of what the word might mean. Contextual clues can often give you all the information you need to decipher the meaning of an unfamiliar word. Even if you can't determine the meaning, you may be able to narrow down the possibilities enough to make a solid guess at the answer to the question.

PREFIXES

If you're having trouble with a word in the question or answer choices, try dissecting it. Take advantage of every clue that the word might include. Prefixes can be a huge help. Usually, they allow you to determine a basic meaning. *Pre-* means before, *post-* means after, *pro-* is positive, *de-* is negative. From prefixes, you can get an idea of the general meaning of the word and try to put it into context.

HEDGE WORDS

Watch out for critical hedge words, such as *likely, may, can, often, almost, mostly, usually, generally, rarely*, and *sometimes*. Question writers insert these hedge phrases to cover every possibility. Often an answer choice will be wrong simply because it leaves no room for exception. Be on guard for answer choices that have definitive words such as *exactly* and *always*.

SWITCHBACK WORDS

Stay alert for *switchbacks*. These are the words and phrases frequently used to alert you to shifts in thought. The most common switchback words are *but, although*, and *however*. Others include *nevertheless, on the other hand, even though, while, in spite of, despite*, and *regardless of*. Switchback words are important to catch because they can change the direction of the question or an answer choice.

FACE VALUE

When in doubt, use common sense. Accept the situation in the problem at face value. Don't read too much into it. These problems will not require you to make wild assumptions. If you have to go beyond creativity and warp time or space in order to have an answer choice fit the question, then you should move on and consider the other answer choices. These are normal problems rooted in reality. The applicable relationship or explanation may not be readily apparent, but it is there for you to figure out. Use your common sense to interpret anything that isn't clear.

Answer Choice Strategies

⊘ Answer Selection

The most thorough way to pick an answer choice is to identify and eliminate wrong answers until only one is left, then confirm it is the correct answer. Sometimes an answer choice may immediately seem right, but be careful. The test writers will usually put more than one reasonable answer choice on each question, so take a second to read all of them and make sure that the other choices are not equally obvious. As long as you have time left, it is better to read every answer choice than to pick the first one that looks right without checking the others.

⊘ Answer Choice Families

An answer choice family consists of two (in rare cases, three) answer choices that are very similar in construction and cannot all be true at the same time. If you see two answer choices that are direct opposites or parallels, one of them is usually the correct answer. For instance, if one answer choice says that quantity *x* increases and another either says that quantity *x* decreases (opposite) or says that quantity *y* increases (parallel), then those answer choices would fall into the same family. An answer choice that doesn't match the construction of the answer choice family is more likely to be incorrect. Most questions will not have answer choice families, but when they do appear, you should be prepared to recognize them.

⊘ Eliminate Answers

Eliminate answer choices as soon as you realize they are wrong, but make sure you consider all possibilities. If you are eliminating answer choices and realize that the last one you are left with is also wrong, don't panic. Start over and consider each choice again. There may be something you missed the first time that you will realize on the second pass.

⊘ Avoid Fact Traps

Don't be distracted by an answer choice that is factually true but doesn't answer the question. You are looking for the choice that answers the question. Stay focused on what the question is asking for so you don't accidentally pick an answer that is true but incorrect. Always go back to the question and make sure the answer choice you've selected actually answers the question and is not merely a true statement.

⊘ Extreme Statements

In general, you should avoid answers that put forth extreme actions as standard practice or proclaim controversial ideas as established fact. An answer choice that states the "process should be used in certain situations, if..." is much more likely to be correct than one that states the "process should be discontinued completely." The first is a calm rational statement and doesn't even make a definitive, uncompromising stance, using a hedge word *if* to provide wiggle room, whereas the second choice is far more extreme.

⊘ Benchmark

As you read through the answer choices and you come across one that seems to answer the question well, mentally select that answer choice. This is not your final answer, but it's the one that will help you evaluate the other answer choices. The one that you selected is your benchmark or standard for judging each of the other answer choices. Every other answer choice must be compared to your benchmark. That choice is correct until proven otherwise by another answer choice beating it. If you find a better answer, then that one becomes your new benchmark. Once you've decided that no other choice answers the question as well as your benchmark, you have your final answer.

✅ Predict the Answer

Before you even start looking at the answer choices, it is often best to try to predict the answer. When you come up with the answer on your own, it is easier to avoid distractions and traps because you will know exactly what to look for. The right answer choice is unlikely to be word-for-word what you came up with, but it should be a close match. Even if you are confident that you have the right answer, you should still take the time to read each option before moving on.

General Strategies

✅ Tough Questions

If you are stumped on a problem or it appears too hard or too difficult, don't waste time. Move on! Remember though, if you can quickly check for obviously incorrect answer choices, your chances of guessing correctly are greatly improved. Before you completely give up, at least try to knock out a couple of possible answers. Eliminate what you can and then guess at the remaining answer choices before moving on.

✅ Check Your Work

Since you will probably not know every term listed and the answer to every question, it is important that you get credit for the ones that you do know. Don't miss any questions through careless mistakes. If at all possible, try to take a second to look back over your answer selection and make sure you've selected the correct answer choice and haven't made a costly careless mistake (such as marking an answer choice that you didn't mean to mark). This quick double check should more than pay for itself in caught mistakes for the time it costs.

✅ Pace Yourself

It's easy to be overwhelmed when you're looking at a page full of questions; your mind is confused and full of random thoughts, and the clock is ticking down faster than you would like. Calm down and maintain the pace that you have set for yourself. Especially as you get down to the last few minutes of the test, don't let the small numbers on the clock make you panic. As long as you are on track by monitoring your pace, you are guaranteed to have time for each question.

✅ Don't Rush

It is very easy to make errors when you are in a hurry. Maintaining a fast pace in answering questions is pointless if it makes you miss questions that you would have gotten right otherwise. Test writers like to include distracting information and wrong answers that seem right. Taking a little extra time to avoid careless mistakes can make all the difference in your test score. Find a pace that allows you to be confident in the answers that you select.

✅ Keep Moving

Panicking will not help you pass the test, so do your best to stay calm and keep moving. Taking deep breaths and going through the answer elimination steps you practiced can help to break through a stress barrier and keep your pace.

Final Notes

The combination of a solid foundation of content knowledge and the confidence that comes from practicing your plan for applying that knowledge is the key to maximizing your performance on test day. As your foundation of content knowledge is built up and strengthened, you'll find that the strategies included in this chapter become more and more effective in helping you quickly sift through the distractions and traps of the test to isolate the correct answer.

Now that you're preparing to move forward into the test content chapters of this book, be sure to keep your goal in mind. As you read, think about how you will be able to apply this information on the test. If you've already seen sample questions for the test and you have an idea of the question format and style, try to come up with questions of your own that you can answer based on what you're reading. This will give you valuable practice applying your knowledge in the same ways you can expect to on test day.

Good luck and good studying!

History

World History Pre-1400

Different Periods of Prehistory

History begins when people started recording their existence with writing systems, but the vast majority of human existence occurred during prehistoric times. Because writing systems were not yet invented, much of our information about prehistory comes from archaeology and anthropology, which use physical remains and environmental evidence to uncover insights into humanity before we developed systems of recording our experiences.

- **Lower Paleolithic or Early Stone Age**— early humans were hunter-gatherers who lived in small groups or tribes and used crude tools like needles, hatchets, awls, and cutting tools made of stone, wood, and other natural materials.
- **Middle Paleolithic or Middle Stone Age**, beginning approximately 300,000 BC—stone tools became more sophisticated, local traditions were developed, and communities became more complex.
- **Upper Paleolithic or Late Stone Age**—Humans began to develop a wider variety of tools. These tools were better made and more specialized. They also began to wear clothes, organize in groups with definite social structures, and practice art. Most lived in caves during this time period.
- **Bronze Age**, beginning approximately 3000 BC—metals are discovered, and the first civilizations emerge as humans become more technologically advanced.
- **Iron Age**, beginning 1200 to 1000 BC—metal tools replace stone tools as humans develop knowledge of smelting.

Anthropology

Anthropology is the study of human culture. Anthropologists study groups of humans, how they relate to each other, and the similarities and differences between these different groups and cultures. Anthropological research takes two approaches: **cross-cultural research** and **comparative research**. Most anthropologists work by living among different cultures and participating in those cultures in order to learn about them.

There are four major **divisions** within anthropology:

- Biological anthropology
- Cultural anthropology
- Linguistic anthropology
- Archaeology

Science of Archaeology

Archaeology is the study of past human cultures by evaluating what they leave behind. This can include bones, buildings, art, tools, pottery, graves, and even trash. Archaeologists maintain detailed notes and records of their findings and use special tools to evaluate what they find. Photographs, notes, maps, artifacts, and surveys of the area can all contribute to the evaluation of an archaeological site. By studying all these elements of numerous archeological sites, scientists have been able to theorize that humans or near-humans have existed for about 600,000 years. Before that, more primitive humans are believed to have appeared about one million years ago. These humans eventually developed into **Cro-Magnon man**, and then **Homo sapiens**, or modern man.

Neolithic Period

The Neolithic period, also known as the **New Stone Age**, refers to that stage of human cultural evolution in which man developed stone tools, settled in villages, and began making crafts. In order to begin living in towns, man had to learn how to domesticate animals and sustain agriculture; formerly, in the Paleolithic and Mesolithic periods, man had subsisted through hunting, fishing, and gathering. The **Neolithic period** is said to have ended when urban civilizations began, or when metal tools or writing began. Because the designation of Neolithic depends on these factors, anthropologists date its occurrence differently for different regions and populations. At present, anthropologists believe that the earliest Neolithic culture was in southwest Asia between 8000 and 6000 BC.

Requirements for Early Civilizations and States

While historians and archaeologists don't all agree on exactly what makes a civilization, many consider the following features defining characteristics of civilizations:

- Urban centers
- Complex social structures
- Centralized government
- Organized religion
- Monumental architecture
- Writing systems
- Economic systems and trade
- Division of labor

The **earliest civilizations** developed in river valleys where reliable, fertile land was easily found, including:

- The Nile River Valley in Egypt
- Mesopotamia
- The Indus Valley
- Hwang Ho in China

The very earliest civilizations developed in the **Tigris-Euphrates valley** in Mesopotamia, which is now part of Iraq, and in Egypt's **Nile valley**. These civilizations arose between 5000 and 3000 BC. The area where these civilizations grew is known as the Fertile Crescent. Geography and the availability of water made large-scale human habitation possible. The walled city of Uruk, which was built in Sumer (southern Mesopotamia), is often considered the first city ever constructed.

Importance of Rivers and Water to the Growth of Early Civilizations

The earliest civilizations are also referred to as **fluvial civilizations** because they were founded near rivers. Rivers and the water they provide were vital to these early groupings, offering:

- Water for drinking, cultivating crops, and caring for domesticated animals
- A gathering place for wild animals that could be hunted
- Rich soil deposits as a result of regular flooding

Irrigation techniques helped direct water where it was most needed, to sustain herds of domestic animals and to nourish crops of increasing size and quality.

Fertile Crescent

James Breasted, an archaeologist from the University of Chicago, popularized the term "**Fertile Crescent**" to describe the area in Southwest Asia and the Mediterranean basin where the earliest civilizations arose. The region includes modern-day Iraq, Syria, Lebanon, Israel, Palestine, and Jordan. It is bordered on the south by the Syrian and Arabian Deserts, the west by the Mediterranean Sea, and to the north and east by the Taurus and Zagros Mountains, respectively. This area not only provided the raw materials for the development of increasingly advanced civilizations but also saw waves of migration and invasion, leading to the earliest wars and genocides as groups conquered and absorbed each other's cultures and inhabitants.

Ancient Civilizations of Mesopotamia and the Near East

The Near East was home to many distinct cultures and civilizations in the ancient world. These cultures controlled different areas of Mesopotamia and the Near East during various time periods but were similar in that they were **autocratic**: a single ruler served as the head of the government and often was the main religious ruler as well. These rulers were often tyrannical, militaristic leaders who controlled all aspects of life, including law, trade, and religious activity. Portions of the legacies of these civilizations remain in cultures today. These include mythologies, religious systems, mathematical innovations, and even elements of various languages.

The Sumerians

Sumer, located in the southern part of Mesopotamia, consisted of a dozen **city-states**. Each city-state had its own patron gods, and the leader of each city-state also served as the high priest. Cultural legacies of Sumer include:

- The invention of writing
- The invention of the wheel
- The first library—established in Assyria by Ashurbanipal
- The Hanging Gardens of Babylon—one of the Seven Wonders of the Ancient World
- First written laws—Ur-Nammu's Codes and the Codes of Hammurabi
- The *Epic of Gilgamesh*—the first recorded epic story

Review Video: Early Mesopotamia: The Sumerians
Visit mometrix.com/academy and enter code: 939880

The Babylonians

The Babylonians conquered the Sumerians and established a city on the Euphrates River in approximately 1750 BC One of the most famous Babylonian rulers was Hammurabi, an Amorite leader who established the famous Code of Hammurabi, an extremely detailed set of laws. This marked the first time that a set of rules governing every aspect of social life was applied to an entire people.

The Amorites

A group of Semitic-speaking people often referred to as the Amorites existed in Mesopotamia for a long time, but the early history of this group is not well known. Some scholars believe the term actually referred to multiple different groups of people from the west. The earliest records of them paint the Amorites as a nomadic, potentially uncivilized, people who made incursions into established territories, oftentimes stealing from communities; however, they eventually assimilated into Mesopotamia and added elements of their own culture. The Amorites are best known for their period of rule over the kingdom of Babylonia.

The Hittites

The Hittites conquered the Babylonian civilization but adopted their religion, laws, and literature. Overall, the Hittites tended to tolerate other religions, unlike many other contemporary cultures, and absorbed foreign gods into their own belief systems rather than forcing their religion onto peoples they conquered. The Hittite Empire reached its peak in 1600-1200 BC. After a war with Egypt, which weakened them severely, they were eventually conquered by the Assyrians.

The Assyrians

The Assyrians developed powerful military technologies, such as horse-drawn chariots and iron weapons, that allowed them to eventually build one of the world's oldest empires. They had a long and complex history, at times being subjects under the rule of other civilizations, like the Babylonians. At their peak (c. 911-612 BC), they were one of the most powerful civilizations in the world, and they were able to maintain their empire for hundreds of years.

THE CHALDEANS

The Chaldeans were a Semitic people who ruled over the Neo-Babylonian Empire. Originally a separate tribal group, they largely assimilated into Babylonian culture. The Neo-Babylonian Empire ultimately fell to the Persian Empire in 539 BC.

THE PERSIAN EMPIRE

The Persian Empire (Achaemenid Empire) were conquerors, but those they conquered were often allowed to keep their own laws, customs, and religious traditions rather than being forced to accept those of their conquerors. They are recognized for their centralized bureaucratic administration and complex infrastructure. They mainly practiced Zoroastrianism, a religion that was heavily influential before it declined after the spread of Islam in the region.

HEBREWS

The Hebrew or ancient Israelite culture emerged in the Levant in the second century BC. They developed the monotheistic religion that eventually developed into modern Judaism and Christianity. The Hebrew history is well-preserved and contains detailed descriptions of conquests against them from Egypt, Assyria, Babylon, Persia, and Rome, many of which can be confirmed from artifacts of other cultures. Despite being conquered by a variety of empires, their cultural identity has survived and still exists today.

EGYPT

Egypt was one of the most powerful and culturally significant civilizations in the ancient world. Its history is often broken up into a few distinct eras: the Old Kingdom, the First Intermediate Period, the Middle Kingdom, the Second Intermediate Period, the New Kingdom, the Third Intermediate Period, and the Late Period. These eras cover a span of around 3,000 years, beginning approximately in the year 3150 BC, when Menes (an Egyptian ruler whose identity is debated) united Upper and Lower Egypt, and ending around 332 BC, when Alexander the Great conquered the region.

Egypt was centered around the Nile River, which had a predictable annual flooding schedule that the Egyptians used to grow large surpluses of crops. The Egyptians traded these surplus crops with nearby civilizations, particularly Mesopotamia. This trade formed one of the chief bases of their wealth and influence.

During its long history, Ancient Egypt contributed many technological and cultural innovations in the fields of religion, art, engineering, astronomy, medicine, and more. They are renowned for their impressive monuments, temples, and tombs, including the Great Pyramids and the Sphinx of Giza. On many of these monuments is a complex script developed by the Egyptians called hieroglyphics. This is a written language that uses pictures and other symbols to represent words, ideas, and sounds. It was often used to record important events, such as battles, and the lives of important people, such as the Pharaoh (the modern title attributed to the king of Egypt).

KUSHITES

Kush, or Cush, was located in Nubia, south of ancient Egypt, and the earliest existing records of this civilization were found in Egyptian texts. At one time, Kush was the largest empire on the Nile River, ruling not only Nubia but Upper and Lower Egypt as well.

In Neolithic times, Kushites lived in villages, with buildings made of mud bricks. They were settled rather than nomadic and practiced hunting and fishing, cultivated grain, and also herded cattle. Kerma, the capital, was a major center of trade.

Kush determined leadership through matrilineal descent of their kings, as did Egypt. Their heads of state, the Kandake or Kentake, were female. Their polytheistic religion included the primary Egyptian gods as well as regional gods, including a lion-headed god, which is commonly found in African cultures. Kush was conquered by the Aksumite Empire in the 4th century AD.

Phoenicians

Skilled seafarers and navigators, the Phoenicians were a maritime civilization mostly along the coast of the Levant region. They were highly skilled in trade and developed a purple dye that was in great demand in the ancient world. They were also skilled glass and metal workers. They devised a phonetic alphabet, using symbols to represent individual sounds rather than whole words or syllables.

Minoans

The Minoans lived on the island of Crete, just off the coast of Greece. This civilization reigned from approximately 4000 to 1400 BC and is considered to be the first advanced civilization in Europe. The Minoans developed writing systems known to linguists as **Linear A** and **Linear B**. Linear A has not yet been translated; Linear B evolved into classical Greek script. "Minoans" is not the name they used for themselves but is instead a variation on the name of King Minos, a king in Greek mythology believed by some to have been a denizen of Crete. The Minoan civilization subsisted on trade, and their way of life was often disrupted by earthquakes and volcanoes. Much is still unknown about the Minoans, and archaeologists continue to study their architecture and archaeological remains. The Minoan culture eventually fell to Greek invaders and was supplanted by the **Mycenaean civilization**.

Mycenaeans

In contrast to the Minoans, whom they displaced, the **Mycenaeans** relied more on conquest than on trade. Mycenaean states included Sparta, Athens, and Corinth. The history of this civilization, including the **Trojan War**, was recorded by the Greek poet **Homer**. His work was largely considered mythical until archaeologists discovered evidence of the city of **Troy** in Hisarlik, Turkey. Archaeologists continue to add to the body of information about this ancient culture, translating documents written in Linear B, a script derived from the Minoan Linear A. It is theorized that the Mycenaean civilization was eventually destroyed in either a Dorian invasion or an attack by Greek invaders from the north.

Dorian Invasion

A Dorian invasion does not refer to an invasion by a particular group of people, but rather is a hypothetical theory to explain the end of the **Mycenaean civilization** and the growth of **classical Greece**. Ancient tradition refers to these events as "the return of the Heracleidae," or the sons (descendants) of Hercules. Archaeologists and historians still do not know exactly who conquered the Mycenaeans, but it is believed to have occurred around 1200 BC, contemporaneous with the destruction of the **Hittite civilization** in what is now modern Turkey. The Hittites speak of an attack by people of the Aegean Sea, or the "Sea People." Only Athens was left intact.

Ancient India

The civilizations of ancient India gave rise to both **Hinduism** and **Buddhism**, major world religions that have influenced countries far from their place of origin. Practices such as yoga, increasingly popular in the West, can trace their roots to these earliest Indian civilizations, and the poses are still formally referred to by Sanskrit names. Literature from ancient India includes the *Mahabharata* containing the *Bhagavad Gita*, the *Ramayana*, *Arthashastra*, and the *Vedas*, a collection of sacred texts. Indo-European languages, including English, find their beginnings in these ancient cultures. Ancient Indo-Aryan languages such as Sanskrit are still used in some formal Hindu practices.

Indus Valley Civilization

The Indus Valley Civilization (IVC) was an urban civilization that arose in the Indus Valley, located in between the modern countries of Iran, India, and Pakistan. These ancient humans developed the concept of zero in mathematics, practiced an early form of the Hindu religion, and developed the caste system which is still prevalent in India today. Archeologists are still uncovering information about this highly developed ancient civilization.

Earliest Civilizations in China

Many historians believe **Chinese civilization** is the oldest uninterrupted civilization in the world. The **Neolithic age** in China goes back to 10,000 BC, with agriculture in China beginning as early as 5000 BC. Their system of writing dates to 1500 BC. The Yellow River served as the center for the earliest Chinese settlements. In Ningxia, in northwest China, there are carvings on cliffs that date back to the Paleolithic Period, indicating the extreme antiquity of Chinese culture. Literature from ancient China includes Confucius' *Analects*, the *Tao Te Ching*, and a variety of poetry.

Ancient Cultures in the Americas

Less is known of ancient American civilizations since less was left behind. Some of the more well-known cultures include:

- The **Norte Chico civilization** in Peru, an agricultural society of up to 30 individual communities, existed over 5,000 years ago. This culture is also known as the Caral-Supe civilization, and is the oldest known civilization in the Americas.
- The **Anasazi**, or Ancestral Pueblo People, lived in what is now the southwestern United States. Emerging about 1200 BC, the Anasazi built complex adobe dwellings and were the forerunners of later Pueblo Indian cultures.
- The **Maya** emerged in southern Mexico and northern Central America as early as 2600 BC. They developed a written language and a complex calendar.

Greece

After the fall of Mycenaean civilization came a dark age out of which would spring one of the most influential cultures in the western world: Greece. While much was lost after the fall of the Mycenaeans, including writing, the Ancient Greeks, in the Archaic Period (800-500 BC) and the Classical Period (500-323 BC), went on to make fundamental achievements in politics, philosophy, history, drama, literature, art, mathematics, and science. They colonized areas all across the Mediterranean and spread their culture around the world. Their culture was heavily influential in shaping the Roman Empire and later civilizations, including those that exist today.

Spartans vs. Athenians

Both powerful Greek city-states, Sparta and Athens fought each other in the **Peloponnesian War** (431-404 BC). Despite their proximity, the Spartans and the Athenians nurtured contrasting cultures:

- The **Spartans**, located in Peloponnesus, were ruled by an oligarchic military state. They practiced farming, disallowed trade for Spartan citizens, and valued military arts and strict discipline. They emerged as the strongest military force in the area and maintained this status for many years. In one memorable encounter, a small group of Spartans held off a huge army of Persians at Thermopylae.
- The **Athenians** were centered in Attica, where the land was rocky and unsuitable for farming. Like the Spartans, they descended from invaders who spoke Greek. Their government was very different from Sparta's; it was in Athens that democracy was created by Cleisthenes of Athens in 508 BC. Athenians excelled in art, theater, architecture, and philosophy.

Contributions of Ancient Greece That Still Exist Today

Ancient Greece made numerous major contributions to cultural development, including:

- **Theater**—Aristophanes and other Greek playwrights laid the groundwork for modern theatrical performance.
- **Alphabet**—the Greek alphabet, derived from the Phoenician alphabet, developed into the Roman alphabet, and then into our modern-day alphabet.
- **Geometry**—Pythagoras and Euclid pioneered much of the system of geometry still taught today. Archimedes made various mathematical discoveries, including calculating a very accurate value of pi.

- **Historical writing**—much of ancient history doubles as mythology or religious texts. Herodotus and Thucydides made use of research and interpretation to record historical events.
- **Philosophy**—Socrates, Plato, and Aristotle served as the fathers of Western philosophy. Their work is still required reading for philosophy students.

Review Video: Ancient Greece Timeline
Visit mometrix.com/academy and enter code: 800829

Alexander the Great

Born to Philip II of Macedon and tutored by Aristotle, **Alexander the Great** is considered one of the greatest conquerors in history. He conquered Egypt and the Achaemenid/Persian Empire, a powerful empire founded by Cyrus the Great that spanned three continents, and he traveled as far as India and the Iberian Peninsula. Alexander the Great died at an early age and, though his cause of death is not known for certain, one hypothesis is that he succumbed to malaria at the early age of 32. His conquering efforts spread Greek culture into the east. This cultural diffusion left a greater mark on history than did his empire, which fell apart due to internal conflict not long after his death. Trade between the East and West increased, as did an exchange of ideas and beliefs that influenced both regions greatly. The **Hellenistic traditions** his conquest spread were prevalent in Byzantine culture until as late as the 15th century.

Persian Wars

The Persian Empire, ruled by **Cyrus the Great**, encompassed an area from the Black Sea to Afghanistan and beyond into Central Asia. After the death of Cyrus, **Darius I** became king in 522 BC. The empire reached its zenith during his reign, and Darius attempted to conquer Greece as well. From 499 to 449 BC, the Greeks and Persians fought in the **Persian Wars**. The **Peace of Callias** brought an end to the fighting, after the Greeks were able to repel the invasion.

Battles of the Persian Wars included:

- The **Battle of Marathon**—heavily outnumbered Greek forces managed to achieve victory.
- The **Battle of Thermopylae**—a small band of Spartans held off a throng of Persian troops for several days before Persia defeated the Greeks and captured an evacuated Athens.
- The **Battle of Salamis**—this was a naval battle that again saw outnumbered Greeks achieving victory.
- The **Battle of Plataea**—this was another Greek victory, but one in which they outnumbered the Persians. This ended the invasion of Greece.

Maurya Empire

The Maurya Empire was a large, powerful empire established in India. It was one of the largest ever to rule in the Indian subcontinent and existed from 322 to 185 BC, ruled by **Chandragupta Maurya** after the withdrawal from India of Alexander the Great. The Maurya Empire was highly developed, including a standardized economic system, waterways, and private corporations. Trade to the Greeks and others became common, with goods including silk, exotic foods, and spices. Religious development included the rise of Buddhism and Jainism. The laws of the Maurya Empire protected not only civil and social rights of the citizens, but they also protected animals, establishing protected zones for economically important creatures such as elephants, lions, and tigers. This period of time in Indian history was largely peaceful, perhaps due to the strong Buddhist beliefs of many of its leaders. The empire finally fell after a succession of weak leaders and was taken over by **Demetrius**, a Greco-Bactrian king who took advantage of this lapse in leadership to conquer southern Afghanistan and Pakistan around 180 BC, forming the **Indo-Greek Kingdom**.

Hinduism

Hinduism is the traditional religion of India. It is expressed in an individual's philosophy and behavior, rather than in the performance of any specific rituals. **Hinduism** does not claim a founder but has evolved slowly over thousands of years; the first Hindu writings date back to the third millennium BC. There are a few concepts that are common to all permutations of Hinduism, such as the **Vedas**, which are considered to be the sacred texts of the religion. The chief aim in life for a Hindu is to be liberated from the cycle of suffering and rebirth. Hindus believe in **reincarnation** and that a person's conduct in this life will affect his or her position in the next (**karma**). Although Hinduism is frequently associated with the caste system, the two are actually unrelated.

Buddhism

Buddhism was created by **Gautama Siddhartha** (otherwise known as Buddha) in about 528 B.C. It was in part a response to Hinduism, which Buddha felt had become bloated with worldliness and politics. Traditional Buddhism is based upon the **Four Noble Truths**: existence is suffering, suffering is caused by desire, an end of suffering will come with Nirvana, and Nirvana will come with the practice of the **Eightfold Path**. The steps of the Eightfold Path are as follows: right views, right resolve, right speech, right action, right livelihood, right effort, right mindfulness, and right concentration. Buddhism did not receive any official sanction for a long time but did eventually spread and take hold in India, China, Japan, and elsewhere.

Development and Growth of the Chinese Empires

In China, history was divided into a series of **dynasties**. The most famous of these, the **Han dynasty**, existed from 206 BC to AD 220. Accomplishments of the Chinese empires included:

- Building the Great Wall of China
- Numerous inventions, including paper, paper money, printing, and gunpowder
- High level of artistic development
- Silk production

The Chinese dynasties were comparable to Rome as far as their artistic and intellectual accomplishments, as well as the size and scope of their influence.

Confucianism and Taoism

Confucianism was founded by Confucius (551–479 BC), who lived around the same time as Buddha. This faith was designed to relieve conflict in all arenas, from that which existed among families to that between Heaven and Earth. Confucius defined "appropriate" social roles for people of different ages, sexes, and social ranks; by assuming these roles, Confucians attempt to create a more peaceful world.

Taoism originated in China at approximately the same time as Confucianism. Taoism strives to create harmony between humans and the natural world. Unlike Confucianism, which has a significant political aspect and is largely monistic, Taoism values natural goodness and expressiveness over social order and is largely dualistic.

Roman Empire and Republic

Rome began humbly, in a single town that grew out of Etruscan settlements and traditions, founded, according to legend, by twin brothers Romulus and Remus, who were raised by wolves. Romulus killed Remus, and from his legacy grew Rome. A thousand years later, the **Roman Empire** covered a significant portion of the known world, from what is now Scotland, across Europe, and into the Middle East. **Hellenization**, or the spread of Greek culture throughout the world, served as an inspiration and a model for the spread of Roman culture. Rome brought in belief systems of conquered peoples as well as their technological and scientific accomplishments, melding the disparate parts into a Roman core. Rome began as a **republic** ruled by consuls, but after the assassination of **Julius Caesar**, it became an **empire** led by emperors. Rome's overall government was autocratic, but local officials came from the provinces where they lived. This limited administrative system was probably a major factor in the long life of the empire.

> **Review Video: Roman Republic Part One**
> Visit mometrix.com/academy and enter code: 360192
>
> **Review Video: Roman Republic Part Two**
> Visit mometrix.com/academy and enter code: 881514

Development of the Byzantine Empire from the Roman Empire

Constantinople developed as the eastern capital of the Roman Empire and later the Byzantine Empire. Its culture and institutions were primarily shaped by the continuation of Roman political structures, the dominance of Greek language and intellectual traditions, and the growing influence of Christianity as the empire's central religious and cultural force. These three elements together defined Byzantine civilization and distinguished it from other ancient regional traditions.

Early Christianity

Early Christianity was a mass of competing doctrines, including various groups such as the Gnostics and Arians who all sought to have their view legitimized as the truth. Eventually, the **orthodox church**, through an ecumenical council of bishops, created in the 4th century AD the canon of New Testament texts which exists today. The apostles had created a hierarchy of bishops, priests, and deacons who stressed obedience to duly constituted church authority. By the middle of the 2nd century, Christianity began to attract intellectuals in the **Roman Empire**. Although Christians were still liable to be persecuted in the farther reaches of the empire, many turned to the Church as the empire crumbled. For many, the christian church was all that was left of civilization and would rebuild Europe over the next millennium.

Significance of the Nicene Creed

The **Byzantine Empire** was Christian-based but incorporated Greek language, philosophy, and literature and drew its law and government policies from Rome. However, there was as yet no unified doctrine of Christianity, as it was a relatively new religion that had spread rapidly and without a great deal of organization. In 325, the **First Council of Nicaea** addressed this issue. From this conference came the **Nicene Creed**, addressing the Trinity and other basic Christian beliefs. The **Council of Chalcedon** in 451 further defined the view of the Trinity.

Factors That Led to the Fall of the Western Roman Empire

Germanic tribes, including the Visigoths, Ostrogoths, Vandals, Saxons, and Franks, controlled most of Europe. The Roman Empire faced major opposition on that front. The increasing size of the empire also made it harder to manage, leading to dissatisfaction throughout the empire as Roman government became less efficient. Germanic tribes refused to adhere to the Nicene Creed, instead following **Arianism**, which led the Roman Catholic Church to declare them heretics. The **Franks** proved a powerful military force in their defeat of the Muslims in 732. In 768, **Charlemagne** became king of the Franks. These tribes waged several wars against Rome, including the invasion of Britannia by the Angles and Saxons. Far-flung Rome lost control over this area of its empire, and eventually, Rome itself was **invaded**.

Iconoclasm and Conflicts of Roman Catholic and Eastern Orthodox Churches

Emperor Leo III ordered the destruction of all icons throughout the Byzantine Empire. Images of Jesus were replaced with crosses, and images of Jesus, Mary, or other religious figures were considered blasphemy on the grounds of idolatry. **Pope Gregory II** called a synod to discuss the issue. The synod declared that the images were not heretical and that strong disciplinary measures would result for anyone who destroyed them. Leo's response was an attempt to kill Pope Gregory, but this plan ended in failure.

Effect of the Viking Invasions on the Culture of England and Europe

Vikings invaded Northern France in the 10th century, eventually becoming the **Normans**. Originating in Scandinavia, the **Vikings** were accomplished seafarers with advanced knowledge of trade routes. With overpopulation plaguing their native lands, they began to travel. From the 8th to the 11th centuries, they spread throughout Europe, conquering and colonizing. Vikings invaded and colonized England in several waves, including the **Anglo-Saxon invasions** that displaced Roman control. Their influence remained significant in England, affecting everything from the language of the country to place names and even the government and social structure. By 900, Vikings had settled in **Iceland**. They proceeded then to **Greenland** and eventually to **North America**, arriving in the New World even before the Spanish and British who claimed the lands several centuries later. They also traded with the Byzantine Empire until the 11th century, when their significant level of activity came to an end.

West vs. East 10th-Century Events

In **Europe**, the years AD 500-1000 are largely known as the **Dark Ages**. In the 10th century, numerous Viking invasions disrupted societies that had been more settled under Roman rule. Vikings settled in Northern France, eventually becoming the Normans. By the 11th century, Europe would rise again into the **High Middle Ages** with the beginning of the **Crusades**.

In **China**, wars also raged. This led the Chinese to make use of gunpowder for the first time in warfare.

In the **Americas**, the **Mayan Empire** was winding down while the **Toltec** became more prominent. **Pueblo** Indian culture was also at its zenith.

In the **East**, the **Muslims** and the **Byzantine Empire** were experiencing a significant period of growth and development.

World History 1400 to 1914

Feudalism in Europe in the Middle Ages

A major element of the social and economic life of Europe, **feudalism** developed as a way to ensure European rulers would have the wherewithal to quickly raise an army when necessary. **Vassals** swore loyalty and promised to provide military service for lords, who in return offered a **fief**, or a parcel of land, for them to use to generate their livelihood. Vassals could work the land themselves, have it worked by **peasants** or **serfs**—workers who had few rights and were little more than slaves—or grant the fief to someone else. The king legally owned all the land, but in return, promised to protect the vassals from invasion and war. Vassals returned a certain percentage of their income to the lords, who in turn, passed a portion of their income on to the king. A similar practice was **manorialism**, in which the feudal system was applied to a self-contained manor. These manors were often owned by the lords who ran them but were usually included in the same system of loyalty and promises of protection that drove feudalism.

Review Video: The Middle Ages: Feudalism
Visit mometrix.com/academy and enter code: 165907

Effect of Black Death on Medieval Politics and Economic Conditions

The Black Death, believed to be **bubonic plague**, most likely came to Europe on fleas carried by rats on sailing vessels. The plague killed more than a third of the entire population of Europe and effectively ended **feudalism** as a political system. Many who had formerly served as peasants or serfs found different work, as a demand for skilled labor grew. Nation-states grew in power, and in the face of the pandemic, many began to turn away from faith in God and toward the ideals of ancient Greece and Rome for government and other beliefs.

Review Video: Black Death (An Overview)
Visit mometrix.com/academy and enter code: 431857

Influence of the Roman Catholic Church Over Medieval Society

The Roman Catholic Church extended significant influence both politically and economically throughout medieval society. The church supplied **education**, as there were no established schools or universities. To a large extent, the church had filled a power void left by various invasions throughout the former Roman Empire, leading it to exercise a role that was far more **political** than religious. Kings were heavily influenced by the pope and other church officials, and churches controlled large amounts of land throughout Europe.

Progression of the Crusades and Major Figures Involved

The Crusades began in the 11th century and continued into the 15th. The major goal of these various military ventures was to slow the progression of Muslim forces into Europe and to expel them from the **Holy Land**, where they had taken control of Jerusalem and Palestine. Alexius I, the Byzantine emperor, called for help from **Pope Urban** II when Palestine was taken. In 1095, the pope, hoping to reunite Eastern and Western Christianity, encouraged all Christians to help the cause. Amidst great bloodshed, this crusade recaptured **Jerusalem**, but over the next centuries, Jerusalem and other areas of the Holy Land changed hands numerous times. The **Second Crusade** (1147-1149) consisted of an unsuccessful attempt to retake Damascus. The **Third Crusade**, under Pope Gregory VIII, attempted to recapture Jerusalem but failed. The **Fourth Crusade**, under Pope Innocent III, attempted to come into the Holy Land via Egypt. The Crusades led to greater power for the pope and the Catholic Church in general and also opened numerous trading and cultural routes between Europe and the East.

Political Developments in India Through the 11th Century

After the Mauryan dynasty, the **Guptas** ruled India, maintaining a long period of peace and prosperity in the area. During this time, the Indian people invented the decimal system and the concept of zero. They produced cotton and calico, as well as other products in high demand in Europe and Asia, and developed a complex system of medicine. The Gupta Dynasty ended in the 6th century. First, the **Huns** invaded, and then the **Hephthalites** (an Asian nomadic tribe) destroyed the weakened empire. In the 14th century, **Tamerlane**, a Muslim who envisioned restoring Genghis Khan's empire, expanded India's borders and founded the **Mogul Empire**. His grandson Akbar promoted freedom of religion and built a widespread number of mosques, forts, and other buildings throughout the country.

Development of Chinese and Japanese Governments Through the 11th Century

After the Mongols, led by Genghis Khan and his grandson Kublai Khan, unified the Mongol Empire, **China** was led by the **Ming Dynasty** (1368-1644) and the **Manchu (also known as Qing) Dynasty** (1644-1912). Both dynasties were isolationist, ending China's interaction with other countries until the 18th century. The Ming Dynasty was known for its porcelain, while the Manchus focused on farming and road construction as the population grew.

Japan developed independently of China but borrowed the Buddhist religion, the Chinese writing system, and other elements of Chinese society. Ruled by the divine emperor, Japan basically functioned on a feudal system led by **daimyo**, or warlords, and soldiers known as **samurai**. Japan remained isolationist, not interacting significantly with the rest of the world until the 1800s.

Ming Dynasty

The Ming dynasty lasted in China from AD 1368 to 1644. This dynasty was established by a Buddhist monk, **Zhu Yuanzhang**, who quickly became obsessed with consolidating power in the central government and was known for the brutality with which he achieved his ends. It was during the **Ming dynasty** that China developed and introduced its famous civil service examinations, rigorous tests on the **Confucian classics**. The future of an ambitious Chinese youth depended on his performance on this exam. The capital was transferred from Nanjing to Beijing during this period, and the **Forbidden City** was constructed inside the new capital. The Ming period, despite its constant expansionary wars, also continued China's artistic resurgence; the porcelain of this period is especially admired.

Developments in Africa Through the 11th Century

Much of Africa was difficult to traverse early on, due to the large amount of desert and other inhospitable terrain. **Egypt** remained important, though most of the northern coast became Muslim as their armies spread through the area. **Ghana** rose as a trade center in the 9th century, lasting into the 12th century, primarily trading in gold, which it exchanged for Saharan salt. **Mali** rose somewhat later, with the trade center Timbuktu becoming an important exporter of goods such as iron, leather, and tin. Mali also dealt in agricultural trade, becoming one of the most significant trading centers in West Africa. The Muslim religion dominated, and technological advancement was sparse.

African culture was largely defined through migration, as Arab merchants and others settled on the continent, particularly along the east coast. Scholars from the Muslim nations gravitated to Timbuktu, which in addition to its importance in trade, had also become a magnet for those seeking Islamic knowledge and education.

History of Islam and Its Role in Bringing Unity to the Middle East

Born in AD 570, **Muhammad** began preaching around 613, leading his followers in a new religion called **Islam**, which means "submission to God's will." Before this time, the Arabian Peninsula was inhabited largely by Bedouins, nomads who battled amongst each other and lived in tribal organizations. But by the time Muhammad died in 632, most of Arabia had become Muslim to some extent.

Muhammad conquered **Mecca**, where a temple called the **Kaaba** had long served as a center of the nomadic religions. He declared this temple the most sacred of Islam, and Mecca as the holy city. His writings became the **Koran**, or **Qur'an**, divine revelations he said had been delivered to him by the angel Gabriel.

Muhammad's teachings gave the formerly tribal Arabian people a sense of unity that had not existed in the area before. After his death, the converted Muslims of Arabia conquered a vast territory, creating an empire and bringing advances in literature, technology, science, and art as Europe was declining under the scourge of the Black Death. Literature from this period includes the *Arabian Nights* and the *Rubaiyat* of Omar Khayyam.

Later in its development, Islam split into two factions; the **Shiite** and the **Sunni** Muslims. Conflict continues today between these groups.

Ottoman Empire

By 1400, the Ottomans had grown in power in Anatolia and had begun attempts to take Constantinople. In 1453, they finally conquered the Byzantine capital and renamed it **Istanbul**. The **Ottoman Empire's** major strength, much like Rome before it, lay in its ability to unite widely disparate people through religious tolerance. This tolerance, which stemmed from the idea that Muslims, Christians, and Jews were fundamentally related and could coexist, enabled the Ottomans to develop a widely varied culture. They also believed in just laws and just government, with government centered in a monarch, known as the **sultan**.

Renaissance

The French word "renaissance" means "rebirth." This is the term used to describe a period of history and cultural movement that occurred after the Middle Ages. During this time, interest rose again in the beliefs and politics of ancient Greece and Rome. Art, literature, music, science, and philosophy all burgeoned during the Renaissance and experience rapid progress.

Many of the ideas of the Renaissance began in **Florence, Italy** in the 14th century, spurred by the **Medici** family. Education for the upper classes expanded to include law, math, reading, writing, and classical Greek and

Roman works. As the Renaissance progressed, the world was presented through art and literature in a realistic way that had never been explored before. This **realism** drove culture to new heights.

Review Video: The Renaissance
Visit mometrix.com/academy and enter code: 123100

Humanism

The term "humanism" was attributed long after the Renaissance but represents a foundational collection of ideas that propelled much of the developments that occurred during the Renaissance in art, politics, education, and many other fields. Humanists believed that the study of classics from Ancient Greece and Rome was essential to understanding humanity, virtues, ethics, and peoples' roles in society. The study of humanity was given precedence over the study of religion, though religion and humanism were not mutually exclusive, and many religious people also held many humanist beliefs. Humanism did not represent a formal school of thought or encompassing philosophy. It was, rather, a general intellectual movement that placed education—specifically of classical texts—at the forefront. Some of the main subjects of Renaissance humanism were:

- Private and civic virtue
- Latin
- Grammar and rhetoric
- Literature and poetry
- Moral philosophy

Renaissance Artists, Authors, and Scientists

Artists of the Renaissance included Leonardo da Vinci, also an inventor; Michelangelo, also an architect; and others who focused on realism in their work. In **literature**, major contributions came from humanist authors like Petrarch, Erasmus, Sir Thomas More, and Boccaccio, who believed man should focus on reality rather than on the ethereal. Shakespeare, Cervantes, and Dante followed in their footsteps, and their works found a wide audience thanks to Gutenberg's development of the printing press.

Scientific developments of the Renaissance included the work of Copernicus, Galileo, and Kepler, who challenged the geocentric philosophies of the day by proving that the earth was not the center of the solar system.

Two Phases of the Reformation Period

The Reformation period arose near the later part of the Renaissance and consisted of both the Protestant and the Catholic Reformation. The **Protestant Reformation** rose in Germany when **Martin Luther** protested abuses of the Catholic Church. **John Calvin** led the movement in Switzerland, while in England, King Henry VIII made use of the Reformation's ideas to further his own political goals. The **Catholic Reformation**, or **Counter-Reformation**, occurred in response to the Protestant movement, leading to various changes in the Catholic Church. Some provided wider tolerance of different religious viewpoints, but others actually increased the persecution of those deemed to be heretics.

From a **religious** standpoint, the Reformation occurred due to abuses by the Catholic Church such as indulgences and dispensations, religious offices being offered up for sale, and an increasingly dissolute clergy. **Politically**, the Reformation was driven by increased power of various ruling monarchs, who wished to take all power to themselves rather than allowing power to remain with the church. They also had begun to chafe at papal taxes and the church's increasing wealth. The ideas of the Protestant Revolution removed power from the Catholic Church and the Pope himself, playing nicely into the hands of those monarchs, such as Henry VIII, who wanted out from under the church's control.

Review Video: Martin Luther and the Reformation
Visit mometrix.com/academy and enter code: 691828

Review Video: The Counter-Reformation
Visit mometrix.com/academy and enter code: 950498

Review Video: The Protestants
Visit mometrix.com/academy and enter code: 583582

Developments of the Scientific Revolution

In addition to holding power in the political realm, church doctrine also governed scientific belief. During the **Scientific Revolution**, however, which began during the renaissance, astronomers and other scientists began to amass evidence that challenged the church's scientific doctrines. These scientists employed the scientific method and emergent theories and technologies to make new discoveries about the universe. It was during the Scientific Revolution that many huge scientific discoveries were made, and the very nature of knowledge gathering changed. Major figures of the Scientific Revolution included:

- **Nicolaus Copernicus**—wrote *On the Revolutions of the Celestial Spheres*, arguing that the earth revolved around the sun
- **Tycho Brahe**—cataloged astronomical observations
- **Johannes Kepler**—developed laws of planetary motion
- **Galileo Galilei**—defended the heliocentric theories of Copernicus and Kepler, discovered four moons of Jupiter, and died under house arrest by the church, charged with heresy
- **Isaac Newton**—discovered gravity; studied optics, calculus, and physics; and believed the workings of nature could be studied and proven through observation

Review Video: The Scientific Revolution
Visit mometrix.com/academy and enter code: 974600

Major Ideas of the Enlightenment

The Enlightenment (also called the Age of Reason) began in the late 17th century and lasted until around the late 18th century. It came partially as a result of the reformation, which diminished some of the power of the Christian Church. This allowed more freedom of expression and thought. During this time in Europe and North America, philosophers and scientists began to rely more and more on **observation** and logic to support their ideas rather than building on past beliefs, particularly those held by the church. A focus on **ethics and reason** drove their work. Through reason, they believed, some of the universe's most difficult questions—be them in ethics, politics, or science — could be answered. Major philosophers of the Enlightenment included:

- **Rene Descartes**—while often considered a pre-Enlightenment thinker, Descartes's philosophical work was instrumental to the development of philosophy in the Enlightenment. He believed that in order to know something, everything must first be put into doubt until it could be proved. He believed the senses could not be fully trusted to represent reality, but that reason may be relied upon to understand the foundational aspects of existence. He famously wrote, "I think, therefore I am," which is his assertion that the very fact that he is thinking is evidence that he really exists.
- **David Hume**—he pioneered empiricism and skepticism, believing that truth could only be found through direct experience and that what others said to be true was always suspect.
- **Immanuel Kant**—he believed in self-examination and observation and that the root of morality lay within human beings.

- **Jean-Jacques Rousseau**—he developed the idea of the social contract, that government existed by the agreement of the people, and that the government was obligated to protect the people and their basic rights. His ideas heavily influenced the founding fathers.

Review Video: Age of Enlightenment
Visit mometrix.com/academy and enter code: 143022

American Revolution vs. French Revolution

Both the American and French Revolution came about as a protest against the excesses and overly controlling nature of their respective monarchs. In **America**, the British colonies had been left mostly to self-govern until the British monarchs began to increase control, spurring the colonies to revolt. In **France**, the nobility's excesses had led to increasingly difficult economic conditions, with inflation, heavy taxation, and food shortages creating great burdens on the lower classes. Both revolutions led to the development of republics to replace the monarchies that were displaced. However, the French Revolution eventually led to the rise of the dictator **Napoleon Bonaparte**, while the American Revolution produced a functioning, though imperfect, **republic** from the beginning.

Events and Figures of the French Revolution

In 1789, **King Louis XVI**, faced with a huge national debt, convened parliament. The **Third Estate**, or Commons, a division of the French parliament, then claimed power, and the king's resistance led to the storming of the **Bastille**, the royal prison. The people established a constitutional monarchy. When King Louis XVI and Marie Antoinette attempted to leave the country, they were executed on the guillotine. From 1793 to 1794, **Robespierre** and extreme radicals, the **Jacobins**, instituted a **Reign of Terror**, executing tens of thousands of nobles as well as anyone considered an enemy of the Revolution. Robespierre was then executed as well, and the **Directory** came into power, leading to a temporary return to bourgeois values. This governing body proved incompetent and corrupt, allowing **Napoleon Bonaparte** to come to power in 1799, first as a dictator, then as emperor. While the French Revolution threw off the power of a corrupt monarchy, its immediate results were likely not what the original perpetrators of the revolt had intended.

Review Video: The French Revolution: Napoleon Bonaparte
Visit mometrix.com/academy and enter code: 876330

Industrial Revolution

Effects of the Industrial Revolution on Society

The Industrial Revolution began in Great Britain in the 18th century, bringing coal- and steam-powered machinery into widespread use. Industry began a period of rapid growth with these developments. Goods that had previously been produced in small workshops or even in homes were produced more efficiently and in much larger quantities in **factories**. Where society had been largely agrarian-based, the focus swiftly shifted to an **industrial** outlook. As electricity and internal combustion engines replaced coal and steam as energy sources, even more drastic and rapid changes occurred. Western European countries, in particular, turned to colonialism, taking control of portions of Africa and Asia to ensure access to the raw materials needed to produce factory goods. Specialized labor became very much in demand, and businesses grew rapidly, creating monopolies, increasing world trade, and developing large urban centers. Even agriculture changed fundamentally as the Industrial Revolution led to a second **Agricultural Revolution** with the addition of new technology to advance agricultural production.

Review Video: Industrialization
Visit mometrix.com/academy and enter code: 893924

First and Second Phases of the Industrial Revolution

The **first phase** of the Industrial Revolution took place from roughly 1750 to 1830. The textile industry experienced major changes as more and more elements of the process became mechanized. Mining benefited from the steam engine. Transportation became easier and more widely available as waterways were improved and the railroad came into prominence. In the **second phase**, from 1830 to 1910, industries further improved in efficiency, and new industries were introduced as photography, various chemical processes, and electricity became more widely available to produce new goods or new, improved versions of old goods. Petroleum and hydroelectricity became major sources of power. During this time, the Industrial Revolution spread out of Western Europe and into the US and Japan.

Political, Social and Economic Side Effects of the Industrial Revolution

The Industrial Revolution led to widespread education, a wider franchise, and the development of mass communication in the political arena. **Economically**, conflicts arose between companies and their employees, as struggles for fair treatment and fair wages increased. Unions gained power and became more active. Government regulation over industries increased, but at the same time, growing businesses fought for the right to free enterprise. In the **social** sphere, populations increased and began to concentrate around centers of industry. Cities became larger and more densely populated. Scientific advancements led to more efficient agriculture, greater supply of goods, and increased knowledge of medicine and sanitation, leading to better overall health.

Review Video: The Industrial Revolution
Visit mometrix.com/academy and enter code: 372796

Causes and Progression of the Russian Revolution of 1905

In Russia, rule lay in the hands of the **czars**, and the overall structure was **feudalistic**. Beneath the czars was a group of rich nobles, landowners whose lands were worked by peasants and serfs. The **Russo-Japanese War** (1904-1905) made conditions much worse for the lower classes. When peasants demonstrated outside the czar's Winter Palace, the palace guard fired upon the crowd. The demonstration had been organized by a trade union leader, and after the violent response, many unions and political parties blossomed and began to lead numerous strikes. When the economy ground to a halt, Czar Nicholas II signed a document known as the **October Manifesto**, which established a constitutional monarchy and gave legislative power to parliament. However, he violated the manifesto shortly thereafter, disbanding parliament and ignoring the civil liberties granted by the manifesto. This eventually led to the **Bolshevik Revolution**.

World History 1914 to Present

Nationalism and Its Effect on Society Through the 18th and 19th Centuries

Nationalism, put simply, is a strong belief in, identification with, and allegiance to a particular nation and people. **Nationalistic belief** unified various areas that had previously seen themselves as fragmented, which led to **patriotism** and, in some cases, **imperialism**. As nationalism grew, individual nations sought to grow, bringing in other, smaller states that shared similar characteristics such as language and cultural beliefs. Unfortunately, a major side effect of these growing nationalistic beliefs was often conflict and outright **war**.

In Europe, imperialism led countries to spread their influence into Africa and Asia. **Africa** was eventually divided among several European countries that wanted certain raw materials. **Asia** also came under European control, with the exception of China, Japan, and Siam (now Thailand). In the US, **Manifest Destiny** became the rallying cry as the country expanded west. Italy and Germany formed larger nations from a variety of smaller states.

Review Video: Historical Nationalism
Visit mometrix.com/academy and enter code: 510185

Review Video: Nationalism
Visit mometrix.com/academy and enter code: 865693

Events of World War I in the European Theater

WWI began in 1914 with the assassination of **Archduke Franz Ferdinand**, heir to the throne of Austria-Hungary, by a Serbian national. This led to a conflict between Austria-Hungary and Serbia that quickly escalated into the First World War. Europe split into the **Allies**—Britain, France, and Russia, and later Italy, Japan, and the US, against the **Central Powers**—Austria-Hungary, Germany, the Ottoman Empire, and Bulgaria. As the war spread, countries beyond Europe became involved. The war left Europe deeply in debt, and particularly devastated the German economy. The ensuing **Great Depression** made matters worse, and economic devastation opened the door for communist, fascist, and socialist governments to gain power.

Combat in World War I

Despite the fact that almost every nation in Europe had entered into World War I, most Europeans thought the conflict would be brief. Instead, advances in **weapons technology** made the war bloody and excruciatingly slow. Fighting during WWI largely took place in a series of **trenches** built along the Eastern and Western Fronts. These trenches added up to more than 24,000 miles. This produced fronts that stretched over 400 miles, from the coast of Belgium to the border of Switzerland. The Allies made use of straightforward open-air trenches with a front line, supporting lines, and communications lines. By contrast, the German trenches sometimes included well-equipped underground living quarters.

Contributions of the American Public and Public Opinion of the War

The **18th amendment** to the Constitution, otherwise known as the **Volstead Act**, outlawed alcohol in 1920. This amendment was purported to conserve food, though it was really an attempt to influence public morality. Through the **Food Administration**, President Wilson encouraged people to plant "victory gardens," and to skip meat one day a week. The war was also supported through the **Espionage and Sedition Acts of 1917-8**, which made it illegal to say negative things about the war or to interfere with the sale of war bonds. In **Schenck v. US** (1919), the arrest of the Socialist leader Charles Schenck for criticizing the war was upheld by the Supreme Court, which asserted that First Amendment rights were only exercisable when they did not present a clear and present danger to the nation. In **Abrams v. US** (1919), a Russian immigrant critical of the US actions in Russia was also declared to be a clear and present danger.

Treaty of Versailles

As the First World War wound down, a disgruntled German populace ousted the emperor and installed a moderate socialist government. This government, known as the **Weimar Republic**, would last until 1933. At the **Paris Peace Conference**, the victors of the war (the US, Britain, France, and Italy) exacted some revenge on Germany. The **Treaty of Versailles** penalized Germany economically and territorially; Alsace-Lorraine became independent, and the German military was dismantled. The Treaty of Versailles would need to be modified by two subsequent agreements: the **Treaty of Locarno,** which outlined a more reasonable reparations plan for Germany, and the **Kellogg-Briand Pact,** which asserted that diplomacy rather than force would be used to resolve conflicts.

Bolshevik Revolution

Factors Leading to the Bolshevik Revolution of 1917

Throughout its modern history, Russia had lagged behind other countries in development. The continued existence of a feudal system, combined with harsh conditions and the overall size of the country, led to massive food shortages and increasingly harsh conditions for the majority of the population. The tyrannical rule of the czars only made this worse, as did repeated losses in various military conflicts. Increasing poverty, decreasing supplies, and the czar's violation of the **October Manifesto,** which had given some political power and civil rights to the people, finally came to a head with the **Bolshevik Revolution**.

Events of the Bolshevik Revolution

A **workers' strike in Petrograd** in 1917 set the revolutionary wheels in motion when the army sided with the workers. While parliament set up a provisional government made up of nobles, the workers and military joined to form their own governmental system known as **soviets**, which consisted of local councils elected by the people. The ensuing chaos opened the doors for formerly exiled leaders Vladimir Lenin, Joseph Stalin, and Leon Trotsky to move in and gain popular support as well as the support of the Red Guard. Overthrowing parliament, they took power, creating a **communist** state in Russia. This development led to the spread of communism throughout Eastern Europe and elsewhere, greatly affecting diplomatic policies throughout the world for several decades.

Communism vs. Socialism

At their roots, socialism and communism both focus on public ownership and distribution of goods and services. However, **communism** works toward revolution by drawing on what it sees to be inevitable class antagonism, eventually overthrowing the upper classes and the systems of capitalism. **Socialism** makes use of democratic procedures, building on the existing order. This was particularly true of the utopian socialists, who saw industrial capitalism as oppressive, not allowing workers to prosper. While socialism struggled between the World Wars, communism took hold, especially in Eastern Europe. After WWII, **democratic socialism** became more common. Later, **capitalism** took a stronger hold again, and today most industrialized countries in the western world function under an economy that mixes elements of capitalism and socialism.

Review Video: Communism vs. Socialism
Visit mometrix.com/academy and enter code: 917677

Conditions that Led to the Rise of the Nazi Party in Germany

The **Great Depression** had a particularly devastating effect on Germany's economy, especially after the US was no longer able to supply reconstruction loans to help the country regain its footing. With unemployment rising rapidly, dissatisfaction with the government grew. Fascist and Communist parties rose, promising change and improvement.

Led by **Adolf Hitler**, the fascist **Nazi Party** eventually gained power in Parliament based on these promises and the votes of desperate German workers. When Hitler became chancellor, he launched numerous expansionist policies, violating the peace treaties that had ended WWI. His military buildup and conquering of neighboring countries sparked the aggression that soon led to WWII.

Belief System of the Nazi Party

Led by **Adolf Hitler**, the Nazi party championed the **Aryan race** as superior to all others, especially the "insidious" Jews. Hitler suggested that the noble ambitions of the true German people required ***lebensraum***, or living space. In other words, Germany needed more territory. In its early days, the Nazi party was part of the German republican system; Nazi candidates ran for office and served in the **Reichstag** (German parliament). As Germany suffered through a terrible economic depression in the early 1930s, however, the people became impatient. In 1933, the Reichstag was set on fire, and the Nazis used the opportunity to claim total control of the government. Hitler had already been appointed Chancellor in January 1933. He was able to quickly improve the German economy, mostly through the expansion of the weapon-building industry. At the same time, the new government began to quietly round up Jews, Gypsies, and homosexuals.

Beginning and Initial Years of World War II in Europe

Still shell-shocked from the First World War, the nations of western Europe were slow to respond to the growing menace of **Nazi Germany**. In general, they pursued a policy of appeasement and isolation. The British prime minister **Neville Chamberlain** was especially committed to using diplomacy over war. Then, in 1936, Hitler sent troops to occupy the **Rhineland**, a strip of territory on the German border. At around the same time, **Mussolini** invaded Ethiopia; the two aggressors, Germany and Italy, entered into an agreement making them the **Axis Powers**. In 1938, Germany annexed Austria and indicated that it was about to attack Czechoslovakia. In response to these actions, Chamberlain brought together Mussolini and Hitler for the **Munich Conference of 1938**. These talks would only briefly suspend German aggression.

After **Chamberlain** had tried to forestall German aggression at the **Munich Conference of 1938**, Germany nevertheless invaded Czechoslovakia in 1939. It was also during this year that Hitler signed a secret agreement with **Stalin** pledging not to attack Russia so long as Russia stayed out of German affairs. Hitler then declared war on and conquered Poland. At this step, Great Britain and France were finally forced to declare war upon Germany. Germany at this point was a dominating military adversary. The **Axis powers** conquered almost the entire European continent, including France, over the course of 1940.

Importance of the German Blitzkrieg to the Progression of World War II

The blitzkrieg, or "lightning war," consisted of fast, powerful surprise attacks that disrupted communications, made it difficult if not impossible for the victims to retaliate, and demoralized Germany's foes. The "blitz," or the aerial bombing of England in 1940, was one example, with bombings occurring in London and other cities 57 nights in a row. The **Battle of Britain** in 1940 also brought intense raids by Germany's air force, the **Luftwaffe**, mostly targeting ports and British air force bases. Eventually, Britain's Royal Air Force blocked the Luftwaffe, ending Germany's hopes for conquering Britain.

Battle of the Bulge

Following the **D-Day Invasion**, Allied forces gained considerable ground and began a major campaign to push through Europe. In December of 1944, Hitler launched a counteroffensive, attempting to retake Antwerp, an important port. The ensuing battle became the largest land battle on the war's Western Front and was known as the Battle of the Ardennes, or the **Battle of the Bulge**. The battle lasted from December 16, 1944, to January 25, 1945. The Germans pushed forward, making inroads into Allied lines, but in the end, the Allies brought the advance to a halt. The Germans were pushed back, with massive losses on both sides. However, those losses proved crippling to the German army. Surrounded and with the war lost, Hitler committed suicide in his bunker in Berlin in April 1945, and the remaining German forces surrendered shortly afterward.

Holocaust

As Germany sank deeper and deeper into dire economic straits, the tendency was to look for a person or group of people to blame for the problems of the country. With distrust of the Jewish people already ingrained, it was easy for German authorities to set up the **Jews** as scapegoats for Germany's problems. Under the rule of Hitler and the Nazi party, the "Final Solution" for the supposed Jewish problem was devised. Millions of Jews, as well as Gypsies, homosexuals, communists, Catholics, the mentally ill, and others, simply named as criminals, were transported to concentration camps during the course of the war. At least six million were slaughtered in death camps such as **Auschwitz**, where horrible conditions and torture of prisoners were commonplace. The Allies were aware of rumors of mass slaughter throughout the war, but many discounted the reports. Only when troops went in to liberate the prisoners was the true horror of the concentration camps brought to light. The **Holocaust** resulted in massive loss of human life, but also in the loss and destruction of cultures. Because the genocide focused on specific ethnic groups, many traditions, histories, knowledge, and other cultural elements were lost, particularly among the Jewish and Gypsy populations. After World War II, the United Nations recognized **genocide** as a "crime against humanity." The UN passed the **Universal Declaration of Human**

Rights in 1948 in order to further specify what rights the organization protected. Nazi war criminals faced justice during the **Nuremberg Trials**. There, individuals, rather than their governments, were held accountable for war crimes.

Review Video: The Holocaust
Visit mometrix.com/academy and enter code: 350695

Pacific Arena in WWII

The **Japanese**, like the Germans, became seduced by the notion of their own racial superiority during the 1930s. As in Germany, this inevitably led to a lust for territorial expansion. By 1941, Japan had conquered Korea, Manchuria, and parts of China. Japan was also threatening to invade American interests in the Philippines. The United States imposed **economic sanctions** on Japan, making it difficult for the Japanese war industry to function. In response, the Japanese launched a surprise attack on the United States by bombing the US naval base of **Pearl Harbor**. After the attack on Pearl Harbor, the United States declared war upon Japan (and Germany, in turn, declared war on the United States). The Japanese made huge territorial gains before the US turned the tide at the **Battles of Midway and Guadalcanal**. The war in the Pacific would take much longer than the war in Europe due to the island-hopping nature of the fight. The unwillingness of the Japanese to surrender made it almost impossible for America to entirely vanquish them without enormous loss of life. So, the United States decided to drop atomic bombs on **Hiroshima** and **Nagasaki** to force Japan to surrender and finally end the war in the Pacific in August 1945.

India and Pakistan After WWII

In 1947, after years of peaceful protests led by **Mahatma Gandhi**, India was given its independence and partitioned into two states, **India** and **Pakistan**. The following year, Gandhi would be assassinated in India. In 1965, border disputes would flare into the **Indo-Pakistani War**. In 1971, Pakistan would fend off attacks from Bengali rebels, who sought to achieve independence. The next year, however, **Bangladesh** would be established as an independent state. In 1984, India had its own internal problems; after the Indian army occupied the **Golden Temple** sacred to the Sikhs, the Indian leader **Indira Gandhi** was assassinated by her Sikh bodyguards. **Anti-Sikh riots** resulted, and much blood was shed.

World War II and the Ensuing Diplomatic Climate that Led to the Cold War

With millions of military and civilian deaths and over 12 million persons displaced, **WWII** left large regions of Europe and Asia in disarray. **Communist** governments moved in with promises of renewed prosperity and economic stability. The **Soviet Union** backed communist regimes in much of Eastern Europe. In China, **Mao Zedong** led communist forces in the overthrow of the Chinese Nationalist Party and instituted a communist government in 1949. While the new communist governments restored a measure of stability to much of Eastern Europe, it brought its own problems, with dictatorial governments and an oppressive police force. The spread of communism also led to several years of tension between communist countries and the democratic West, as the West fought to slow the spread of oppressive regimes throughout the world. With both sides in possession of nuclear weapons, tensions rose. Each side feared the other would resort to nuclear attack. This standoff lasted until 1989, when the **Berlin Wall** fell. The Soviet Union was dissolved two years later.

Truman Doctrine, Marshall Plan, NATO, and Warsaw Pact

In order to stop the spread of communism in Europe and elsewhere, President Truman asserted his policy of "containment" in the so-called **Truman Doctrine**. This meant that the US would support anticommunist governments throughout the world. The **Marshall Plan** advanced this policy by supplying aid to war-ravaged countries in Western Europe. When the **Eastern Bloc countries** prevented aid from reaching West Berlin, the US, England, and France organized the **Berlin Airlift** to overcome this obstacle. In 1949, the Western European and North American nations entered into a mutual defense treaty, NATO (North Atlantic Treaty Organization). As a response, the Eastern Bloc nations joined with the Soviet Union in the **Warsaw Pact**.

Origins of the United Nations

The United Nations (**UN**) came into being toward the end of World War II. A successor to the less-than-successful League of Nations formed after World War I, the UN built and improved on those ideas. Since its inception, the UN has worked to bring the countries of the world together for **diplomatic solutions** to international problems, including sanctions and other restrictions. It has also initiated military action, calling for peacekeeping troops from member countries to move against countries violating UN policies. The **Korean War** was the first example of UN involvement in an international conflict.

Effects of Decolonization on the Post-War Period

A rise of nationalism among European colonies led to many of them declaring independence. **India** and **Pakistan** became independent of Britain in 1947, and numerous African and Asian colonies declared independence as well. This period of **decolonization** lasted into the 1960s. Some colonies moved successfully into independence, but many, especially in Africa and Asia, struggled to create stable governments and economies and suffered from ethnic and religious conflicts, some of which continue today.

Factors and Shifts in Power that Led to the Korean War

In 1910, Japan annexed Korea and maintained this control until 1945. After WWII, Soviet and US troops occupied Korea, with the **Soviet Union** controlling North Korea and the **US** controlling South Korea. In 1947, the UN ordered elections in Korea to unify the country, but the Soviet Union refused to allow them to take place in North Korea, instead setting up a communist government. In 1950, the US withdrew troops, and the North Korean troops moved to invade South Korea. The **Korean War** was the first war in which the UN—or any international organization—played a major role. The US, Australia, Canada, France, Netherlands, Great Britain, Turkey, China, the USSR, and other countries sent troops at various times, for both sides, throughout the war. In 1953, the war ended in a truce, but no peace agreement was ever achieved, and Korea remains divided.

Events that Led to the Vietnam War

Vietnam had previously been part of a French colony called French Indochina. The **Vietnam War** began with the **First Indochina War** from 1946 to 1954, in which France battled with the Democratic Republic of Vietnam, ruled by Ho Chi Minh.

In 1954, a siege at Dien Bien Phu ended in a Vietnamese victory. Vietnam was then divided into North and South, much like Korea. Communist forces controlled the North, and the South was controlled by South Vietnamese forces, supported by the US. Conflict ensued, leading to another war. US troops eventually led the fight, in support of South Vietnam. The war became a major political issue in the US, with many citizens protesting American involvement. In 1975, South Vietnam surrendered, and Vietnam became the **Socialist Republic of Vietnam.**

Middle East from 1947 to 1977

After WWII, the United Nations announced that **Palestine** would be partitioned in order to make room for a new Jewish state. **Israel** was created in 1948. In 1951, the Iranian leader **Mossadegh** nationalized the oil interests, making his government extremely wealthy and powerful. This move would be emulated by future leaders. In 1967, in the **Six-Day War**, Israel routed a coalition of Arab nations, seizing the West Bank, Sinai, and Jerusalem. In 1972, Palestinian terrorists murdered 12 Israeli athletes at the Olympics in Munich. In 1973, the oil-producing Arab nations placed an embargo on shipments to the West, causing major energy crises in the US and Europe. Also, in 1973, Israelis and Arabs battled again in the **Yom Kippur War**. In 1977, Egyptian leader **Anwar Sadat** became the first Arab leader to visit Israel.

Middle East from 1978 to 1985

In 1978, American President **Jimmy Carter** hosted successful peace talks between Egypt and Israel at **Camp David**. The next year, however, a fundamentalist Islamist regime would take power in Iran, and many

Americans would be taken hostage, only released upon the election of **Ronald Reagan**. Between 1980 and 1988, Iran and Iraq engaged in a bloody and brutal war, begun when the Iraqi leader **Saddam Hussein** seized territory in eastern Iran. Also, during this period, Afghan rebels were engaged in a prolonged, ultimately successful fight for independence from the Soviets. In 1982, Israel attacked Lebanon, which was harboring the Palestinian leader **Yasser Arafat**. Lebanon would be forced to oust Arafat the next year. Israel would continue attacking Arafat and the **Palestinian Liberation Organization**, and the PLO would continue to sponsor terrorist activities against Israel.

End of the Cold War

Over time, the leaders of the Soviet Union and United States began to realize the total annihilation that would ensue if nuclear war was declared, and it was agreed that both sides would **disarm**. The two treaties that were signed during the 1970s are known as the **Strategic Arms Limitation Talks (SALT) I and II**. When **Mikhail Gorbachev** came into power in the USSR in 1985, he established a policy of **glasnost**, or "openness." In response to US President Ronald Reagan's military build-up using the might of the US economy, Gorbachev understood that the Soviet Union could not economically compete militarily under a communist system and overcome the military might of the United States. He thus advocated **perestroika**, a gradual metamorphosis of the Soviet economy. In 1991, these reforms culminated in the disintegration of the ruling Communist party, and the **disbanding of the Soviet Union**. This occurred two years after the **Berlin Wall**, which for more than forty years had separated communist and anticommunist Germany, was finally torn down.

Globalism

In the modern era, globalism has emerged as a popular political ideology. **Globalism** is based on the idea that all people and all nations are **interdependent**. Each nation is dependent on one or more other nations for production of and markets for goods, and for income generation. Today's ease of international travel and communication, including technological advances such as the airplane, has heightened this sense of interdependence. The global economy and the general idea of globalism have shaped many economic and political choices since the beginning of the 20th century. Many of today's issues, including environmental awareness, economic struggles, and continued warfare, often require the cooperation of many countries if they are to be dealt with effectively.

Effect of Globalization on the Way Countries Interact With Each Other

Countries worldwide often seek the same resources, leading to high demand, particularly for **nonrenewable resources**. This can result in heavy fluctuations in price. One major example is the demand for petroleum products such as oil and natural gas. Increased travel and communication make it possible to deal with diseases in remote locations; however, this also allows diseases to be spread via travelers.

A major factor contributing to increased globalization over the past few decades has been the **internet**. By allowing instantaneous communication with anyone nearly anywhere on the globe, the internet has led to interaction between far-flung individuals and countries, and an ever-increasing awareness of events all over the world.

Review Video: Globalization
Visit mometrix.com/academy and enter code: 551962

Role of the Middle East in International Relations and Economics

The location on the globe, with ease of access to Europe and Asia, and its preponderance of oil deposits, makes the **Middle Eastern countries** crucial in many international issues, both diplomatic and economic. Because of its central location, the Middle East has been a hotbed for violence since before the beginning of recorded history. Conflicts over land, resources, and religious and political power continue in the area today, spurred by conflict over control of the area's vast oil fields as well as over territories that have been disputed for thousands of years.

Middle East from 1987 to 2003

In 1987, Syrian troops entered Lebanon and stopped the civil war. Also, during this year, 402 pilgrims died during riots in the Saudi Arabian sacred city of Mecca. In 1988, the Palestinian resistance (known as the Intifada) began in earnest against Israel. Iraq invaded Kuwait in 1990, and after UN sanctions were levied, the US invaded in 1991. The Iraqi soldiers set fire to thousands of Kuwaiti oil wells while retreating. In 1992, Arafat and Israeli PM Yitzhak Rabin shook hands in Washington, and Arafat would soon return to Gaza after years of exile. In 1995, the Israelis and Palestinians signed an agreement giving the Palestinians autonomy in the West Bank and Gaza areas. Despite continuing violence, another agreement was reached in 1998, this one stating that the Palestinians would be granted land in exchange for keeping the peace. Violence continued, however, and in 2003, Israel began construction of a barrier between itself and the Palestinian territories.

War on Terror

Following the terrorist attacks on the United States on September 11, 2001, the United States invaded Afghanistan, marking the start of the Global War on Terrorism. This was a global campaign led by the Americans to oust Islamic extremist terrorist groups mainly situated in the Middle East. On the side of the Americans was a large coalition of other countries, many of whom were members of NATO. American allies that fought in the War on Terror included the United Kingdom, Australia, Canada, Denmark, France, Italy, the Netherlands, New Zealand, and Norway. Major wars occurred in Afghanistan and Iraq against al-Qaeda, the Taliban, and their allies.

While stopping terrorism was the main stated goal of the War on Terror, the American government invaded Iraq under the claims that Saddam Hussein's government had weapons of mass destruction, but these claims were found to be false. The goal of removing extremist groups from the region has also not been entirely successful, as the Taliban took control of Afghanistan in 2021, and militant groups continue to have heavy influence in the region.

New Europe after 1991 through 1998

In 1991, **Gorbachev** resigned as the last president of the USSR, and a number of the Soviet provinces, including Lithuania and Latvia, declared independence. The **Maastricht Treaty**, formally announcing the creation of the European Union, was signed in 1992, and the next year a unified European stock market opened. In the **"Velvet" Revolution of 1993**, Slovakia separated from Czechoslovakia, which became the Czech Republic. Meanwhile, the former USSR was enduring civil strife until **Boris Yeltsin** seized power in 1993. In 1994, Russian troops attacked **Chechnya**, which was trying to achieve independence. In 1998, President Clinton helped broker a peace agreement between the **British** and **North Irish rebels**.

New Europe After 1999

In 1999, the Czech Republic, Poland, and Hungary all joined **NATO**, further eliminating the old divides between western and eastern Europe. The conflict in Chechnya increased during this year, and Yeltsin was succeeded as Russian leader by the former KGB agent Vladimir Putin. An **International Criminal Court** was created in the Hague (Netherlands) in 2002, despite the vehement opposition of the United States. In the late '90s, many of the western European governments had become quasi-socialist, and they spent much of their time debating the immense increase in **immigration**. Meanwhile, the former Soviet states have had a rough transition from command to market economies, and are still somewhat economically depressed.

The Russo-Ukrainian War

The Russo-Ukrainian war began in February of 2014 when Russia annexed the Crimea region of Ukraine following Ukraine's Revolution of Dignity, in which the pro-Russian president of Ukraine was ousted. This resulted in pro-Russian unrest in the Donbas region of Ukraine. A war eventually broke out between Ukraine and Russian-backed separatists in the region. This conflict is referred to as the Donbas War.

In 2022, the war was escalated by Russia's invasion of Ukraine, sparking the biggest conflict in Europe since WWII. Russia's actions in starting the invasion have been internationally condemned. The Ukrainians have since been fighting a costly war to maintain their independence, with casualties estimated to be in the tens of thousands. Russia has been accused of many war crimes, including deliberately targeting large numbers of civilians throughout the course of the war.

Human-Induced Global Climate Change and Further Climate Change

Today, the climate change debate mostly focuses on whether it is specifically **human activities** that have wrought **changes in our world climate**; in other words, is mankind directly responsible for causing the change in global temperature and thus directly responsible for implementing choices to counteract the impact of its actions. For example, the United Nations Intergovernmental Panel on Climate Change, a multinational group of the world's leading environmental scientists, has documented increases in the average tidal levels, increasing temperatures at ground level, concentrations of greenhouse gases in the atmosphere, glaciers whose ice is melting, explorations of the Arctic ice core, and so forth. Based on this data, this panel has made predictions of variations in patterns of weather and temperatures in the near future. They believe these variations to be directly caused by emissions from human use of fossil fuels. These foremost scientists state that the climate likely will change dramatically within 50-100 years, almost completely due to human actions and their impact on the natural environment.

Major Occurrences of Genocide in Modern History

Five major occurrences of genocide in modern history other than the Holocaust are:

- **Armenian genocide**—from 1914 to 1918, the Young Turks, heirs to the Ottoman Empire, slaughtered between 800,000 and 1.5 million Armenians. This constituted approximately half of the Armenian population at the time.
- **Holodomor**—from 1932 to 1933, the people of Ukraine suffered the effects of a famine created by Joseph Stalin's collectivization of agriculture. Millions of Ukranians starved to death due to a lack of access to food.
- **Cambodian genocide**—from 1975 to 1979, the Khmer Rouge, a communist group, inflicted violence on the people of Cambodia. Between 1.5 million and 3 million Cambodians were killed. The Khmer Rouge were removed from power when the Vietnamese military took the capital of Cambodia.
- **Rwandan genocide**—in 1994, hundreds of thousands of Tutsis and Hutu sympathizers were slaughtered during the Rwandan Civil War. The UN did not act or authorize intervention during these atrocities.
- **Darfur genocide**—In 2003, militias tasked with combating rebel activity in Darfur kept the people of Darfur from accessing food and resources. This resulted in the death of hundreds of thousands of people in Darfur.

American History Pre-Columbian to 1789

Prior to European colonization, the land that would become the United States was populated by millions of Native Americans belonging to hundreds of distinct tribes. Native American societies were diverse and sophisticated, with political structures, religious beliefs, domesticated animals, agricultural practices, and trade networks. Native Americans adapted their societies and cultures to the environments in which they settled, which led to distinct cultures, beliefs, practices, and languages all across the continent.

Well-Known Native Americans

The following are five well-known Native Americans and their roles in early US history:

1. **Squanto**, an Algonquian, helped early English settlers survive the hard winter by teaching them the native methods of planting corn, squash, and pumpkins.
2. **Pocahontas**, also Algonquian, became famous as a liaison with John Smith's Jamestown colony in 1607.

3. **Sacagawea**, a Shoshone, served a vital role in the Lewis and Clark expedition when the two explorers hired her as their guide in 1805.
4. **Crazy Horse** and **Sitting Bull** led Sioux and Cheyenne troops in the Battle of the Little Bighorn in 1876, soundly defeating George Armstrong Custer.
5. **Chief Joseph**, a leader of the Nez Perce who supported peaceful interaction with white settlers, attempted to relocate his tribe to Canada rather than move them to a reservation.

Major Regional Native American Groups

The major regional Native American groups and the major traits of each are as follows:

- The **Algonquians** in the eastern part of the United States lived in wigwams. The northern tribes subsisted on hunting and gathering, while those who were farther south grew crops such as corn.
- The **Iroquois**, also an east coast tribe, spoke a different language from the Algonquians and lived in rectangular longhouses.
- The **Plains tribes** lived between the Mississippi River and the Rocky Mountains. These nomadic tribes lived in teepees and followed the buffalo herds. Plains tribes included the Sioux, Cheyenne, Comanche, and Blackfoot.
- **Pueblo tribes** included the Zuni, Hopi, and Acoma. They lived in the Southwest deserts in homes made of stone or adobe. They domesticated animals and cultivated corn and beans.
- On the Pacific coast, tribes such as the **Tlingit**, **Chinook**, and **Salish** lived on fish,deer, native berries, and roots. Their rectangular homes housed large family groups, and they used totem poles.
- In the far north, the **Aleuts** and **Inuit** lived in skin tents or igloos. Talented fishermen, they built kayaks and umiaks and also hunted caribou, seals, whales, and walrus.

Review Video: Major Regional Native American Groups
Visit mometrix.com/academy and enter code: 550136

Age of Exploration

The Age of Exploration is also called the **Age of Discovery**. It is generally considered to have begun in the early 15th century and continued into the 17th century. Major developments of the **Age of Exploration** included technological advances in navigation, mapmaking, and shipbuilding. These advances led to expanded European exploration of the rest of the world. Explorers set out from several European countries, including Portugal, Spain, France, and England, seeking new routes to Asia. These efforts led to the discovery of new lands, as well as colonization in India, Asia, Africa, and North America.

Review Video: Age of Exploration
Visit mometrix.com/academy and enter code: 612972

Impact of Technological Advances in Navigation and Seafaring Exploration

For long ocean journeys, it was important for sailors to be able to find their way home even when their vessels sailed far out to sea. A variety of navigational tools enabled them to launch ambitious journeys over long distances. The **compass** and **astrolabe** were particularly important advancements. Chinese navigators used the magnetic compass in approximately 200 BC, and knowledge of the astrolabe came to Europe from Arab navigators and traders who had refined designs developed by the ancient Greeks. The Portuguese developed a ship called a **caravel** in the 1400s that incorporated navigational advancements with the ability to make long sea journeys. Equipped with this advanced vessel, the Portuguese achieved a major goal of the Age of Exploration by discovering a **sea route** from Europe to Asia in 1498.

Significance of Christopher Columbus's Voyage

In 1492, Columbus, a Genoan explorer, obtained financial backing from King Ferdinand and Queen Isabella of Spain to seek a sea route to Asia. He sought a trade route with the Asian Indies to the west. With three ships, the *Niña*, the *Pinta*, and the *Santa Maria*, he eventually landed in the **West Indies**. While Columbus failed in his effort to discover a western route to Asia, he is credited with the discovery of the **Americas**.

> **Review Video: Christopher Columbus**
> Visit mometrix.com/academy and enter code: 496598

French, Spanish, Dutch, and British Goals in Colonization of the Americas

France, Spain, the Netherlands, and England each had specific goals in the colonization of the Americas:

- Initial **French colonies** were focused on expanding the fur trade. Later, French colonization led to the growth of plantations in Louisiana, which brought numerous African slaves to the New World.
- **Spanish colonists** came to look for wealth and to convert the natives to Christianity. For some, the desire for gold led to mining in the New World, while others established large ranches.
- The **Dutch** were also involved in the fur trade and imported slaves as the need for laborers increased.
- **British colonists** arrived with various goals. Some were simply looking for additional income, while others were fleeing Britain to escape religious persecution.

> **Review Video: European Colonization of the Americas**
> Visit mometrix.com/academy and enter code: 438412

Interactions Between the Colonies and Native Americans

While there were examples of peaceful relations between Native Americans and European colonists, these two groups were often in conflict. The colonists constantly attempted to expand their territories and take Native American land. Native Americans often tried to stop the expansion of European colonies via war and diplomacy, both of which usually resulted in failure due to European advantages in technology and shifting alliances. Both the colonists and the Native Americans committed atrocities against the other in these conflicts. Many Native Americans captured in war were made slaves; however, the most fatal attack suffered by the Native Americans came in the form of disease. Foreign diseases like small pox ravaged through the Native American population. Some researchers estimate that up to 90% of the Native American population died as a result of foreign diseases brought to America by colonists.

New England Colonies

The New England colonies were New Hampshire, Connecticut, Rhode Island and Massachusetts. These colonies were founded largely to escape **religious persecution** in England. The beliefs of the **Puritans**, who migrated to America in the 1600s, significantly influenced the development of these colonies. Situated in the northeast coastal areas of America, the New England colonies featured numerous harbors as well as dense forests. The soil, however, was rocky and had a very short growing season, so was not well suited for agriculture. The economy of New England during the colonial period centered around fishing, shipbuilding and trade along with some small farms and lumber mills. Although some groups congregated in small farms, life centered mainly in towns and cities where **merchants** largely controlled the trade economy. Coastal cities such as Boston grew and thrived.

> **Review Video: The Massachusetts Bay Colony**
> Visit mometrix.com/academy and enter code: 407058

Middle or Middle Atlantic Colonies

The Middle or Middle Atlantic Colonies were New York, New Jersey, Pennsylvania, and Delaware. Unlike the New England colonies, where most colonists were from England and Scotland, the Middle Colonies founders were from various countries, including the Netherlands and Sweden. Various factors led these colonists to America. More fertile than New England, the Middle Colonies became major producers of **crops**, including rye, oats, potatoes, wheat, and barley. Some particularly wealthy inhabitants owned large farms and/or businesses.

Farmers, in general, were able to produce enough to have a surplus to sell. Tenant farmers also rented land from larger landowners.

Southern Colonies

The Southern Colonies were Maryland, Virginia, North Carolina, South Carolina, and Georgia. Of the Southern Colonies, Virginia was the first permanent English colony and Georgia the last. The warm climate and rich soil of the south encouraged **agriculture**, and the growing season was long. As a result, economy in the south was based largely on labor-intensive **plantations**. Crops included tobacco, rice, and indigo, all of which became valuable cash crops. Most land in the south was controlled by wealthy plantation owners and farmers. Labor on the farms came in the form of indentured servants and African slaves. The first of these **African slaves** arrived in Virginia in 1619.

Review Video: The Southern Colonies
Visit mometrix.com/academy and enter code: 703830

Review Video: The English Colony of Virginia
Visit mometrix.com/academy and enter code: 537399

Significance of the French and Indian Wars

The **British defeat of the Spanish Armada** in 1588 led to the decline of Spanish power in Europe. This, in turn, led the British and French into battle several times between 1689 and 1748. These wars were:

- King William's War, or the Nine Years War, 1689-1697. This war was fought largely in Flanders.
- The War of Spanish Succession, or Queen Anne's War, 1702-1713
- War of Austrian Succession, or King George's War, 1740-1748

The fourth and final war, the **French and Indian War** (1754-1763), was fought largely in the North American territory and resulted in the end of France's reign as a colonial power in North America. Although the French held many advantages, including more cooperative colonists and numerous Native American allies, the strong leadership of **William Pitt** eventually led the British to victory. Costs incurred during the wars eventually led to discontent in the colonies and helped spark the **American Revolution**.

Review Video: French and Indian Wars
Visit mometrix.com/academy and enter code: 502183

Navigation Acts

The Navigation Acts, enacted in 1651, were an attempt by Britain to dominate international trade. Aimed largely at the Dutch, the acts banned foreign ships from transporting goods to the British colonies and from transporting goods to Britain from elsewhere in Europe. While the restrictions on trade angered some colonists, these acts were helpful to other American colonists who, as members of the British Empire, were legally able to provide ships for Britain's growing trade interests and use the ships for their own trading ventures. By the time the French and Indian War had ended, one-third of British merchant ships were built in the American colonies. Many colonists amassed fortunes in the shipbuilding trade.

Acts of British Parliament that Occurred After the French and Indian Wars

After the French and Indian Wars, the British Parliament passed four major acts:

1. The **Sugar Act**, 1764—this act not only required taxes to be collected on molasses brought into the colonies but gave British officials the right to search the homes of anyone suspected of violating it.
2. The **Stamp Act**, 1765—this act taxed printed materials such as newspapers and legal documents. Protests led the Stamp Act to be repealed in 1766, but the repeal also included the Declaratory Act, which stated that Parliament had the right to govern the colonies.

3. The **Quartering Act**, 1765—this act required colonists to provide accommodations and supplies for British troops. In addition, colonists were prohibited from settling west of the Appalachians until given permission by Britain.
4. The **Townshend Acts**, 1767—these acts taxed paper, paint, lead, and tea that came into the colonies. Colonists led boycotts in protest, and in Massachusetts leaders like Samuel and John Adams began to organize resistance against British rule.

Britain's Taxation of the American Colonies After the French and Indian War

The French and Indian War created circumstances for which the British desperately needed more revenue. These needs included:

- Paying off the war debt
- Defending the expanding empire
- Governing Britain's 33 far-flung colonies, including the American colonies

To meet these needs, the British passed additional laws, increasing revenues from the colonies. Because they had spent so much money to defend the American colonies, the British felt it was appropriate to collect considerably higher **taxes** from them. The colonists felt this was unfair, and many were led to protest the increasing taxes. Eventually, protest led to violence.

Triangular Trade

Triangular trade began in the colonies with ships setting off for **Africa**, carrying rum. In Africa, the rum was traded for gold or slaves. Ships then went from Africa to the **West Indies**, trading slaves for sugar, molasses, or money. To complete the triangle, the ships returned to the **colonies** with sugar or molasses to make more rum, as well as stores of gold and silver. This trade triangle violated the Molasses Act of 1733, which required the colonists to pay high duties to Britain on molasses acquired from French, Dutch, and Spanish colonies. The colonists ignored these duties, and the British government adopted a policy of salutary neglect by not enforcing them.

Review Video: The Triangular Trade
Visit mometrix.com/academy and enter code: 415470

Effects of New Laws on British-Colonial Relations

While earlier revenue-generating acts such as the Navigation Acts brought money to the colonists, the new laws after 1763 required colonists to pay money back to **Britain**. The British felt this was fair since the colonists were British subjects and since they had incurred debt protecting the Colonies. The colonists felt it was not only unfair but illegal.

The development of **local government** in America had given the colonists a different view of the structure and role of government. This made it difficult for the British to understand the colonists' protests against what the British felt was a fair and reasonable solution to the mother country's financial problems.

Factors that Led to Increasing Discontent in the American Colonies

More and more colonists were born on American soil, decreasing any sense of kinship with the far-away British rulers. Their new environment had led to new ideas of government and a strong view of the colonies as a separate entity from Britain. Colonists were allowed to **self-govern** in domestic issues, but **Britain** controlled international issues. In fact, the American colonies were largely left to form their own local government bodies, giving them more freedom than any other colonial territory. This gave the colonists a sense of **independence**, which led them to resent control from Britain. Threats during the French and Indian War led the colonists to call for unification in order to protect themselves.

Colonial and British Government Differences That Caused Tension

As new towns and other legislative districts developed in America, the colonists began to practice **representative government**. Colonial legislative bodies were made up of elected representatives chosen by male property owners in the districts. These individuals represented the interests of the districts from which they had been elected.

By contrast, in Britain, the **Parliament** represented the entire country. Parliament was not elected to represent individual districts. Instead, they represented specific classes. Because of this drastically different approach to government, the British did not understand the colonists' statement that they had no representation in the British Parliament.

Factors That Led to the Boston Massacre

With the passage of the **Stamp Act**, nine colonies met in New York to demand its repeal. Elsewhere, protest arose in New York City, Philadelphia, Boston, and other cities. These protests sometimes escalated into violence, often targeting ruling British officials. The passage of the **Townshend Acts** in 1767 led to additional tension in the colonies. The British sent troops to New York City and Boston. On March 5, 1770, protesters began to taunt the British troops, throwing snowballs. The soldiers responded by firing into the crowd. This clash between protesters and soldiers led to five deaths and eight injuries, and was christened the **Boston Massacre**. Shortly thereafter, Britain repealed the majority of the Townshend Acts.

Tea Act That Led to the Boston Tea Party

The majority of the **Townshend Acts** were repealed after the Boston Massacre in 1770, but Britain kept the tax on tea. In 1773, the **Tea Act** was passed. This allowed the East India Company to sell tea for much lower prices and also allowed them to bypass American distributors, selling directly to shopkeepers instead. Colonial tea merchants saw this as a direct assault on their business. In December of 1773, the **Sons of Liberty** boarded ships in Boston Harbor and dumped 342 chests of tea into the sea in protest of the new laws. This act of protest came to be known as the **Boston Tea Party**.

Coercive Acts Passed After the Boston Tea Party

The Coercive Acts passed by Britain in 1774 were meant to punish Massachusetts for defying British authority. These became collectively known as the **Intolerable Acts** in the colonies and mandated the following:

- Shut down ports in Boston until the city paid back the value of the tea destroyed during the Boston Tea Party
- Required that local government officials in Massachusetts be appointed by the governor rather than being elected by the people
- Allowed trials of British soldiers to be transferred to Britain rather than being held in Massachusetts
- Required locals to provide lodging for British soldiers any time there was a disturbance, even if lodging required them to stay in private homes

These acts led to the assembly of the First Continental Congress in Philadelphia on September 5, 1774. Fifty-five delegates met, representing 12 of the American colonies. They sought compromise with England over England's increasingly harsh efforts to control the colonies.

First Continental Congress

The goal of the First Continental Congress was to achieve a peaceful agreement with Britain. Made up of delegates from 12 of the 13 colonies, the Congress affirmed loyalty to Britain and the power of Parliament to dictate foreign affairs in the colonies. However, they demanded that the **Intolerable Acts** be repealed, and instituted a trade embargo with Britain until this came to pass.

In response, George III of England declared that the American colonies must submit or face military action. The British sought to end assemblies that opposed their policies. These assemblies gathered weapons and began to form militias. On April 19, 1775, the British military was ordered to disperse a meeting of the Massachusetts Assembly. A battle ensued on Lexington Common as the armed colonists resisted. The resulting battles became the **Battle of Lexington and Concord**—the first battles of the **American Revolution**.

Significance of the Second Continental Congress

The Second Continental Congress met in Philadelphia on May 10, 1775, a month after Lexington and Concord. Their discussions centered on the defense of the American colonies and how to conduct the growing war, as well as local government. The delegates also discussed declaring independence from Britain, with many members in favor of this drastic move. They established an army, and on June 15, named **George Washington** as its commander in chief. By 1776, it was obvious that there was no turning back from full-scale war with Britain. The colonial delegates of the Continental Congress signed the **Declaration of Independence** on July 4, 1776.

> **Review Video:** The First and Second Continental Congress
> Visit mometrix.com/academy and enter code: 835211

Origins and Basic Ideas of the Declaration of Independence

Penned by Thomas Jefferson and signed on July 4, 1776, the **Declaration of Independence** stated that King George III had violated the rights of the colonists and was establishing a tyrannical reign over them. Many of Jefferson's ideas of natural rights and property rights were shaped by 17th-century philosopher **John Locke**. Jefferson asserted all people's rights to "life, liberty and the pursuit of happiness." Locke's comparable idea asserted "life, liberty, and private property." Both felt that the purpose of government was to protect the rights of the people, and that individual rights were more important than individuals' obligations to the state.

> **Review Video:** Declaration of Independence
> Visit mometrix.com/academy and enter code: 256838

Battles of the Revolutionary War

The following are five major battles of the Revolutionary War and their significance:

- The **Battle of Lexington and Concord** (April 1775) is considered the first engagement of the Revolutionary War.
- The **Battle of Bunker Hill** (June 1775) was one of the bloodiest of the entire war. Although American troops withdrew, about half of the British army was lost. The colonists proved they could stand against professional British soldiers. In August, Britain declared that the American colonies were officially in a state of rebellion.
- The first colonial victory occurred in Trenton, New Jersey, when Washington and his troops **crossed the Delaware River** on Christmas Day, 1776, for a December 26 surprise attack on British and Hessian troops.
- The **Battle of Saratoga** effectively ended a plan to separate the New England colonies from their Southern counterparts. The surrender of British general John Burgoyne led to France joining the war as allies of the Americans and is generally considered a turning point of the war.
- On October 19, 1781, General Cornwallis surrendered after a defeat in the **Battle of Yorktown**, ending the Revolutionary War.

> **Review Video:** The American Revolutionary War
> Visit mometrix.com/academy and enter code: 935282

Significance of the Treaty of Paris

The Treaty of Paris was signed on September 3, 1783, bringing an official end to the Revolutionary War. In this document, Britain officially recognized the United States of America as an **independent nation**. The treaty established the Mississippi River as the country's western border. The treaty also restored Florida to Spain, while France reclaimed African and Caribbean colonies seized by the British in 1763. On November 25, 1783, the last British troops departed from the newly born United States of America.

Significance of the Articles of Confederation

A precursor to the Constitution, the **Articles of Confederation** represented the first attempt of the newly independent colonies to establish the basics of government. The Continental Congress approved the Articles on November 15, 1777. They went into effect on March 1, 1781, following ratification by the thirteen states. The articles prevented a central government from gaining too much power, instead giving power to a **congressional body** made up of **delegates** from all thirteen states. However, the individual states retained final authority.

Without a strong central **executive**, though, this weak alliance among the new states proved ineffective in settling disputes or enforcing laws. The idea of a weak central government needed to be revised. Recognition of these weaknesses eventually led to the drafting of a new document, the **Constitution**.

Review Video: Articles of Confederation
Visit mometrix.com/academy and enter code: 927401

Initial Proposition and Draft of the Constitution

Delegates from twelve of the thirteen states (Rhode Island was not represented) met in Philadelphia in May of 1787, initially intending to revise the Articles of Confederation. However, it quickly became apparent that a simple revision would not provide the workable governmental structure the newly formed country needed. After vowing to keep all the proceedings secret until the final document was completed, the delegates set out to draft what would eventually become the **Constitution of the United States of America**. By keeping the negotiations secret, the delegates were able to present a completed document to the country for ratification, rather than having every small detail hammered out by the general public.

General Structure of Government Proposed by the Delegates

The delegates agreed that the new nation required a **strong central government** but that its overall power should be **limited**. The various branches of the government should have **balanced power**, so that no one group could control the others. Final power belonged to the **citizens** who voted officials into office based on who would provide the best representation.

Objections Against the Constitution

Once the Constitution was drafted, it was presented for approval by the states. Nine states needed to approve the document for it to become official. However, debate and discussion continued. Major **concerns** included:

- There was no bill of rights to protect individual freedoms.
- States felt too much power was being handed over to the central government.
- Voters wanted more control over their elected representatives.

Discussion about necessary changes to the Constitution was divided into two camps: Federalists and Anti-Federalists. **Federalists** wanted a strong central government. **Anti-Federalists** wanted to prevent a tyrannical government from developing if a central government held too much power

Major Players in the Federalist and Anti-Federalist Camps

Major Federalist leaders included Alexander Hamilton, John Jay, and James Madison. They wrote a series of letters, called the **Federalist Papers**, aimed at convincing the states to ratify the Constitution. These were published in New York papers. Anti-Federalists included Thomas Jefferson and Patrick Henry. They argued against the Constitution as it was originally drafted in a series of **Anti-Federalist Papers**.

The final compromise produced a strong central government controlled by checks and balances. A **Bill of Rights** was also added, becoming the first ten amendments to the Constitution. These amendments protected rights such as freedom of speech, freedom of religion, and other basic rights. Aside from various amendments added throughout the years, the United States Constitution has remained unchanged.

Individuals Who Formed the First Administration of the New Government

The individuals who formed the first administration of the new government were:

- **George Washington**—elected as the first President of the United States in 1789
- **John Adams**—finished second in the election and became the first Vice President
- **Thomas Jefferson**—appointed by Washington as Secretary of State
- **Alexander Hamilton**—appointed Secretary of the Treasury

The Virginia Plan, the New Jersey Plan, and the Great Compromise

Disagreement immediately occurred between delegates from large states and those from smaller states. James Madison and Edmund Randolph (the governor of Virginia) felt that representation in Congress should be based on state population. This was the **Virginia Plan**. The **New Jersey Plan**, presented by William Paterson from New Jersey, proposed that each state should have equal representation. Finally, Roger Sherman from Connecticut formulated the **Connecticut Compromise**, also called the Great Compromise. The result was the familiar structure we have today. Each state has the equal representation of two Senators in the Senate, with the number of representatives in the House of Representatives based on population. This is called a **bicameral congress**. Both houses may draft bills, but financial matters must originate in the House of Representatives.

The Three-fifths Compromise and Number of Representatives for Each State

During debate on the US Constitution, a disagreement arose between the Northern and Southern states involving how **slaves** should be counted when determining a state's quota of representatives. In the South, large numbers of slaves were commonly used to run plantations. Delegates wanted slaves to be counted to determine the number of representatives but not counted to determine the amount of taxes the states would pay. The Northern states wanted exactly the opposite arrangement. The final decision was to count three-fifths of the slave population both for tax purposes and to determine representation. This was called the **Three-fifths Compromise**.

Provisions of the Commerce Compromise

The Commerce Compromise also resulted from a North/South disagreement. In the North, the economy was centered on **industry and trade**. The Southern economy was largely **agricultural**. The Northern states wanted to give the new government the ability to regulate exports as well as trade between the states. The South opposed this plan. Another compromise was in order. In the end, Congress received regulatory power over all trade, including the ability to collect **tariffs** on exported goods. In the South, this raised another red flag regarding the slave trade, as they were concerned about the effect on their economy if tariffs were levied on slaves. The final agreement allowed importing slaves to continue for twenty years without government intervention. Import taxes on slaves were limited, and after the year 1808, Congress could decide whether to allow continued imports of slaves.

American History 1790 to 1898

Alien and Sedition Acts

When **John Adams** became president, a war was raging between Britain and France. While Adams and the Federalists backed the British, Thomas Jefferson and the Democratic-Republican Party supported the French. The United States nearly went to war with France during this time period, while France worked to spread its international standing and influence under the leadership of **Napoleon Bonaparte**. The **Alien and Sedition Acts** grew out of this conflict and made it illegal to speak in a hostile fashion against the existing government.

They also allowed the president to deport anyone in the US who was not a citizen and who was suspected of treason or treasonous activity. When Jefferson became the third president in 1800, he repealed these four laws and pardoned anyone who had been convicted under them.

Development of Political Parties in Early US Government

Many in the US were against political parties after seeing the way parties, or factions, functioned in Britain. The factions in Britain were more interested in personal profit than the overall good of the country, and they did not want this to happen in the US.

However, the differences of opinion between Thomas Jefferson and Alexander Hamilton led to the formation of **political parties.** Hamilton favored a stronger central government, while Jefferson felt that more power should remain with the states. Jefferson was in favor of strict Constitutional interpretation, while Hamilton believed in a more flexible approach. As others joined the two camps, Hamilton backers began to call themselves **Federalists**, while those supporting Jefferson became identified as **Democratic-Republicans**.

Development of the Whig, the Democratic, and the Republican Parties

Thomas Jefferson was elected president in 1800 and again in 1804. The **Federalist Party** began to decline, and its major figure, Alexander Hamilton, died in a duel with Aaron Burr in 1804. By 1816, the Federalist Party had virtually disappeared.

New parties sprang up to take its place. After 1824, the **Democratic-Republican Party** suffered a split. The **Whigs** rose, backing John Quincy Adams and industrial growth. The new Democratic Party formed in opposition to the Whigs, and their candidate, Andrew Jackson, was elected as president in 1828.

By the 1850s, issues regarding slavery led to the formation of the **Republican Party**, which was anti-slavery, while the Democratic Party, with a larger interest in the South, favored slavery. This Republican/Democrat division formed the basis of today's **two-party system**.

Significance of Marbury v. Madison

The main duty of the Supreme Court today is **judicial review**. This power was largely established by **Marbury v. Madison**. When John Adams was voted out of office in 1800, he worked during his final days in office to appoint Federalist judges to Supreme Court positions, knowing Jefferson, his replacement, held opposing views. As late as March 3, the day before Jefferson was to take office, Adams made last-minute appointments referred to as "Midnight Judges." One of the late appointments was William Marbury. The next day, March 4, Jefferson ordered his Secretary of State, James Madison, not to deliver Marbury's commission. This decision was backed by Chief Justice Marshall, who determined that the **Judiciary Act of 1789**, which granted the power to deliver commissions, was illegal in that it gave the Judicial Branch powers not granted in the Constitution. This case set precedent for the Supreme Court to nullify laws it found to be **unconstitutional**.

Review Video: Marbury v Madison
Visit mometrix.com/academy and enter code: 573964

Political Motivations Behind France Selling the Louisiana Purchase

With tension still high between France and Britain, Napoleon was in need of money to support his continuing war efforts. To secure necessary funds, he decided to sell the **Louisiana Territory** to the US. President **Thomas Jefferson** wanted to buy New Orleans, feeling US trade was made vulnerable to both Spain and France at that port. Instead, Napoleon sold him the entire territory for the bargain price of $15 million. The Louisiana Territory was larger than all the rest of the United States put together, and it eventually became 15 additional states.

Federalists in Congress were opposed to the purchase. They feared that the Louisiana Purchase would extend slavery, and that further western growth would weaken the power of the northern states.

Lewis and Clark Expedition

The purchase of the **Louisiana Territory** from France in 1803 more than doubled the size of the United States. President Thomas Jefferson wanted to have the area mapped and explored, since much of the territory was wilderness. He chose Meriwether Lewis and William Clark to head an expedition into the Louisiana Territory. After two years, Lewis and Clark returned, having traveled all the way to the Pacific Ocean. They brought maps, detailed journals, and a multitude of information about the wide expanse of land they had traversed. The **Lewis and Clark Expedition** opened up the west in the Louisiana Territory and beyond for further exploration and settlement.

Review Video: Purpose of the Lewis and Clark Expedition
Visit mometrix.com/academy and enter code: 570657

Causes and Result of the War of 1812

The War of 1812 grew out of the continuing tension between France and Great Britain. Napoleon continued striving to conquer Britain, while the US continued trade with both countries but favored France and the French colonies. Because of what Britain saw as an alliance between America and France, they determined to bring an end to trade between the two nations.

With the British preventing US trade with the French and the French preventing trade with the British, James Madison's presidency introduced acts to **regulate international trade**. If either Britain or France removed their restrictions, America would not trade with the other country. Napoleon acted first, and Madison prohibited trade with England. England saw this as the US formally siding with the French, and war ensued in 1812.

The **War of 1812** has been called the **Second American Revolution**. It established the superiority of the US naval forces and reestablished US independence from Britain and Europe.

The British had two major objections to America's continued trade with France. First, they saw the US as helping France's war effort by providing supplies and goods. Second, the United States had grown into a competitor, taking trade and money away from British ships and tradesmen. In its attempts to end American trade with France, the British put into effect the **Orders in Council**, which made any and all French-owned ports off-limits to American ships. They also began to seize American ships and conscript their crews.

Review Video: Overview of the War of 1812
Visit mometrix.com/academy and enter code: 507716

Review Video: Opinions About the War of 1812
Visit mometrix.com/academy and enter code: 274558

Major Military Events of the War of 1812

Two major naval battles, at **Lake Erie** and **Lake Champlain**, kept the British from invading the US via Canada. American attempts to conquer Canadian lands were not successful.

In another memorable British attack, the British invaded Washington, DC and burned the White House on August 24, 1814. Legend has it that **Dolley Madison**, the First Lady, salvaged the portrait of George Washington from the fire. On Christmas Eve, 1814, the **Treaty of Ghent** officially ended the war. However, Andrew Jackson, unaware that the war was over, managed another victory at New Orleans on January 8, 1815. This victory improved American morale and led to a new wave of national pride and support known as the "**Era of Good Feelings**."

Influence of the American System on American Economics

Spurred by the trade conflicts of the War of 1812 and supported by Henry Clay among others, the **American System** set up tariffs to help protect American interests from competition with overseas products. Reducing competition led to growth in employment and an overall increase in American industry. The higher tariffs also provided funds for the government to pay for various improvements. Congress passed high tariffs in 1816 and also chartered a federal bank. The **Second Bank of the United States** was given the job of regulating America's money supply.

McCulloch v. Maryland

Judicial review was further exercised by the Supreme Court in **McCulloch v. Maryland**. When Congress chartered a national bank, the **Second Bank of the United States**, Maryland voted to tax any bank business dealing with banks chartered outside the state, including the federally chartered bank. Andrew McCulloch, an employee of the Second Bank of the US in Baltimore, refused to pay this tax. The resulting lawsuit from the State of Maryland went to the Supreme Court for judgment.

John Marshall, Chief Justice of the Supreme Court, stated that Congress was within its rights to charter a national bank. In addition, the State of Maryland did not have the power to levy a tax on the federal bank or on the federal government in general. In cases where state and federal government collided, precedent was set for the **federal government** to prevail.

Effects of the Missouri Compromise on the Tensions Between the North and South

By 1819, the United States had developed a tenuous balance between slave and free states, with exactly 22 senators in Congress from each faction. However, Missouri was ready to join the union. As a slave state, it would tip the balance in Congress. To prevent this imbalance, the **Missouri Compromise** brought the northern part of Massachusetts into the union as Maine, establishing it as a free state to balance the admission of Missouri as a slave state. In addition, the remaining portion of the Louisiana Purchase was to remain free north of **latitude 36°30'**. Since cotton did not grow well this far north, this limitation was acceptable to congressmen representing the slave states.

However, the proposed Missouri constitution presented a problem, as it outlawed immigration of free blacks into the state. Another compromise was in order, this time proposed by **Henry Clay**. According to this new compromise, Missouri would never pass a law that prevented anyone from entering the state. Through this and other work, Clay earned his title of the "**Great Compromiser**."

> **Review Video: The Missouri Compromise**
> Visit mometrix.com/academy and enter code: 848091

Monroe Doctrine

On December 2, 1823, President Monroe delivered a message to Congress in which he introduced the **Monroe Doctrine**. In this address, he stated that any attempts by European powers to establish new colonies on the North American continent would be considered interference in American politics. The US would stay out of European matters, and expected Europe to offer America the same courtesy. This approach to foreign policy stated in no uncertain terms that America would not tolerate any new European colonies in the New World, and that events occurring in Europe would no longer influence the policies and doctrines of the US.

> **Review Video: What was the Monroe Doctrine?**
> Visit mometrix.com/academy and enter code: 953021

Effect of the Treaty of Paris on Native Americans

After the Revolutionary War, the **Treaty of Paris**, which outlined the terms of surrender of the British to the Americans, granted large parcels of land to the US that were occupied by Native Americans. The new government attempted to claim the land, treating the natives as a conquered people. This approach proved unenforceable.

Next, the government tried purchasing the land from the Native Americans via a series of **treaties** as the country expanded westward. In practice, however, these treaties were not honored, and Native Americans were simply dislocated and forced to move farther and farther west, often with military action, as American expansion continued.

Indian Removal Act of 1830 and the Treaty of New Echota

The Indian Removal Act of 1830 gave the new American government power to form treaties with Native Americans. In theory, America would claim land east of the Mississippi in exchange for land west of the Mississippi, to which the natives would relocate voluntarily. In practice, many tribal leaders were forced into signing the treaties, and relocation at times occurred by force.

The **Treaty of New Echota** in 1835 was supposedly a treaty between the US government and Cherokee tribes in Georgia. However, the treaty was not signed by tribal leaders but rather by a small portion of the represented people. The leaders protested and refused to leave, but President Martin Van Buren enforced the treaty by sending soldiers. During their forced relocation, more than 4,000 Cherokees died on what became known as the **Trail of Tears**.

Review Video: Indian Removal Act
Visit mometrix.com/academy and enter code: 666738

Jacksonian Democracy vs. Preceding Political Climate

Jacksonian Democracy is largely seen as a shift from politics favoring the wealthy to politics favoring the common man. The right to vote was given to all free white males, not just property owners, as had been the case previously. Jackson's approach favored the patronage system, laissez-faire economics, and relocation of the Native American tribes from the Southeast portion of the country. Jackson opposed the formation of a federal bank and allowed the Second Bank of the United States to collapse by vetoing a bill to renew the charter. Jackson also faced the challenge of the **Nullification Crisis** when South Carolina claimed that it could ignore or nullify any federal law it considered unconstitutional. Jackson sent troops to the state to enforce the protested tariff laws, and a compromise engineered by Henry Clay in 1833 settled the matter for the time being.

Second Great Awakening

Led by Protestant evangelical leaders, the **Second Great Awakening** occurred between 1800 and 1830. Several missionary groups grew out of the movement, including the **American Home Missionary Society**, which formed in 1826. The ideas behind the Second Great Awakening focused on personal responsibility, both as an individual and in response to injustice and suffering. The **American Bible Society** and the **American Tract Society** provided literature, while various traveling preachers spread the word. New denominations arose, including the Latter-day Saints and Seventh-day Adventists.

Another movement associated with the Second Great Awakening was the **temperance movement**, focused on ending the production and use of alcohol. One major organization behind the temperance movement was the **Society for the Promotion of Temperance**, formed in 1826 in Boston.

Attitudes Toward Education in the Early 19th Century

Horace Mann, among others, felt that schools could help children become better citizens, keep them away from crime, prevent poverty, and help American society become more unified. His *Common School Journal* brought his ideas of the importance of education into the public consciousness and proposed his suggestions for an improved American education system. Increased literacy led to increased awareness of current events, Western expansion, and other major developments of the time period. Public interest and participation in the arts and literature also increased. By the end of the 19th century, all children had access to a **free public elementary education**.

Development of Economic Trends as the US Continued to Grow

In the Northeast, the economy mostly depended on **manufacturing, industry, and industrial development**. This led to a dichotomy between rich business owners and industrial leaders and the much poorer workers who supported their businesses. The South continued to depend on **agriculture**, especially on large-scale farms or plantations worked mostly by slaves and indentured servants. In the West, where new settlements had begun to develop, the land was largely wild. Growing communities were essentially **agricultural**, raising crops and livestock. The differences between regions led each to support different interests both politically and economically.

Industrial Activity Before and After 1800

During the 18th century, goods were often manufactured in houses or small shops. With increased technology allowing for the use of machines, **factories** began to develop. In factories, a large volume of salable goods could be produced in a much shorter amount of time. Many Americans, including increasing numbers of **immigrants**, found jobs in these factories, which were in constant need of labor. Another major invention was the **cotton gin**, which significantly decreased the processing time of cotton and was a major factor in the rapid expansion of cotton production in the South.

Development of Labor Movements in the 1800s

In 1751, a group of bakers held a protest in which they stopped baking bread. This was technically the first American **labor strike**. In the 1830s and 1840s, labor movements began in earnest. Boston's masons, carpenters, and stoneworkers protested the length of the workday, fighting to reduce it to ten hours. In 1844, a group of women in the textile industry also fought to reduce their workday to ten hours, forming the **Lowell Female Labor Reform Association**. Many other protests occurred and organizations developed through this time period with the same goal in mind.

Major Ideas Driving American Foreign Policy

The three major ideas driving American foreign policy during its early years were:

- **Isolationism**—the early US government did not intend to establish colonies, though they did plan to grow larger within the bounds of North America.
- **No entangling alliances**—both George Washington and Thomas Jefferson were opposed to forming any permanent alliances with other countries or becoming involved in other countries' internal issues.
- **Nationalism**—a positive patriotic feeling about the United States blossomed quickly among its citizens, particularly after the War of 1812, when the US once again defeated Britain. The Industrial Revolution also sparked increased nationalism by allowing even the most far-flung areas of the US to communicate with each other via telegraph and the expanding railroad.

Effects of Manifest Destiny on American Politics

In the 1800s, many believed America was destined by God to expand west, bringing as much of the North American continent as possible under the umbrella of the US government. With the Northwest Ordinance and the Louisiana Purchase, over half of the continent became American. However, the rapid and relentless expansion brought conflict with the Native Americans, Great Britain, Mexico, and Spain. One result of "**Manifest Destiny**" was the **Mexican-American War** from 1846 to 1848. By the end of the war, Texas, California, and a large portion of what is now the American Southwest joined the growing nation. Conflict also arose over the **Oregon Territory**, shared by the US and Britain. In 1846, President James Polk resolved this problem by compromising with Britain, establishing a US boundary south of the 49th parallel.

> **Review Video: Manifest Destiny**
> Visit mometrix.com/academy and enter code: 957409

Mexican-American War

Spain had held colonial interests in America since the 1540s—earlier even than Great Britain. In 1810, **Mexico** revolted against Spain, becoming a free nation in 1821. **Texas** followed suit, declaring its independence after an 1836 revolution. In 1844, the Democrats pressed President Tyler to annex Texas. Unlike his predecessor, Andrew Jackson, Tyler agreed to admit Texas into the Union, and in 1845, Texas became a state.

During Mexico's war for independence, the nation incurred $4.5 million in war debts to the US. Newly elected James K. Polk offered to forgive the debts in return for New Mexico and Upper California, but Mexico refused. In 1846, war was declared in response to a Mexican attack on American troops that President Polk had moved into a disputed zone between the Rio Grande and Nueces River. As US victory grew more certain, dispute arose over how to handle slavery in any newly acquired territory. The **Wilmot Proviso**, though it was never passed, was a large source of contention, as it aimed to prohibit slavery in any territory acquired from Mexico—sowing further seeds of tension between the North and the South. The Mexican-American War ended in 1848 with Mexico agreeing to sell California and its remaining territory north of the Rio Grande.

> **Review Video: The Mexican-American War**
> Visit mometrix.com/academy and enter code: 271216
>
> **Review Video: Sectional Crisis: The Wilmot Proviso**
> Visit mometrix.com/academy and enter code: 974842

Popular Sovereignty and the Compromise of 1850

In addition to the pro-slavery and anti-slavery factions, a third group rose, who felt that each individual state should decide whether to allow or permit slavery within its borders. The idea that a state could make its own choices was referred to as **popular sovereignty**.

When California applied to join the union in 1849, the balance of congressional power was again threatened. The **Compromise of 1850** introduced a group of laws meant to bring an end to the conflict:

- California's admittance as a free state
- The outlaw of the slave trade in Washington, DC
- An increase in efforts to capture escaped slaves
- The right of New Mexico and Utah territories to decide individually whether to allow slavery

In spite of these measures, debate raged each time a new state prepared to enter the union.

Gadsden Purchase and the 1853 Post-War Treaty with Mexico

After the Mexican-American war, a **second treaty** in 1853 determined hundreds of miles of America's southwest borders. In 1854, the **Gadsden Purchase** was finalized, providing even more territory to aid in the building of the transcontinental railroad. This purchase added what would eventually become the southernmost regions of Arizona and New Mexico to the growing nation. The modern outline of the United States was by this time nearly complete.

Kansas-Nebraska Act Trigger of Additional Conflict

With the creation of the Kansas and Nebraska territories in 1854, another debate began. Congress allowed popular sovereignty in these territories, but slavery opponents argued that the Missouri Compromise had already made slavery illegal in this region. In Kansas, two separate governments arose, one pro-slavery and one anti-slavery. Conflict between the two factions rose to violence, leading Kansas to gain the nickname of "**Bleeding Kansas**."

Review Video: Sectional Crisis: The Kansas-Nebraska Act
Visit mometrix.com/academy and enter code: 982119

Early Leaders in the Women's Rights Movement

The women's rights movement began in the 1840s, with leaders including Elizabeth Cady Stanton, Sojourner Truth, Ernestine Rose, and Lucretia Mott. In 1869, Elizabeth Cady Stanton and Susan B. Anthony formed the **National Woman Suffrage Association**, fighting for women's right to vote.

In 1848, in Seneca Falls, the first women's rights convention was held, with about 300 attendees. The two-day **Seneca Falls Convention** discussed the rights of women to vote (suffrage) as well as equal treatment in careers, legal proceedings, etc. The convention produced a "Declaration of Sentiments," which outlined a plan for women to attain the rights they deserved. **Frederick Douglass** supported the women's rights movement, as well as the abolition movement. In fact, women's rights and abolition movements often went hand-in-hand during this time period.

Review Video: The Women's Rights Movement in America
Visit mometrix.com/academy and enter code: 987734

Events and Developments that Brought the North and South into Conflict

The conflict between the North and South coalesced around the issue of **slavery**, but other elements contributed to the growing disagreement. Though most farmers in the South worked small farms with little or no slave labor, the huge plantations run by the South's rich depended on slaves or indentured servants to remain profitable. They had also become more dependent on **cotton**, with slave populations growing in concert with the rapid increase in cotton production. In the North, a more diverse agricultural economy and the growth of **industry** made slaves rarer. The **abolitionist movement** grew steadily, with Harriet Beecher Stowe's *Uncle Tom's Cabin* giving many an idea to rally around. A collection of anti-slavery organizations formed, with many actively working to free slaves in the South, often bringing them to the northern states or Canada.

Dred Scott Decision

Abolitionist factions coalesced around the case of **Dred Scott**, using his case to test the country's laws regarding slavery. Scott, a slave, had been taken by his owner from Missouri, which was a slave state. He then traveled to Illinois, a free state, then on to the Minnesota Territory, also free based on the Missouri Compromise. After several years, he returned to Missouri, and his owner subsequently died. Abolitionists took Scott's case to court, stating that Scott was no longer a slave but free, since he had lived in free territory. The case went to the Supreme Court.

The Supreme Court stated that, because Scott, as a slave, was not a US citizen, his time in free states did not change his status. He also did not have the right to sue. In addition, the Court determined that the **Missouri Compromise** was unconstitutional, stating that Congress had overstepped its bounds by outlawing slavery in the territories.

Review Video: The Dred Scott Act
Visit mometrix.com/academy and enter code: 364838

Anti-Slavery Organizations

Five anti-slavery organizations and their significance are:

- **American Colonization Society**—Protestant churches formed this group, aimed at returning black slaves to Africa. Former slaves subsequently formed Liberia, but the colony did not do well, as the region was not well-suited for agriculture.
- **American Anti-Slavery Society**—William Lloyd Garrison, a Quaker, was the major force behind this group and its newspaper, *The Liberator*.
- **Philadelphia Female Anti-Slavery Society**—this women-only group was formed by Margaretta Forten because women were not allowed to join the Anti-Slavery Society formed by her father.
- **Anti-Slavery Convention of American Women**—this group continued meeting even after pro-slavery factions burned down their original meeting place.
- **Female Vigilant Society**—this organization raised funds to help the Underground Railroad, as well as slave refugees.

Incidents at Harper's Ferry and John Brown's Role

John Brown, an abolitionist, had participated in several anti-slavery activities, including killing five pro-slavery men in retaliation, after the sacking of Lawrence, Kansas, an anti-slavery town. He and other abolitionists also banded together to pool their funds and build a runaway slave colony.

In 1859, Brown seized a federal arsenal in **Harper's Ferry**, located in what is now West Virginia. Brown intended to seize guns and ammunition and lead a slave rebellion. **Robert E. Lee** captured Brown and 21 followers, who were subsequently tried and hanged. While Northerners took the executions as an indication that the government supported slavery, Southerners were of the opinion that most of the North supported Brown and were, in general, anti-slavery.

Presidential Candidates for the 1860 Election

The 1860 presidential candidates represented four different parties, each with a different opinion on slavery:

- **John Breckinridge**, representing the Southern Democrats, was pro-slavery but urged compromise to preserve the Union.
- **Abraham Lincoln**, of the Republican Party, was anti-slavery.
- **Stephen Douglas**, of the Northern Democrats, felt that the issue should be determined locally, on a state-by-state basis.
- **John Bell**, of the Constitutional Union Party, focused primarily on keeping the Union intact.

In the end, Abraham Lincoln won both the popular and electoral election. Southern states, who had sworn to secede from the Union if Lincoln was elected, did so, led by South Carolina and followed by the rest of the Deep South (Mississippi, Alabama, Georgia, Louisiana, Florida, and Texas). These states established the **Confederate States of America**, with its capital in Montgomery, Alabama. The president of the CSA was **Jefferson Davis**. Outgoing US President Buchanan claimed that he had no constitutional authority to stop the secession, but upon entering office, Lincoln attempted to maintain control of all Southern forts. This led to the firing on **Ft. Sumter** (SC) by the Confederates. As Lincoln called for aid, the Upper South (Virginia, Arkansas, North Carolina, and Tennessee) seceded as well, and the CSA made Richmond, Virginia its new capital.

Compromises to Save the Union

The US government made a number of compromises in an attempt to preserve the Union after Lincoln's election. The **Crittenden Compromise** extended the line of the Missouri Compromise and promised federal protection of slavery south of that line. The **House of Representatives Compromise** offered an extension of the Missouri Compromise and a Constitutional amendment to protect slavery. The **Virginia Peace Convention** produced an offer to extend the line of the Missouri Compromise and establish that slavery can never be outlawed except by the permission of the owner. Finally, Congress offered $300 for each slave. The South said that this was not enough money, and the North was appalled by the offer, regardless. It became clear that such compromises would not be enough to save the Union.

North vs. South in the Civil War

The Northern states had significant advantages, including:

- **Larger population**—the North consisted of 24 states, while the South had 11.
- **Better transportation and finances**—with railroads primarily in the North, supply chains were much more dependable, as was overseas trade.
- **Raw materials**—the North held the majority of America's gold, as well as iron, copper, and other minerals vital to wartime.

The South's advantages included the following:

- **Better-trained military officers**—many of the Southern officers were West Point trained and had commanded in the Mexican and Indian wars.
- **Familiarity with weapons**—the climate and lifestyle of the South meant most of the people were experienced with both guns and horses. The industrial North had less extensive experience.
- **Defensive position**—the South felt that victory was guaranteed, since they were protecting their own lands, while the North would be invading.
- **Well-defined goals**—the South fought an ideological war to be allowed to govern themselves and preserve their way of life. The North originally fought to preserve the Union and later to free the slaves.

Review Video: American Civil War: North vs. South Overview
Visit mometrix.com/academy and enter code: 370788

Benefit of the Emancipation Proclamation on the Union's Military Strategy

The Emancipation Proclamation, issued by President Lincoln on January 1, 1863, freed all slaves in **Confederate states** that were still in rebellion against the Union. While the original proclamation did not free any slaves in the states actually under Union control, it did set a precedent for the emancipation of slaves as the war progressed.

The **Emancipation Proclamation** worked in the Union's favor, as many freed slaves and other black troops joined the **Union Army**. Almost 200,000 blacks fought in the Union army, and over 10,000 served in the navy. By the end of the war, over 4 million slaves had been freed, and in 1865 slavery was abolished in the **13th amendment** to the Constitution.

Review Video: The Civil War: The Emancipation Proclamation
Visit mometrix.com/academy and enter code: 181778

Major Events of the Civil War

Six major events of the Civil War and their outcomes or significance are:

- The **First Battle of Bull Run** (July 21, 1861)—this was the first major land battle of the war. Observers, expecting to enjoy an entertaining skirmish, set up picnics nearby. Instead, they found themselves witness to a bloodbath. Union forces were defeated, and the battle set the course of the Civil War as long, bloody, and costly.
- The **Capture of Fort Henry** by Ulysses S. Grant—this battle in February of 1862 marked the Union's first major victory.

- The **Battle of Gettysburg** (July 1-3, 1863)—often seen as the turning point of the war, Gettysburg also saw the largest number of casualties of the war, with over 50,000 dead, wounded, or missing. Robert E. Lee was defeated, and the Confederate army, significantly crippled, withdrew.
- The **Overland Campaign** (May and June of 1864)—Grant, now in command of all the Union armies, led this high casualty campaign that eventually positioned the Union for victory.
- **Sherman's March to the Sea**—William Tecumseh Sherman, in May of 1864, conquered Atlanta. He then continued to Savannah, destroying vast amounts of property as he went.
- Following Lee's defeat at the Appomattox Courthouse, General Grant accepted **Lee's surrender** in the home of Wilmer McLean in Appomattox, Virginia on April 9, 1865.

Impact of the Civil War across America

The Civil War impacted various people in America in remarkable ways. The people most affected were likely African Americans, who were at the center of the divide between the North and the South. Many African Americans directly fought in the war on both sides. Those in the Southern states were ultimately freed as a result of the Emancipation Proclamation of 1863. Soldiers in the war saw brutal warfare and faced physical and psychological repercussions of combat. It has long been said about the Civil War that soldiers often knew or were related to the very people they were fighting. This was especially so in states that hosted battles or lied on the borders between Southern and Northern states, such as Virginia and Tennessee. Others affected included women and children who were, in some cases, located fairly near the fights and played roles as suppliers, medics, and activists, leading to some precursors to the women's rights movement. In the reconstruction, economic, political, legal, and emotional fallout had to be dealt with, leading to many decades of repair following the war.

Circumstances of Lincoln's Assassination

The Civil War ended with the surrender of the South on April 9, 1865. Five days later, Lincoln and his wife, Mary, went to the play *Our American Cousin* at the Ford Theater. John Wilkes Booth, who did not know that the war was over, did his part in a plot to help the Confederacy by shooting Lincoln. He was carried from the theater to a nearby house, where he died the next morning. Booth was tracked down and killed by Union soldiers twelve days later.

Review Video: Overview of the American Civil War
Visit mometrix.com/academy and enter code: 239557

Goals of Reconstruction and the Freedmen's Bureau

In the aftermath of the Civil War, the South was left in chaos. From 1865 to 1877, government on all levels worked to help restore order to the South, ensure civil rights to the freed slaves, and bring the Confederate states back into the Union. This became known as the **Reconstruction period**. In 1866, Congress passed the **Reconstruction Acts**, placing former Confederate states under military rule and stating the grounds for readmission into the Union.

The **Freedmen's Bureau** was formed to help freedmen both with basic necessities like food and clothing and also with employment and finding of family members who had been separated during the war. Many in the South felt the Freedmen's Bureau worked to set freed slaves against their former owners. The Bureau was intended to help former slaves become self-sufficient, and to keep them from falling prey to those who would take advantage of them. It eventually closed due to lack of funding and to violence from the **Ku Klux Klan**.

Policies of the Radical and Moderate Republicans

The **Radical Republicans** wished to treat the South quite harshly after the war. **Thaddeus Stevens**, the House Leader, suggested that the Confederate states be treated as if they were territories again, with ten years of military rule and territorial government before they would be readmitted. He also wanted to give all black men the right to vote. Former Confederate soldiers would be required to swear they had never supported the Confederacy (knows as the "Ironclad Oath") in order to be granted full rights as American citizens.

In contrast, the **moderate Republicans** wanted only black men who were literate or who had served as Union troops to be able to vote. All Confederate soldiers except troop leaders would also be able to vote. Before his death, **Lincoln** had favored a more moderate approach to Reconstruction, hoping this approach might bring some states back into the Union before the end of the war.

Phases of Reconstruction

The three phases of Reconstruction are:

- **Presidential Reconstruction**—largely driven by President Andrew Johnson's policies, the presidential phase of Reconstruction was lenient on the South and allowed continued discrimination against and control over blacks.
- **Congressional Reconstruction**—Congress, controlled largely by Radical Republicans, took a different stance, providing a wider range of civil rights for blacks and greater control over Southern government. Congressional Reconstruction is marked by military control of the former Confederate States.
- **Redemption**—gradually, the Confederate states were readmitted into the Union. During this time, white Democrats took over the government of most of the South. In 1877, President Rutherford Hayes withdrew the last federal troops from the South.

Carpetbaggers and Scalawags

The chaos in the South attracted a number of people seeking to fill the power vacuums and take advantage of the economic disruption. **Scalawags** were southern whites who aligned with freedmen to take over local governments. Many in the South who could have filled political offices refused to take the necessary oath required to grant them the right to vote, leaving many opportunities for Scalawags and others. **Carpetbaggers** were Northerners who traveled to the South for various reasons. Some provided assistance, while others sought to make money or to acquire political power during this chaotic period.

Black Codes and the Civil Rights Bill

The Black Codes were proposed to control freed slaves. They would not be allowed to bear arms, assemble, serve on juries, or testify against whites. Schools would be segregated, and unemployed blacks could be arrested and forced to work. The **Civil Rights Act** countered these codes, providing much wider rights for the freed slaves.

Andrew Johnson, who became president after Lincoln's death, supported the Black Codes and vetoed the Civil Rights Act in 1865 and again in 1866. The second time, Congress overrode his veto, and it became law.

Two years later, Congress voted to **impeach** Johnson, the culmination of tensions between Congress and the president. He was tried and came within a single vote of being convicted, but ultimately was acquitted and finished his term in office.

Purpose of the Thirteenth, Fourteenth, and Fifteenth Amendments

The Thirteenth, Fourteenth and Fifteenth Amendments were all passed shortly after the end of the Civil War:

- The **Thirteenth Amendment** was ratified by the states on December 6, 1865. This amendment prohibited slavery in the United States.
- The **Fourteenth Amendment** overturned the Dred Scott decision and was ratified July 9, 1868. American citizenship was redefined: a citizen was any person born or naturalized in the US, with all citizens guaranteed equal legal protection by all states. It also guaranteed citizens of any race the right to file a lawsuit or serve on a jury.
- The **Fifteenth Amendment** was ratified on February 3, 1870. It states that no citizen of the United States can be denied the right to vote based on race, color, or previous status as a slave.

Black Southerners and Segregation

Most Southern Democrats supported **segregation**, or the separation of the races. Although the **Civil Rights Act of 1875** had outlawed segregated restaurants and hotels, among other things, the Supreme Court ruled in 1883 that this act violated the 14th amendment because only states, and not individuals, could be forbidden from segregation. The **Jim Crow laws** were those rules that segregated black people and white people. Although de facto (by custom) segregation had existed in the North for years, the South began to implement segregation de jure (by law). In **Plessy v. Ferguson** (1896), the Supreme Court ruled that accommodations should be "separate but equal." In **Cummings v. Board of Education** (1898), the Supreme Court allowed public schools to be segregated.

Developments in Transportation

As America expanded its borders, it also developed new technology to travel the rapidly growing country. Roads and railroads traversed the nation, with the **Transcontinental Railroad** eventually allowing travel from one coast to the other. Canals and steamboats simplified water travel and made shipping easier and less expensive. The **Erie Canal** (1825) connected the Great Lakes to the Hudson River. Other canals connected other major waterways, further facilitating transportation and the shipment of goods.

Transcontinental Railroad

In 1869, the **Union Pacific Railroad** completed the first section of a planned **transcontinental railroad**. This section went from Omaha, Nebraska to Sacramento, California. Ninety percent of the workers were Chinese, working in very dangerous conditions for very low pay. With the rise of the railroad, products were much more easily transported across the country. While this was positive overall for industry throughout the country, it was often damaging to family farmers, who found themselves paying high shipping costs for smaller supply orders while larger companies received major discounts.

Measures to Limit Immigration in the 19th Century

In 1870, the **Naturalization Act** put limits on US citizenship, allowing full citizenship only to whites and those of African descent. The **Chinese Exclusion Act of 1882** put limits on Chinese immigration. The **Immigration Act of 1882** taxed immigrants, charging 50 cents per person. These funds helped pay administrative costs for regulating immigration. **Ellis Island** opened in 1892 as a processing center for those arriving in New York. The year 1921 saw the **Emergency Quota Act** passed, also known as the **Johnson Quota Act**, which severely limited the number of immigrants allowed into the country.

Agriculture in the 19th Century

Technological Advances in Agricultural Changes

During the mid-1800s, irrigation techniques improved significantly. Advances occurred in cultivation and breeding, as well as fertilizer use and crop rotation. In the Great Plains, also known as the Great American Desert, the dense soil was finally cultivated with steel plows. In 1892, gasoline-powered tractors arrived, and they were widely used by 1900. Other advancements in agriculture's toolset included barbed wire fences, combines, silos, deep-water wells, and the cream separator.

Major Actions that Helped Improve Agriculture

Four major government actions that helped improve US agriculture in the 19th century are:

- The **Department of Agriculture** came into being in 1862, working for the interests of farmers and ranchers across the country.
- The **Morrill Land-Grant Acts** were a series of acts passed between 1862 and 1890, allowing land-grant colleges.
- In conjunction with land-grant colleges, the **Hatch Act of 1887** brought agriculture experiment stations into the picture, helping discover new farming techniques.

- In 1914, the **Smith-Lever Act** provided cooperative programs to help educate people about food, home economics, community development, and agriculture. Related agriculture extension programs helped farmers increase crop production to feed the rapidly growing nation.

Inventors from the 1800s

Major inventors from the 1800s and their inventions include:

- Alexander Graham Bell—the telephone
- Orville and Wilbur Wright—the airplane
- Richard Gatling—the machine gun
- Walter Hunt, Elias Howe, and Isaac Singer—the sewing machine
- Nikola Tesla—alternating current motor
- George Eastman—the Kodak camera
- Thomas Edison—the first commercially practical light bulbs, motion pictures, and the phonograph
- Samuel Morse—the telegraph
- Charles Goodyear—vulcanized rubber
- Cyrus McCormick—the reaper
- George Westinghouse—the transformer, the air brake

This was an active period for invention, with about 700,000 patents registered between 1860 and 1900.

Gilded Age

The time period from the end of the Civil War to the beginning of the First World War is often referred to as the **Gilded Age**, or the **Second Industrial Revolution**. The US was changing from an agricultural-based economy to an **industrial economy**, with rapid growth accompanying the shift. In addition, the country itself was expanding, spreading into the seemingly unlimited west.

This time period saw the beginning of banks, department stores, chain stores, and trusts—all familiar features of the modern-day landscape. Cities also grew rapidly, and large numbers of immigrants arrived in the country, swelling the urban ranks.

Review Video: The Gilded Age: An Overview
Visit mometrix.com/academy and enter code: 684770

Factors Leading to the Development of the Populist Party

A major **recession** struck the United States during the 1890s, with crop prices falling dramatically. **Drought** compounded the problems, leaving many American farmers in crippling debt. The **Farmers' Alliance** formed in 1875, drawing the rural poor into a single political entity.

Recession also affected the more industrial parts of the country. The **Knights of Labor**, formed in 1869 by **Uriah Stephens**, was able to unite workers into a union to protect their rights. Dissatisfied by views espoused by industrialists, the Farmers Alliance and the Knights of Labor, joined to form the **Populist Party**, also known as the People's Party, in 1892. Some of the elements of the party's platform included:

- National currency
- Graduated income tax
- Government ownership of railroads as well as telegraph and telephone systems
- Secret ballots for voting
- Immigration restriction
- Single-term limits for president and vice-president

The Populist Party was in favor of decreasing elitism and making the voice of the common man more easily heard in the political process.

Growth of the Labor Movement Through the Late 19th Century

One of the first large, well-organized strikes occurred in 1892. Called the **Homestead Strike**, it occurred when the Amalgamated Association of Iron and Steel Workers struck against the Carnegie Steel Company. Gunfire ensued, and Carnegie was able to eliminate the plant's union. In 1894, workers in the American Railway Union, led by Eugene Debs, initiated the **Pullman Strike** after the Pullman Palace Car Co. cut their wages by 28 percent. President Grover Cleveland called in troops to break up the strike on the grounds that it interfered with mail delivery. Mary Harris "Mother" Jones organized the **Children's Crusade** to protest child labor. A protest march proceeded to the home of President Theodore Roosevelt in 1903. Jones also worked with the United Mine Workers of America and helped found the **Industrial Workers of the World**.

Panic of 1893

Far from a US-centric event, the **Panic of 1893** was an economic crisis that affected most of the globe. As a response, President Grover Cleveland repealed the **Sherman Silver Purchase Act**, afraid it had caused the downturn rather than boosting the economy as intended. The Panic led to bankruptcies, with banks and railroads going under and factory unemployment rising as high as 25 percent. In the end, the **Republican Party** regained power due to the economic crisis.

Progressive Era

From the 1890s to the end of the First World War, **Progressives** set forth an ideology that drove many levels of society and politics. The Progressives were in favor of workers' rights and safety and wanted measures taken against waste and corruption. They felt science could help improve society and that the government could—and should—provide answers to a variety of social problems. Progressives came from a wide variety of backgrounds but were united in their desire to improve society.

Muckrakers and the Progressive Movement

"Muckrakers" was a term used to identify aggressive investigative journalists who exposed scandals, corruption, and many other wrongs in late 19th-century society. Among these intrepid writers were:

- **Ida Tarbell**—she exposed John D. Rockefeller's Standard Oil Trust.
- **Jacob Riis**—a photographer, he brought the living conditions of the poor in New York to the public's attention.
- **Lincoln Steffens**—he worked to expose political corruption in municipal government.
- **Upton Sinclair**—his book *The Jungle* led to reforms in the meat-packing industry.

Through the work of these journalists, many new policies came into being, including workmen's compensation, child labor laws, and trust-busting.

Dealings with Native Americans Through the End of the 19th Century

America's westward expansion led to conflict and violent confrontations with Native Americans such as the **Battle of Little Bighorn**. In 1876, the American government ordered all Native Americans to relocate to reservations. Lack of compliance led to the **Dawes Act** in 1887, which ordered assimilation rather than separation: Native Americans were offered American citizenship and a piece of their tribal land if they would accept the lot chosen by the government and live on it separately from the tribe. This act remained in effect until 1934. Reformers also forced Native American children to attend **boarding schools**, where they were not allowed to speak their native language and were immersed into a Euro-American culture and religion. Children were often abused in these schools and were indoctrinated to abandon their identity as Native Americans.

In 1890, the massacre at **Wounded Knee**, accompanied by Geronimo's surrender, led the Native Americans to work to preserve their culture rather than fight for their lands.

> **Review Video: Government Dealings with Native Americans Through 1900**
> Visit mometrix.com/academy and enter code: 635645

Native Americans in Wartime Through the Beginning of the 20th Century

The **Spanish-American War** (1898) saw a number of Native Americans serving with Teddy Roosevelt in the Rough Riders. Apache scouts accompanied General John J. Pershing to Mexico, hoping to find **Pancho Villa**. More than 17,000 Native Americans were drafted into service for **World War I**, though at the time, they were not considered legal citizens. In 1924, Native Americans were finally granted official citizenship by the **Indian Citizenship Act**.

After decades of relocation, forced assimilation, and genocide, the number of Native Americans in the US has greatly declined. Though many Native Americans have chosen—or have been forced—to assimilate, about 300 reservations exist today, with most of their inhabitants living in abject poverty.

> **Review Video: Wartime Role of Native Americans**
> Visit mometrix.com/academy and enter code: 419128

Events Leading up to the Spanish-American War

Spain had controlled **Cuba** since the 15th century. Over the centuries, the Spanish had quashed a variety of revolts. In 1886, slavery ended in Cuba, and another revolt was rising.

In the meantime, the US had expressed interest in Cuba, offering Spain $130 million for the island in 1853, during Franklin Pierce's presidency. In 1898, the Cuban revolt was underway. In spite of various factions supporting the Cubans, the US President, William McKinley, refused to recognize the rebellion, preferring negotiation over involvement in war. Then, the *Maine*, a US battleship in Havana Harbor, was blown up, killing 266 crew members. The US declared war two months later, and the war ended with a **Spanish surrender** in less than four months.

American History 1899 to Present

Influence of Big Stick Diplomacy on American Foreign Policy in Latin America

Theodore Roosevelt's famous quote, "Speak softly and carry a big stick," is supposedly of African origins, at least according to Roosevelt. He used this proverb to justify expanded involvement in foreign affairs during his tenure as President. The US military was deployed to protect American interests in **Latin America**. Roosevelt also worked to maintain an equal or greater influence in Latin America than those held by European interests. As a result, the US Navy grew larger, and the US generally became more involved in foreign affairs. Roosevelt felt that if any country was left vulnerable to control by Europe due to economic issues or political instability, the US had not only a right to intervene but was **obligated** to do so. This led to US involvement in Cuba, Nicaragua, Haiti, and the Dominican Republic over several decades leading into the First and Second World Wars.

Importance of the Panama Canal

Initial work began on the **Panama Canal** in 1881, though the idea had been discussed since the 1500s. The canal greatly reduces the length and time needed to sail from one ocean to the other by connecting the Atlantic to the Pacific through the Isthmus of Panama, which joins South America to North America. Before the canal was built, travelers had to sail around the entire perimeter of South America to reach the West Coast of the US. The French began the work after successfully completing the **Suez Canal**, which connected the Mediterranean Sea to the Red Sea. However, due to disease and high expense, the work moved slowly, and after eight years, the company went bankrupt, suspending work. The US purchased the holdings, and the first ship sailed through the canal in 1914. The Panama Canal was constructed as a lock-and-lake canal, with ships lifted on locks to travel from one lake to another over the rugged, mountainous terrain. In order to maintain control of the Canal Zone, the US assisted Panama in its battle for independence from **Colombia**.

Taft's Dollar Diplomacy vs. Roosevelt's Diplomatic Theories

During William Howard Taft's presidency, Taft instituted "**Dollar Diplomacy**." This approach was America's effort to influence Latin America and East Asia through economic rather than military means. Taft saw past efforts in these areas to be political and warlike, while his efforts focused on peaceful economic goals. His justification of the policy was to protect the **Panama Canal**, which was vital to US trade interests.

In spite of Taft's assurance that Dollar Diplomacy was a peaceful approach, many interventions proved violent. During Latin American revolts, such as those in **Nicaragua**, the US sent troops to settle the revolutions. Afterward, bankers moved in to help support the new leaders through loans. Dollar Diplomacy continued until 1913, when Woodrow Wilson was elected president.

Growth of Civil Rights for African Americans

Marcus Garvey founded the **Universal Negro Improvement Association and African Communities League (UNIA-ACL)**, which became a large and active organization focused on building black nationalism. In 1909, the **National Association for the Advancement of Colored People (NAACP)** came into being, working to defeat Jim Crow laws. The NAACP also helped prevent racial segregation from becoming federal law, fought against lynchings, helped black soldiers in WWI become officers, and helped defend the Scottsboro Boys, who were unjustly accused of rape.

Wilson's Approach to International Diplomacy

Turning away from Taft's "Dollar Diplomacy," Wilson instituted a foreign policy he referred to as "**moral diplomacy**." This approach still influences American foreign policy today.

Wilson felt that **representative government and democracy** in all countries would lead to worldwide stability. Democratic governments, he felt, would be less likely to threaten American interests. He also saw the US and Great Britain as the great role models in this area, as well as champions of world peace and self-government. Free trade and international commerce would allow the US to speak out regarding world events.

Main elements of Wilson's policies included:

- Maintaining a strong military
- Promoting democracy throughout the world
- Expanding international trade to boost the American economy

The Sixteenth, Seventeenth, Eighteenth, and Nineteenth Amendments

The early 20th century saw several amendments made to the US Constitution:

- The **Sixteenth Amendment** (1913) established a federal income tax.
- The **Seventeenth Amendment** (1913) allowed popular election of senators.
- The **Eighteenth Amendment** (1919) prohibited the sale, production, and transportation of alcohol. This amendment was later repealed by the Twenty-first Amendment.
- The **Nineteenth Amendment** (1920) gave women the right to vote.

These amendments largely grew out of the Progressive Era, as many citizens worked to improve American society.

Goals of the Anti-Defamation League

In 1913, the Anti-Defamation League was formed to prevent anti-Semitic behavior and practices. Its actions also worked to prevent all forms of racism and to prevent individuals from being discriminated against for any reason involving their race. They spoke against the Ku Klux Klan, as well as other racist or anti-Semitic organizations. This organization still works to fight discrimination against all minorities.

Role of the Federal Trade Commission in Eliminating Trusts

Muckrakers such as Ida Tarbell and Lincoln Steffens brought to light the damaging trend of trusts—huge corporations working to monopolize areas of commerce so they could control prices and distribution. The **Sherman Antitrust Act** and the **Clayton Antitrust Act** set out guidelines for competition among corporations and set out to eliminate these trusts. The **Federal Trade Commission** was formed in 1914 in order to enforce antitrust measures and ensure that companies were operated fairly and did not create controlling monopolies.

Major Events of World War I

World War I occurred from 1914 to 1918 and was fought largely in Europe. The rise in **nationalism** at the beginning of the 20th century helped contribute to the possibility of war. There was also some conflict between the **imperialist** (France, Britain, and the US) and the **non-imperialist** (Germany, Italy) nations. Many large nations were seeking economic expansion outside of their own borders, and the competition for foreign markets was intense. There was also a complex system of entangling alliances; many countries were involved in several different alliances at the same time. The spark for World War I, though, was the assassination of **Archduke Franz Ferdinand**, heir to the throne of Austria-Hungary, in April of 1914 by a Serbian nationalist. When Emperor Franz Joseph declared war on Serbia, it set off a chain reaction that involved virtually every nation in Europe. At the beginning of the conflict, Woodrow Wilson declared the US neutral. Eventually, however, the US joined the war. Major events influencing US involvement included:

- **Sinking of the *Lusitania***—the British passenger liner RMS *Lusitania* was sunk by a German U-boat in 1915. Among the 1,000 civilian victims were over 100 American citizens. Outraged by this act, many Americans began to push for US involvement in the war, using the *Lusitania* as a rallying cry.
- **German U-boat aggression**—Wilson continued to keep the US out of the war, using as his 1916 reelection slogan, "He kept us out of war." While he continued to work toward an end of the war, German U-boats began to indiscriminately attack American and Canadian merchant ships carrying supplies to Germany's enemies in Europe.
- **Zimmerman Telegram** —the final event that brought the US into World War I was the interception of the Zimmerman Telegram (also known as the Zimmerman Note) on January 17th, 1917. In this telegram, Germany proposed forming an alliance with Mexico if the US entered the war.

Efforts in the US During World War I Supporting the War Effort

American **railroads** came under government control in December 1917. The widespread system was consolidated into a single system, with each region assigned a director. This greatly increased the efficiency of the railroad system, allowing the railroads to supply both domestic and military needs. Control returned to private ownership in 1920. In 1918, **telegraph, telephone, and cable services** also came under Federal control, to be returned to private management the next year. The **American Red Cross** supported the war effort by knitting clothes for Army and Navy troops. They also helped supply hospital and refugee clothing and surgical dressings. Over 8 million people participated in this effort. To generate wartime funds, the US government sold **Liberty Bonds**. In four issues, they sold nearly $25 billion—more than one-fifth of Americans purchased them. After the war, a fifth bond drive was held but sold "**Victory Liberty Bonds**."

Review Video: WWI Overview
Visit mometrix.com/academy and enter code: 659767

Influence of Wilson's Fourteen Points on Final Peace Treaties

President Woodrow Wilson proposed **Fourteen Points** as the basis for a peace settlement to end the war. Presented to the US Congress in January 1918, the Fourteen Points included:

- Five points outlining **general ideals**
- Eight points to resolve **immediate problems** of political and territorial nature
- One point proposing an **organization of nations** (the League of Nations) with the intent of maintaining world peace

In November of that same year, Germany agreed to an **armistice**, assuming the final treaty would be based on the Fourteen Points. However, during the peace conference in Paris 1919, there was much disagreement, leading to a final agreement that punished Germany and the other Central Powers much more than originally intended. Henry Cabot Lodge, who had become the Foreign Relations Committee chairman in 1918, wanted an unconditional surrender from Germany and was concerned about the article in the **Treaty of Versailles** that gave the League of Nations power to declare war without a vote from the US Congress. A **League of Nations** was included in the Treaty of Versailles at Wilson's insistence. The Senate rejected the Treaty of Versailles, and in the end, Wilson refused to concede to Lodge's demands. As a result, the US did not join the League of Nations.

Origins of the Red Scare

World War I created many jobs, but after the war ended, these jobs disappeared, leaving many unemployed. In the wake of these employment changes, the **International Workers of the World** and the **Socialist Party**, headed by Eugene Debs, became more and more visible. Workers initiated strikes in an attempt to regain the favorable working conditions that had been put into place before the war. Unfortunately, many of these strikes became violent, and the actions were blamed on "Reds," or Communists, for trying to spread their views into America. With the recent Bolshevik Revolution in Russia, many Americans feared a similar revolution might occur in the US. The **Red Scare** ensued, with many individuals jailed for supposedly holding communist, anarchist, or socialist beliefs.

Major Changes and Events that Took Place in America During the 1920s

The post-war 1920s saw many Americans moving from the farm to the city, with growing prosperity in the US. The **Roaring Twenties**, or the **Jazz Age**, was driven largely by growth in the automobile and entertainment industries. Individuals like Charles Lindbergh, the first aviator to make a solo flight across the Atlantic Ocean, added to the American admiration of individual accomplishment. Telephone lines, distribution of electricity, highways, the radio, and other inventions brought great changes to everyday life.

Review Video: 1920's
Visit mometrix.com/academy and enter code: 124996

Prohibition

The Eighteenth Amendment was ratified by most states in 1919, making the manufacture, sale, transportation, importation, and exportation of alcohol illegal; however, this change was not enforced with much success. Instead of curbing the production and consumption of alcohol, Prohibition led to the creation of a large, illegal alcohol market dominated by organized crime. Criminal organizations, like the Mafia crime syndicate, grew massively in power and influence during the 1920s and 1930s by cornering the market on the production, distribution, and sale of alcohol. Americans continued to drink alcohol in speakeasies—hidden, illegal drinking establishments. The huge illegal market for alcohol contributed to increased crime and unregulated, sometimes dangerous, alcohol.

Major Cultural Movements of the 1920s Influenced by African Americans

The **Harlem Renaissance** saw a number of African-American artists settling in Harlem in New York. This community produced a number of well-known artists and writers, including Langston Hughes, Nella Larsen,

Zora Neale Hurston, Claude McKay, Countee Cullen, and Jean Toomer. The growth of jazz, also largely driven by African Americans, defined the **Jazz Age**. Its unconventional, improvisational style matched the growing sense of optimism and exploration of the decade. Originating as an offshoot of the blues, jazz began in New Orleans. Some significant jazz musicians were Duke Ellington, Louis Armstrong, and Jelly Roll Morton. **Big Band** and **Swing Jazz** also developed in the 1920s. Well-known musicians of this movement included Bing Crosby, Frank Sinatra, Count Basie, Benny Goodman, Billie Holiday, Ella Fitzgerald, and The Dorsey Brothers.

American Civil Liberties Union

The American Civil Liberties Union (**ACLU**), founded in 1920, grew from the American Union Against Militarism. The ACLU helped conscientious objectors avoid going to war during WWI, and also helped those being prosecuted under the **Espionage Act** (1917) and the **Sedition Act** (1918), many of whom were immigrants. Their major goals were to protect immigrants and other citizens who were threatened with prosecution for their political beliefs, and to support labor unions, which were also under threat by the government during the Red Scare.

Womens' Suffrage

The Nineteenth Amendment gave **women the right to vote**. This amendment was proposed on June 4, 1919, and was ratified on August 18, 1920. An amendment to give women the right to vote was first introduced in Congress in 1878, but it failed to pass. For the next four decades, the amendment was reintroduced in every session of Congress but was defeated each time. The involvement of women in the war effort during World War I spawned increased support for women's suffrage. Finally, in 1918, the House of Representatives approved the amendment to grant women suffrage, but the Senate defeated it. In 1919, the Senate also passed the amendment and sent it to the states for approval, where it was ratified in 1920.

Provisions and Importance of the National Origins Act of 1924

The National Origins Act (Johnson-Reed Act) placed limitations on **immigration**. The number of immigrants allowed into the US was based on the population of each nationality of immigrants who were living in the country in 1890. Only two percent of each nationality's 1890 population numbers were allowed to immigrate. This led to great disparities between immigrants from various nations, and Asian immigration was not allowed at all. Some of the impetus behind the Johnson-Reed Act came as a result of paranoia following the **Russian Revolution**. Fear of communist influences in the US led to a general fear of immigrants.

Ku Klux Klan

In 1866, Confederate Army veterans came together to fight against Reconstruction in the South, forming a group called the **Ku Klux Klan (KKK)**. With white supremacist beliefs, including anti-Semitism, nativism, anti-Catholicism, and overt racism, this organization relied heavily on violence to get its message across. In 1915, they grew again in power, using a film called *The Birth of a Nation*, by D.W. Griffith, to spread their ideas. In the 1920s, the reach of the KKK spread far into the north and midwest, and members controlled a number of state governments. Its membership and power began to decline during the Great Depression but experienced a resurgence later.

The Great Depression

The **Great Depression** was the largest economic downturn in the history of the United States. It began in 1929 with the stock market crash and ended around 1939. The Great Depression grew out of several factors that had developed over the previous years, including:

- Growing economic disparity between the rich and middle classes, with the rich amassing wealth much more quickly than the lower classes
- Disparity in economic distribution in industries
- Growing use of credit, leading to an inflated demand for some goods
- Government support of new industries rather than agriculture
- Risky stock market investments, leading to the stock market crash

Additional factors contributing to the Depression also included the **Labor Day Hurricane** in the Florida Keys (1935) and the **Great Hurricane of 1938** in New England, along with the **Dust Bowl** in the Great Plains, which destroyed crops and resulted in the displacement of as many as 2.5 million people.

Review Video: Causes of the Great Depression
Visit mometrix.com/academy and enter code: 635912

The Dust Bowl

The Dust Bowl (1930-1941) was a period of American history characterized by a high incidence of dust storms in the Great Plains region. The instability of the world agriculture market during World War I led to overproduction in the 1920s. Even lands previously considered unsuitable for agricultural use were leveled and developed. This excessive activity devastated the Great Plains, eliminating the natural vegetation that could have prevented the massive soil movement that occurred during the drought and strong winds of the 1930s, and resulted in widespread crop failure. In turn, the Dust Bowl led to millions of people being displaced from their homes and hundreds of thousands migrating to California in search of work and better living conditions. On their journeys, however, these migrants faced poor conditions, starvation, and dehydration. Even when they arrived in California, many of them struggled to find work. The work that was available was often hard labor, like picking cotton. Migrants also faced hostility and even phyisical violence from locals. They were often forced to live in roadside camps, which were sometimes the target of arson.

Franklin D. Roosevelt's Election and New Deal

Franklin D. Roosevelt was elected president in 1932 with his promise of a "**New Deal**" for Americans. His goals were to provide government work programs to provide jobs, wages, and relief to numerous workers throughout the beleaguered US. Congress gave Roosevelt almost free rein to produce relief legislation. The goals of this legislation were:

- **Relief**—creating jobs for the high numbers of unemployed
- **Recovery**—stimulating the economy through the National Recovery Administration
- **Reform**—passing legislation to prevent future, similar economic crashes

The Roosevelt Administration also passed legislation regarding ecological issues, including the Soil Conservation Service, aimed at preventing another Dust Bowl.

Roosevelt's Alphabet Organizations

So-called "alphabet organizations" set up during Roosevelt's administration included:

- **Civilian Conservation Corps** (CCC)—provided jobs in the forestry service
- **Agricultural Adjustment Administration** (AAA)—increased agricultural income by adjusting both production and prices
- **Tennessee Valley Authority** (TVA)—organized projects to build dams in the Tennessee River for flood control and production of electricity, resulting in increased productivity for industries in the area, and easier navigation of the Tennessee River
- **Public Works Administration** (PWA) and Civil Works Administration (CWA)—provided a multitude of jobs, initiating over 34,000 projects
- **Works Progress Administration** (WPA)—helped unemployed persons to secure employment on government work projects or elsewhere

Actions Taken During the Roosevelt Administration to Prevent Future Crashes

The Roosevelt administration passed several laws and established several institutions to initiate the "reform" portion of the New Deal, including:

- **Glass-Steagall Act**—separated investment from commercial banking
- **Securities Exchange Commission (SEC)**—helped regulate Wall Street investment practices, making them less dangerous to the overall economy
- **Wagner Act**—provided worker and union rights to improve relations between employees and employers
- **Social Security Act of 1935**—provided pensions as well as unemployment insurance

Other actions focused on insuring bank deposits and adjusting the value of American currency. Most of these regulatory agencies and government policies and programs still exist today.

Major Regulations Regarding Labor During the Great Depression

Three major regulations regarding labor that were passed after the Great Depression are:

- **Davis-Bacon Act** (1931)—provided fair compensation for contractors and subcontractors.
- The **Wagner Act** (1935)—also known as the National Labor Relations Act, it established that unions were legal, protected members of unions, and required collective bargaining. This act was later amended by the Taft-Hartley Act of 1947 and the Landrum-Griffin Act of 1959, which further clarified certain elements.
- **Walsh-Healey Act** (1936)—established a minimum wage, child labor laws, safety standards, and overtime pay.

World War II

America's Introduction to WWII

After the First World War, the US became obsessed with isolating itself from foreign conflicts. The **Nye Committee** studied the war and determined that it had been fought for financial reasons and could have been avoided. Isolationist parties achieved some popularity during this period, including the **America First Committee**, led by Charles Lindbergh, and **SOS** (Stop Organized Slaughter). The **Neutrality Laws** of 1935-7 declared that the US could not sell weapons to another country in a time of war and that US citizens could not travel on the ships of a nation at war. In 1937, FDR delivered the **Quarantine Speech**, in which he asserted that the Nazi "disease" must be contained. Finally, after conflict in Europe had escalated considerably, FDR declared that the US needed to help Britain and be an "arsenal of democracy in the world." The **Neutrality Act of 1940** made it legal for the US to sell weapons on a cash and carry basis. In August of 1941, FDR and Churchill drew up the **Atlantic Charter**, which vowed to destroy Nazism, protect the right of self-determination, and create a World Peace Organization.

Buildup to the Attack on Pearl Harbor

A number of events had created a stormy relationship between the US and Japan long before the invasion of Pearl Harbor, but the conflict reached a boiling point after President Roosevelt froze all Japanese assets in the US and cut Japan off from US oil and steel. America also had a cordial relationship at this time with Japan's longtime rival, China. The Japanese launched surprise attacks both on the American naval base at **Pearl Harbor** and on the **Philippines**, where they hoped to secure some oil.

US Involvement in WWII Concerning Europe and Africa

After the Japanese attack on Pearl Harbor in 1941, the US declared **war** on Japan, after which Germany declared war on the US. Before going after Japan, however, the US first attacked Germany; this was done because the US underestimated Japan industrially and militarily, and because the US feared Britain was on the verge of defeat. **Operation Overlord**, the Allied invasion of the European continent at Normandy, was led in part by General **Dwight D. Eisenhower**. The American generals Omar Bradley and George Patton took part in the **Allied Operation Torch**, aimed at taking back North Africa. At the **Battle of the Bulge**, in Belgium, the Germans tried to break the Allied lines, but were unsuccessful, in part because of the heroism of American soldiers.

US Involvement in WWII Concerning Asia and the Pacific

The US strategy for controlling the Pacific was known as "island hopping." In the **Coral Sea Battle of 1942**, Americans stopped the Japanese from taking Australia and New Guinea. In the same year, the **Doolittle raids** of Japanese naval bases boosted American morale. In the **Battle of Midway** (1942), the US sunk four Japanese aircraft carriers. In the **Battle of Leyte Gulf**, General Douglas MacArthur took back the Philippines and also took control of Iwo Jima and Okinawa. During this period, a team of American scientists led by Robert Oppenheimer was developing the **atomic bomb** in Los Alamos, New Mexico. Japan was warned several times by President Truman that the bomb would be used if they did not surrender. Surely enough, Americans dropped atomic bombs on **Hiroshima** on August 6, 1945, and on **Nagasaki** three days later. Japanese leaders surrendered aboard the USS Missouri on August 15, 1945.

The Holocaust is the name given to the systematic killing of Jews, Gypsies, homosexuals, and others by the Nazis. **Anti-Semitism** had existed in Europe for a long time, but the Nazis gave it renewed emphasis and, after making numerous false claims about Jews, began persecuting them upon Hitler's rise to power in 1933. Jews were disenfranchised, forced into ghettos, had their property taken, and were finally sent to work and be killed in **concentration camps**. Approximately 6 million Jews were killed during the **Holocaust**. As the situation for the Germans became more dire in the Second World War, Hitler sought to implement what he called the "final solution," in which hundreds of thousands were killed just before the fall of Nazi Germany.

Interventionist and Isolationist Approaches in World War II

When war broke out in Europe in 1939, President Roosevelt stated that the US would remain **neutral**. However, his overall approach was considered "**interventionist**," as he was willing to provide aid to the Allies without actually entering the conflict. Thus, the US supplied a wide variety of war materials to the Allied nations in the early years of the war.

Isolationists believed the US should not provide any aid to the Allies, including supplies. They felt Roosevelt, by assisting the Allies, was leading the US into a war for which it was not prepared. Led by Charles Lindbergh, the Isolationists believed that any involvement in the European conflict endangered the US by weakening its national defense.

Sequence of Events that Led the US to Declare War and Enter World War II

In 1937, Japan invaded China, prompting the US to eventually halt exports to Japan. Roosevelt also did not allow Japanese interests to withdraw money held in US banks. In 1941, **General Tojo** rose to power as the Japanese prime minister. Recognizing America's ability to bring a halt to Japan's expansion, he authorized the bombing of **Pearl Harbor** on December 7. The US responded by declaring war on Japan. Partially because of the **Tripartite Pact** among the Axis Powers, Germany and Italy then declared war on the US, later followed by Bulgaria, Hungary, and other Axis nations.

Review Video: World War II Overview
Visit mometrix.com/academy and enter code: 759402

Occurrences of World War II that Led to the Surrender of Germany

In 1941, **Hitler** violated the non-aggression pact he had signed with Stalin two years earlier by invading the USSR. **Stalin** then joined the **Allies**. Stalin, Roosevelt, and Winston Churchill planned to defeat Germany first, then Japan, bringing the war to an end.

In 1942-1943, the Allies drove **Axis** forces out of Africa. In addition, the Germans were soundly defeated at Stalingrad.

The **Italian Campaign** involved Allied operations in Italy between July 1943 and May 1945, including Italy's liberation. On June 6, 1944, known as **D-Day**, the Allies invaded France at Normandy. Soviet troops moved on the eastern front at the same time, driving German forces back. By April 25, 1945, Berlin was surrounded by Soviet troops. On May 7, Germany surrendered.

Major Events of World War II that Led to the Surrender of Japan

War continued with **Japan** after Germany's surrender. Japanese forces had taken a large portion of Southeast Asia and the Western Pacific, all the way to the Aleutian Islands in Alaska. **General Doolittle** bombed several Japanese cities while American troops scored a victory at Midway. Additional fighting in the Battle of the Coral Sea further weakened Japan's position. As a final blow, the US dropped two **atomic bombs** on Japan, one on Hiroshima and the other on Nagasaki. This was the first time atomic bombs had been used in warfare, and the devastation was horrific and demoralizing. Japan surrendered on September 2, 1945, which became **V-J Day** in the US.

The 442nd Regimental Combat Team, Tuskegee Airmen, and Navajo Code Talkers

The 442nd Regimental Combat Team consisted of Japanese-Americans fighting in Europe for the US. The most highly decorated unit per member in US history, they suffered a 93% casualty rate during the war. The **Tuskegee Airmen** were African American aviators, the first black Americans allowed to fly for the military. In spite of being ineligible to become official navy pilots, they flew over 15,000 missions and were highly decorated. The **Navajo Code Talkers** were native Navajo who used their traditional language to transmit information among Allied forces. Because Navajo is a highly-complex and unwritten language and not simply a code, the Axis powers were never able to translate it. The use of Navajo Code Talkers to transmit information was instrumental in the taking of Iwo Jima and other major victories of the war.

Circumstances and Opportunities for Women During World War II

Women served widely in the military during WWII, working in numerous positions, including the **Flight Nurses Corps**. Women also moved into the workforce while men were overseas, leading to over 19 million women in the US workforce by 1944. **Rosie the Riveter** stood as a symbol of these women and a means of recruiting others to take needed positions. Women, as well as their families left behind during wartime, also grew **Victory Gardens** to help provide food.

Japanese-American Internment During World War II

Following the attack on Pearl Harbor, the American government began to suspect that people of Japanese ancestry in America may be operating as spies for Japan, though there was little evidence for this. Just a couple of months after the attack, President Franklin D. Roosevelt signed Executive Order 9066, which allowed the government to declare Military Exclusion Zones for the purpose of national security. This made it legal for the military to remove people or other perceived threats from these exclusion zones. As a result, over 100,000 people of Japanese ancestry were removed from their homes in these areas and placed into internment camps. These camps were hastily built and offered poor living conditions. Children interned in these camps did not have access to a full education, and many Japanese-Americans lost their businesses and homes as a result of their internment.

In **Korematsu v. US** (1944), the Supreme Court ruled that the internment camps were legal, but in **ex parte Endo** (1944), the Court adjusted its decision to state that the US could only intern those whose disloyalty could be proven. Japanese internment ended in 1945, but the effects of internment on Japanese-Americans endured.

Importance of the Atomic Bomb During World War II

The atomic bomb, developed during WWII, was the most powerful bomb ever invented. A single bomb, carried by a single plane, held enough power to destroy an entire city. This devastating effect was demonstrated with the bombing of **Hiroshima** and **Nagasaki** in 1945 in what later became a controversial move, but ended the war. The bombings resulted in as many as 150,000 immediate deaths and many more as time passed after the bombings, mostly due to **radiation poisoning**.

Whatever the arguments against the use of "The Bomb," the post-WWII era saw many countries develop similar weapons to match the newly expanded military power of the US. The impact of those developments and use of nuclear weapons continues to haunt international relations today.

IMPORTANCE OF THE YALTA CONFERENCE AND THE POTSDAM CONFERENCE

In February 1945, Joseph Stalin, Franklin D. Roosevelt, and Winston Churchill met in Yalta to discuss the post-war treatment of the **Axis nations**, particularly Germany. Though Germany had not yet surrendered, its defeat was imminent. After Germany's official surrender, Joseph Stalin, Harry Truman (Roosevelt's successor), and Clement Attlee (replacing Churchill partway through the conference) met to formalize those plans. This meeting was called the **Potsdam Conference**. Basic provisions of these agreements included:

- Dividing Germany and Berlin into four zones of occupation
- Demilitarization of Germany
- Poland remaining under Soviet control
- Outlawing the Nazi Party
- Trials for Nazi leaders
- Relocation of numerous German citizens
- The USSR joining the United Nations, established in 1945
- Establishment of the United Nations Security Council, consisting of the US, the UK, the USSR, China, and France

AGREEMENTS MADE WITH POST-WAR JAPAN

General Douglas MacArthur led the American **military occupation of Japan** after the country surrendered. The goals of the US occupation included removing Japan's military and making the country a democracy. A 1947 constitution removed power from the emperor and gave it to the people, as well as granting voting rights to women. Japan was no longer allowed to declare war, and a group of 28 government officials were tried for war crimes. In 1951, the US finally signed a peace treaty with Japan. This treaty allowed Japan to rearm itself for purposes of self-defense but stripped the country of the empire it had built overseas.

US TREATMENT OF IMMIGRANTS DURING AND AFTER WORLD WAR II

In 1940, the US passed the **Alien Registration Act**, which required all aliens older than fourteen to be fingerprinted and registered. They were also required to report changes of address within five days.

Tension between whites and Japanese immigrants in **California**, which had been building since the beginning of the century, came to a head with the bombing of **Pearl Harbor** in 1941. Believing that even those Japanese living in the US were likely to be loyal to their native country, the president ordered numerous Japanese to be arrested on suspicion of subversive action and isolated in exclusion zones known as **War Relocation Camps**. Approximately 120,000 Japanese-Americans, two-thirds of them US citizens, were sent to these camps during the war.

GENERAL STATE OF THE US AFTER WORLD WAR II

Following WWII, the US became the strongest political power in the world, becoming a major player in world affairs and foreign policies. The US determined to stop the spread of **communism**, having named itself the "**arsenal of democracy**" during the war. In addition, America emerged with a greater sense of itself as a single, integrated nation, with many regional and economic differences diminished. The government worked for greater equality, and the growth of communications increased contact among different areas of the country. Both the aftermath of the Great Depression and the necessities of WWII had given the government greater **control** over various institutions as well as the economy. This also meant that the American government took on greater responsibility for the well-being of its citizens, both in the domestic arena, such as providing basic needs, and in protecting them from foreign threats. This increased role of providing basic necessities for all Americans has been criticized by some as "**the welfare state.**"

Fear of Communism Following World War II

After World War II, America became greatly concerned with the spread of communism, which was being propagated mainly by the Soviet Union and the communist party in China. A series of policies in America, Western Europe, and the Soviet Union brought the anti-communist and communist groups ever closer to open conflict. As these tensions grew in the international community, Americans became increasingly paranoid about the spread of **Communism**. There were numerous investigations aimed at weeding Communist spies out of the government, and two people, Julius and Ethel Rosenberg, were executed for spying. The leader of much of this was Senator **Joseph McCarthy**, who was famous for promoting and prolonging the "**Red Scare**" as the often-termed witch-hunt for communists in the government was known (Soviet communications released after the fall of the Soviet Union confirmed the vast majority of his accusations). The tide of anti-communism extended into a general disapproval of organized labor. The **Taft-Hartley Act** restricted the ability of labor unions markedly. In order to survive, the nation's two largest labor unions combined, forming the **AFL-CIO**.

US Policy Toward Immigrants After World War II

Prior to WWII, the US had been limiting **immigration** for several decades. After WWII, policy shifted slightly to accommodate political refugees from Europe and elsewhere. So many people were displaced by the war that in 1946, the UN formed the **International Refugee Organization** to deal with the problem. In 1948, the US Congress passed the **Displaced Persons Act**, which allowed over 400,000 European refugees to enter the US, most of them concentration camp survivors and refugees from Eastern Europe.

In 1952, the **United States Escapee Program (USEP)** increased the quotas, allowing refugees from communist Europe to enter the US, as did the **Refugee Relief Act**, passed in 1953. At the same time, however, the **Internal Security Act of 1950** allowed deportation of declared communists, and Asians were subjected to a quota based on race, rather than country of origin. Later changes included:

- **Migration and Refugee Assistance Act** (1962)—provided aid for refugees in need
- **Immigration and Nationality Act** (1965)—ended quotas based on nation of origin
- **Immigration Reform and Control Act** (1986)—prohibited the hiring of illegal immigrants but also granted amnesty to about three million illegals already in the country

Accomplishments of Harry S. Truman

Harry S. Truman took over the presidency from Franklin D. Roosevelt near the end of WWII. He made the final decision to drop atomic bombs on Japan and played a major role in the final decisions regarding the treatment of post-war Germany. On the domestic front, Truman initiated a 21-point plan known as the **Fair Deal**. This plan expanded Social Security, provided public housing, and made the Fair Employment Practice Committee permanent. Truman helped support Greece and Turkey (which were under threat from the USSR), supported South Korea against communist North Korea, and helped with recovery in Western Europe. He also participated in the formation of **NATO**, the North Atlantic Treaty Organization.

Events and Importance of the Korean War

The Korean War began in 1950 and ended in 1953. For the first time in history, a world organization—the **United Nations**—played a military role in a war. North Korea sent communist troops into South Korea, seeking to bring the entire country under communist control. The UN sent out a call to member nations, asking them to support South Korea. Truman sent troops, as did many other UN member nations. The war ended three years later with a **truce** rather than a peace treaty, and Korea remains divided at the **38th parallel north**, with communist rule remaining in the North and a democratic government ruling the South.

Effects of US Cold War Foreign Policy Acts on the International Relationships

The following are US Cold War foreign policy acts and how they affected international relationships, especially between the US and the Soviet Union:

- **Marshall Plan**—this sent aid to war-torn Europe after WWII, largely focusing on preventing the spread of communism.
- **Containment Policy**—proposed by George F. Kennan, the containment policy focused on containing the spread of Soviet communism.
- **Truman Doctrine**—Harry S. Truman stated that the US would provide both economic and military support to any country threatened by Soviet takeover.
- **National Security Act**—passed in 1947, this act reorganized the government's military departments into the Department of Defense and created the Central Intelligence Agency and the National Security Council.

The combination of these acts led to the **Cold War**, with Soviet communists attempting to spread their influence and the US and other countries trying to contain or stop this spread.

Accomplishments of Dwight D. Eisenhower

Eisenhower carried out a middle-of-the-road foreign policy and brought the US several steps forward in equal rights. He worked to minimize tensions during the Cold War and negotiated a peace treaty with Russia after the death of Stalin. He enforced desegregation by sending troops to Little Rock Central High School in Arkansas, as well as ordering the desegregation of the military. Organizations formed during his administration included the Department of Health, Education, and Welfare, and the National Aeronautics and Space Administration (NASA).

Effect of the Arms Race on Post WWII International Relations

After World War II, major nations, particularly the US and USSR, rushed to develop highly advanced weapons systems such as the **atomic bomb** and later the **hydrogen bomb**. These countries seemed determined to outpace each other with the development of numerous, deadly weapons. These weapons were expensive and extremely dangerous, and it is possible that the war between US and Soviet interests remained "cold" due to the fear that one side or the other would use these powerful weapons.

Technological Advances that Occurred Throughout the 1900s

Numerous technological advances throughout the 1900s led to more effective treatment of diseases, more efficient communication and transportation, and new means of generating power. Advances in **medicine** increased the human lifespan in developed countries, and near-instantaneous **communication** opened up a myriad of possibilities. Some of these advances include:

- Discovery of penicillin (1928)
- Supersonic air travel (1947)
- Nuclear power plants (1951)
- Orbital satellite leading to manned space flight (Sputnik, 1957)
- First man on the moon (1969)

NATO, Warsaw Pact, and the Berlin Wall

NATO, the **North Atlantic Treaty Organization**, came into being in 1949. It essentially amounted to an agreement among the US and Western European countries that an attack on any one of these countries was to be considered an attack against the entire group. Under the influence of the Soviet Union, the Eastern European countries of the USSR, Bulgaria, East Germany, Poland, Romania, Albania, Hungary, and Czechoslovakia responded with the **Warsaw Pact**, which created a similar agreement among those nations. In 1961, a wall was built to separate communist East Berlin from democratic West Berlin. This was a literal representation of the "**Iron Curtain**" that separated the democratic and communist countries throughout the world.

Presidency of John F. Kennedy

Although his term was cut short by his assassination, **JFK** instituted economic programs that led to a period of continuous expansion in the US unmatched since before WWII. He formed the Alliance for Progress and the Peace Corps, organizations intended to help developing nations. He also oversaw the passage of new civil rights legislation and drafted plans to attack poverty and its causes, along with support of the arts. Kennedy's presidency ended when he was assassinated by **Lee Harvey Oswald** in 1963.

Events of the Cuban Missile Crisis

The Cuban Missile Crisis occurred in 1962, during John F. Kennedy's presidency. Russian Premier **Nikita Khrushchev** decided to place nuclear missiles in **Cuba** to protect the island from invasion by the US. An American U-2 plane flying over the island photographed the missile bases as they were being built. Tensions rose, with the US concerned about nuclear missiles so close to its shores, and the USSR concerned about American missiles that had been placed in **Turkey**. Eventually, the missile sites were removed, and a US naval blockade turned back Soviet ships carrying missiles to Cuba. During negotiations, the US agreed to remove their missiles from Turkey and agreed to sell surplus wheat to the USSR. A telephone hotline between Moscow and Washington was set up to allow instant communication between the two heads of state to prevent similar incidents in the future.

Accomplishments of the Lyndon B. Johnson Presidency

Kennedy's vice president, **Lyndon Johnson**, assumed the presidency after Kennedy's **assassination**. He supported civil rights bills, tax cuts, and other wide-reaching legislation that Kennedy had also supported. Johnson saw America as a "**Great Society**," and enacted legislation to fight disease and poverty, renew urban areas, and support education and environmental conservation. Medicare and Medicaid were instituted under his administration. He continued Kennedy's support of space exploration, and he is also known, although less positively, for his handling of the **Vietnam War**.

Factors that Led to the Growth of the Civil Rights Movement

In the 1950s, post-war America was experiencing a rapid growth in prosperity; however, African Americans found themselves left behind. Racial segregation and discrimination were still legalized at this time and disproportionately affected black Americans and other minority groups. The civil rights movement arose to abolish legalized discrimination and provide equality for all Americans. While there were many different ideologies that made up the civil rights movement, the movement is largely characterized by peaceful protest and civil disobedience.

- **Rosa Parks**—often called the "mother of the Civil Rights Movement," her refusal to give up her seat on the bus to a white man served as a seed from which the movement grew.
- **Martin Luther King, Jr.**—the best-known leader of the movement, King drew on Gandhi's beliefs and encouraged non-violent opposition. He led a march on Washington in 1963, received the Nobel Peace Prize in 1964, and was assassinated in 1968.
- **Malcolm X**—espousing less peaceful means of change, Malcolm X became a Black Muslim and supported black nationalism.

Policies and Legislation Enacted Expanding Minority Rights

Several major acts have been passed, particularly since WWII, to protect the rights of minorities in America. These include:

- Civil Rights Act (1964)
- Voting Rights Act (1965)

- Age Discrimination Act (1967)
- Americans with Disabilities Act (1990)

Other important movements for civil rights included a prisoner's rights movement, movements for immigrant rights, and the women's rights movement. The National Organization for Women (NOW) was established in 1966 and worked to pass the Equal Rights Amendment. The amendment was passed, but not enough states ratified it for it to become part of the US Constitution.

Impact of Stokely Carmichael, Adam Clayton Powell, and Jesse Jackson

- **Stokely Carmichael**—Carmichael originated the term "Black Power" and served as head of the Student Nonviolent Coordinating Committee. He believed in black pride and black culture and felt separate political and social institutions should be developed for blacks.
- **Adam Clayton Powell**—chairman of the Coordinating Committee for Employment, he led rent strikes and other actions, as well as a bus boycott, to increase the hiring of blacks.
- **Jesse Jackson**—Jackson was selected to head the Chicago Operation Breadbasket in 1966, and went on to organize boycotts and other actions. He also had an unsuccessful run for president.

Events of the Civil Rights Movement

Major events of the Civil Rights Movement include:

- **Montgomery Bus Boycott**—in 1955, Rosa Parks refused to give her seat on the bus to a white man. As a result, she was tried and convicted of disorderly conduct and of violating local ordinances. A 381-day bus boycott ensued, protesting segregation on public buses.
- **Desegregation of Little Rock**—in 1957, after the Supreme Court decision on Brown v. Board of Education, which declared "separate but equal" unconstitutional, the Arkansas school board voted to desegregate their schools. Even though Arkansas was considered progressive, its governor brought in the Arkansas National Guard to prevent nine black students from entering Central High School in Little Rock. President Eisenhower responded by federalizing the National Guard and ordering them to stand down.
- **Birmingham Campaign**—protestors organized a variety of actions such as sit-ins and an organized march to launch a voting campaign. When the City of Birmingham declared the protests illegal, the protestors, including Martin Luther King, Jr., persisted and were arrested and jailed.
- **March on Washington**—on August 28, 1963, more than 200,000 people marched on Washington, D.C. to advocate for civil and economic rights for African Americans. Dr. Martin Luther King Jr., positioned near the Lincoln Memorial, gave his famous "I Have a Dream" speech. This march was heavily influential in passing the Civil Rights Act of 1964.

Pieces of Legislation Passed as a Result of the Civil Rights Movement

Other pieces of legislation passed as a result of the Civil Rights movement include:

- **Brown v. Board of Education** (1954)—the Supreme Court declared that "separate but equal" accommodations and services were unconstitutional.
- **Civil Rights Act of 1964**—this declared discrimination illegal in employment, education, or public accommodation.
- **Voting Rights Act of 1965**—this act ended various activities practiced, mostly in the South, to bar blacks from exercising their voting rights. These included poll taxes and literacy tests.
- **Fair Housing Act of 1968**—this act prohibited discrimination in the sale, purchase, and rental of housing.

Other pieces of legislation that expanded minority rights include the Age Discrimination Act (1967) and the Americans with Disabilities Act (1990). Other important movements for civil rights included prisoners' rights movements, movements for immigrant rights, and the women's rights movement. The National Organization for Women (NOW) was established in 1966 and worked to pass the Equal Rights Amendment. The amendment was passed, but not enough states ratified it for it to become part of the US Constitution.

Events of the Richard Nixon Presidency

Richard Nixon is best known for the **Watergate scandal** during his presidency, but other important events marked his tenure as president, including:

- End of the Vietnam War
- Improved diplomatic relations between the US and China, and the US and the USSR
- National Environmental Policy Act passed, providing for environmental protection
- Compulsory draft ended
- Supreme Court legalized abortion in Roe v. Wade (subsequently overturned in 2022)
- Watergate

The Watergate scandal of 1972 ended Nixon's presidency. Rather than face impeachment and removal from office, he **resigned** in 1974.

US Perspective on the Progression of the Vietnam War

After World War II, the US pledged, as part of its foreign policy, to come to the assistance of any country threatened by **communism**. When Vietnam was divided into a communist North and democratic South, much like Korea before it, the eventual attempts by the North to unify the country under Communist rule led to intervention by the US. On the home front, the **Vietnam War** became more and more unpopular politically, with Americans growing increasingly discontent with the inability of the US to achieve the goals it had set for the Asian country. When President **Richard Nixon** took office in 1969, his escalation of the war led to protests at Kent State in Ohio, during which several students were killed by National Guard troops. Protests continued, eventually resulting in the end of the compulsory draft in 1973. In that same year, the US departed Vietnam. In 1975, the South surrendered, and Vietnam became a unified country under communist rule.

Events of the Gerald Ford Presidency

Gerald Ford was appointed to the vice presidency after Nixon's vice president **Spiro Agnew** resigned in 1973 under charges of tax evasion. With Nixon's resignation, Ford became president.

Ford's presidency saw negotiations with Russia to limit nuclear arms, as well as struggles to deal with inflation, economic downturn, and energy shortages. Ford's policies sought to reduce governmental control of various businesses and reduce the role of government overall. He also worked to prevent escalation of conflicts in the Middle East.

End of the Cold War and the Dissolution of the Soviet Union

In the late 1980s, **Mikhail Gorbachev** led the Soviet Union. He introduced a series of reform programs. **Ronald Reagan** famously urged Gorbachev to tear down the **Berlin Wall** as a gesture of growing freedom in the Eastern Bloc, and in 1989 it was demolished, ending the separation of East and West Germany. The Soviet Union relinquished its power over the various republics in Eastern Europe, and they became independent nations with their own individual governments. In 1991, the **USSR** was dissolved and the Cold War also came to an end.

Review Video: The End of the Cold War
Visit mometrix.com/academy and enter code: 278032

EVENTS OF THE JIMMY CARTER PRESIDENCY

Jimmy Carter was elected as president in 1976. Faced with a budget deficit, high unemployment, and continued inflation, Carter also dealt with numerous matters of international diplomacy, including:

- **Torrijos-Carter Treaties**—the US gave control of the Panama Canal to Panama.
- **Camp David Accords**—negotiations between Anwar el-Sadat, the president of Egypt, and Menachem Begin, the Israeli Prime Minister, led to a peace treaty between Egypt and Israel.
- **Strategic Arms Limitation Talks (SALT)**—these led to agreements and treaties between the US and the Soviet Union.
- **Iran Hostage Crisis**—after the Shah of Iran was deposed, an Islamic cleric, Ayatollah Khomeini, came to power. The shah came to the US for medical treatment, and Iran demanded his return so he could stand trial. In retaliation, a group of Iranian students stormed the US Embassy in Iran. Fifty-two American hostages were held for 444 days.

Jimmy Carter was awarded the **Nobel Peace Prize** in 2002.

EVENTS OF THE RONALD REAGAN PRESIDENCY

Ronald Reagan, at 69, became the oldest American president. The two terms of his administration included notable events such as:

- Reaganomics, also known as supply-side, trickle-down, or free-market economics, involving major tax cuts
- Economic Recovery Tax Act of 1981
- First female justice appointed to the Supreme Court—Sandra Day O'Connor
- Massive increase in the national debt—from $1 trillion to $3 trillion
- Reduction of nuclear weapons via negotiations with Mikhail Gorbachev
- Iran-Contra scandal—cover-up of US involvement in revolutions in El Salvador and Nicaragua
- Deregulation of savings and loan industry
- Loss of the space shuttle *Challenger*

EVENTS OF THE GEORGE H. W. BUSH PRESIDENCY

Reagan's presidency was followed by a term under his former vice president, **George H. W. Bush**. Bush's run for president included the famous "**thousand points of light**" speech, which was instrumental in increasing his standing in the election polls. During Bush's presidency, numerous international events took place, including:

- Fall of the Berlin wall and Germany's unification
- Panamanian dictator Manuel Noriega captured and tried on drug and racketeering charges
- Dissolution of the Soviet Union
- Gulf War, or Operation Desert Storm, triggered by Iraq's invasion of Kuwait
- Tiananmen Square Massacre in Beijing, China
- Ruby Ridge
- The arrival of the World Wide Web

EVENTS OF THE WILLIAM CLINTON PRESIDENCY

William Jefferson "Bill" Clinton was the second president in US history to be impeached, but he was not convicted, and maintained high approval ratings in spite of the impeachment. Major events during his presidency included:

- Family and Medical Leave Act
- "Don't Ask, Don't Tell," a compromise position regarding homosexuals serving in the military

- North American Free Trade Agreement, or NAFTA
- Defense of Marriage Act
- Oslo Accords
- Siege at Waco, Texas, involving the Branch Davidians led by David Koresh
- Bombing of the Murrah Federal Building in Oklahoma City, Oklahoma
- Troops sent to Haiti, Bosnia, and Somalia to assist with domestic problems in those areas

Events of the George W. Bush Presidency

George W. Bush, son of George H. W. Bush, became president after Clinton. Major events during his presidency included:

- September 11, 2001, al-Qaeda terrorists hijack commercial airliners and fly into the World Trade Center towers and the Pentagon, killing nearly 3,000 Americans
- US troops sent to Afghanistan to hunt down al-Qaeda leaders, including the head of the organization, Osama Bin Laden; beginning of the War on Terror
- US troops sent to Iraq, along with a multinational coalition, to depose Saddam Hussein and prevent his deployment of suspected weapons of mass destruction
- Subprime mortgage crisis and near collapse of the financial industry, leading to the Great Recession; first of multiple government bailouts of the financial industry

Events of the Barack Obama Presidency

In 2008, Barack Obama, a senator from Illinois, became the first African American US president. His administration focused on improving the lot of a country suffering from a major recession. His major initiatives included:

- Economic bailout packages
- Improvements in women's rights
- Moves to broaden LGBT rights
- Health care reform legislation
- Reinforcement of the war in Afghanistan

Events of the Donald Trump Presidency

In 2016, Donald Trump, previously a real estate developer and television personality, was elected 45th president after a tumultuous election in which he won the electoral college but lost the popular vote. Marked by tension between the administration and domestic media, Trump's initiatives included:

- Appointing three Supreme Court Justices: Neil Gorsuch, Brett Kavanaugh, and Amy Coney Barrett
- Passing a major tax reform bill
- Enacting travel and emigration restrictions on eight nations: Iran, Libya, Syria, Yemen, Somalia, Chad, North Korea, and Venezuela
- Recognizing Jerusalem, rather than Tel Aviv, as the capital of Israel
- Responding to the novel coronavirus (SARS-CoV-2) outbreak

Almost completely along party lines, Donald Trump was impeached by the House on charges of abuse of power and obstruction of Congress; he was acquitted by the Senate.

Texas History

History of Texas

The history of Texas (as part of the United States) began in 1845, but settlement of the region dates back to the end of the **Upper Paleolithic Period**, around 10,000 BC. Its history has been shaped by being part of **six independent countries**: Spain, France, Mexico, the Republic of Texas, the Confederacy, and the United States. Starting in the 1820s, American and European immigrants began arriving in the area; joined by Hispanic Tejanos they revolted against a very culturally distant Mexico in 1836 in search of state freedom and defeated an invasion army led by General Antonio López de Santa Anna. After nearly a decade as an independent country, the Republic of Texas joined the **Union** (the United States) in 1845. The name Texas derives from táysha, a word in the **Caddoan** language of the Hasinai, which means "friends" or "allies."

People Indigenous to Texas

Texas lies within the regions of three North American civilizations which had reached their developmental peak prior to the arrival of European explorers: the **Pueblo** from the upper Rio Grande region, the **Mound Builder** of the Mississippi Valley region, and the civilizations of the **pre-Colombian** cultures of Mexico and Central America. Native American tribes that lived inside the boundaries of present-day Texas include the Alabama, Apache, Atakapan, Bidai, Caddo, Coahuiltecan, Comanche, Cherokee, Choctaw, Coushatta, Hasinai, Jumano, Karankawa, Kickapoo, Kiowa, Tonkawa, and Wichita. No one culture was dominant in the present-day Texas region and many different peoples inhabited the area.

First Established Europeans in Texas

The first Europeans established in the main part of Texas were the **French**. However, the French colonial presence was short-lived. After exploring the interior of what is now the United States, French nobleman **La Salle** returned with a large expedition designed to establish a French colony on the Gulf of Mexico, at the mouth of the Mississippi River. They left France in 1684 with four ships and 300 colonists. The expedition, however, was plagued by pirates, hostile Native Americans, and poor navigation. They set up **Fort Saint Louis** of Texas, near Victoria, Texas. La Salle led a group eastward on foot on three occasions to try to find the shortest route from Texas to the Mississippi. During the last such search his remaining 36 followers mutinied, and he was murdered by four of them near the site of modern Navasota, Texas. The colony lasted only until 1688, when Karankawa-speaking Native Americans massacred the twenty remaining adults and took five children as captives. Tonti sent out search missions in 1689 when he learned of the expedition's fate, but failed to reach a fort with survivors. Despite the failure of their colony in Texas, the French continued to claim Texas, even after the Spanish had arrived and colonized it. The failure of the French colony became known throughout the world. This French period of Texan history is memorialized in the Texas state seal and as the first (or second) of the traditional "six flags over Texas."

Texas Towards End of 18th Century

Towards the end of the 18th century Texas remained a sparsely settled territory, heavily dependent on the military and continually exposed to the depredations of Native Americans who resisted Spanish sovereignty in the region. Crown efforts during much of the 18th century to bolster the small population and thus improve the province's viability proved in general unsuccessful. The population remained a mixture of hispanized Native Americans centered on the missions, Spanish and Mexican soldiers with their families, Spanish colonial officials and their families, and various communities of French, British, Italian, German, and American settlers who had been assimilated into the Spanish system. Then in the early years of the 19th century Spain once again faced concerted efforts by rivals, now including the United States, to wrest from it important parts of its North American empire. Relations with the United States had come dangerously close to war over navigation rights on the Mississippi River and the expansion of Anglo-American frontier settlements into the Spanish Floridas. Napoleon's coerced acquisition of Louisiana in 1800 and his subsequent sale of the vast territory to the United States in 1803 left Spanish North America divided and vulnerable.

EARLY 19TH CENTURY TEXAS

The early 19th century position of Spanish Texas did not look promising. Foreign encroachments, Native American warfare, and insurrectionary activity all contributed to demographic and economic **collapse**. In the end, desperate Spanish authorities authorized Anglo-American **colonization** in an effort to bolster the province and so produced a new set of problems for the Mexican authorities who soon replaced them. In the years following the Louisiana Purchase and the acquisition of New Orleans by the US, American settlers had begun to move westward into Mexican claimed territory. Some settlers were active filibusters, who sought the long-term annexation of the area by the US In 1812-1813; the **Gutiérrez-Magee Expedition** attempted to separate Texas from the Spanish Empire. In response the Spanish government in Mexico ordered a virtual genocide of the entire Tejano-American population and any of their collaborators amongst the Tejano-Spanish population. The result was the utter devastation of Texas which left it with a population size it had at the beginning of the 18th century. Spanish Texas was a failing colonial policy.

OLDEST AND LARGEST COLONIAL TEXAS COMMUNITY

Spanish Texas had solidified upon three primary centers. The oldest and largest of colonial Texas communities was **San Antonio de Béxar**. In its eighty-year history the settlement had evolved from a presidio-mission complex to the first chartered municipality and finally to the provincial capital. Its population of approximately 2,000 was composed chiefly of Mexican settlers from Coahuila, Nuevo León, and other frontier provinces mixed with a small number of Canary Islanders. After the United States acquired Louisiana, reinforcement of the Spanish military presence in Texas resulted in the transfer of the Second Flying Company of San Carlos de Parras (the Álamo de Parras company) to San Antonio, where it was headquartered in 1803 at San Antonio de Valero Mission, which had been closed. Other units from Nuevo Santander and Nuevo León swelled the population to over 3,000 by 1810.

TEXAS IN THE 1820S AND 1830S

In the 1820s, the population in Texas was very sparse and the Mexican government had difficulty in attracting Mexicans to the area. Thus, in order to populate and develop the area Mexico sought **settlers** from Europe and especially the neighboring United States. When Mexico reached an agreement with **Stephen F. Austin**, it allowed several hundred families from the United States, known as **Texians**, to move into the region. Thousands of additional settlers soon flooded into Texas. When Mexico abolished slavery nationwide, some immigrants from the US refused to comply with the law. This was coupled with complaints about the tightening political and economic control over the territory by the central government in Mexico City, which expected its citizens to be members in good standing of the Catholic Church, whereas the settlers from the United States were Protestant. In 1835, Mexican President **Antonio López de Santa Anna** abolished the Constitution of 1824 and sought to centralize national power in Mexico City. This caused much political unrest throughout Mexico, an example of which was the rebellion and resulting massacre in Zacatecas. As a result, the new government's efforts to tighten political and economic control over the territory of Texas would only rouse emotions in the Texian settlers and local Tejanos, leading to the **Texas Revolution**.

MEXICAN TEXAS

Mexican Texas is the name given by Texas historians to the brief period between 1821—1835, when Texas was part of Mexico, as a part of the **State of Coahuila y Tejas**. The period begins with Mexico's victory over Spain in its war of independence in 1821 and ends with Texas's **Declaration of Independence** from Mexico in 1836, forming the **Republic of Texas**. The Rio Grande and South Texas areas have a long and turbulent history of independence movements by the local Mexican population on account of unitary and perceived dictatorial and unconstitutional practices by the central Mexican government. North Texas and East Texas, meanwhile, remained largely in the hands of Native American tribes, some of whom were hostile to Spanish and then Mexican rule.

Battles of the Texas Revolution

Four days after the first declaration of independence, the two-week long **Battle of the Alamo** ended as Mexican General **Antonio López de Santa Anna's** forces defeated the nearly 200 Texans defending the small mission (which would eventually become the center of the city of San Antonio). "Remember the Alamo!" became the battle cry of the Texas Revolution. The **Battle of San Jacinto** was fought on April 21, 1836 (interestingly, the anniversary for the founding of the city of Rome) near the present-day city of Houston. General Santa Anna's entire force of 1,600 men was killed or captured by Texas General **Sam Houston's** army of 800 Texans; only nine Texans died. This decisive battle resulted in Texas's independence from Mexico. Sam Houston, a native of Virginia, was **President** of the Republic of Texas for two separate terms, 1836–1838 and 1841–1844. He also was **Governor** of the state of Texas from 1859 to 1861.

Third Center of Colonial Spanish Power in Texas

The third center of Spanish power and the one with the most limited amount of Spanish royal control was far to the northeast, near the Louisiana border. **North-Eastern Texas** had traditionally been a community of English, French, and Spanish settlers who had established the Presidio de Las Adaes as the first capital of Texas. However, North-East Texas was even further removed from Mexico City than San Antonio de Bexar. Consequently, the area was downgraded in colonial status and by Imperial edict the settlement was ordered abandoned. The viceroy eventually did permit the resettlement of East Texas, but would not consent to dwellings within 100 leagues of Natchitoches (Nacogdoches), Louisiana. Nevertheless, the refugees in San Antonio viewed any concession as encouraging. In August 1774 they founded the settlement of **Bucareli** on the Trinity River at a site in what is now Madison County. The town had attracted 347 inhabitants by 1777, but it was plagued by floods and Comanche raids. Without authorization, the population moved again in 1779 to **Nacogdoches**. The new town began to be garrisoned in 1795 by a detachment from Bexar as a means of further solidifying the interests of San Antonio over the province. By the beginning of the 19th century, the settlement was attracting increasing numbers of immigrants, legal and otherwise, from the Anglo-American frontier.

Legacies of Spanish Texas

The Spanish occupation of Texas lasted for just 105 years. However, the **legacies of Spanish Texas** are lasting and significant. Perhaps most obvious, yet superficial in importance, is the use of **Spanish names** for hundreds of towns, cities, counties, and geographic features in Texas. San Antonio, the first formal municipality in Texas, is one of the ten largest cities in the United States. Forty-two of the 254 counties in Texas bear either Hispanic names, or an Anglicized derivation such as Galveston or a misspelling such as Uvalde. The names of physiographical features such as Llano Estacado, Guadalupe Mountains, and Padre Island serve as reminders of Spanish explorers and conquistadors who crossed portions of Texas well before the English settled the Atlantic Coast of North America. Spaniards introduced numerous European crops, irrigation at San Antonio and other mission sites, livestock, and livestock-handling techniques. **Farming**, initially practiced by some Native American groups in Texas, was likewise expanded and improved by Spanish missionaries and settlers. The restored **missions** at San Antonio and Goliad stand as enduring monuments to the Franciscans who brought the mantle of Christianity to Native Americans in Texas. With the exception of those in California, the finest examples of Spanish mission architecture in the United States are found in Texas.

Beginning of Republic of Texas

The first declaration of independence for modern Texas, by both Anglo-Texan settlers and local Tejanos, was signed in Goliad on December 20, 1835. The **Texas Declaration of Independence** was enacted at Washington-on-the-Brazos on March 2, 1836, effectively creating the **Republic of Texas**.

Historiography

Introduction to Historiography

Historiography is the study of the methods and approaches that historians use to create histories. It involves examining how historical evidence is chosen, interpreted, evaluated, analyzed, and used in the writing of history. Historiography is not concerned with the events that make up history but rather the manner in which that history was recorded. The sources, techniques, and theoretical frameworks used to record the history of a certain subject constitute that subject's historiography.

Common Terminology Used When Studying History

When studying history, it is important to have a clear understanding of various terms that can be used interchangeably. The term **time** refers to the continuous passing of events in the past, present, and future. Time is a scientific measure that conventionally uses minutes, hours, days, and years as its **standard measures**. Time passes with or without significant events taking place. **History** is distinct from time as it is the record of **significant events** throughout the past. The term **chronology** refers to the arrangement of events in their correct order. As history contains uncertainty, the chronology of particular events is up for debate. Terms used to describe the ebb and flow of history are change and continuity. **Continuity** refers to periods of time that are relatively stable in history with no major changes, whereas times of **change** refer to rich periods in history with significant events that alter the common practices of that time, often leading into a new era. When describing what has changed for a civilization over time, it is common to focus on political, economic, social, and technological aspects. For instance, the United States government was established in 1776 and continues today. This demonstrates a change at the beginning of the timeline related the United States, but since then, there has been political continuity as it has existed for roughly 250 years. Other aspects of life in this period may have experienced other changes, such as the innovation of electricity, steam engines, and automobiles. When a portion of time has relatively stable conditions such that it can be summed up by a common characterization, it is called a **period of time**; this process of summing up time into periods is called **periodization**.

Civilization, City-States, and Empires

Since history is the study of recorded events throughout time, it is naturally tied to organized society with a developed language to record the events. The development necessary to record history generally coincides with early civilization. A **civilization** is a human society that has established complex means of surviving as a group. These **functions** are developing a food supply, a social structure, a shared language, a culture, and technology. The first known complex civilization is Mesopotamia, which was more easily developed due to its fertile farmlands, access to water through an available river. Mesopotamia is a good example of a **city-state**, which is essentially an independently sovereign city that does not depend on another government. Mesopotamia, as an early civilization, was the central hub and government in its region. The model of city-states still exists today, though they are often comparatively less significant in size and economy compared to other nation-states. Examples of modern city-states include Monaco, Vatican City, and Singapore. As the early civilizations continued to develop, they would eventually grow into **empires**, which are larger sovereign states with multiple territories, though they are usually governed centrally by a monarch or emperor.

Interpreting Timelines

Timelines are a useful tool for visualizing the chronology of events as well as a great method to map out periods and view changes or continuity throughout history. Timelines can focus on either small or large ranges and can be multifaceted so that one period or type of event can be compared with another. A key element of a timeline is having a consistent interval mapped out. For instance, if we wanted to construct a timeline to map the events that happened for a single day, we would likely use hours to plot out the continuum. One might start the timeline at 12am and end the timeline at 12am the next night to show the picture of the entire day. Each event or period, such as sleeping, waking up, eating, going to work, and special occurrences can be marked on the timeline to plot out the day. If someone wanted to compare multiple days, these timelines could be lined up and compared and contrasted to find what is common to all days and what is unique. These same concepts can be applied to historical timelines as well. Instead of mapping just one day, one might consider mapping the events leading up to and throughout a particular war. The significance of events should change with the focus of the timeline. Seeing events plotted on a steady continuum of time can be very helpful in understanding the pacing of events throughout history.

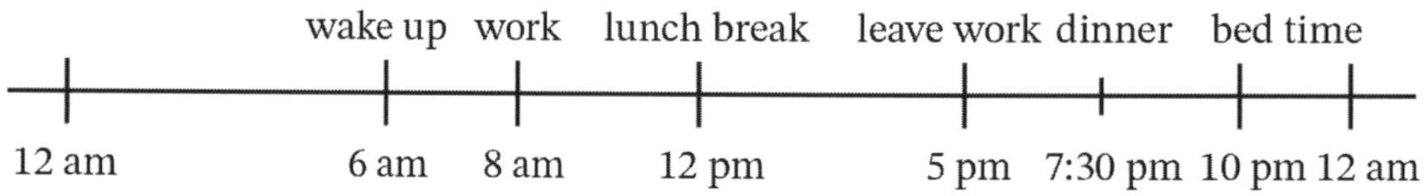

Relationships Between Historical Events and Their Implications

As one aspect of society changes, it frequently proves to have significant effects on other parts of society. One of the easiest ways to see this effect is the innovation of new technologies. An example of a highly impactful technology is the printing press. Prior to this invention, all written documents had to be written by hand, which was time-consuming and costly. Books were very expensive and rare, which put the burden of education on mainly religious authorities and very wealthy classes of people. This new innovation allowed for more written works to be spread, which caused a need for literacy and education, ultimately evoking huge cultural and political changes. Technology tends to be a much quicker influencer of change in civilization, as it is sudden and can have dramatic impacts on how things are done. Cultural, political, and economic effects tend to move more gradually but likewise have strong effects that can change civilization forever.

Primary and Secondary Sources of Historical Information

When studying history, it is important to consider the reliability, validity, and availability of sources of information. **Primary sources** are first-hand accounts of an event, such as a transcript of a speech, a recording, statistics, or a work of art. **Secondary sources** are indirect records, such as text books, newspapers, and other forms of reviews of the primary sources. Secondary sources of information can still be valid and useful, but are more open to **interpretation** and **bias**. Information from recent history, such as the election of a president in the 2010s is very reliable, as there are many sources of information that are in consensus about the objective event. Furthermore, many people still alive are primary sources since they were alive and witnessed the election. This is not true of less modern history, such as the election of Abraham Lincoln in 1860. There are still plentiful records of the information, but all witnesses to the election have passed away at this point. This event took place in an era where newspapers and legitimate documentation was widespread and available. The clarity and objectivity of sources are indisputable because they are so abundant. If, however, we only had political cartoons and election campaign brochures to go by, the reliability and accuracy of the information may be up for debate because the source materials are only secondary sources of information and are likely to contain biases. Generally, the further back in history one researches, the fewer sources are available due to lack of documentation, technological limitations, and language barriers. With fewer sources, and possibly conflicting information, historians must put together the most reasonable explanation of what took place during the period in question, given the amount of information available to them.

Types of Sources of Information Used in Historical Research

- **Almanacs**—books that are published each year to express current information for consideration in the coming year. These often act as time capsules for that particular year and can give historians insight into economic and technological details of the time.
- **Encyclopedias**—resources that cover a variety of topics broadly for the purpose of giving the reader an overview. Wikipedia is an internet-based version of an encyclopedia that is useful for finding leads or obtaining general information about a topic.
- **Bibliographies**—a list of resources used in composing a scholarly work. These are usually primary and secondary sources that can be used to check an author's sources or to give leads on similar research. Similar concepts include works-cited pages and literature reviews.

- **Periodical Guides**—a series of publications over time, usually in the form of magazines or journals. These usually broach a more specific category of information, such as on research methods, psychology, or medical procedures, and are intended to help members of a particular field stay up-to-date with current research in their field.
- **Biographical Dictionaries**—a resource that contains a list of important names to know about the given subject and a description of how they contributed to the field. For instance, if one were interested in the Revolutionary War, a biographical dictionary would include information on each of the founding fathers and other significant individuals of the time.
- **Maps**—representations of land and territories that can display a variety of factors, including geographical features, political features, economics, demographics, and many more aspects. Digital maps can generally be manipulated to show multiple features at once.

Uses and Limitations of Various Historical Source Materials

Historical source materials are a type of primary source material that offer historians the opportunity to study people, places, and events that occurred in the past. Unfortunately, there are limitations to what these materials can tell us. A limitation of **historical source materials** is that they may be biased by those who created them. For example, those who create historical documents such as letters may leave out details or exaggerate parts in order to make their points more convincing. Another limitation might be that some historical sources only provide evidence for certain points of view, as they were recorded by those with specific interests and perspectives.

- An **oral history** provides an account of an event that happened in the past, which is told by the person who was there when it happened. Oral histories are important because they allow us to learn about things that may not be written in books or recorded in documents.
- **Newspapers** are important source materials for scholars because they provide a detailed account of the past, which cannot be found in books or other sources. Newspapers are not always reliable as they may not be based on fact, while others might omit certain information or give undue weight towards one side of an issue at the expense of another.
- **Diaries** and personal **journals** can provide valuable information for historians because they are detailed histories of people's lives. However, the reliability of these accounts is always in question because they were created by just one person and aren't always written with the intention of sharing.
- **Artifacts** can be defined as objects created by humans, which can give hints at the peoples' material culture and intangible culture. Material culture includes things like buildings or furniture while intangible culture includes things like music or dance. The benefits of artifacts are that they can offer insights into how people lived in the past. They can also be used to shed light on the thoughts, feelings, fears, tensions, customs, rituals, and other social practices at that time.
- **Tax lists** and **census data** are useful sources of insight into how people lived during a certain time. They provide us with reliable information about the income, demographics, and beliefs of the people living in a particular time.
- **Personal correspondence** has been an important form of historical information for historians. It gives an insight into the lives and interactions of ordinary people. The main benefits of using personal correspondence as a source for history is that it provides an authentic portrayal of the author's thoughts and feelings during a time period or in response to significant events.

Historical Interpretation and Biases

History is a discipline that relies on the interpretation of **facts** to create **narratives**. Due to the types and availability of sources, history tends to leave itself open to **subjectivity**. Often, this means that **biases** are introduced at either the source of information, the interpretation of the information, or at the explanation of the information. For instance, if the only **sources of information** about an event are newspapers, the author of these historical sources may have been biased, causing the **interpretation** of the actual events to be skewed from the start. Similarly, the person interpreting the source may have their own biases that they introduce or even **teach** to others in the process of communicating the historical narrative. Commonly described biases in modern interpretation of history generally revolve around sociopolitical issues such as Eurocentrism, popular political parties, economic biases, and cultural favoritism.

HISTORICAL REVISIONISM

Historical revisionism is the act of reinterpreting a historical account through established historical methodologies. This is often done when new information is discovered or old information is reinterpreted in such a way that it warrants reconsidering the previously accepted history of an event or period. Historical revisionism is an essential and necessary process in creating accurate histories. Revisionism can, sometimes, be used incorrectly and in a way that leads to a less accurate interpretation of historical events. An example of this would be when the historical record is denied or deliberately distorted. This can involve using falsified records, purposefully misrepresenting the meaning of a piece of historical evidence, manipulating statistics, or unjustly denying the validity of historical evidence. A common example of this is Holocaust denial, which is an antisemitic theory that the Holocaust was either fabricated or greatly exaggerated.

Chapter Quiz

Ready to see how well you retained what you just read? Scan the QR code to go directly to the chapter quiz interface for this study guide. If you're using a computer, simply visit the online resources page at **mometrix.com/resources719/texessocst4-8** and click the Chapter Quizzes link.

Geography

Geography

Geography is the study of Earth. Geographers study **physical characteristics** of Earth as well as man-made borders and boundaries. They also study the **distribution of life** on the planet, such as where certain species of animals can be found or how different forms of life interact. Major elements of the study of geography include:

- Locations
- Regional characteristics
- Spatial relations
- Natural and man-made forces that change elements of Earth

These elements are studied from regional, topical, physical, and human perspectives. Geography also focuses on the origins of Earth, as well as the history and backgrounds of different human populations.

Physical vs. Cultural Geography

Physical geography is the study of the physical characteristics of Earth: how they relate to each other, how they were formed, and how they develop. These characteristics include climate, land, and water, and also how they affect human population in various areas. Different landforms, in combination with various climates and other conditions, determine the characteristics of various cultures.

Cultural geography is the study of how the various aspects of physical geography affect individual cultures. Cultural geography also compares various cultures: how their lifestyles and customs are affected by their geographical location, climate, and other factors, as well as how they interact with their environment.

Review Video: Regional Geography
Visit mometrix.com/academy and enter code: 350378

Divisions of Geographical Study and Tools Used

The four divisions of geographical study and tools used are:

- **Topical**—the study of a single feature of Earth or one specific human activity that occurs worldwide.
- **Physical**—the various physical features of Earth, how they are created, the forces that change them, and how they are related to each other and to various human activities.
- **Regional**—specific characteristics of individual places and regions.
- **Human**—how human activity affects the environment. This includes the study of political, historical, social, and cultural activities.

Tools used in geographical study include special research methods like mapping, field studies, statistics, interviews, mathematics, and the use of various scientific instruments.

Important Ancient Geographers

The following are three important ancient geographers and their contributions to the study of geography:

- **Eratosthenes** lived in ancient Greek times and mathematically calculated the circumference of Earth and the tilt of Earth's axis. He also created the first map of the world.
- **Strabo** wrote a description of the ancient world called *Geographica* in seventeen volumes.
- **Ptolemy**, primarily an astronomer, was an experienced mapmaker. He wrote a treatise entitled *Geography*, which was used by Christopher Columbus in his travels.

Ways Geographers Analyze Areas of Human Population

In cities, towns, or other areas where many people have settled, geographers focus on the **distribution** of populations, neighborhoods, industrial areas, transportation, and other elements important to the society in question. For example, they would map out the locations of hospitals, airports, factories, police stations, schools, and housing groups. They would also make note of how these facilities are distributed in relation to the areas of habitation, such as the number of schools in a certain neighborhood or how many grocery stores are located in a specific suburban area. Another area of study and discussion is the distribution of **towns** themselves, from widely spaced rural towns to large cities that merge into each other to form a megalopolis.

Role of a Cartographer

A cartographer is a mapmaker. Mapmakers produce detailed illustrations of geographic areas to record where various features are located within that area. These illustrations can be compiled into maps, charts, graphs, and even globes. When constructing maps, **cartographers** must take into account the problem of **distortion**. Because Earth is round, a flat map does not accurately represent the correct proportions, especially if a very large geographical area is being depicted. Maps must be designed in such a way as to minimize this distortion and maximize accuracy. Accurately representing Earth's features on a flat surface is achieved through **projection**.

Types of Projection Used in Creating World Maps

The three major types of projection used in creating world maps are:

- **Cylindrical projection**—this is created by wrapping the globe of Earth in a cylindrical piece of paper, then using a light to project the globe onto the paper. The largest distortion occurs at the outermost edges.
- **Conical projection**—the paper is shaped like a cone and contacts the globe only at the cone's base. This type of projection is most useful for middle latitudes.
- **Flat-Plane projections**—also known as a gnomonic projection, this type of map is projected onto a flat piece of paper that only touches the globe at a single point. Flat-plane projections make it possible to map out Great-Circle routes, or the shortest route between one point and another on the globe, as a straight line.

Specific Types of Map Projections

Four specific types of map projections that are commonly used today are:

- **Winkel Tripel projection**—The Winkel Tripel projection balances size and shape, greatly reducing distortion. In 1998, the National Geographic Society accepted the Winkel Tripel projection as a standard, though other map forms have remained popular.
- **Robinson projection**—east and west sections of the map are less distorted, but continental shapes are somewhat inaccurate.
- **Goode homolosine projection**—sizes and shapes are accurate, but distances are not. This projection basically represents a globe that has been cut into connected sections so that it can lie flat.
- **Mercator projection**—though distortion is high, particularly in areas farther from the equator, this cylindrical projection is commonly used by seafarers.

Major Elements of Any Map

The five major elements of any map are:

- **Title**—this tells basic information about the map, such as the area represented.
- **Legend**—also known as the key, the legend explains what symbols used on a particular map represent, such as symbols for major landmarks.

- **Grid**—this most commonly represents the geographic grid system, or latitude and longitude marks used to precisely locate specific locations.
- **Directions**—a compass rose or other symbol is used to indicate the cardinal directions.
- **Scale**—this shows the relation between a certain distance on the map and the actual distance. For example, one inch might represent one mile, or ten miles, or even more, depending on the size of the map.

Review Video: Elements of a Map
Visit mometrix.com/academy and enter code: 437727

Equal-Area Maps vs. Conformal Maps

An equal-area map is designed such that the proportional sizes of various areas are accurate. For example, if one landmass is one-fifth the size of another, the lines on the map will be shifted to accommodate for distortion so that the proportional size is accurate. In many maps, areas farther from the equator are greatly distorted; this type of map compensates for this phenomenon. A **conformal map** focuses on representing the correct shape of geographical areas, with less concern for comparative size.

Consistent Scale Maps and Thematic Maps

With a consistent scale map, the same scale, such as one inch being equal to ten miles, is used throughout the entire map. This is most often used for maps of smaller areas, as maps that cover larger areas, such as the full globe, must make allowances for distortion. Maps of very large areas often make use of more than one scale, with scales closer to the center representing a larger area than those at the edges.

A **thematic map** is constructed to show very specific information about a chosen theme. For example, a thematic map might represent political information, such as how votes were distributed in an election, or could show population distribution or climatic features.

Relief Maps

A relief map is constructed to show details of various **elevations** across the area of the map. Higher elevations are represented by different colors than lower elevations. **Relief maps** often also show additional details, such as the overall ruggedness or smoothness of an area. Mountains would be represented as ridged and rugged, while deserts would be shown as smooth.

Elevation in relief maps can also be represented by contour lines, or lines that connect points of the same elevation. Some relief maps even feature textures, reconstructing details in a sort of miniature model.

Geographical Features

- **Mountains** are elevated areas that measure 2,000 feet or more above sea level. Often steep and rugged, they usually occur in groups called chains or ranges. Six of the seven continents on Earth contain at least one range.
- **Hills** are of lower elevation than mountains, at about 500-2,000 feet. Hills are usually more rounded and are found throughout every continent.
- **Plains** are large, flat areas and are usually very fertile. The majority of Earth's population is supported by crops grown on vast plains.
- **Valleys** lie between hills and mountains. Depending on their location, their specific features can vary greatly, from fertile and habitable to rugged and inhospitable.
- **Plateaus** are elevated, but flat on top. Some plateaus are extremely dry, such as the Kenya Plateau, because surrounding mountains prevent them from receiving moisture.
- **Deserts** receive less than ten inches of rain per year. They are usually large areas, such as the Sahara Desert in Africa or the Australian Outback.
- **Deltas** occur at river mouths. Because the rivers carry sediment to the deltas, these areas are often very fertile.

- **Mesas** are flat, steep-sided mountains or hills. The term is sometimes used to refer to plateaus.
- **Basins** are areas of low elevation where rivers drain.
- **Foothills** are the transitional area between plains and mountains, usually consisting of hills that gradually increase in size as they approach a mountain range.
- **Marshes** and **swamps** are also lowlands, but they are very wet and largely covered in vegetation such as reeds and rushes.

Geographical Terms Referring to Bodies of Water

- The **ocean** refers to the salt water that covers about two-thirds of Earth's surface.
- **Ocean basins** are named portions of the ocean. The five major ocean basins are the Atlantic, Pacific, Indian, Southern, and Arctic.
- **Seas** are generally also salt water, but are smaller than ocean basins and surrounded by land. Examples include the Mediterranean Sea, the Caribbean Sea, and the Caspian Sea.
- **Lakes** are bodies of fresh water found inland. Sixty percent of all lakes are located in Canada.
- **Rivers** are moving bodies of water that flow from higher elevations to lower. They usually start as rivulets or streams and grow until they finally empty into a sea or the ocean.
- **Canals**, such as the Panama Canal and the Suez Canal, are man-made waterways connecting two large bodies of water.

How Communities Develop

Communities, or groups of people who settle together in a specific area, typically gather where certain conditions exist. These conditions include:

- Easy access to resources such as food, water, and raw materials
- Ability to easily transport raw materials and goods, such as access to a waterway
- Room to house a sufficient workforce

People also tend to form groups with others who are similar to them. In a typical **community**, people can be found who share values, a common language, and common or similar cultural characteristics and religious beliefs. These factors will determine the overall composition of a community as it develops.

Differences Between Cities in Various Areas of the World

Cities develop and grow as an area develops. Modern statistics show that over half of the world's people live in **cities**. That percentage is even higher in developed areas of the globe. Cities are currently growing more quickly in developing regions, and even established cities continue to experience growth throughout the world. In developing or developed areas, cities often are surrounded by a metropolitan area made up of both urban and suburban sections. In some places, cities have merged into each other and become a **megalopolis**—a single, huge city.

Cities develop differently in different areas of the world. The area available for cities to grow, as well as cultural and economic forces, drives how cities develop. For example, North American cities tend to cover wider areas. European cities tend to have better-developed transportation systems. In Latin America, the richest inhabitants can be found in the city centers, while in North America, wealthier inhabitants tend to live in suburban areas.

In other parts of the world, transportation and communication between cities are less developed. Technological innovations such as the cell phone have increased communication even in these areas. Urban areas must also maintain communication with rural areas in order to procure food, resources, and raw materials that cannot be produced within the city limits.

WEATHER VS. CLIMATE

Weather and climate are physical systems that affect geography. Though they deal with similar information, the way this information is measured and compiled is different.

Weather involves daily conditions in the atmosphere that affect temperature, precipitation (rain, snow, hail, or sleet), wind speed, air pressure, and other factors. Weather focuses on the short-term—what the conditions will be today, tomorrow, or over the next few days.

In contrast, **climate** aggregates information about daily and seasonal weather conditions in a region over a long period of time. The climate takes into account average monthly and yearly temperatures, average precipitation over long periods of time, and the growing season of an area. Climates are classified according to latitude, or how close they lie to Earth's equator. The three major divisions are:

- **Low Latitudes**, lying from 0 to approximately 23.5 degrees
- **Middle Latitudes**, found from approximately 23.5 to 66.5 degrees
- **High Latitudes**, found from approximately 66.5 degrees to the poles

Review Video: Climates
Visit mometrix.com/academy and enter code: 991320

CLIMATES FOUND IN THE LOW LATITUDES

Rainforests, savannas, and deserts occur in low latitudes:

- **Rainforest** climates, near the equator, experience high average temperatures and humidity, as well as relatively high rainfall.
- **Savannas** are found on either side of the rainforest region. Mostly grasslands, they typically experience dry winters and wet summers.
- Beyond the savannas lie the **desert** regions, with hot, dry climates, sparse rainfall, and temperature fluctuations of up to fifty degrees from day to night.

CLIMATE REGIONS FOUND IN THE MIDDLE LATITUDES

The climate regions found in the middle latitudes are:

- **Mediterranean**—the Mediterranean climate occurs between 30- and 40-degrees latitude, both north and south, on the western coasts of continents. Characteristics include a year-long growing season; hot, dry summers followed by mild winters; and sparse rainfall that occurs mostly during the winter months.
- **Humid-subtropical**—humid-subtropical regions are located in southeastern coastal areas. Winds that blow in over warm ocean currents produce long summers, mild winters, and a long growing season. These areas are highly productive and support a larger part of Earth's population than any other climate.
- **Humid-continental**—the humid continental climate produces the familiar four seasons typical of a good portion of the US. Some of the most productive farmlands in the world lie in these climates. Winters are cold, and summers are hot and humid.

MARINE, STEPPE, AND DESERT CLIMATES

The climate regions found in the middle latitudes are:

- **Marine**—marine climates are found near water or on islands. Ocean winds help make these areas mild and rainy. Summers are cooler than humid-subtropical summers, but winters also bring milder temperatures due to the warmth of the ocean winds.
- **Steppe**—steppe climates, or prairie climates, are found far inland on large continents. Summers are hot and winters are cold, but rainfall is sparser than in continental climates.
- **Desert**—desert climates occur where steppe climates receive even less rainfall. Examples include the Gobi Desert in Asia as well as desert areas of Australia and the southwestern US.

CLIMATES FOUND IN THE HIGH LATITUDES

The high latitudes consist of two major climate areas, the tundra and taiga:

- **Tundra** means "marshy plain." The ground is frozen throughout long, cold winters, but there is little snowfall. During the short summers, it becomes wet and marshy. Tundras are not amenable to crops, but many plants and animals have adapted to the conditions.
- **Taigas** lie south of tundra regions and include the largest forest areas in the world, as well as swamps and marshes. Large mineral deposits exist here, as well as many animals valued for their fur. In the winter, taiga regions are colder than the tundra, and summers are hotter. The growing season is short.

A **vertical climate** exists in high mountain ranges. Increasing elevation leads to varying temperatures, growing conditions, types of vegetation and animals, and occurrence of human habitation, often encompassing elements of various other climate regions.

FACTORS AFFECTING CLIMATE

Because Earth is tilted, its **rotation** brings about changes in **seasons**. Regions closer to the equator, and those nearest the poles, experience very little change in seasonal temperatures. Mid-range latitudes are most likely to experience distinct seasons. Large bodies of water also affect climate. Ocean currents and wind patterns can change the climate for an area that lies in a typically cold latitude, such as England, to a much more temperate climate. Mountains can affect both short-term weather and long-term climates. Some deserts occur because precipitation is stopped by the wall of a mountain range.

Over time, established **climate patterns** can shift and change. While the issue is hotly debated, it has been theorized that human activity has also led to climate change.

EFFECT OF HUMAN SYSTEMS

HUMAN SYSTEMS THAT GEOGRAPHERS INCORPORATE INTO THE STUDY OF EARTH

Human systems affect geography in the way in which they settle, form groups that grow into large-scale habitations, and even create permanent changes in the landscape. **Geographers** study movements of people, how they distribute goods among each other and to other settlements or cultures, and how ideas grow and spread. Migrations, wars, forced relocations, and trade can all spread cultural ideas, language, goods, and other practices to widespread areas. Throughout history, cultures have been changed due to a wide range of events, including major migrations and the conquering of one people by another. In addition, **human systems** can lead to various conflicts or alliances to control access to and the use of natural resources.

HUMAN SYSTEMS THAT FORM THE BASIS OF CULTURES IN NORTH AMERICA

North America consists of 23 countries, including (in decreasing population order) the United States of America, Mexico, Canada, Guatemala, Cuba, Haiti, and the Dominican Republic. The US and Canada support similarly diverse cultures, as both were formed from groups of native races and large numbers of immigrants. Many **North American cultures** come from a mixture of indigenous and colonial European influences. Agriculture is important to North American countries, while service industries and technology also play a large part in the economy. On average, North America supports a high standard of living and a high level of development and supports trade with countries throughout the world.

Human Systems that Shape South America

Home to twelve sovereign states, including Brazil (largest in area and population), Colombia, Argentina, Venezuela, and Peru; two independent territories; and one internal territory, **South America** is largely defined by its prevailing languages. The majority of countries in South America speak Spanish or Portuguese. Most of South America has experienced a similar history, having been originally dominated by Native cultures and then conquered by European nations. The countries of South America have since gained independence, but there is a wide disparity between various countries' economic and political factors. Most South American countries rely on only one or two exports, usually agricultural, with suitable lands often controlled by rich families. Most societies in South America feature major separations between classes, both economically and socially. Challenges faced by developing South American countries include geographical limitations, economic issues, and sustainable development, including the need to preserve the existing rainforests.

Human Systems Influencing Europe

Europe contains a wide variety of cultures, ethnic groups, physical geographical features, climates, and resources, all of which have influenced the distribution of its varied population. **Europe**, in general, is industrialized and developed, with cultural differences giving each individual country its own unique characteristics. Greek and Roman influences played a major role in European culture, as did Christianity. European countries spread their beliefs and cultural elements throughout the world by means of migration and colonization. They have had a significant influence on nearly every other continent in the world. While Western Europe has been largely democratic, Eastern Europe functioned under communist rule for many years. The formation of the European Union (EU) in 1993 has increased stability and positive diplomatic relations among European nations. Like other industrialized regions, Europe is now focusing on various environmental issues.

Human Systems that Have Shaped Russia

After numerous conflicts, Russia became a Communist state, known as the **USSR**. With the collapse of the USSR in 1991, the country has struggled in its transition to a market-driven economy. Attempts to build a workable system have led to the destruction of natural resources as well as problems with nuclear power, including accidents such as Chernobyl. To complete the transition to a market economy, Russia would need to improve its transportation and communication systems and find a way to more efficiently use its natural resources.

The population of Russia is not distributed evenly, with three-quarters of the population living west of the Ural Mountains. The people of Russia encompass over a hundred different ethnic groups. Over eighty percent of the population is ethnically Russian, and Russian is the official language of the country.

Human Systems that Have Shaped North Africa and Southwest and Central Asia

The largely desert climate of these areas has led most population centers to rise around sources of **water**, such as the Nile River. This area is the home of the **earliest known civilizations** and the origin of Christianity, Judaism, and Islam. After serving as the site of huge, independent civilizations in ancient times, North Africa and Southwest and Central Asia were largely parceled out as **European colonies** during the 18th and 19th centuries. The beginning of the 20th century saw many of these countries gain their independence. **Islam** has served as a unifying force for large portions of these areas, and many of the inhabitants speak Arabic. In spite of the arid climate, agriculture is a large business, but the most valuable resource is **oil**. Centuries of conflict throughout this area have led to ongoing political problems. These political problems have also contributed to environmental issues.

Human Systems that Shape and Influence the Culture of Sub-Saharan Africa

South of the Sahara Desert, **Africa** is divided into a number of culturally diverse nations. The inhabitants are unevenly distributed due to geographical limitations that prevent settlement in vast areas. **AIDS** has become a major plague throughout this part of Africa, killing millions, largely due to restrictive beliefs that prevent education about the disease, as well as abject poverty and unsettled political situations that make it impossible to manage the pandemic. The population of this area of Africa is widely diverse due to extensive **migration**. Many of the people still rely on **subsistence farming** for their welfare. Starvation and poverty are rampant due to drought and political instability. Some areas are far more stable than others due to the greater availability of resources. These areas have been able to begin the process of **industrialization**.

Human Systems that Determine the Cultural Makeup of South Asia

South Asia is home to one of the first human civilizations, which grew up in the **Indus River Valley**. With a great deal of disparity between rural and urban life, South Asia has much to do to improve the quality of life for its lower classes. Two major religions, **Hinduism** and **Buddhism**, have their origins in this region. Parts of South Asia, most notably India, were subject to **British rule** for several decades and are still working to improve independent governments and social systems. Overall, South Asia is very culturally diverse, with a wide mix of religions and languages throughout. Many individuals are **farmers**, but a growing number have found prosperity in the spread of **high-tech industries**. Industrialization is growing in South Asia but continues to face environmental, social, religious, and economic challenges.

Human Systems Shaping the Culture of East Asia

Governments in East Asia are varied, ranging from communist to democratic governments, with some governments that mix both approaches. **Isolationism** throughout the area limited the countries' contact with other nations until the early 20th century. The unevenly distributed population of East Asia consists of over one and a half billion people with widely diverse ethnic backgrounds, religions, and languages. More residents live in **urban** areas than in **rural** areas, creating shortages of farmworkers at times. Japan, Taiwan, and South Korea are overall more urban, while China and Mongolia are more rural. Japan stands as the most industrial country in East Asia. Some areas of East Asia are suffering from major environmental issues. Japan has dealt with many of these problems and now has some of the strictest environmental laws in the world.

Human Systems that Have Influenced Southeast Asia

Much of Southeast Asia was **colonized** by European countries during the 18th and 19th centuries, with the exception of Siam, now known as Thailand. All Southeast Asian countries are now independent, but the 20th century saw numerous conflicts between **communist** and **democratic** forces.

Southeast Asia has been heavily influenced by both Buddhist and Muslim religions. Industrialization is growing, with the population moving in large numbers from rural to urban areas. Some have moved to avoid conflict, oppression, and poverty.

Natural disasters, including volcanoes, typhoons, and flash flooding, are fairly common in Southeast Asia, creating extensive economic damage and societal disruption.

Human Systems that Affect the Development and Culture of Australia, Oceana, and Antarctica

South Pacific cultures originally migrated from Southeast Asia, creating hunter-gatherer or sometimes settled agricultural communities. **European** countries moved in during later centuries, seeking the plentiful natural resources of the area. Today, some South Pacific islands remain under the control of foreign governments, and culture in these areas mixes modern, industrialized society with indigenous culture. Population is unevenly distributed, largely due to the inhabitability of many parts of the South Pacific, such as the extremely hot desert areas of Australia. **Agriculture** still drives much of the economy, with **tourism** growing. **Antarctica** remains the only continent that has not been claimed by any country. There are no permanent human habitations in Antarctica, but scientists and explorers visit the area on a temporary basis.

Human-Environment Interaction

Geography also studies the ways people interact with, use, and change their **environment**. The effects, reasons, and consequences of these changes are studied, as are the ways the environment limits or influences human behavior. This kind of study can help determine the best course of action when a nation or group of people is considering making changes to the environment, such as building a dam or removing natural landscape to build or expand roads. Study of the **consequences** can help determine if these actions are manageable and how long-term, detrimental results can be mitigated.

Physical Geography and Climates

Physical Geography and Climate of North America

Together, the US and Canada make up the majority of North America and both have a similar distribution of geographical features: mountain ranges in both the east and the west, stretches of fertile plains through the center, and lakes and waterways. Both areas were shaped by **glaciers**, which also deposited highly fertile soil. Because they are so large, Canada and the US experience several varieties of **climate**, including continental climates with four seasons in median areas, tropical climates in the southern part of the US, and arctic climes in the far north. The remaining area of North America includes Mexico, Central America, the Caribbean Isles, and Greenland.

Physical Geography and Climate of South America

South America contains a wide variety of geographical features, including high **mountains** such as the Andes, wide **plains**, and high-altitude **plateaus**. The region contains numerous natural resources, but many of them have remained unused due to various obstacles, including political issues, geographic barriers, and lack of sufficient economic power. Climate zones in South America are largely **tropical**, with rainforests and savannas, but vertical climate zones and grasslands also exist in some places.

Physical Geography and Climate of Europe

Europe spans a wide area with a variety of climate zones. In the east and south are **mountain** ranges, while the north is dominated by a **plains** region. The long coastline and the island nature of some countries, such as Britain, mean the climate is often warmer than other lands at similar latitudes, as the area is warmed by **ocean currents**. Many areas of western Europe have a moderate climate, while areas of the south are dominated by the classic Mediterranean climate. Europe carries a high level of natural resources. Numerous waterways help connect the inner regions with the coastal areas. Much of Europe is **industrialized**, and **agriculture** has been developed for thousands of years.

Physical Geography and Climate of Russia

Russia's area encompasses part of Asia and Europe. From the standpoint of square footage alone, **Russia** is the largest country in the world. Due to its size, Russia encompasses a wide variety of climatic regions, including **plains**, **plateaus**, **mountains**, and **tundra**.

Russia's **climate** can be quite harsh, with rivers that are frozen most of the year, making transportation of the country's rich natural resources more difficult. Siberia, in northern Russia, is dominated by **permafrost**. Native peoples in this area still follow a hunting and gathering lifestyle, living in portable yurts and subsisting largely on herds of reindeer or caribou. Other areas include taiga with extensive, dense woods in north-central Russia and more temperate steppes and grasslands in the southwest.

Physical Geography and Climate of North Africa, Southwest, and Central Asia

This area of the world is complex in its geographical structure and climate, incorporating seas, peninsulas, rivers, mountains, and numerous other features. **Earthquakes** are common, with tectonic plates in the area remaining active. Much of the world's **oil** lies in this area. The tendency of the large rivers of North Africa, especially the Nile, to follow a set pattern of **drought** and extreme **fertility**, led people to settle there from prehistoric times. As technology has advanced, people have tamed this river, making its activity more predictable and the land around it more productive. The extremely arid nature of many other parts of this area has also led to **human intervention** such as irrigation to increase agricultural production.

PHYSICAL GEOGRAPHY AND CLIMATE OF THE SOUTHERN PORTION OF AFRICA

South of the Sahara Desert, the high elevations and other geographical characteristics have made it very difficult for human travel or settlement to occur. The geography of the area is dominated by a series of **plateaus**. There are also mountain ranges and a large rift valley in the eastern part of the country. Contrasting the wide desert areas, sub-Saharan Africa contains numerous lakes, rivers, and world-famous waterfalls. The area has **tropical** climates, including rainforests, savannas, steppes, and desert areas. The main natural resources are minerals, including gems and water.

PHYSICAL GEOGRAPHY AND CLIMATE OF SOUTH ASIA

The longest **alluvial plain**, a plain caused by shifting floodplains of major rivers and river systems over time, exists in South Asia. South Asia boasts three major **river systems** in the Ganges, Indus, and Brahmaputra. It also has large deposits of **minerals**, including iron ore that is in great demand internationally. South Asia holds mountains, plains, plateaus, and numerous islands. The climates range from tropical to highlands and desert areas. South Asia also experiences monsoon winds that cause a long rainy season. Variations in climate, elevation, and human activity influence agricultural production.

GEOGRAPHY AND CLIMATE OF EAST ASIA

East Asia includes North and South Korea, Mongolia, China, Japan, and Taiwan. Mineral resources are plentiful but not evenly distributed throughout. The coastlines are long, and while the population is large, farmlands are sparse. As a result, the surrounding ocean has become a major source of sustenance. East Asia is large enough to encompass several climate regions. **Ocean currents** provide milder climates to coastal areas, while **monsoons** provide the majority of the rainfall for the region. **Typhoons** are somewhat common, as are **earthquakes**, **volcanoes**, and **tsunamis**. The latter occur because of the tectonic plates that meet beneath the continent and remain somewhat active.

GEOGRAPHY AND CLIMATE OF SOUTHEAST ASIA

Southeast Asia lies largely on the **equator**, and roughly half of the countries of the region are island nations. These countries include Indonesia, the Philippines, Vietnam, Thailand, Myanmar, and Malaysia (which is partially on the mainland and partially an island country). The island nations of Southeast Asia feature mountains that are considered part of the **Ring of Fire**, an area where tectonic plates remain active, leading to extensive volcanic activity as well as earthquakes and tsunamis. Southeast Asia boasts many rivers and abundant natural resources, including gems, fossil fuels, and minerals. There are basically two seasons: wet and dry. The wet season arrives with the **monsoons**. In general, Southeast Asia consists of **tropical rainforest climates**, but there are some mountain areas and tropical savannas.

GEOGRAPHY AND CLIMATE OF AUSTRALIA, OCEANIA, AND ANTARCTICA

In the far southern hemisphere of the globe, Australia and Oceania present their own climatic combinations. **Australia**, the only island on Earth that is also a continent, has extensive deserts as well as mountains and lowlands. The economy is driven by agriculture, including ranches and farms, and minerals. While the steppes bordering extremely arid inland areas are suitable for livestock, only the coastal areas receive sufficient rainfall for crops without using irrigation. **Oceania** refers to over 10,000 Pacific islands created by volcanic activity. Most of these have tropical climates with wet and dry seasons. **New Zealand**, Australia's nearest neighbor, boasts rich forests, mountain ranges, and relatively moderate temperatures, including rainfall throughout the year. **Antarctica** is covered with ice. Its major resource consists of scientific information. It supports some wildlife, such as penguins, and little vegetation, primarily mosses or lichens.

THEORY OF PLATE TECTONICS

According to the geological theory of plate tectonics, Earth's crust is made up of ten major and several minor **tectonic plates**. These plates are the solid areas of the crust. They float on top of Earth's mantle, which is made up of molten rock. Because the plates float on this liquid component of Earth's crust, they move, creating major changes in Earth's surface. These changes can happen very slowly over a long time period, such as in continental drift, or rapidly, such as when earthquakes occur. **Interaction** between the different continental plates can create mountain ranges, volcanic activity, major earthquakes, and deep rifts.

TYPES OF PLATE BOUNDARIES

Plate tectonics defines three types of plate boundaries, determined by how the edges of the plates interact. These **plate boundaries** are:

- **Convergent boundaries**—the bordering plates move toward one another. When they collide directly, this is known as continental collision, which can create very large, high mountain ranges such as the Himalayas and the Andes. If one plate slides under the other, this is called subduction. Subduction can lead to intense volcanic activity. One example is the Ring of Fire that lies along the northern Pacific coastlines.
- **Divergent boundaries**—plates move away from each other. This movement leads to rifts such as the Mid-Atlantic Ridge and East Africa's Great Rift Valley.
- **Transform boundaries**—plate boundaries slide in opposite directions against each other. Intense pressure builds up along transform boundaries as the plates grind along each other's edges, leading to earthquakes. Many major fault lines, including the San Andreas Fault, lie along transform boundaries.

EROSION, WEATHERING, TRANSPORTATION, AND DEPOSITION

Erosion involves movement of any loose material on Earth's surface. This can include soil, sand, or rock fragments. These loose fragments can be displaced by natural forces such as wind, water, ice, plant cover, and human factors. **Mechanical erosion** occurs due to natural forces. **Chemical erosion** occurs as a result of human intervention and activities. **Weathering** occurs when atmospheric elements affect Earth's surface. Water, heat, ice, and pressure all lead to weathering. **Transportation** refers to loose material being moved by wind, water, or ice. Glacial movement, for example, carries everything from pebbles to boulders, sometimes over long distances. **Deposition** is the result of transportation. When material is transported, it is eventually deposited, and builds up to create formations like moraines and sand dunes.

EFFECTS OF HUMAN INTERACTION AND CONFLICT ON GEOGRAPHICAL BOUNDARIES

Human societies and their interaction have led to divisions of territories into **countries** and various other subdivisions. While these divisions are at their root artificial, they are important to geographers in discussing various populations' interactions.

Geographical divisions often occur through conflict between different human populations. The reasons behind these divisions include:

- Control of resources
- Control of important trade routes
- Control of populations

Conflict often occurs due to religious, political, language, or race differences. Natural resources are finite and so often lead to conflict over how they are distributed among populations.

STATE SOVEREIGNTY

State sovereignty recognizes the division of geographical areas into areas controlled by various governments or groups of people. These groups control not only the territory but also all its natural resources and the inhabitants of the area. The entire planet Earth is divided into **political** or **administratively sovereign areas** recognized to be controlled by a particular government, with the exception of the continent of Antarctica.

Alliances

Alliances form between different countries based on similar interests, political goals, cultural values, or military issues. Six existing **international alliances** include:

- North Atlantic Treaty Organization (NATO)
- Common Market
- European Union (EU)
- United Nations (UN)
- Caribbean Community
- Council of Arab Economic Unity

In addition, very large **companies** and **multi-national corporations** can create alliances and various kinds of competition based on the need to control resources, production, and the overall marketplace.

Ways Agricultural Revolution Changed Society

The agricultural revolution began approximately 6,000 years ago when the **plow** was invented in **Mesopotamia**. Using a plow drawn by animals, people were able to cultivate crops in large quantities rather than gathering available seeds and grains and planting them by hand. Because large-scale agriculture was labor-intensive, this led to the development of stable communities where people gathered to make farming possible. As **stable farming communities** replaced groups of nomadic hunter-gatherers, human society underwent profound changes. Societies became dependent on limited numbers of crops as well as subject to the vagaries of weather. Trading livestock and surplus agricultural output led to the growth of large-scale **commerce** and **trade routes**.

Ways Human Populations Modify Their Surrounding Environment

The agricultural revolution led human societies to begin changing their surroundings to accommodate their needs for shelter and room to cultivate food and to provide for domestic animals. Clearing ground for crops, redirecting waterways for irrigation purposes, and building permanent settlements all create major changes in the **environment**. Large-scale agriculture can lead to loose topsoil and damaging erosion. Building large cities leads to degraded air quality, water pollution from energy consumption, and many other side effects that can severely damage the environment. Recently, many countries have taken action by passing laws to **reduce human impact** on the environment and reduce the potentially damaging side effects. This is called **environmental policy**.

Ecology

Ecology is the study of the way living creatures interact with their environment. **Biogeography** explores the way physical features of Earth affect living creatures.

Ecology bases its studies on three different levels of the environment:

- **Ecosystem**—this is a specific physical environment and all the organisms that live there.
- **Biome**—this is a group of ecosystems, usually consisting of a large area with similar flora and fauna as well as similar climate and soil. Examples of biomes include deserts, tropical rain forests, taigas, and tundra.
- **Habitat**—this is an area in which a specific species usually lives. The habitat includes the necessary soil, water, and resources for that particular species, as well as predators and other species that compete for the same resources.

Types of Interactions Occurring Between Species in an Individual Habitat

Different interactions occur among species and members of single species within a habitat. These **interactions** fall into three categories:

- **Competition** — competition occurs when different animals, either of the same species or of different species, compete for the same resources. Robins can compete with other robins for available food, but other insectivores also compete for these same resources.
- **Predation**— predation occurs when one species depends on the other species for food, such as a fox who subsists on small mammals.
- **Symbiosis** — symbiosis occurs when two different species exist in the same environment without negatively affecting each other. Some symbiotic relationships are beneficial to one or both organisms without harm occurring to either.

Importance of an Organism's Ability to Adapt

If a species is relocated from one habitat to another, it must **adapt** in order to survive. Some species are more capable of adapting than others. Those that cannot adapt will not survive. There are different ways a creature can adapt, including behavior modification and structural or physiological changes. Adaptation is also vital if an organism's environment changes around it. Although the creature has not been relocated, it finds itself in a new environment that requires changes in order to survive. The more readily an organism can adapt, the more likely it is to survive. The almost infinite ability of **humans** to adapt is a major reason why they are able to survive in almost any habitat in any area of the world.

Biodiversity

Biodiversity refers to the variety of habitats that exist on the planet, as well as the variety of organisms that can exist within these habitats. A greater level of **biodiversity** makes it more likely that an individual habitat will flourish along with the species that depend upon it. Changes in habitat, including climate change, human intervention, or other factors, can reduce biodiversity by causing the extinction of certain species.

Texas Geography

Geography of Texas

Occupying about 7% of the total water and land area of the US, it is the **second largest state** after Alaska, and is the southernmost part of the Great Plains. Texas is in the south-central part of the United States of America, and is considered to form part of both the US **South** and **Southwest**. The Rio Grande, Red and Sabine Rivers all provide natural state lines where Texas borders Oklahoma on the north, Louisiana and Arkansas on the east, New Mexico on the west and the Mexican states of Chihuahua, Coahuila, Nuevo León, and Tamaulipas to the south. Austin, the state capital, is farther south than all other US state capitals except Honolulu. By residents, the state is generally divided into North, East, Central, South, and West Texas, but according to the Texas Almanac, Texas has four major physical regions: the **Gulf Coastal Plains**, **Interior Lowlands**, **Great Plains**, and **Basin and Range Province**. This has been cited as the difference between human geography and physical geography. Some regions of Texas are associated with the South (primarily East Texas and North Texas), while other regions share more similarities with the Southwest (primarily West Texas and South Texas). Even the northwestern part of the state seems to have more in common with parts of the United States (Kansas and Nebraska) that are considered "midwestern" and never "southern." The size of Texas prohibits easy categorization of the entire state wholly in any recognized region of the United States.

With 10 climatic regions, 14 soil regions, and 11 distinct ecological regions, **classifying** regions becomes problematic with differences in soils, topography, geology, rainfall, and plant and animal communities. The geographic center of Texas is about 15 miles northeast of Brady in northern McCulloch County. Guadalupe Peak, at 8,749 feet above sea level is the highest point in Texas. The lowest being sea level where Texas meets the Gulf of Mexico. Texas has five state forests and 120 state parks for a total of over 605,000 acres. There are 3,700 named streams and 15 major river systems flowing through 191,000 miles of Texas. Eventually emptying into seven major estuaries, these rivers support over 212 reservoirs. Texas is so large in its east-west expanse that El Paso, in the western corner of the state, is closer to San Diego, California than to Beaumont, near the Louisiana state line; Beaumont, in turn, is closer to Jacksonville, Florida than it is to El Paso.

Climate in Texas

Continental, Mountain, and Modified Marine are the three major **climatic types** of Texas, with no distinguishable boundaries. **Modified Marine**, or subtropical, dominates the majority of the state. Texas has an annual precipitation range from 60.57 inches in Jasper County, East Texas, to 9.43 inches in El Paso. The record high of 120 °F (49 °C) was reached at Seymour on Aug. 12, 1936, and Monahans on June 28, 1994. The low also ties at -23 °F (-31 °C) in Tulia on Feb. 12, 1899, and Seminole on Feb. 8, 1933. Most of Texas is under direct threat from drought, heat, hail, high winds, flash floods, hurricanes, and tornadoes. Select areas occasionally suffer from dust storms, river floods, snow and ice. Amarillo has the highest average wind speed in Texas at 14.3 mph (23 km/h).

Gulf Coastal Plains of Texas

The Gulf Coastal Plains range from the Gulf of Mexico inland to the Balcones Fault and the Eastern Cross Timbers. This large area stretches from the cities of Paris to San Antonio to Del Rio but shows a large variety in vegetation. The thick pineywoods of east Texas and the brush country south of San Antonio are found here. With about 20 to 50 inches annual rainfall, this is a nearly level, drained plain dissected by streams and rivers flowing into estuaries and marshes. Windblown sands and dunes, grasslands, oak mottes and salt marshes make up the seaward areas.

Interior Lowlands of Texas

The Interior Lowlands are bounded by the Caprock Escarpment to the west, the Edwards Plateau to the south, and the Eastern Cross Timbers to the east. This area includes the North Central Plains around the cities of Abilene and Wichita Falls, the Western Cross Timbers to the west of Fort Worth, the Grand Prairie, and the Eastern Cross Timbers to the east of Dallas. With about 35 to 50 inches annual rainfall, gently rolling to hilly forested land is part of a larger pine-hardwood forest of oaks, hickories, elm and gum trees. Soils vary from coarse sands to tight clays or red-bed clays and shales.

Great Plains of Texas

The Great Plains include the Llano Estacado, the Panhandle, Edwards Plateau, Toyah Basin, and the Llano Uplift. It is bordered on the east by the Caprock Escarpment in the panhandle and by the Balcones Fault to the southeast. Cities in this region include Austin, San Angelo, Midland and Odessa, Lubbock, and Amarillo. The Hill Country is a popular name for the area of hills along the Balcones Escarpment and is a transitional area between the Great Plains and the Gulf Coastal Plains. With about 15 to 31 inches annual rainfall, the southern end of the Great Plains are gently rolling plains of shrub and grassland, and home to the dramatic Caprock Canyons and Palo Duro Canyon state parks. The largest concentration of playa lakes in the world (nearly 22,000) is on the Southern High Plains of Texas and Eastern New Mexico.

Texas's **Blackland Prairie** were some of the first areas farmed in Texas. Highly expansive clays with characteristic dark coloration, called the Houston Black series, occur on about 1.5 million acres extending from north of Dallas south to San Antonio. The Professional Soil Scientists Association of Texas has recommended to the State Legislature that the Houston Black series be designated the State soil.

Basin and Range Province of Texas

The most complex Natural Region, it includes Sand Hills, the Stockton Plateau, desert valleys, wooded mountain slopes and desert grasslands. The **Basin and Range Province** in extreme western Texas stretches west of the Pecos River beginning with the Davis Mountains on the east and the Rio Grande to its west and south. The Trans-Pecos region is the only part of Texas regarded as mountainous and includes seven named peaks in elevation greater than 8,000 feet. With less than 12 inches annual rainfall, this region includes sand hills, desert valleys, wooded mountain slopes and desert grasslands.The vegetation diversity includes at least 268 grass species and 447 species of woody plants.

Chapter Quiz

Ready to see how well you retained what you just read? Scan the QR code to go directly to the chapter quiz interface for this study guide. If you're using a computer, simply visit the online resources page at **mometrix.com/resources719/texessocst4-8** and click the Chapter Quizzes link.

Economics

Economics is the study of the ways specific societies **allocate** resources to individuals and groups within that society. Also important are the choices society makes regarding what efforts or initiatives are funded and which are not. Since resources in any society are finite, allocation becomes a vivid reflection of that society's values. In general, the economic system that drives an individual society is based on:

- What goods are produced
- How those goods are produced
- Who acquires the goods or benefits from them

Economics consists of two main categories: **macroeconomics**, which studies larger systems, and **microeconomics**, which studies smaller systems.

Scarcity and Choice

Economics could rightfully be called the study of **scarcity**. Limited resources are available to satisfy the wants and needs of both individuals and states. Economics involves the **choices** made by an economy to satisfy these wants and needs. Every economy must choose what goods and services to produce, how to produce them, and for whom they are intended. Limitations of the factors of production—land, labor, and capital—sometimes make these choices difficult. When an economic choice is made, there is an "**opportunity cost**" implicit in the choice. The opportunity cost is what is given up by making a choice. If a country chooses to manufacture automobiles, it may not have the industrial capacity to produce tanks or aircraft. Thus, the economic choice to make automobiles involves the opportunity cost of not making tanks or aircraft. Individuals and countries continually make economic choices and sacrifice opportunist costs in the process. An individual may choose to attend a film rather than go out to dinner. Choices are driven by what people and countries feel is in their best interest.

Marginalism

Marginalism concerns itself with the economic worth of the last (or next) product or service provided. The cost of making the last product, the cost of hiring the last employee, and the cost of selling the last product, determine the **marginal cost** of that next good. Presumably, a company will continue to produce goods and services until it becomes unprofitable. Production will cease when the marginal return of a product does not yield a profit. From the consumer's viewpoint, the **marginal utility** of the purchase is the crucial factor. How much satisfaction does an individual get from each purchase? When this marginal utility decreases too much, the buyer will not buy the next unit. The idea of diminishing returns often determines how many units of a good or service a buyer will purchase. For example, after eating a piece of pie, the want-satisfying power of the next piece of pie is decreased. When this marginal utility reaches a certain point, the consumer will stop buying.

Costs

Costs and revenues are the two determinants of income, the most common measuring tools for assessing business success. Firms incur **fixed costs**, which are constant and do not depend on that amount of production. Examples would be physical plants and heavy equipment, which must be paid for even if production is zero. **Variable costs** are tied directly to the production of finished goods and services. As more goods are produced, variable costs rise. Examples of variable costs are raw materials used in the production process, extra labor needed in peak production periods, and additional capital if expansion is needed.

Exchange

Economic exchange is the basic activity of economics. The circular cycle of exchange from consumer to suppliers and back are the transactions that move an economy. The field of exchange is the marketplace, and money is the medium through which these transactions move. Building an **infrastructure** for market transactions is necessary to allow an orderly and dependable mechanism for economic exchange.

Traditional Economy

In a traditional economy, determinations of the types and amounts of goods produced, methods of production, and distribution of goods are based on long-established customs and habits. Such economies are sometimes referred to as subsistence economies because little surplus is produced, which negates the need for markets.

Market Economy

A market economy is based on supply and demand. **Demand** has to do with what customers want and need, as well as what quantity those consumers are able to purchase based on other economic factors. **Supply** refers to how much can be produced to meet demand, or how much suppliers are willing and able to sell. Where the needs of consumers meet the needs of suppliers is referred to as a market equilibrium price. This price varies depending on many factors, including the overall health of a society's economy and the overall beliefs and considerations of individuals in society. The following is a list of terms defined in the context of a market economy:

- **Elasticity**—this is based on how the quantity of a particular product responds to the price demanded for that product. If quantity responds quickly to changes in price, the supply/demand for that product is said to be elastic. If it does not respond quickly, then the supply/demand is inelastic.
- **Market efficiency**—this occurs when a market is capable of producing output high enough to meet consumer demand.
- **Comparative advantage**—in the field of international trade, this refers to a country focusing on a specific product that it can produce more efficiently and more cheaply, or at a lower opportunity cost, than another country, thus giving it a comparative advantage in production.

Review Video: Basics of Market Economy
Visit mometrix.com/academy and enter code: 791556

Planned Economy vs. Market Economy

In a **market economy**, supply and demand are determined by consumers. In a **planned economy**, a public entity or planning authority makes the decisions about what resources will be produced, how they will be produced, and who will be able to benefit from them. The means of production, such as factories, are also owned by a public entity rather than by private interests. In **market socialism**, the economic structure falls somewhere between the market economy and the planned economy. Planning authorities determine the allocation of resources at higher economic levels, while consumer goods are driven by a market economy.

Microeconomics

While economics generally studies how resources are allocated, **microeconomics** focuses on economic factors such as the way consumers behave, how income is distributed, and output and input markets. Studies are limited to the industry or firm level rather than an entire country or society. Among the elements studied in microeconomics are factors of production, costs of production, and factor income. These factors determine production decisions of individual firms, based on resources and costs.

Classification of Various Markets by Economists

The conditions prevailing in a given market are used to **classify** markets. Conditions considered include:

- Existence of competition
- Number and size of suppliers
- Influence of suppliers over price

- Variety of available products
- Ease of entering the market

Once these questions are answered, an economist can classify a certain market according to its structure and the nature of competition within the market.

Market Failure

When any of the elements for a successfully competitive market are missing, this can lead to a **market failure**. Certain elements are necessary to create what economists call "**perfect competition**." If one of these factors is weak or lacking, the market is classified as having "**imperfect competition**." Worse than imperfect competition, though, is a market failure. There are five major types of market failure:

- Inadequate competition
- Inadequate information
- Immobile resources
- Negative externalities, or side effects
- Failure to provide public goods

Externalities are side effects of a market that affect third parties. These effects can be either negative or positive.

Factors of Production and Costs of Production

Every good and service requires certain resources, or **inputs**. These inputs are referred to as **factors of production**. Every good and service requires four factors of production:

- Labor
- Capital
- Land
- Entrepreneurship

These factors can be fixed or variable and can produce fixed or variable costs. Examples of **fixed costs** include land and equipment. **Variable costs** include labor. The total of fixed and variable costs makes up the cost of production.

Factor Income

Factors of production each have an associated **factor income**. Factors that earn income include:

- **Labor**—earns wages
- **Capital**—earns interest
- **Land**—earns rent
- **Entrepreneurship**—earns profit

Each factor's income is determined by its **contribution**. In a market economy, this income is not guaranteed to be equal. How scarce the factor is and the weight of its contribution to the overall production process determines the final factor income.

Kinds of Market Structures in an Output Market.

The four kinds of market structures in an output market are:

- **Perfect competition**—all existing firms sell an identical product. The firms are not able to control the final price. In addition, there is nothing that makes it difficult to become involved in or leave the industry. Anything that would prevent entering or leaving an industry is called a barrier to entry. An example of this market structure is agriculture.
- **Monopoly**—a single seller controls the product and its price. Barriers to entry, such as prohibitively high fixed cost structures, prevent other sellers from entering the market.
- **Monopolistic competition**—a number of firms sell similar products, but they are not identical, such as different brands of clothes or food. Barriers to entry are low.
- **Oligopoly**—only a few firms control the production and distribution of products, such as automobiles. Barriers to entry are high, preventing large numbers of firms from entering the market.

Types of Monopolies

Four types of monopolies are:

- **Natural monopoly**—a single supplier has a distinct advantage over the others.
- **Geographic monopoly**—only one business offers the product in a certain area.
- **Technological monopoly**—a single company controls the technology necessary to supply the product.
- **Government monopoly**—a government agency is the only provider of a specific good or service.

Actions Taken by the US Government to Control Monopolies

The US government has passed several acts to regulate businesses, including:

- **Sherman Antitrust Act (1890)**—this prohibited trusts, monopolies, and any other situations that eliminated competition.
- **Clayton Antitrust Act (1914)**—this prohibited price discrimination.
- **Robinson-Patman Act (1936)**—this strengthened provisions of the Clayton Antitrust Act, requiring businesses to offer the same pricing on products to any customer.

The government has also taken other actions to ensure competition, including requirements for public disclosure. The **Securities and Exchange Commission (SEC)** requires companies that provide public stock to provide financial reports on a regular basis. Because of the nature of their business, banks are further regulated and required to provide various information to the government.

Marketing and Utility

Marketing consists of all of the activity necessary to convince consumers to acquire goods. One major way to move products into the hands of consumers is to convince them that any single product will satisfy a need. The ability of a product or service to satisfy the need of a consumer is called **utility**. There are four types of utility:

- **Form utility**—a product's desirability lies in its physical characteristics.
- **Place utility**—a product's desirability is connected to its location and convenience.
- **Time utility**—a product's desirability is determined by its availability at a certain time.
- **Ownership utility**—a product's desirability is increased because ownership of the product passes to the consumer.

Marketing behavior will stress any or all of these types of utility when marketing to the consumer.

Producers Determining What Customers Desire for Their Products

Successful marketing depends not only on convincing customers they need the product but also on focusing the marketing towards those who already have a need or desire for the product. Before releasing a product into the general marketplace, many producers will **test** markets to determine which will be the most receptive to the product. There are three steps usually taken to evaluate a product's market:

- **Market research**—this involves researching a market to determine if it will be receptive to the product.
- **Market surveys**—a part of market research, market surveys ask consumers specific questions to help determine the marketability of a product to a specific group.
- **Test marketing**—this includes releasing the product into a small geographical area to see how it sells. Often test marketing is followed by wider marketing if the product does well.

Major Elements of a Marketing Plan

The four major elements of a marketing plan are:

- **Product**—this includes any elements pertaining directly to the product, such as packaging, presentation, or services to include along with it.
- **Price**—this calculates the cost of production, distribution, advertising, etc., as well as the desired profit to determine the final price.
- **Place**—this determines which outlets will be used to sell the product, whether traditional outlets such as brick and mortar stores or through direct mail or internet marketing.
- **Promotion**—this involves ways to let consumers know the product is available, through advertising and other means.

Once these elements have all been determined, the producer can proceed with production and distribution of his product.

Distribution Channels

Distribution channels determine the route a product takes on its journey from producer to consumer, and can also influence the final price and availability of the product. There are two major forms of distributions: wholesale and retail. A **wholesale distributor** buys in large quantities and then resells smaller amounts to other businesses. **Retailers** sell directly to the consumers rather than to businesses. In the modern marketplace, additional distribution channels have grown up with the rise of markets such as club warehouse stores as well as purchasing through catalogs or over the internet. Most of these newer distribution channels bring products more directly to the consumer, eliminating the need for middlemen.

Distribution of Income in a Society

Distribution of income in any society ranges from poorest to richest. In most societies, income is not distributed evenly. To determine **income distribution**, family incomes are ranked from lowest to highest. These rankings are divided into five sections called **quintiles**, which are compared to each other. The uneven distribution of income is often linked to higher levels of education and ability in the upper classes but can also be due to other factors such as discrimination and existing monopolies. The **income gap** in America continues to grow, largely due to growth in the service industry, changes in the American family unit, and reduced influence of labor unions. **Poverty** is defined by comparing incomes to poverty guidelines. Poverty guidelines determine the level of income necessary for a family to function. Those below the poverty line are often eligible for assistance from government agencies.

Macroeconomics

Macroeconomics examines economies on a much larger level than microeconomics. While **microeconomics** studies economics on a firm or industry level, **macroeconomics** looks at economic trends and structures on a national level. Variables studied in macroeconomics include:

- Output
- Consumption
- Investment
- Government spending
- Net exports

The overall economic condition of a nation is defined as the **Gross Domestic Product**, or GDP. GDP measures a nation's economic output over a limited time period, such as a year.

Review Video: Microeconomics and Macroeconomics
Visit mometrix.com/academy and enter code: 538837

Review Video: Gross Domestic Product
Visit mometrix.com/academy and enter code: 409020

Taxes

Any assessment or charge to an individual economic unit by a government or quasi-government may be termed a **tax**. Some taxes are **direct**, such as a sales tax on goods and services sold. Other taxes may be **indirect**, property taxes being a prime example. Earlier economic systems received "taxes" as goods and services rendered to a ruling authority. In contemporary economics, we usually think of taxes in terms of legal currency. Taxes have caused revolutions ("No taxation without representation"), have overturned governments, and have become a social and political issue of controversy and debate. Who should pay taxes, how much should be paid, and the use of tax revenue are all critical issues in the fabric of society. The branch of formal economics most concerned with taxes is public finance.

Types of Consumer Behavior

The two major types of consumer behavior as defined in macroeconomics are:

- **Marginal propensity to consume (MPC)** defines the tendency of consumers to increase spending in conjunction with increases in income. In general, individuals with greater income will buy more. As individuals increase their income through job changes or growth of experience, they will also increase spending.
- **Utility** is a term that describes the satisfaction experienced by a consumer in relation to acquiring and using a good or service. Providers of goods and services will stress utility to convince consumers they want the products being presented.

Ways to Measure the Gross Domestic Product of a Country

Gross domestic product (GDP) is the total value of all the goods and services produced within a country during a certain time period. It is often used as a measurement of a country's economic health.

The two major ways to measure the Gross Domestic Product of a country are:

- The **expenditures approach** calculates the GDP based on how much money is spent in each individual sector.
- The **income approach** calculates the GDP based on how much money is earned in each sector.

Both methods yield the same results, and both of these calculation methods are based on four **economic sectors** that make up a country's macro-economy:

- Consumers
- Business
- Government
- Foreign sector

Types of Earnings Generated by an Economy Considered to Calculate GDP

Several factors must be considered in order to accurately calculate the GDP using the incomes approach. **Income factors** are:

- Wages paid to laborers, or compensation of employees (CE)
- Rental income derived from land
- Interest income derived from invested capital
- Entrepreneurial income

Entrepreneurial income consists of two forms. **Proprietor's income** is income that comes back to the entrepreneur himself. **Corporate profit** is income that goes back into the corporation as a whole. Corporate profit is divided by the corporation into corporate profits taxes, dividends, and retained earnings. Two other figures must be subtracted in the incomes approach. These are **indirect business taxes**, including property and sales taxes, and **depreciation**.

Effects of Population of a Country on the Gross Domestic Product

Changes in population can affect the calculation of a nation's **GDP**, particularly since GDP and GNP (Gross National Product) are generally measured per capita. If a country's economic production is low but the population is high, the income per individual will be lower than if the income is high and the population is lower. Also, if the population grows quickly and the income grows slowly, individual income will remain low or even drop drastically.

Population growth can also affect overall **economic growth**. Economic growth requires both that consumers purchase goods and workers produce them. A population that does not grow quickly enough will not supply enough workers to support rapid economic growth.

Problems with Equating GDP Per Capita and Economic Well-Being

Several economic factors may interfere with equating GDP per capita with individual well-being. A significant allocation of assets is used to combat the negative effects of economic growth such as the destruction of natural habitats and air and water pollution. Economic growth increases such **intangibles** as the increase in commuting, which affects quality of life. Perhaps most importantly, GDP does not account for a significant amount of **domestic production,** such as child-raising and homemaking. The money equivalents for these tasks are omitted from the GDP calculation. There are numerous markets that are left out of GDP, including black markets, criminal activity, and alternative economies. There is also no provision in GDP for volunteer activity, "do it yourself" tasks such as home improvements and landscape management. All of these economic activities are omitted from the formal measurement of per capita GDP and fail to give an accurate picture of individual well-being.

Ideal Balance to be Obtained in an Economy

Ideally, an economy functions efficiently, with the **aggregate supply**, or the amount of national output, equal to the **aggregate demand**, or the amount of the output that is purchased. In these cases, the economy is stable and prosperous. However, economies more typically go through **phases**. These phases are:

- **Boom**—GDP is high and the economy prospers
- **Recession**—GDP falls and unemployment rises
- **Trough**—the recession reaches its lowest point
- **Recovery**—unemployment lessens, prices rise, and the economy begins to stabilize again

These phases tend to repeat in cycles that are not necessarily predictable or regular.

Measures of National Income and Output

National income may be defined as the aggregate figure of all consumption, individual, business, and governmental income, plus total investments and the balance of trade accounts for a country. This aggregate number, derived from adding these categories together, is called the **expenditure method** of national income determination. Another calculation to determine the national income is to account for all the goods and services produced in a country during a fixed period. This is called the **production accounting** of national income. Yet another way of computing national income is to total all income received by individuals, businesses, and governments to arrive at total national income. This is the **income approach** to national income accounting. To summarize, there are three ways of calculating national income: total expenditures, total value of production, and the aggregate consumption figures for a country.

Consumer Price Indices

A price index, such as the **Consumer Price Index**, can be used as a measuring tool to compare prices at different times. A fictional "market basket" of commonly consumed staples is measured and charted over a period of time (usually one year). If the price of the representative market basket has gone up, **inflation** has occurred. For example, if a typical basket costs $500 this year as compared to $400 last year for the same basket, inflation has risen over a year. Inflation reduces the buying power of money, and if uncontrolled, can threaten the entire economy.

Unemployment and Inflation

When demand outstrips supply, prices are driven artificially high, or are **inflated**. This occurs when too much spending causes an imbalance in the economy. In general, inflation occurs because an economy is growing too quickly. When there is too little spending, and supply has moved far beyond demand, a **surplus** of product results. Companies cut back on production and reduce the number of employees, and **unemployment** rises as people lose their jobs. This imbalance occurs when an economy becomes sluggish. In general, both these economic instability situations are caused by an imbalance between supply and demand. Government intervention may be necessary to stabilize an economy when either inflation or unemployment becomes too serious.

Different Forms of Unemployment

- **Frictional**—when workers change jobs and are unemployed while waiting for new jobs
- **Structural**—when economic shifts reduce the need for workers
- **Cyclical**—when natural business cycles bring about loss of jobs
- **Seasonal**—when seasonal cycles reduce the need for certain jobs
- **Technological**—when advances in technology result in the elimination of certain jobs

Any of these factors can increase unemployment in certain sectors.

Inflation is classified by the overall rate at which it occurs:

- **Creeping inflation**—this is an inflation rate of about 1%-3% annually.
- **Walking inflation**—this is an inflation rate of 3%-10% annually.
- **Galloping inflation**— a severe inflation rate above 10 percent (to upwards of 100 percent and beyond) annually. Highly detrimental to the economy, this deeply impacts the lower and middle class populus.
- **Hyperinflation**— an inflation rate over 50% monthly or 500+ percent annually. Hyperinflation usually leads to complete monetary collapse in a society. Individuals are unable to have enough income to purchase their needed goods.

Government Intervention Policies That Mitigate Inflation and Unemployment

When an economy becomes too imbalanced, either due to excessive spending or not enough spending, **government intervention** often becomes necessary to put the economy back on track. Government fiscal policy can take several forms, including:

- Contractionary policy
- Expansionary policy
- Monetary policy

Contractionary policies help counteract inflation. These include increasing taxes and decreasing government spending to slow spending in the overall economy. **Expansionary policies** increase government spending and lower taxes in order to reduce unemployment and increase the level of spending in the economy overall. **Monetary policy** can take several forms and affects the amount of funds available to banks for making loans.

Study and Quantification of Populations and Population Growth

Populations are studied by **size**, rates of **growth** due to immigration, the overall **fertility rate**, and **life expectancy**. For example, though the population of the United States is considerably larger than it was two hundred years ago, the rate of population growth has decreased greatly, from about three percent per year to less than one percent per year.

In the US, the fertility rate is fairly low, with most choosing not to have large families, and life expectancy is high, creating a projected imbalance between older and younger people in the near future. In addition, immigration and the mixing of racially diverse cultures are projected to increase the percentages of Asians, Hispanics, and African Americans.

Functions and Types of Money

Money is used in three major ways:

- As an accounting unit
- As a store of value
- As an exchange medium

In general, money must be acceptable throughout a society in exchange for debts or to purchase goods and services. Money should be relatively scarce, its value should remain stable, and it should be easily carried, durable, and easy to divide up. There are three basic types of money: commodity, representative, and fiat. **Commodity money** includes gems or precious metals. **Representative money** can be exchanged for items such as gold or silver that have inherent value. **Fiat money**, or legal tender, has no inherent value but has been declared to function as money by the government. It is often backed by gold or silver but not necessarily on a one-to-one ratio.

Investment and Credit

Investment is committing financial resources to a particular account or asset in order to earn a return at a later time. Each type of **investment** carries a different level of risk and a different potential return, though it can be difficult to determine exactly how profitable a particular endeavor will be in the long run. **Credit** is the process by which a financial institution lends funds to an individual for the purchase of a particular product or service. This means that the financial institution will cover the cost of the product or service in exchange for the individual agreeing to pay back that money, and any interest associated with the loan or credit, at a later time.

Types of Money Available in the US and Economists' Measure of It

Money in the US is not just currency. When economists calculate the amount of money available, they must take into account other factors, such as deposits that have been placed in checking accounts, debit cards, and "near moneys," such as savings accounts, that can be quickly converted into cash. Currency, checkable deposits and traveler's checks, referred to as **M1**, are added up, and then **M2** is calculated by adding savings deposits, CDs, and various other monetary deposits. The final result is the total quantity of available money.

Aspects of Monetary Policy and the Role of the Federal Reserve System

The Federal Reserve System, also known as the **Fed**, implements all monetary policy in the US. Monetary policy regulates the amount of money available in the American banking system. The Fed can decrease or increase the amount of available money for loans, thus helping regulate the national economy. Monetary policies implemented by the Fed are part of expansionary or contractionary monetary policies that help counteract inflation or unemployment. The **discount rate** is an interest rate charged by the Fed when banks borrow money from them. A lower discount rate leads banks to borrow more money, leading to increased spending. A higher discount rate has the opposite effect.

How Banks Function

Banks earn their income by **loaning** out money and charging **interest** on those loans. If less money is available, fewer loans can be made, which affects the amount of spending in the overall economy. While banks function by making loans, they are not allowed to loan out all the money they hold in deposit. The amount of money they must maintain in reserve is known as the **reserve ratio**. If the reserve ratio is raised, less money is available for loans and spending decreases. A lower reserve ratio increases available funds and increases spending. This ratio is determined by the Federal Reserve System.

Central Banks

Central banks of countries are the institutions that control currency (and the money supply) through monetary and fiscal policy. These central banks or other monetary authorities (set up as an agency by the government) control and implement monetary policy and activity. Such authorities differ in their power from country to country. For example, in the United States, the Federal Reserve is a wholly independent agency free of political controls. Although Congress legislated the Federal Reserve into existence, it remains completely independent in its activity.

Open Market Operations

The Federal Reserve System can also expand or contract the overall money supply through **open market operations**. In this case, the Fed can buy or sell **bonds** it has purchased from banks or individuals. When the Fed buys bonds, more money is put into circulation, creating an expansionary situation to stimulate the economy. When the Fed sells bonds, money is withdrawn from the system, creating a **contractionary** situation to slow an economy suffering from inflation. Because of international financial markets, however, American banks often borrow and lend money in markets outside the US. By shifting their attention to international markets, domestic banks and other businesses can circumvent whatever contractionary policies the Fed may have put into place.

Major Characteristics of International Trade

International trade can take advantage of broader markets, bringing a wider variety of products within easy reach. By contrast, it can also allow individual countries to specialize in particular products that they can produce easily, such as those for which they have easy access to raw materials. Other products, more difficult to make domestically, can be acquired through trade with other nations. **International trade** requires efficient use of **native resources** as well as sufficient **disposable income** to purchase native and imported products. Many countries in the world engage extensively in international trade, but others still face major economic challenges.

Major Characteristics of a Developing Nation

The five major characteristics of a developing nation are:

- Low GDP
- Rapid growth of population
- Economy that depends on subsistence agriculture
- Poor conditions, including high infant mortality rates, high disease rates, poor sanitation, and insufficient housing
- Low literacy rate

Developing nations often function under oppressive governments that do not provide private property rights and withhold education and other rights from women. They also often feature an extreme disparity between upper and lower classes, with little opportunity for the lower classes to improve their position.

Stages of Economic Development

Economic development occurs in three stages that are defined by the activities that drive the economy:

- Agricultural stage
- Manufacturing stage
- Service sector stage

In developing countries, it is often difficult to acquire the necessary funding to provide equipment and training to move into the advanced stages of economic development. Some can receive help from developed countries via foreign aid and investment or international organizations such as the **International Monetary Fund** or the **World Bank**. Having developed countries provide monetary, technical, or military assistance can help developing countries move forward to the next stage in their development.

Controls

An imposition of wage and price controls is a more drastic way to slow or halt inflation. These measures have many drawbacks, including the possibility of depressing the economy too far. Controls also promote hoarding and artificial shortages and sometimes encourage the creation of alternative marketplaces that impair economic growth.

Labor Demand

The totality of all firms' demand for labor is called the **total market demand for labor**. The market supply of labor depends on the population, level of skill required, prevalent economic condition, and effective wage rate. When the demand and supply curves for labor intersect, the **competitive equilibrium wage rate** is determined. Firms will continue to hire labor until the marginal revenue product of labor, or its demand for labor, reaches the wage rate. **Labor unions** can distort the supply and demand for labor, and thus the wage determination, by increasing productivity, reducing the labor force with excessive union dues, and bargaining with businesses and threatening strikes.

Obstacles Developing Nations Face Regarding Economic Growth

Developing nations typically struggle to overcome obstacles that prevent or slow economic development. Major **obstacles** can include:

- Rapid, uncontrolled population growth
- Trade restrictions
- Misused resources, often perpetrated by the government
- Traditional beliefs that can slow or reject change

Corrupt, oppressive governments often hamper the economic growth of developing nations, creating huge **economic disparities** and making it impossible for individuals to advance, in turn preventing overall growth. Governments sometimes export currency, called **capital flight**, which is detrimental to a country's economic development. In general, countries are more likely to experience economic growth if their governments encourage entrepreneurship and provide private property rights.

Problems When Industrialization Occurs Too Quickly

Rapid growth throughout the world leaves some nations behind and sometimes spurs their governments to move forward too quickly into **industrialization** and **artificially rapid economic growth**. While slow or nonexistent economic growth causes problems in a country, overly rapid industrialization carries its own issues. Four major problems encountered due to rapid industrialization are:

- Use of technology not suited to the products or services being supplied
- Poor investment of capital
- Lack of time for the population to adapt to new paradigms
- Lack of time to experience all stages of development and adjust to each stage

Economic failures in Indonesia were largely due to rapid growth that was poorly handled.

Importance of E-Commerce in Today's Marketplace

The growth of the internet has brought many changes to our society, not the least of which is the modern way of business. Where supply channels used to move in certain necessary ways, many of these channels are now bypassed as **e-commerce** makes it possible for nearly any individual to set up a direct market to consumers, as well as direct interaction with suppliers. Competition is fierce. In many instances, e-commerce can provide nearly instantaneous gratification, with a wide variety of products. Whoever provides the best product most quickly often rises to the top of a marketplace. How this added element to the marketplace will affect the economy in the future remains to be seen. Many industries are still struggling with the best ways to adapt to the rapid, continuous changes.

Knowledge Economy and Possible Effect on Future Economic Growth

The knowledge economy is a growing sector in the economy of developed countries, and includes the trade and development of:

- Data
- Intellectual property
- Technology, especially in the area of communications

Knowledge as a resource is steadily becoming more and more important. What is now being called the **Information Age** may prove to bring about changes in life and culture as significant as those brought on by the Agricultural and Industrial Revolutions.

CYBERNOMICS

Related to the knowledge economy is what has been dubbed "**cybernomics**," or economics driven by e-commerce and other computer-based markets and products. Marketing has changed drastically with the growth of cyber communication, allowing suppliers to connect one-on-one with their customers. Other issues coming to the fore regarding cybernomics include:

- Secure online trade
- Intellectual property rights
- Rights to privacy
- Bringing developing nations into the fold

As these issues are debated and new laws and policies developed, the face of many industries continues to undergo drastic change. Many of the old ways of doing business no longer work, leaving industries scrambling to function profitably within the new system.

Chapter Quiz

Ready to see how well you retained what you just read? Scan the QR code to go directly to the chapter quiz interface for this study guide. If you're using a computer, simply visit the online resources page at **mometrix.com/resources719/texessocst4-8** and click the Chapter Quizzes link.

Government and Citizenship

US Government and Citizenship

Political Science and Its Ties to Other Major Disciplines

Political science focuses on studying different governments and how they compare to each other, general political theory, ways political theory is put into action, how nations and governments interact with each other, and a general study of governmental structure and function. Other elements of **political science** include the study of elections, governmental administration at various levels, development and action of political parties, and how values such as freedom, power, justice, and equality are expressed in different political cultures. Political science also encompasses elements of other disciplines, including:

- **History**—how historical events have shaped political thought and process
- **Sociology**—the effects of various stages of social development on the growth and development of government and politics
- **Anthropology**—the effects of governmental process on the culture of an individual group and its relationships with other groups
- **Economics**—how government policies regulate the distribution of products and how they can control and/or influence the economy in general

General Political Theory

Based on general political theory, the four major purposes of any given government are:

- **Ensuring national security**—the government protects against international, domestic, and terrorist attacks and also ensures ongoing security through negotiating and establishing relationships with other governments.
- **Providing public services**—the government should "promote the general welfare," as stated in the Preamble to the US Constitution, by providing whatever is needed to its citizens.
- **Ensuring social order**—the government supplies means of settling conflicts among citizens as well as making laws to govern the nation, state, or city.
- **Making decisions regarding the economy**—laws help form the economic policy of the country, regarding both domestic and international trade and related issues. The government also has the ability to distribute goods and wealth to some extent among its citizens.

Main Theories Regarding the Origin of the State

There are four main theories regarding the origin of the state:

- **Evolutionary**—the state evolved from the family, with the head of state the equivalent of the family's patriarch or matriarch.
- **Force**—one person or group of people brought everyone in an area under their control, forming the first government.
- **Divine Right**—certain people were chosen by the prevailing deity to be the rulers of the nation, which is itself created by the deity or deities.
- **Social Contract**—there is no natural order. The people allow themselves to be governed to maintain social order, while the state, in turn, promises to protect the people they govern. If the government fails to protect its people, the people have the right to seek new leaders.

Public Policy

Public policy is the study of how the various levels of government formulate and implement policies. **Public policy** also refers to the set of policies that a government adopts and implements, including laws, plans, actions, and behaviors, for the purpose of governing society. Public policy is developed and adapted through the process of **policy analysis**. Public policy analysis is the systematic evaluation of alternative means of reaching social goals. Public policy is divided into various policy areas, including domestic policy, foreign policy, healthcare policy, education policy, criminal policy, national defense policy, and energy policy.

Influences of Philosophers on Political Study

Ancient Greek philosophers **Aristotle** and **Plato** believed political science would lead to order in political matters and that this scientifically organized order would create stable, just societies.

- **Thomas Aquinas** adapted the ideas of Aristotle to a Christian perspective. His ideas stated that individuals should have certain rights but also certain duties, and that these rights and duties should determine the type and extent of government rule. In stating that laws should limit the role of government, he laid the groundwork for ideas that would eventually become modern constitutionalism.
- **Niccolò Machiavelli**, author of *The Prince*, was a proponent of politics based on power. He is often considered the founder of modern political science.
- **Thomas Hobbes**, author of *Leviathan* (1651), believed that individuals' lives were focused solely on a quest for power and that the state must work to control this urge. Hobbes felt that people were completely unable to live harmoniously without the intervention of a powerful, undivided government.

Contributions of John Locke, Montesquieu, and Rousseau to Political Science

John Locke published *Two Treatises of Government* in 1689. This work argued against the ideas of Thomas Hobbes. He put forth the theory of *tabula rasa*—that people are born with minds like blank slates. Individual minds are molded by experience, not innate knowledge or intuition. He also believed that all men should be independent and equal. Many of Locke's ideas found their way into the Constitution of the United States.

The two French philosophers, **Montesquieu** and **Rousseau**, heavily influenced the French Revolution (1789-1799). They believed government policies and ideas should change to alleviate existing problems, an idea referred to as "liberalism." Rousseau, in particular, directly influenced the Revolution with writings such as *The Social Contract* (1762) and *Declaration of the Rights of Man and of the Citizen* (1789). Other ideas Rousseau and Montesquieu espoused included:

- Individual freedom and community welfare are of equal importance
- Man's innate goodness leads to natural harmony
- Reason develops with the rise of civilized society
- Individual citizens carry certain obligations to the existing government

Political Ideologies of Famous Philosophers

David Hume and **Jeremy Bentham** believed politics should have as its main goal maintaining "the greatest happiness for the greatest number." Hume also believed in empiricism, or that ideas should not be believed until the proof has been observed. He was a natural skeptic and always sought out the truth of matters rather than believing what he was told.

John Stuart Mill, a British philosopher and economist, made significant contributions to the fields of social and economic theory. A majorly influential thinker in the realm of classical liberalism, Mill believed in progressive policies such as women's suffrage, emancipation, and the development of labor unions and farming cooperatives. His ideas on free speech and the harm principle were the basis for the "clear and present danger" test outlined by Oliver Wendell Holmes Jr. when determining if speech is protected by the First Amendment of the US Constitution.

Johann Fichte and **Georg Hegel**, German philosophers in the late 18th and early 19th centuries, supported a form of liberalism grounded largely in socialism and a sense of nationalism.

Main Political Orientations

The four main political orientations are:

- **Liberal**—liberals believe that government should work to increase equality, even at the expense of some freedoms. Government should assist those in need, focusing on enforced social justice and free basic services for everyone.
- **Conservative**—a conservative believes that government should be limited in most cases. The government should allow its citizens to help one another and solve their own problems rather than enforcing solutions. Business should not be overregulated, allowing a free market.
- **Moderate**—this ideology incorporates some liberal and some conservative values, generally falling somewhere between in overall belief.
- **Libertarian**—libertarians believe that the government's role should be limited to protecting the life and liberty of citizens. Government should not be involved in any citizen's life unless that citizen is encroaching upon the rights of another.

Major Principles of Government as Outlined in the United States Constitution

The six major principles of government as outlined in the United States Constitution are:

- **Federalism**—the power of the government does not belong entirely to the national government but is divided between federal and state governments.
- **Popular sovereignty**—the government is determined by the people and gains its authority and power from the people.
- **Separation of powers**—the government is divided into three branches (executive, legislative, and judicial) with each having its own set of powers.
- **Judicial review**—courts at all levels of government can declare laws invalid if they contradict the constitutions of individual states, or the US Constitution, with the Supreme Court serving as the final judicial authority on decisions of this kind.
- **Checks and balances**—no single branch can act without input from another, and each branch has the power to "check" any other, as well as balance other branches' powers.
- **Limited government**—governmental powers are limited, and certain individual rights are defined as inviolable by the government.

Types of Powers Delegated to the National Government by the US Constitution

The structure of the US government divides power between national and state governments. Powers delegated to the federal government by the Constitution are:

- **Expressed powers**—powers directly defined in the Constitution, including power to declare war, regulate commerce, make money, and collect taxes
- **Implied powers**—powers the national government must have in order to carry out the expressed powers
- **Inherent powers**—powers inherent to any government, not expressly defined in the Constitution

Some of these powers, such as collection and levying of taxes, are also granted to the individual state governments.

Primary Positions of Federalism and Development through the Years in the US

The way federalism should be practiced has been the subject of debate since the writing of the Constitution. There were—and still are—two main factions regarding this issue:

- **States' rights**—those favoring the states' rights position feel that the state governments should take the lead in performing local actions to manage various problems.
- **Nationalist**—those favoring a nationalist position feel the national government should take the lead to deal with those same matters.

The flexibility of the Constitution has allowed the US government to shift and adapt as the needs of the country have changed. Power has often shifted from the state governments to the national government and back again, and both levels of government have developed various ways to influence each other.

Effects of Federalism on Policy-Making and the Balance of Politics in the US

Federalism has three major effects on **public policy** in the US:

- Determining whether the local, state, or national government originates policy
- Affecting how policies are made
- Ensuring policy-making functions under a set of limitations

Federalism also influences the **political balance of power** in the US by:

- Making it difficult, if not impossible, for a single political party to seize total power
- Ensuring that individuals can participate in the political system at various levels
- Making it possible for individuals working within the system to be able to affect policy at some level, whether local or more widespread

Three Branches of the US Federal Government

The following are the three branches of the US Federal government and the individuals that belong to each branch:

- **Legislative Branch**—this consists of the two houses of Congress: the House of Representatives and the Senate. All members of the Legislative Branch are elected officials.
- **Executive Branch**—this branch is made up of the president, vice president, presidential advisors, and other various cabinet members. Advisors and cabinet members are appointed by the president, but they must be approved by Congress.
- **Judicial Branch**—the federal court system, headed by the Supreme Court.

Review Video: What Does the Executive Branch Do?
Visit mometrix.com/academy and enter code: 210629

Review Video: What Does the Judicial Branch Do?
Visit mometrix.com/academy and enter code: 278093

Review Video: What Does the Legislative Branch Do?
Visit mometrix.com/academy and enter code: 405303

Major Responsibilities of the Three Branches of the Federal Government

The three branches of the federal government each have specific roles and responsibilities:

- The **Legislative Branch** is largely concerned with lawmaking. All laws must be approved by Congress before they go into effect. They are also responsible for regulating money and trade, approving presidential appointments, and establishing organizations like the postal service and federal courts. Congress can also propose amendments to the Constitution, and can impeach, or bring charges against, the president. Only Congress can declare war.
- The **Executive Branch** carries out laws, treaties, and war declarations enacted by Congress. The president can also veto bills approved by Congress, and serves as commander in chief of the US military. The president appoints cabinet members, ambassadors to foreign countries, and federal judges.
- The **Judicial Branch** makes decisions on challenges as to whether laws passed by Congress meet the requirements of the US Constitution. The Supreme Court may also choose to review decisions made by lower courts to determine their constitutionality.

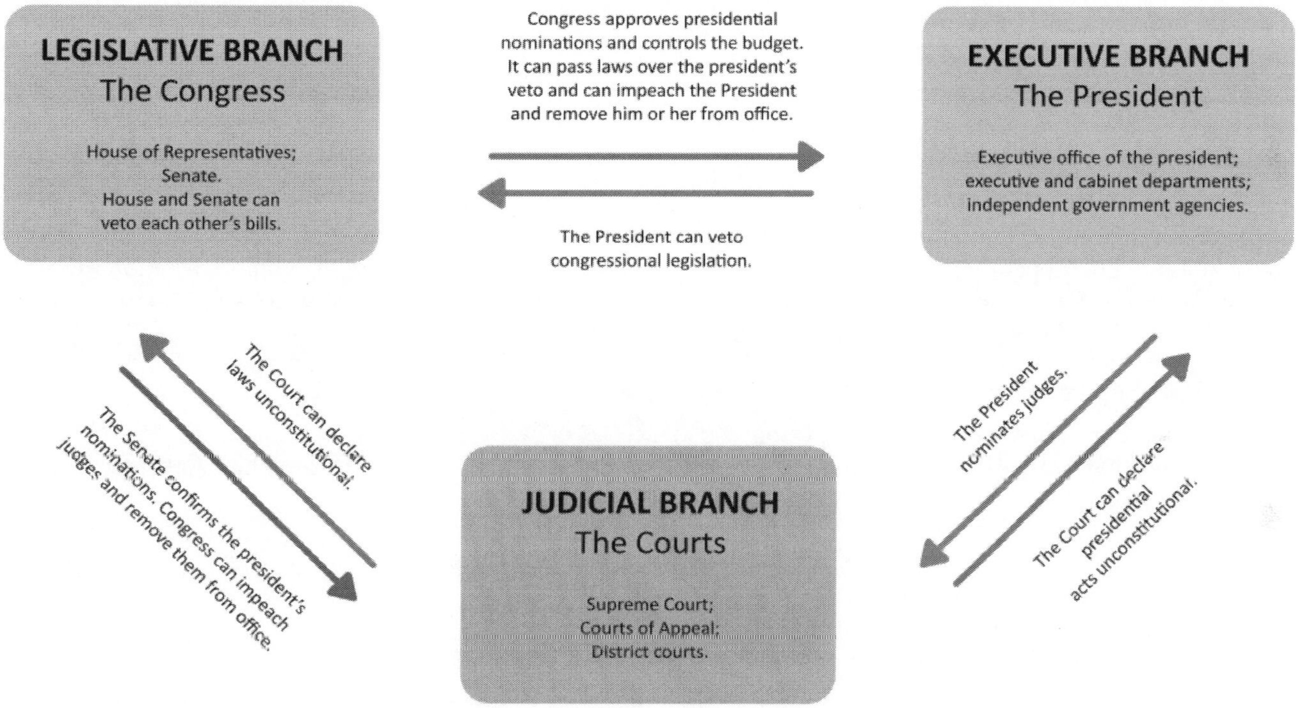

US Citizenship

Qualifications of a US citizen/How Citizenship May Be Lost

Anyone born in the US, born abroad to a US citizen, or who has gone through a process of naturalization is considered a **citizen** of the United States. It is possible to lose US citizenship as a result of conviction of certain crimes such as treason. Citizenship may also be lost if a citizen pledges an oath to another country or serves in the military of a country engaged in hostilities with the US. A US citizen can also choose to hold dual citizenship, work as an expatriate in another country without losing US citizenship, or even to renounce citizenship if he or she so chooses.

Rights, Duties, and Responsibilities Granted to or Expected from Citizens

Citizens are granted certain rights under the US government. The most important of these are defined in the **Bill of Rights**, and include freedom of speech, religion, assembly, and a variety of other rights the government is not allowed to remove. A US citizen also has a number of **duties**:

- Paying taxes
- Loyalty to the government (though the US does not prosecute those who criticize or seek to change the government)
- Support and defense of the Constitution
- Serving in the Armed Forces when required by law
- Obeying laws as set forth by the various levels of government.

Responsibilities of a US citizen include:

- Voting in elections
- Respecting one another's rights and not infringing on them
- Staying informed about various political and national issues
- Respecting one another's beliefs

Bill of Rights

Importance of the Bill of Rights

The first ten amendments of the US Constitution are known as the **Bill of Rights**. These amendments prevent the government from infringing upon certain freedoms that the Founding Fathers felt were natural rights that already belonged to all people. These rights included freedom of speech, freedom of religion, freedom of assembly, and the right to bear arms. Many of the rights were formulated in direct response to the way the colonists felt they had been mistreated by the British government.

Rights Granted in the Bill of Rights

The first ten amendments were passed by Congress in 1789. Three-fourths of the existing thirteen states had ratified them by December of 1791, making them official additions to the Constitution. The rights granted in the Bill of Rights are:

- **First Amendment**—freedom of religion, speech, freedom of the press, and the right to assemble and to petition the government
- **Second Amendment**—the right to bear arms
- **Third Amendment**—Congress cannot force individuals to house troops
- **Fourth Amendment**—protection from unreasonable search and seizure
- **Fifth Amendment**—no individual is required to testify against himself, and no individual may be tried twice for the same crime
- **Sixth Amendment**—the right to criminal trial by jury and the right to legal counsel
- **Seventh Amendment**—the right to civil trial by jury
- **Eighth Amendment**—protection from excessive bail or cruel and unusual punishment
- **Ninth Amendment**—prevents rights not explicitly named in the Constitution from being taken away because they are not named
- **Tenth Amendment**—any rights not directly delegated to the national government, or not directly prohibited by the government from the states, belong to the states or to the people

Review Video: Bill of Rights
Visit mometrix.com/academy and enter code: 585149

SITUATIONS WHERE THE GOVERNMENT RESTRICTS THE FIRST AMENDMENT FREEDOMS

In some cases, the government restricts certain elements of First Amendment rights. Some examples include:

- **Freedom of religion**—when a religion espouses illegal activities, the government often restricts these forms of religious expression. Examples include polygamy, animal sacrifice, and use of illicit drugs or illegal substances.
- **Freedom of speech**—this can be restricted if exercise of free speech endangers other people.
- **Freedom of the press**—laws prevent the press from publishing falsehoods.

In **emergency situations** such as wartime, stricter restrictions are sometimes placed on these rights, especially rights to free speech and assembly, and freedom of the press, in order to protect national security.

CONSTITUTION'S ADDRESS OF THE RIGHTS OF THOSE ACCUSED OF CRIMES

The US Constitution makes allowances for the **rights of criminals**, or anyone who has transgressed established laws. There must be laws to protect citizens from criminals, but those accused of crimes must also be protected and their basic rights as individuals preserved. In addition, the Constitution protects individuals from the power of authorities to prevent police forces and other enforcement organizations from becoming oppressive. The fourth, fifth, sixth, and eighth amendments specifically address these rights.

SUPREME COURT'S PROVISION OF EQUAL PROTECTION FOR ALL INDIVIDUALS

When the Founding Fathers wrote in the Declaration of Independence that "all men are created equal," they actually were referring to men, and, in fact, defined citizens as white men who owned land. However, as the country has developed and changed, the definition has expanded to more wholly include all people.

"**Equality**" does not mean all people are inherently the same, but it does mean they all should be granted the same rights and should be treated the same by the government. Amendments to the Constitution have granted citizenship and voting rights to all Americans regardless of race or gender. The Supreme Court evaluates various laws and court decisions to determine if they properly represent the idea of **equal protection**. One sample case was Brown v. Board of Education in 1954, which declared separate-but-equal treatment to be unconstitutional.

PROTESTS

A protest is an expression of opposition to, and sometimes of support of, events or circumstances. **Protests** represent a means for individuals to publicly make their views heard in an effort to influence public opinion or government policy, or as a means to enact **change**. Protests generally result when self-expression of opposing views is restricted by government policy, political or economic circumstances, religion, social structures, or the media, and people react by declaring their views through cultural mechanisms or on the streets. There are numerous forms of protest, including boycotts, civil disobedience, demonstrations, non-violent protests, picketing, protest marches, protest songs, riots, sit-ins, teach-ins, strikes, and others.

CIVIL LIBERTY CHALLENGES ADDRESSED IN CURRENT POLITICAL DISCUSSIONS

The **civil rights movements** of the 1960s and the ongoing struggle for the rights of women and other minorities have sparked **challenges to existing law**. In addition, debate has raged over how much information the government should be required to divulge to the public. Major issues in the 21st century political climate include:

- Continued debate over women's rights, especially regarding equal pay for equal work
- Debate over affirmative action to encourage hiring of minorities
- Debate over civil rights of homosexuals, including marriage and military service
- Decisions as to whether minorities should be compensated for past discriminatory practices
- Balance between the public's right to know and the government's need to maintain national security
- Balance between the public's right to privacy and national security

Civil Liberties vs. Civil Rights

While the terms *civil liberties* and *civil rights* are often used interchangeably, in actuality, their definitions are slightly different. The two concepts work together, however, to define the basics of a free state:

- **"Civil liberties"** define the constitutional freedoms guaranteed to citizens. Examples include freedoms such as free speech, privacy, or free thought.
- **"Civil rights"** are guarantees of or protections of civil liberties. One comparison can be found in the case of freedom of religion. The civil liberty is that one has the freedom to practice the religion of his or her choice, whereas the civil right would protect that individual from being denied a job on the basis of their religion.

Suffrage, Franchise, and the Change of Voting Rights Over American History

Suffrage and franchise both refer to the right to **vote**. As the US developed as a nation, there was much debate over which individuals should hold this right. In the early years, only white male landowners were granted suffrage. By the 19th century, most states had franchised, or granted the right to vote, to all adult white males. The **Fifteenth Amendment** of 1870 granted suffrage to formerly enslaved men. The **Nineteenth Amendment** gave women the right to vote in 1920, and in 1971 the **Twenty-sixth Amendment** expanded voting rights to include any US citizen over the age of eighteen. However, those who have not been granted full citizenship and citizens who have committed certain crimes do not have voting rights.

Ways in Which the Voting Process Has Changed Over the Years

The first elections in the US were held by **public ballot**. However, election abuses soon became common, since public ballot made it easy to intimidate, threaten, or otherwise influence the votes of individuals or groups of individuals. New practices were put into play, including **registering voters** before elections took place and using a **secret or Australian ballot**. In 1892, the introduction of the **voting machine** further privatized the voting process, since it allowed complete privacy for voting. Today, debate continues about the accuracy of various voting methods, including high-tech voting machines and even low-tech punch cards.

Effect of Political Parties on the Functioning of an Individual Government

Different types and numbers of political parties can have a significant effect on how a government is run. If there is a **single party**, or a one-party system, the government is defined by that one party, and all policy is based on that party's beliefs. In a **two-party system**, two parties with different viewpoints compete for power and influence. The US is basically a two-party system, with checks and balances to make it difficult for one party to gain complete power over the other. There are also **multiparty systems**, with three or more parties. In multiparty systems, various parties will often come to agreements in order to form a majority and shift the balance of power.

Development of Political Parties in the US.

George Washington was adamantly against the establishment of **political parties**, based on the abuses perpetrated by such parties in Britain. However, political parties developed in US politics almost from the beginning. Major parties throughout US history have included:

- **Federalists and Democratic-Republicans**—these parties formed in the late 1700s and disagreed on the balance of power between national and state government.
- **Democrats and Whigs**—these developed in the 1830s, and many political topics of the time centered on national economic issues.
- **Democrats and Republicans**—the Republican Party developed before the Civil War, after the collapse of the Whig party, and the two parties debated issues centering on slavery and economic issues, such as taxation.

While third parties sometimes enter the picture in US politics, the government is basically a two-party system, dominated by the Democrats and Republicans.

Functions of Political Parties

Political parties form organizations at all levels of government. Activities of individual parties include:

- Recruiting and backing candidates for offices
- Discussing various issues with the public, increasing public awareness
- Working toward compromise on difficult issues
- Staffing government offices and providing administrative support

At the administrative level, parties work to ensure that viable candidates are available for elections and that offices and staff are in place to support candidates as they run for office and afterward, when they are elected.

Processes of Selecting Political Candidates

Historically, in the quest for political office, a potential candidate has followed one of the following four processes:

- **Nominating convention**—an official meeting of the members of a party for the express purpose of nominating candidates for upcoming elections. The Democratic National Convention and the Republican National Convention, convened to announce candidates for the presidency, are examples of this kind of gathering.
- **Caucus**—a meeting, usually attended by a party's leaders. Some states still use caucuses, but not all.
- **Primary election**—the most common method of choosing candidates today, the primary is a publicly held election to choose candidates.
- **Petition**—signatures gathered to place a candidate on the ballot. Petitions can also be used to place legislation on a ballot.

Ways the Average Citizen Participates in the Political Process

In addition to voting for elected officials, American citizens are able to participate in the political process through several other avenues. These include:

- Participating in local government
- Participating in caucuses for large elections
- Volunteering to help political parties
- Running for election to local, state, or national offices

Individuals can also donate money to political causes or support political groups that focus on specific causes such as abortion, wildlife conservation, or women's rights. These groups often make use of **representatives** who lobby legislators to act in support of their efforts.

Ways in Which Political Campaign Gains Funding

Political campaigns are very expensive. In addition to the basic necessities of a campaign office, including office supplies, office space, etc., a large quantity of the money that funds a political campaign goes toward **advertising**. Money to fund a political campaign can come from several sources, including:

- The candidate's personal funds
- Donations by individuals
- Special interest groups

The most significant source of campaign funding is **special interest groups**. Groups in favor of certain policies will donate money to candidates they believe will support those policies. Special interest groups also do their own advertising in support of candidates they endorse.

Presidential Elections

The President of the United States is elected **indirectly** by members of an **electoral college**. Members of the electoral college nearly always vote along the lines of the popular vote of their respective states. The winner of a presidential election is the candidate with at least 270 **Electoral College votes**. It is possible for a candidate to win the electoral vote and lose the popular vote. Incumbent Presidents and challengers typically prefer a balanced ticket, where the President and Vice President are elected together and generally balance one another with regard to geography, ideology, or experience working in government. The nominated Vice Presidential candidate is referred to as the President's **running mate**.

Importance of Free Press and the Media

The right to free speech guaranteed in the first amendment to the Constitution allows the media to report on **government and political activities** without fear of retribution. Because the media has access to information about the government, the government's policies and actions, and debates and discussions that occur in Congress, it can keep the public informed about the inner workings of the government. The media can also draw attention to injustices, imbalances of power, and other transgressions the government or government officials might commit. However, media outlets may, like special interest groups, align themselves with certain political viewpoints and skew their reports to fit that viewpoint. The rise of the **internet** has made media reporting even more complex, as news can be found from an infinite variety of sources, both reliable and unreliable.

Forms of Government

Anarchism, Communism, and Dictatorship

Anarchists believe that all government should be eliminated and that individuals should rule themselves. Historically, anarchists have used violence and assassination to further their beliefs.

Communism is based on class conflict, revolution, and a one-party state. Ideally, a communist government would involve a single government for the entire world. Communist government controls the production and flow of goods and services rather than leaving this to companies or individuals.

Dictatorship involves rule by a single individual. If rule is enforced by a small group, this is referred to as an oligarchy. Dictators tend to rule with a violent hand, using a highly repressive police force to ensure control over the populace.

Fascism and Monarchy

Fascism centers on a single leader and is, ideologically, an oppositional belief to communism. **Fascism** includes a single-party state and centralized control. The power of the fascist leader lies in the "cult of personality," and the fascist state often focuses on expansion and conquering of other nations. **Monarchy** was the major form of government for Europe through most of its history.

A monarchy is led by a king or a queen. This position is hereditary, and the rulers are not elected. In modern times, constitutional monarchy has developed, where the king and queen still exist, but most of the governmental decisions are made by democratic institutions such as a parliament.

Parliamentary and Democratic Systems

In a parliamentary system, government involves a legislature and a variety of political parties. The head of government, usually a prime minister, is typically the head of the dominant party. A head of state can be elected, or this position can be taken by a monarch, as in Great Britain's constitutional monarchy system.

In a **democratic system** of government, the people elect their government representatives. The word *democracy* is a Greek term that means "rule of the people." There are two forms of democracy: direct and indirect. In a direct democracy, each issue or election is decided by a vote where each individual is counted separately. An indirect democracy employs a legislature that votes on issues that affect large numbers of people whom the legislative members represent. Democracy can exist as a parliamentary system or a presidential system. The US is a presidential, indirect democracy.

Presidential System and Socialism

A presidential system, like a parliamentary system, has a legislature and political parties, but there is no difference between the head of state and the head of government. Instead of separating these functions, an elected president performs both. Election of the president can be direct or indirect, and the president may not necessarily belong to the largest political party. In **socialism**, the state controls the production of goods, though it does not necessarily own all means of production. The state also provides a variety of social services to citizens and helps guide the economy. A democratic form of government often exists in socialist countries.

Review Video: Communism vs. Socialism
Visit mometrix.com/academy and enter code: 917677

Totalitarian and Authoritarian Systems

A totalitarian system believes everything should be under the control of the government—from resource production, to the press, to religion, and other social institutions. All aspects of life under a totalitarian system must conform to the ideals of the government. **Authoritarian** governments practice widespread state authority but do not necessarily dismantle all public institutions. If a church, for example, exists as an organization but poses no threat to the authority of the state, an authoritarian government might leave it as it is. While all totalitarian governments are by definition authoritarian, a government can be authoritarian without becoming totalitarian.

Review Video: Totalitarianism vs. Authoritarianism
Visit mometrix.com/academy and enter code: 104046

Parliamentary and Democratic Systems

In a parliamentary system, government involves a legislature and a variety of political parties. The head of government, usually a prime minister, is typically the head of the dominant party. A head of state can be elected, or this position can be taken by a monarch, as in Great Britain's constitutional monarchy system.

In a **democratic system** of government, the people elect their government representatives. The word *democracy* is a Greek term that means "rule of the people." There are two forms of democracy: direct and indirect. In a direct democracy, each issue or election is decided by a vote where each individual is counted separately. An indirect democracy employs a legislature that votes on issues that affect large numbers of people whom the legislative members represent. Democracy can exist as a parliamentary system or a presidential system. The US is a presidential, indirect democracy.

Realism, Liberalism, Institutionalism, and Constructivism

The theory of realism states that nations are by nature aggressive and work in their own self-interest. Relations between nations are determined by military and economic strength. The nation is seen as the highest authority. **Liberalism** believes states can cooperate and that they act based on capability rather than power. This term was originally coined to describe Woodrow Wilson's theories on international cooperation. In **institutionalism**, institutions provide structure and incentive for cooperation among nations. Institutions are defined as a set of rules used to make international decisions. These institutions also help distribute power and determine how nations will interact. **Constructivism**, like liberalism, is based on international cooperation but recognizes that perceptions countries have of each other can affect their relations.

Effects of Foreign Policy on a Country's Position in World Affairs

Foreign policy is a set of goals, policies, and strategies that determine how an individual nation will interact with other countries. These strategies shift, sometimes quickly and drastically, according to actions or changes occurring in the other countries. However, a nation's **foreign policy** is often based on a certain set of ideals and national needs. Examples of US foreign policy include isolationism versus internationalism. In the 1800s, the US leaned more toward isolationism, exhibiting a reluctance to become involved in foreign affairs. The World Wars led to a period of internationalism, as the US entered these wars in support of other countries and joined the United Nations. Today's foreign policy tends more toward **interdependence**, or **globalism**, recognizing the widespread effects of issues like economic health.

Major Figures Involved in Determining and Enacting US Foreign Policy

US foreign policy is largely determined by Congress and the president, influenced by the secretary of state, secretary of defense, and the national security adviser. Executive officials carry out policies. The main departments in charge of these day-to-day issues are the **US Department of State**, also referred to as the State Department. The Department of State carries out policy, negotiates treaties, maintains diplomatic relations, assists citizens traveling in foreign countries, and ensures that the president is properly informed of any international issues. The **Department of Defense**, the largest executive department in the US, supervises the armed forces and provides assistance to the president in his role as commander-in-chief.

Major Types of International Organizations

Two types of international organizations are:

- **Intergovernmental organizations (IGOs)**. These organizations are made up of members from various national governments. The UN is an example of an intergovernmental organization. Treaties among the member nations determine the functions and powers of these groups.
- **Nongovernmental organizations (NGOs)**. An NGO lies outside the scope of any government and is usually supported through private donations. An example of an NGO is the International Red Cross, which works with governments all over the world when their countries are in crisis but is formally affiliated with no particular country or government.

Role of Diplomats in International Relations

Diplomats are individuals who reside in foreign countries in order to maintain communications between that country and their home country. They help negotiate trade agreements and environmental policies, as well as conveying official information to foreign governments. They also help to resolve conflicts between the countries, often working to sort out issues without making the conflicts official in any way. **Diplomats**, or **ambassadors**, are appointed in the US by the president. Appointments must be approved by Congress.

Role of the United Nations in International Relations and Diplomacy

The United Nations (**UN**) helps form international policies by hosting representatives of various countries who then provide input into policy decisions. Countries that are members of the UN must agree to abide by all final UN resolutions, but this is not always the case in practice, as dissent is not uncommon. If countries do not follow UN resolutions, the UN can decide on sanctions against those countries, often economic sanctions, such as trade restriction. The UN can also send military forces to problem areas, with "peacekeeping" troops brought in from member nations. An example of this function is the Korean War, the first war in which an international organization played a major role.

Texas Government

MUNICIPALITIES IN TEXAS

LARGE

Larger cities (those exceeding 225,000) have a unique authority: that of "**limited annexation**," whereby an adjoining area may be annexed for purposes of imposing city ordinances related to safety and building codes. The residents can vote for mayor and council races but cannot vote in bond elections (and, consequently, the city cannot collect city sales tax from businesses or city property tax from owners). The purpose of limited annexation is to allow the city to control development in an area that it eventually will fully annex; it must do so within three years (though it can arrange "non-annexation agreements" with local property owners). During each of the three years, the city must develop a land use plan, identify needed capital improvements, and identify the financing for such improvements as well as to provide essential services. Municipal elections in Texas are **nonpartisan** in the sense that candidates do not appear on the ballot on party lines, and do not run as party tickets. However, a candidate's party affiliation is usually known or can be discerned with minimal effort (as the candidate most likely has supported other candidates on partisan tickets). In some instances, an informal citizen's group will support a slate of candidates that it desires to see elected. However, each candidate must be voted on individually.

SMALL

Texas does not have townships; areas within a county are either incorporated or unincorporated. **Incorporated areas** are part of a city, though the city may contract with the county for needed services. **Unincorporated areas** are not part of a city; in these areas the county has authority for law enforcement and road maintenance. Cities are classified as either "general law" or "home rule." A city may elect **home rule status** once it exceeds 5,000 population and the voters agree to home rule. Otherwise, it is classified as **general law** and has very limited powers. One example of the difference in the two structures regards annexation. General law cities cannot annex adjacent unincorporated areas without the property owner's consent; home rule cities may annex without consent but must provide essential services within a specified period of time (generally within three years) or the property owner may file suit to be deannexed. Once a city adopts home rule it may continue to keep this status even if the population later falls below 5,000.

FOUNDERS OF REPUBLIC OF TEXAS

The following are some of the founders of the Republic of Texas and their contributions:

- Stephen F. Austin (1793–1836), "Father of Texas"
- Edward Burleson (1798–1851), Texas soldier, general, and statesman
- David G. Burnet (1788–1870), interim President of the Republic of Texas
- Lorenzo de Zavala (1788–1836), first vice-president of the Republic of Texas and signer of the Texas Declaration of Independence
- Sam Houston (1793–1863), first President of Republic of Texas, later US Senator from Texas and Governor of Texas
- Anson Jones (1798–1858), last President of the Republic of Texas, called the "Architect of Annexation"
- Mirabeau B. Lamar (1798–1859), second President of Republic of Texas
- Jose Antonio Navarro (1795–1871), Texas statesman, revolutionary and politician
- Thomas Jefferson Rusk (1803–1857), Secretary of War between Texas and Mexico, chief justice of the Supreme Court of Texas and Senator from Texas after admission to the Union.
- Edwin Waller (1800–1881), judge, signer of the Texas Declaration of Independence

Important People from Texas During Civil War

The following are some important people from Texas during the Civil War and their contributions:

- Dick Dowling (1838–1867), commander at Sabine Pass and famous Houstonian
- John "Rip" Ford (1815–1897), Texas Rangers legend and commander at the Battle of Palmito Ranch
- John Bell Hood (1831–1879), commander of Hood's Texas Brigade and Confederate General
- Albert Sidney Johnston (1803–1862), Confederate General and commander of the Confederate western forces
- John B. Magruder (1807–1871), Confederate General at the Battle of Galveston
- Pleasant Tackitt (1803–1886), Confederate Officer and county official at Fort Belknap, Texas. One of the founders of Parker County, Texas.
- Charles S. West (1829–1885), Confederate officer and judge advocate general for the Trans-Mississippi Department
- Louis T. Wigfall (1816–1874), Confederate General and Senator from Texas, secured the surrender of Fort Sumter

Important People from the Texas Revolution

The following are some important people from the Texas Revolution and their contributions:

- Jim Bowie (1796–1836), frontiersman, died at the Battle of the Alamo
- Davy Crockett (1786–1836), frontiersman and US Congressman, died at the Alamo
- James Fannin (1804? –1836), key figure during the Texas Revolution
- Benjamin McCulloch (1811–1862), soldier in the Texas Revolution, Texas Ranger, US Marshal and brigadier general in the army of the Confederate States during the American Civil War
- Henry Eustace McCulloch (1816–1895), soldier in the Texas Revolution, Texas Ranger, and brigadier general in the army of the Confederate States during the American Civil War
- Juan Seguin (1806–1890), Tejano hero during the Texas Revolution
- William B. Travis (1809–1836), commander of Texas forces at the Alamo
- Logan Vandeveer (1815–1855), Hero of San Jacinto

Internal Politics of the Republic

Internal politics of the Republic were based on the conflict between two factions. The **nationalist faction**, led by **Mirabeau B. Lamar** advocated the continued independence of Texas, the expulsion of the Native Americans, and the expansion of Texas to the Pacific Ocean. Their opponents, led by **Sam Houston**, advocated the annexation of Texas to the United States and peaceful coexistence with Native Americans. The first flag of the republic was the "Burnet Flag" (a gold star on an azure field), followed shortly thereafter by official adoption of the Lone Star Flag. The Republic received diplomatic recognition from the United States, France, the United Kingdom, the Netherlands, and the Republic of Yucatán.

Important Texans in Science and Medicine

The following are some important people in the fields of science and medicine who are from Texas:

- Denton Cooley (b. 1920), pioneering heart surgeon
- Michael E. DeBakey (b. 1908), pioneering heart surgeon
- Chu Ching-wu, physicist
- Robert Dennard (b. 1932), computer scientist.
- Bryce DeWitt, physicist, co-developed Wheeler-DeWitt equation ("wave function of the Universe")
- Leonard Eugene Dickson, mathematician
- G.B. Halsted, mathematician
- M. King Hubbert (1903–1989), geophysicist
- Jack Kilby, electrical engineer

- Hermann Joseph Muller, geneticist, Nobel Laureate in Physiology or Medicine
- Ilya Prigogine, physicist and chemist, Nobel Laureate in Chemistry
- John Tate, mathematician, Wolf Prize in Mathematics
- Beatrice Tinsley, astronomer
- Karen Uhlenbeck, mathematician, National Medal of Science
- Harry Vandiver, mathematician
- Steven Weinberg, Nobel Laureate in Physics
- Spencer Wells, geneticist and anthropologist
- John A. Wheeler, physicist, Wolf Prize in Physics, coined the term 'black hole'

Statehood of Texas

On February 28, 1845, the US Congress passed a bill that would authorize the United States to **annex** the Republic of Texas and on March 1 US President **John Tyler** signed the bill. The legislation set the date for annexation for December 29 of the same year. On October 13 of the same year, a majority of voters in the Republic approved a proposed constitution that specifically endorsed slavery and the slave trade. This constitution was later accepted by the US Congress, making Texas a US state on the same day annexation took effect (therefore bypassing a territorial phase). One of the primary motivations for annexation was that the Texas government had incurred huge debts which the United States agreed to assume upon annexation. In the **Compromise of 1850**, in return for this assumption of $10 million of debt, a large portion of Texas-claimed territory, now parts of Colorado, Kansas, Oklahoma, New Mexico, and Wyoming, was ceded to the Federal government.

Spindletop

Anthony F. Lucas, an experienced mining engineer, drilled the first major oil well at **Spindletop** on the morning of January 10, 1901 on the little hill south of Beaumont, Texas. The **East Texas Oil Field**, discovered on October 5, 1930 is located in east central part of the state, and is the largest and most prolific oil reservoir in the contiguous United States. Other oil fields were later discovered in West Texas and under the Gulf of Mexico. The resulting "Oil Boom" permanently transformed the economy of Texas, and led to the first significant economic expansion after the Civil War.

Texas Secession from United States During Civil War

Texas **seceded** from the United States on February 1, 1861, and joined the **Confederate States of America** on March 2, 1861. Texas was mainly a "supply state" for the Confederate forces until mid 1863, when the Union capture of the Mississippi River made large movements of men, horses or cattle impossible. Texas regiments fought in every major battle throughout the war. The last battle of the Civil War, the **Battle of Palmito Ranch**, was fought in Texas on May 12, 1865.

Capital of Texas

Austin is the capital of Texas. The State Capitol resembles the federal Capitol Building in Washington, D.C., but is faced in Texas pink granite and is topped by a statue of the "Goddess of Liberty" holding aloft a five-point Texas star. The capitol is also notable for facing south toward Mexico City and for purposefully being built seven feet taller than the US national capitol.

Texas Constitution

The Texas Constitution, adopted in 1876, is the second oldest state constitution still in effect. As with many state constitutions, it explicitly provides for the **separation of powers** and incorporates its **bill of rights** directly into the text of the constitution (as Article I). The bill of rights is considerably lengthier and more detailed than the federal Bill of Rights, and includes some provisions unique to Texas.

Offices of US Government in Texas

Texas has a **Governor**, elects two US **Senators** and 32 US **Representatives**.

Legislature of Texas

The Legislature of Texas, like the legislature of every other state except Nebraska, is **bicameral** (that is, it has two chambers). The **House of Representatives** has 150 members, while the **Senate** has 31. The speaker of the house leads the House, and the lieutenant governor leads the state Senate. The Legislature meets in regular session only once every two years. The Legislature cannot call itself into special session; only the governor may call a special session, and may call as many sessions as often as desired.

Executive Branch of Government in Texas

The executive branch consists of the Governor, Lieutenant Governor, Comptroller of Public Accounts, Land Commissioner, Attorney General, Agriculture Commissioner, the three-member Texas Railroad Commission, the State Board of Education, and the Secretary of State. The comptroller decides whether expected state income is sufficient to cover the proposed state budget. Except for the secretary of state—who is appointed by the governor with the advice and consent of the Senate—each of these officials is **elected** (the three Railroad Commission members are voted at-large; the State Board of Education members are voted in single-member districts). There are also many state agencies and numerous boards and commissions. Partly because of many elected officials, the governor's powers are quite **limited** in comparison to other state governors or the US President. In popular lore and belief the lieutenant governor, who heads the Senate and appoints its committees, has more power than the governor. The governor commands the state militia and can veto bills passed by the Legislature and call special sessions of the Legislature (this power is exclusive to the governor and can be exercised as often as desired). The governor also appoints members of various executive boards and fills judicial vacancies between elections.

County Government in Texas

Texas has a total of 254 **counties**, by far the most counties of any state. Each county is run by a **commissioners court** consisting of four elected **commissioners** (one from each of four precincts drawn based on population) and a **county judge** elected from all the voters of the county. The county judge does not have the authority to veto a decision of the commissioners court; the judge votes along with the commissioners. In smaller counties, the county judge actually does perform judicial duties, but in larger counties the judge's role is limited to serving on the commissioners court. Certain officials, such as the sheriff and tax collector, are elected separately by the voters, but the commissioners court determines their office budgets and sets overall county policy. All county elections are partisan. Counties also have much less legal power than municipalities. For instance, counties in Texas do not have zoning power. However, counties do have eminent domain power. Counties do not have "home rule" authority; whatever powers are not specifically granted by the state are not permitted. Unlike other states, Texas does not allow for consolidated city-county governments. Cities and counties are permitted to enter "interlocal agreements" to share services.

Judicial Branch

The judicial system of Texas has a reputation as one of the most complex in the United States, with many layers and many overlapping jurisdictions. Texas has two courts of last resort: the **Texas Supreme Court**, which hears civil cases, and the **Texas Court of Criminal Appeals**. Except in the case of some municipal benches, partisan elections choose all of the judges at all levels of the judiciary; the governor fills vacancies by appointment.

Chapter Quiz

Ready to see how well you retained what you just read? Scan the QR code to go directly to the chapter quiz interface for this study guide. If you're using a computer, simply visit the online resources page at **mometrix.com/resources719/texessocst4-8** and click the Chapter Quizzes link.

Culture, Science, Technology, and Society

Anthropology, Sociology, and Psychology

Importance of Socialization to Individuals Within a Specific Culture

Individuals learn how to function within a specific culture, group, or society via a process called **socialization**. Social contact with other human beings is vitally important to early development so that children can grow up to function in society as expected.

During the early years, children receive socialization from their families, siblings, peers, and schoolmates, as well as from exposure to mass media when applicable. Observing the behavior of others and adapting it to their own use helps children learn to interact with others. This process continues throughout life as individuals learn to adapt to various situations and interact with new groups.

Processes That Bring Cultural Change and Traits That Appear in All Cultures

Three major processes bring about the majority of changes in a culture:

1. **Discovery**—finding things that already exist, such as fire, a major cultural transformer
2. **Invention**—creating new equipment, machinery, etc., that changes the way tasks are accomplished
3. **Diffusion**—borrowing elements from other cultures

Over 70 **traits** have been identified that are found in nearly every culture to some level. These traits can be divided into four categories that determine the basic structure, mores, norms, and other characteristics of a culture:

- Language and cognition
- Society
- Myth, ritual, and aesthetics
- Technology

Culture

Culture refers to all learned human behaviors and behavioral patterns and is made up of:

- **Cultural universals**—traits shared by all human beings, such as language
- **Culture**—all traditions that define a society
- **Subculture**—groups within a culture that share specific traits

While culture serves as a survival mechanism by bringing people together in groups and helping individuals identify with each other, it also undergoes frequent and sometimes profound **change** as groups respond to new technologies, knowledge, or contact with other cultures.

Characteristics and Importance of Religion in an Anthropological Sense

Strictly defined, **religion** consists of a belief system and usually a set of rituals involving worship of a supernatural force or forces that have some effect on both everyday life and the overall structure and functioning of the world around us. Religion provides meaning and explanation for various life events and profoundly affects a culture's **worldviews**. Religion provides emotional support for individuals and a sense of **community** within a group that has shared religious views. Religious organization also provides structured sets of **moral norms** and motivation to abide by these norms and rules.

Increased **secularization**, particularly in developed countries, has reduced the role of religion in everyday life, leading individuals to find other systems to fill these basic human needs.

Behaviorism

John B. Watson, an American, developed the idea of **behaviorism**. In his theory, growth, learning, and training would always win out over any possible inborn tendencies. He believed that any person, regardless of origin, could learn to perform any type of art, craft, or enterprise with sufficient training and experience.

Science of Sociology

Sociology is a scientific discipline that focuses on the study of societies. Human societies are made up of institutions, groups, and individuals. How all these levels of organization **interact** is the major interest of sociologists. The way individuals organize themselves, how they interact with each other, and the attitudes and beliefs different groups develop all define those groups' cultural backgrounds. Groups of people in the same geographical area often develop similar organizational structures, beliefs, and attitudes.

Impact of Technology and Media on Culture

Technology is one of the primary means through which culture is developed, exchanged, spread, and experienced. Historically, the introduction of new technologies have made culture more accessible to people. An early example of this is the printing press, which allowed cultural products, such as poetry, novels, and histories, to be accessed by people outside of the elite and rich classes. In the modern era, the invention of the internet and propagation of social media has led to the world's cultures becoming more interconnected than ever before. In addition to connecting people and providing access to certain elements of culture, the internet has bred its own unique cultural products, such as memes and online activism. While current technologies have connected the various cultures of the world, some social scientists believe that the internet and social media could lead to the homogenization of culture and the disappearance of tradition, as certain dominant cultures overpower others in the digital landscape.

Major Study Areas Covered by Sociology

The five major study areas covered by sociology are:

1. **Population studies**—these studies involve observing social patterns of groups of people who live in the same area.
2. **Social behaviors**—sociologists study how general behaviors change over time, as well as attitudes such as morale, need for conformity, and other elements of social interaction.
3. **Cultural influences**—the influences of culture on social groups include art, religion, language, and overall knowledge and learning.
4. **Social change**—this involves the ways societies change over time, including major events such as wars and revolutions, or the way technology changes how people interact.
5. **Social institutions**—large groups of people are organized to fit specific niches in society, such as churches, hospitals, government, businesses, and schools. These organizations change over time and according to the overall needs and beliefs of an individual society.

How Sociologists Gather and Test Data

The three major methods of gathering data for sociological studies are:

1. **Surveys**—gathering information via direct questioning of members of the social group being studied
2. **Controlled experiments**—performing experiments that change an element of society
3. **Field observations**—living among members of a particular group or culture and observing how they interact and live their everyday lives

Major Classifications of Social Groups

Social groups are defined based on how they come into being, how they develop, and how they interact with wider society. The five major classifications are:

1. **Primary groups**—focused on members' need for support, such as a family or friend grouping
2. **Secondary groups**—form around the need to complete a task
3. **Reference groups**—help form an individual's identity
4. **In-groups and out-groups**—oppose each other or exclude members of other groups
5. **Social networks**—provide multiple links to an often large number of other individuals

Major Types of Social Interaction

Five main forms of social interaction help define social groups:

1. Cooperation
2. Coercion
3. Conflict
4. Conformity
5. Social exchange

All of these elements can bring a group into existence, break it apart, or transform it.

Major Social Institutions that Characterize and Meet the Needs of Any Society

Six major social institutions that characterize and meet the needs of any society are:

1. **Family**—this is the basic unit of any society and the most important social institution in all sociological study.
2. **Education**—in many societies, the values and norms of culture are communicated through institutionalized education as well as via the family.
3. **Political institutions**—political institutions in a society determine the distribution of power.
4. **Economic institutions**—these institutions determine the distribution of wealth.
5. **Religion**—this provides mores and beliefs that help unify a culture. Unfortunately, many religions also function in an in-group/out-group capacity.
6. **Sport**—this reflects values of society, promotes unity, and provides an outlet for aggression.

Various Patterns to Define Relationships Involving Race and Ethnicity

In general, relationships within cultures involving race and ethnicity are defined by either assimilation or conflict. **Assimilation** in the US can involve:

- **Anglo-conformity**—immigrants and racial minorities conform to the expectations of Anglo-American society, whether by choice, necessity, or force.
- **Cultural pluralism**—this involves the acceptance of varieties of racial and ethnic groups.
- **Accommodation**—this is mutual adaptation between majority and minority groups.
- **Melting pot**—the mixing together of various ethnic groups will bring about a new cultural group.

Patterns of **conflict** include:

- **Population transfer**—one group is required or forced to leave by another group.
- **Subjugation**—one group exercises control over the other.
- **Genocide**—one group slaughters another.

Ways Gender and Age Lead to Discrimination

In spite of legislation, education, and other attempts to bring about a higher level of equality, **discrimination** still exists against women and the elderly, particularly as it involves law, politics, and economic standing. Discrimination against **women** is particularly profound in most developing countries. It is believed that increasing the standing of women in a society is a major element in increasing the overall livelihood of that society.

While some societies value the **elderly** for their knowledge and experience, others discriminate against older people because of their decreased physical ability and ability to contribute economically. In the US, the poverty level for the elderly still stands at about ten percent. As lifespan increases, all societies must find a way to accommodate the needs of the elderly population.

Importance of Auguste Comte

Auguste Comte, a French philosopher, first used the term *sociology* to describe the study of human organizations and culture. His major theory was **positivism**. Positivism relies entirely on physical and sensory data to describe and evaluate human experience, completely discounting anything metaphysical. **Social behavior**, according to Comte, could be measured scientifically, as could major events that occurred in different populations. Comte is considered to be the first sociologist in the Western world.

Influence of Émile Durkheim on Sociology and Sociological Study

Through Durkheim's efforts, sociology eventually came to be considered a discipline in major universities. Heavily influenced by Comte's views of positivism, Durkheim felt the larger world was influenced by group beliefs, attitudes, and cultural aspects rather than by individuals. He performed in-depth studies on the cause of higher suicide rates among certain social groups. In the course of this study, he discussed **anomie**, a condition when people are affected by larger changes in society, such as unemployment or alienation of social groups, and receive little moral guidance from society.

Philosophy of Karl Marx and Friedrich Engels

According to Marx and Engels, society worldwide could be boiled down to a constant struggle between **classes**. This socioeconomic battle, as explained in *The Communist Manifesto*, would eventually lead to a revolution by the working class, since work itself is a social organization that involves large groups of people.

Herbert Spencer

Herbert Spencer is credited with the idea known as **Social Darwinism**. Though he and Darwin were technically rivals, Spencer applied Darwin's idea of "**survival of the fittest**" (a term actually coined by Spencer) to the way society develops. According to Spencer, **competition** is the major driving force behind the development and changes inherent in human society.

Max Weber

Weber's major thesis stated that the differing **religions** of the East and West led to differences in societal development. Weber believed **Protestantism** as a religion influenced the development of **capitalism** in the West. He also stated that the organization of the state felt **violence** was a legitimate means of protecting citizenry or enforcing rule. Police action, military action, and violence of individuals against each other in order to protect themselves or property demonstrate the state's propensity to solve problems through violence.

Science of Anthropology

While archaeology studies the physical remains of populations, **anthropology,** in contrast, is the study of human culture, its development, and how various cultural groups are similar or different. Anthropologists often engage in direct study of cultures by living among them, observing and participating in everyday activities. This is referred to as "**participant observation.**" Anthropologists also perform cross-cultural and comparative research.

Anthropology can be divided into four major areas of study. Each one addresses a slightly different approach to culture and how it affects human beings, as well as how culture develops over time:

- **Archaeology**—this is the study of materials and physical items left behind by human settlements
- **Social-cultural anthropology**—focuses on cultural standards, beliefs, values, and norms
- **Biological anthropology**—this is the study of specific genetic characteristics of different populations
- **Linguistics**— this is the study of the development of languages over time

Subsistence Patterns and Its Major Classifications

The term *subsistence pattern* refers to ways in which societies obtain the necessities of life, such as food and shelter. The **subsistence pattern** of a society often directly correlates to its economy, population size, political systems, and overall technological development. Certain subsistence patterns can only support lower levels of societal development, while others can support a much more developed culture. The four major subsistence patterns are:

1. **Foraging**—the hunter-gatherer lifestyle
2. Pastoralism—herding
3. **Horticulture**—small-scale farming
4. Intensive agriculture—large-scale farming

Hunter-gatherer societies by nature are nomadic and do not tend to support highly developed cultures. Intensive agriculture, in contrast, can support a large population to a high subsistence level, allowing for the development of a sophisticated, modern culture.

Evolution in Anthropology

Darwin's theory of evolution had considerable effects on early anthropology. One theory that was inspired by Darwin's work was cultural evolutionism, which in the 19th century was the idea that societies evolved from simpler to more complex forms in a unilinear fashion. Those who believed in this form of cultural evolution often turned to Darwin's theory of evolution as a biological analogue for the types of changes that cultures underwent; however, this unilinear theory of cultural evolutionism eventually fell out of favor due to its ethnocentrism and was replaced by a more nuanced, multilinear theory of cultural evolution.

Ethnocentrism

Ethnocentrism is the conscious or unconscious cultural or ethnic bias in which someone views the world through his or her group's perspective, often resulting in placing that group above another group. One's group becomes the reference point to which other groups are compared. This can lead to inaccurate views of other groups and in-group/out-group bias. In anthropology, this has historically led to some European anthropologists viewing cultures from other parts of the world as being less developed or less sophisticated simply because their cultures differed from those of Europe.

Cultural Relativism

Cultural relativism is the belief that cultural concepts and morals should be viewed within the cultural contexts in which they appear and should not be judged according to the standards of another culture. Franz Boas, an anthropologist, first developed this concept in the late 19th and early 20th centuries. He believed that civilization was relative and that the morals, laws, and standards of one society were not absolute.

Margaret Mead

Margaret Mead studied sexual beliefs and norms among **South Pacific** and **Southeast Asian** cultures. Her first book on the subject was *Coming of Age in Samoa*. She acquired a PhD from Columbia University, and her work popularized sociology. She studied how children were treated and brought up in different cultures and how breastfeeding was viewed in different population groups.

Mary and Louis Leakey and Discoveries at Olduvai Gorge

The Leakeys made major discoveries regarding the **origin of the human species** during their excavations in Olduvai Gorge in Tanzania, Africa, excavating wide varieties of stone tools and other artifacts dating back as far as two million years. Mary Leakey discovered footprints belonging to early humans at **Laetoli**, a palaeontological site in Tanzania, and developed a system to classify early human tools. The Leakeys also discovered prehistoric remains of humans, including early humans dating to nearly four million years ago, fifteen new species, and one new genus of early human ancestors. They also discovered the first fossil ape skull, and only three similar specimens exist to this day. Their findings fundamentally changed theories regarding the development and evolution of ancient humans.

Psychology

Psychology is the study of **human behavior** and how the **mind** works. Some psychologists pursue scientific psychology, while others focus on applied psychology. Psychologists correlate human behavior and can make use of this data to predict behavior or determine why a particular behavior has occurred. Psychologists also help work with people who have specific problems with relationships or with how they perceive the world. By observing patterns and recording them in detail, psychologists can apply these patterns to predictions about human behavior in individuals, groups, cultures, and even countries.

Techniques Used by Psychologists in Research

Psychological researchers study their discipline in various ways. Based on what they are studying, they generally use one of the following methods:

- **Naturalistic observation**—much as with sociological study, psychologists observe people and their natural behavior without interfering.
- **Survey method**—surveys are distributed among a wide range of people, and the answers are correlated.
- **Case studies**—specific individuals or groups are studied in depth over a period of time, sometimes for many years.
- **Experimental method**—this involves experimental and control groups and the use of specific experiments to prove or disprove a theory.
- **Correlational design**—this is concerned with relationships between variables, such as whether one factor causes or influences another.

Importance of Aristotle to the Science of Psychology

Aristotle is often cited as founding the science of **psychology** through his overall interest in the working of the human mind. His beliefs stated that the mind was part of the body, while the psyche functioned as a receiver of knowledge. He felt psychology's major focus was to uncover the soul. Later philosophers and scientists built on these ideas to eventually develop the modern science of psychology.

Nativism

Nativism is a theory that states that there is a certain **body of knowledge** all people are born with. This knowledge requires no learning or experience on the part of the individual. **René Descartes**, a French philosopher, developed this concept. He believed the body and mind affected each other profoundly, largely because they are separate from each other. The physical site of this interaction took place in the **pineal gland** (a small gland in the brain), according to his theory. Descartes developed several theories in the fields of philosophy and psychology that are still studied in modern universities.

Empiricism

Empiricism is in direct opposition to Descartes' theory of nativism, theorizing that all knowledge is acquired through **life experience**, impressing itself on a mind and brain that are **blank** at the time of birth. Major proponents of empiricism were Thomas Hobbes, John Locke, David Hume, and George Berkeley.

Johannes P. Müller, Hermann L. F. von Helmholtz, William James, and Wilhelm Wundt

Johannes P. Müller and Hermann L. F. von Helmholtz conducted scientific, organized studies of sensation and perception. As the first psychologists to attempt this kind of study, they showed that it was possible to study actual physical processes that work to produce mental activity.

William James was the founder of the world's first psychology laboratory. **Wilhelm Wundt**, a student of Helmholtz, published the first experimental psychology journal and is known as the father of modern psychology. Together, James and Wundt helped bring psychology into its own, separating it from philosophy. The method of psychological study called introspection grew out of their work.

Sigmund Freud

An Austrian doctor, Freud developed a number of theories regarding human mental processes and behavior. He believed the **subconscious** to hold numerous repressed experiences and feelings that drive behavior without the individual's awareness, and that these subconscious motivators could lead to severe personality problems and disorders. He particularly stressed sexual desire as a motivating force. Freud developed the method of **psychoanalysis** to help discover the hidden impulses driving individual behavior. Freud's psychoanalytic theory proposed three major components to an individual's psychological makeup:

- **Id**—driven by instinct and basic drives
- **Ego**—most conscious and producing self-awareness
- **Superego**—strives for perfection and appropriate behavior

The **ego** acts as mediator between the **id** and **superego**, which function in opposition to each other.

Review Video: Sigmund Freud
Visit mometrix.com/academy and enter code: 473747

Carl Jung

A student of Freud, Jung eventually developed different theories regarding the workings of the human mind. With an intense interest in both Eastern and Western philosophy, he incorporated ideas from both into his psychological explorations. He developed the theories of **extroversion** and **introversion**, as well as proposing the existence of the **collective unconscious** and the occurrence of **synchronicity**.

Cognitive Psychology

Cognitive psychology is the study of how the brain thinks, remembers, processes information, and learns. It developed as a departure from behaviorism and focuses on internal mental processes instead of observable behaviors. Cognitive psychologists investigate higher-order mental processes and how they contribute to our thinking and emotions.

Humanistic Psychology

Humanistic psychology was developed partially as a response to psychoanalysis and behaviorism, which previously dominated the field. It arose in the middle of the twentieth century and emphasizes human potential and the ability for individuals to reach self-actualization. Humanist psychologists take a holistic approach to therapy and prioritize the experiences and desires of individuals rather than attempt to analyze their subconscious thoughts or change their behaviors. Humanist psychologists aim to help people achieve self-actualization through their relationships and personal insights.

Abraham Maslow

Abraham Maslow was an American humanist psychologist. His most notable contribution to the field of psychology was his hierarchy of needs. Maslow suggested that human needs were arranged in a hierarchy. At the bottom of the hierarchy are physiological needs, such as breathing, eating, and sleeping. Above strictly physiological needs are the needs for safety, love, and self-esteem. At the top of the hierarchy is self-actualization, which involves morality, creativity, acceptance, meaning, and reaching one's potential. The lower needs must usually be met before focus can be placed on the higher needs, but Maslow admitted that there is often some overlap in the real world.

Ivan Pavlov and B. F. Skinner

Ivan Pavlov and B. F. Skinner both built on Watson's theories of behaviorism. This work came about largely as a counter to the growing importance of introspective techniques to psychological study. Believing **environment** strongly influenced individual behavior, Pavlov and Skinner searched for connections between outside stimuli and behavioral patterns. Pavlov's experiments proved the existence of **conditioned response**. His most famous experiment conditioned dogs to salivate at the sound of a ringing bell. Skinner went on to build further on these ideas, developing the "Skinner box," a device used to develop and study conditioned response in rats.

Gestalt Psychology, Social Psychology, and Modern Psychology

Gestalt psychology is a school of psychology that was developed in the 20th century by **Max Wertheimer, Kurt Koffka, and Wolfgang Kohler**. In **Gestalt theory**, events are not considered individually but as part of a larger pattern. **Social psychology** is the study of how social conditions affect individuals. **Modern psychology**, as it has developed, combines earlier schools of psychology, including Freudian, Jungian, behaviorism, cognitive, humanistic, and stimulus-response theories.

Divisions of the Human Lifespan

Developmental psychologists divide the human lifespan into stages and list certain developmental milestones that generally take place during these stages:

- **Infancy and childhood**—this is the most rapid period of human development, during which the child learns to experience its world, relate to other people, and perform tasks necessary to function in its native culture. Debate exists as to which characteristics are inborn and which are learned.
- **Adolescence**—this period represents the shift from child to adult. Changes are rapid and can involve major physical and emotional shifts.
- **Adulthood**—individuals take on new responsibilities, become self-sufficient, and often form their own families and other social networks.
- **Old age**—priorities shift again as children become adults and no longer require support and supervision.

Types of Learning

Psychologists define learning as a **permanent change in behavior**. Learning is divided into three basic categories, based on how the behavioral change is acquired:

- **Classical conditioning**—this is a learning process in which a specific stimulus is associated with a specific response over time.
- **Operant conditioning**—this is a learning process in which behavior is punished or rewarded, leading to a desired long-term behavior.
- **Social learning**—this refers to learning based on observation of others and modeling others' behavior.

These three learning processes work together to produce the wide variety of human behavior.

Factors Involved in Social Psychology and Effects on Various Groups of People

Social psychology studies how people **interact** as well as why and how they decide whom to interact with. The ways people react with each other are defined in several ways, including:

- **Social perception**—this describes how we perceive others and their behavior as we make judgments based on our own experiences and prejudices.
- **Personal relationships**—close relationships develop among people for various reasons, including the desire to reproduce and form a family unit.
- **Group behavior**—people gather into groups with similar beliefs, needs, or other characteristics. Sometimes group behavior differs greatly from behavior that would be practiced by individuals.
- **Attitudes**—individual attitudes toward others develop over time based on individual history, experience, knowledge, and other factors. Attitudes can change over time, but some are deeply ingrained and can lead to prejudice.

Texas Culture

Houston Livestock Show and Rodeo

The annual Houston Livestock Show and Rodeo is America's largest rodeo. It is held over 20 days from late February through early March. The event begins with trail rides that originate from several points throughout the state, all of which convene at Reliant Park for a barbecue cook-off. The rodeo includes typical rodeo events, as well as concert performances from major artists and carnival rides.

Music in Texas

Texas has a vibrant **live music scene** in Austin boasting more music venues per capita than any other US city, befitting the city's official slogan as **The Live Music Capital of the World**. Austin's music revolves around the many nightclubs on 6th Street and an annual film, music, and multimedia festival known as South by Southwest. The longest-running concert music program on American television, Austin City Limits, is videotaped on The University of Texas at Austin campus. Austin City Limits and Waterloo Records run the Austin City Limits Music Festival, an annual music and art festival held at Zilker Park in Austin.

Arts and Theatre in Houston Area

Known for the vibrancy of its visual and performing arts, the **Houston Theater District**—a 17-block area in the heart of Downtown Houston—is ranked second in the country (behind New York City) in the number of theatre seats in a concentrated downtown area with 12,948 seats for live performances and 1,480 movie seats. Houston is also one of only five cities in the United States with permanent professional resident companies in all of the major performing arts disciplines (the Houston Grand Opera, the Houston Symphony Orchestra, the Houston Ballet, and The Alley Theatre). Houston is widely recognized as the nation's third most important city for **contemporary visual arts**.

Arts and Theatre in Dallas and Fort Worth Area

Dallas and Fort Worth serve as epicenters of the North Texas region's **art scene**. The Modern (formerly the Modern Art Museum of Fort Worth), founded in 1892, is the oldest art museum in Texas. The city is also home to the Kimbell Art Museum, the Amon Carter Museum, the National Cowgirl Museum and Hall of Fame, the Will Rogers Memorial Center and the Bass Performance Hall downtown. The Arts District of Downtown Dallas is home to several arts venues. Notable venues in the district include the Dallas Museum of Art, the Morton H. Meyerson Symphony Center, The Trammell & Margaret Crow Collection of Asian Art, and the Nasher Sculpture Center.

Also within Dallas is the notable **Deep Ellum district** which originally became popular during the 1920s and 1930s as the prime jazz and blues hotspot in the Southern United States. The name Deep Ellum is thought to have originally derived from local tongues saying "Deep Elm", but that came out as "Deep Ellum." Artists such as Blind Lemon Jefferson, Robert Johnson, Huddie "Leadbelly" Ledbetter, and Bessie Smith played in original Deep Ellum clubs like The Harlem and The Palace. Today, Deep Ellum is home to hundreds of artists who live in lofts and operate in studios throughout the district alongside bars, pubs, and concert venues. One major art infusion in the area is the city's lax stance on graffiti, thusly several public ways including tunnels, sides of buildings, sidewalks, and streets are covered in murals.

TEXAS FOOTBALL

Texas is known for its love of American **football** and is noted for the intensity with which people follow high school and college football teams—often dominating over all else for the purposes of socializing and leisure. School districts in Texas are sometimes criticized for the amount of money spent on their sports programs and facilities. For example, the turf of the football field at Duncanville High School cost hundreds of thousands of dollars. Such facilities and programs can garner a school attention, however. In May of 2005, Sports Illustrated also named the high school's sports program as one of the top 25 in the nation. Texas has two professional football teams, the **Houston Texans** and the **Dallas Cowboys**.

BASEBALL IN TEXAS

Baseball is also very popular in Texas with Major League Baseball, with the **Texas Range**rs and **Houston Astros** being equally popular in the state. North Texas, West Texas, and Panhandle residents are predominantly Rangers fans, while Southeast Texas, Central Texas, and South Texas is predominantly inhabited by Astros fans. Minor league baseball is also closely followed. Texas is home to eight minor league baseball teams affiliated with the Houston Astros, Texas Rangers, San Diego Padres, and Oakland Athletics.

POPULAR SPORTS IN TEXAS

Other popular sports in Texas include **golf** (which can be played year-round because of the South's mild climate), **basketball** (the state has three NBA teams: the Houston Rockets, San Antonio Spurs, and Dallas Mavericks, as well as one WNBA team, the Dallas Wings), **fishing**, **hunting**, and **auto racing**. **Lacrosse**, originally played by some of the indigenous tribes, is a visible sport and growing. **Soccer** is a popular participatory sport—especially among children—but as a spectator sport, it does not yet have a large following despite three Texan teams in Major League Soccer (the Houston Dynamo, FC Dallas, and Austin FC) and the Houston Dash of the National Women's Soccer League. **Hockey** has been a growing participatory sport in the Dallas/Fort Worth area since the Minnesota North Stars became the Dallas Stars in 1993. Minor league pro hockey has become quite popular in the last decade. Texas is home to the Allen Americans of the ECHL and the Texas Stars of the AHL.

RACE AND ETHNIC ORIGINS IN TEXAS

The largest reported **ancestry groups** in Texas include: Mexican (25.3%), German (10.9%), African American (10.5%), English (7.2%), and Scots-Irish (7.2%). Much of east, central, and north Texas is inhabited by Texans of White Protestant heritage, primarily Anglo, while much of central and southeast-central Texas is inhabited by Texans of German descent. African Americans, who historically made up one-third of the state population, are concentrated in those parts of East Texas where the cotton plantation culture was most prominent prior to the American Civil War, as well as in the Dallas-Fort Worth and Houston metropolitan areas. Frontier Texas saw settlements of Germans, particularly in Fredericksburg and New Braunfels. After the European revolutions of 1848, German, Polish, Swedish, Norwegian, Czech and French immigration grew and continued until World War I. More than one-third of Texas residents are of **Hispanic** origin and may be of any racial group. The Hispanic population in Texas is increasing as more illegal immigrants from certain Latin American countries—primarily from Mexico—look for work in Texas. The state has the second-largest Hispanic population in the United States, behind California. This influx of immigrants is partially responsible for Texas having a population younger than the Union average. In recent years, the **Asian American** population in Texas has grown, especially in Houston and in Dallas, with the largest groups from Vietnam, India, China, Korea, and Japan.

Official Language of Texas

Texas does not have an official language; nevertheless, **English** (specifically, American English) is the language used for legislation, regulations, executive orders, treaties, education, federal court rulings, and all other official pronouncements. **Spanish** is also heavily spoken in Texas due to the large number of ethnic Mexicans and other Hispanics (Puerto Ricans, Guatemalans, Colombians, etc.).

Popular Events That Celebrate Cultures of Texans

The following are some popular events that celebrate the cultures of Texans:

- The Houston Livestock Show and Rodeo
- The Fort Worth Livestock Show and Rodeo
- The Mexican Rodeo
- The State Fair of Texas
- The OU and Texas State Football Game
- The University of Texas and Texas A&M rivalry

Recognized Native American Tribes in Texas

Currently, there are three federally-recognized Native American tribes that reside in Texas:

1. the Alabama-Coushatta Tribes of Texas
2. the Kickapoo Traditional Tribe of Texas
3. the Ysleta Del Sur Pueblo of Texas

There is a remnant of the Choctaw tribe in East Texas that still lives in the Mt. Tabor Community near Overton, Texas.

Spanish Efforts Towards Expansion During 1731-1762

During most of the period of **Spanish Texas**, the region assumed a geopolitical importance vastly disproportionate to its economic or demographic place in the Spanish Empire. Spanish civilization gained toeholds via missions and presidios. Little was known about the area outside of unsubstantiated reports from the early Conquistador period. Spanish power was thus not geared as much toward civilizing the area than toward delineating its own extent. A system of **mission-presidios** were established at present day San Antonio, La Bahia, Los Adaes, El Paso, Laredo, Nacogdoches, and San Luis de las Amarillas. This initial expansion, however, was met with immediate setback in the 1718 **War of the Quadruple Alliance** in Europe, during which France managed to briefly capture the capital of Texas, Los Adaes, in modern Northwest Louisiana. Due to Indian depredations, the Presidios of San Luis de las Amarillas had to be abandoned in 1770 after a period of economic inviability. Most Spanish efforts toward expansion in Texas during the years 1731-62 were a failure, except at La Bahía, San Antonio de Bexar, and along the lower Rio Grande. Missions and presidios, although proven frontier institutions, had clearly failed north of San Antonio.

Spanish Texas

Spanish Texas was largely an effort by the Spanish Crown to keep its assets in the New World secure from the French in Louisiana. Texas was thus a sparsely populated buffer between the claims of these two nations. Texas was **Spanish territory** from 1690, the expedition of the governor of Coahuila to destroy the ruins of the French colony of Fort Saint Louis and establish a Spanish presence, until independence movements in 1821 began to shatter the Spanish Empire, resulting in the independence of Mexico. During this period, Texas was a part of four provinces in the **Viceroyalty of New Spain** (Colonial Mexico): New Mexico, Nueva Vizcaya, Nuevo Santander after 1749, and initially joint jurisdiction with the province of Coahuila. Slightly more than three centuries elapsed between the time the Texas shoreline was first viewed by a Spaniard in 1519 and July 21, 1821, when the flag of Castile and León was lowered for the last time at San Antonio. These three hundred years may be divided into the **era of early exploration**, in which there was a preliminary evaluation of the land and its resources; the **period of cultural absorption**, in which the Texas Indians began to acquire

Hispanic cultural elements directly from the Spanish themselves; and the **time of defensive occupation**, in which the Spanish presence in Texas was more dictated by international considerations than caused by the momentum of an expanding empire.

Secondary Center of Colonial Power in Spanish Texas

The secondary center of Spanish colonial power, **La Bahía** (present-day Goliad), was the second oldest settlement in the province. It was originally established in 1721 at the site of La Salle's Fort St. Louis, then moved in 1749 to the San Antonio River, where the presidio and two missions had the task of guarding the Texas Gulf Coast against foreign encroachment. In 1803 the settlement's population of approximately 618 soldiers and civilians continued to live under military jurisdiction.

Chapter Quiz

Ready to see how well you retained what you just read? Scan the QR code to go directly to the chapter quiz interface for this study guide. If you're using a computer, simply visit the online resources page at **mometrix.com/resources719/texessocst4-8** and click the Chapter Quizzes link.

Social Studies Foundations and Skills

Social Studies Skills

Collecting Information and Organizing and Reporting Results

The first step of compiling data for useful implementation requires narrowing down on a **topic**. The student should first read background information to identify areas that are interesting or need further study and that the student does not have a strong opinion about. The research question should be identified, and the student should refer to general sources that can point to more specific information. When he or she begins to take notes, his or her information must be **organized** with a clear system to identify the source. Any information from outside sources must be acknowledged with **footnotes** or a **bibliography**. To gain more specific information about his or her topic, the student can then research bibliographies from general sources to narrow down on information pertinent to the topic at hand. He or she should draft a thesis statement that summarizes the main point of the research. This should lead to a working **outline** that incorporates all the ideas needed to support the main point in a logical order. A rough draft should incorporate the results of the research in the outlined order, with all citations clearly inserted. The paper should then be edited for clarity, style, flow, and content.

Formulating Research Questions or Hypotheses

Formulating research questions or hypotheses is the process of finding questions to answer that have not yet been asked. The first step in the process is reading **background information**. Knowing about a general topic and reading about how other people have addressed it helps identify areas that are well understood. Areas that are not as well understood may either be lightly addressed in the available literature or distinctly identified as a topic that is not well understood and deserves further study. Research questions or hypotheses may address such an unknown aspect, or they may focus on drawing parallels between similar, well-researched topics that have not been connected before. Students usually need practice in developing research questions that are of the appropriate scope so that they will find enough information to answer the question, yet not so much that they become overwhelmed. Hypotheses tend to be more specific than research questions.

Identifying Main Ideas in a Document

Main ideas in a paragraph are often found in the **topic sentence**, which is usually the first or second sentence in the paragraph. Every following sentence in the paragraph should relate to that initial information. Sometimes, the first or second sentence doesn't obviously set up the main idea. When that happens, each sentence in the paragraph should be read carefully to find the **common theme** between them all. This common theme is the main idea of the paragraph. Main ideas in an entire document can be found by analyzing the structure of the document. Frequently, the document begins with an introductory paragraph or abstract that will summarize the main ideas. Each paragraph often discusses one of the main ideas and contributes to the overall goal of the document. Some documents are divided up into chapters or sections, each of which discusses a main idea. The way that main ideas are described in a document (either in sentences, paragraphs, or chapters) depends on the length of the document.

Using Electronic Resources and Periodicals for Reference

Electronic resources are often the quickest, most convenient way to get background information on a topic. One of the particular strengths of **electronic resources** is that they can also provide primary-source multimedia video, audio, or other visual information on a topic that would not be accessible in print. Information available on the internet is not often carefully screened for accuracy or for bias, so choosing the **source** of electronic information is often very important. Electronic encyclopedias can provide excellent overview information, but publicly edited resources like Wikipedia are open to error, rapid change, incompleteness, or bias. Students should be made aware of the different types and reliabilities of electronic resources, and they should be taught how to distinguish between them. Electronic resources can often be too detailed and overwhelm students with irrelevant information. **Periodicals** provide current information on social science events, but they too must be screened for bias. Some amount of identifiable bias can actually be an important source of information, because it indicates prevailing culture and standards. Periodicals generally have tighter editorial standards than electronic resources, so completeness and overt errors are not usually as problematic. Periodicals can also provide primary-source information with interviews and photographs.

Using Encyclopedias, Bibliographies, or Almanacs for Social Science Research

Encyclopedias are ideal for getting background information on a topic. They provide an overview of the topic and link it to other concepts that can provide additional keywords, information, or subjects. They can help students narrow their topic by showing the subtopics within the overall topic and by relating it to other topics. **Encyclopedias** may sometimes prove to be more useful than the internet because they provide a clearly organized, concise overview of material. **Bibliographies** are bound collections of references to periodicals and books, organized by topic. Students can begin researching more efficiently after they identify a topic, look it up in a bibliography, and look up the references listed there. This provides a branching network of information a student can follow. A pitfall of bibliographies is that when in textbooks or other journal articles, the references in them are chosen to support the author's point of view and so may be limited in scope. **Almanacs** are volumes of facts published annually. They provide numerical information on just about every topic, and are organized by subject or geographic region. They are often helpful for supporting arguments made using other resources and do not provide any interpretation of their own.

Primary and Secondary Resources

Primary resources provide information about an event from the perspective of people who were present at the event. They might be letters, autobiographies, interviews, speeches, artworks, or anything created by people with first-hand experience. **Primary resources** are valuable because they provide not only facts about the event but also information about the surrounding circumstances; for example, a letter might provide commentary about how a political speech was received. The internet is a source of primary information, but care must be taken to evaluate the perspective of the website providing that information. Websites hosted by individuals or special-interest organizations are more likely to be biased than those hosted by public organizations, governments, educational institutions, or news associations. **Secondary resources** provide information about an event but were not written at the time the event occurred. They draw information from primary sources. Because secondary sources were written later, they have the added advantage of historical perspective, multiple points of view, or resultant outcomes. Newsmagazines that write about an event even a week after it occurred count as secondary sources. Secondary sources tend to analyze events more effectively or thoroughly than primary sources.

Review Video: Primary and Secondary Sources
Visit mometrix.com/academy and enter code: 383328

Organizing Information Chronologically and Analyzing the Sequence of Events

To organize information chronologically, each piece of information must be associated with a time or a date. Events are ordered according to the time or date at which they happened. In social sciences, chronological organization is the most straightforward way to arrange information, because it relies on a uniform, fixed scale—the passage of time. Information can also be organized based on any of the "who, what, when, where, why?" principles.

Analyzing the sequence of chronological events involves not only examining the event itself but the preceding and following events. This can put the event in question into perspective, showing how a certain thing might have happened based on preceding history. One large disadvantage of chronological organization is that it may not highlight important events clearly relative to less important events. Determining the relative importance of events depends more strongly on interpreting their relationships to neighboring events.

Recognizing Cause-and-Effect and Comparing Similarities and Differences

Cause-and-effect relationships are simply linkages between an event that happened (the **effect**) because of some other event (the **cause**). Effects are always chronologically ordered after causes. Effects can be found by asking why something happened or looking for information following words like *so, consequently, since, because, therefore, this led to, as a result,* and *thus*. Causes can also be found by asking what happened. **Comparing similarities and differences** involves mentally setting two concepts next to each other and then listing the ways they are the same and the ways they are different. The level of comparison varies by student level; for example, younger students may compare the physical characteristics of two animals while older students compare the themes of a book. Similarity/difference comparisons can be made by listing written descriptions in a point-by-point approach, or they can be done in several graphic ways. Venn diagrams are commonly used to organize information, showing non-overlapping clouds filled with information about the different characteristics of A and B, and the overlapping area shows ways in which A and B are the same. Idea maps using arrows and bubbles can also be developed to show these differences.

Distinguishing Between Fact and Opinion

Students easily recognize that **facts** are true statements that everyone agrees on, such as an object's name or a statement about a historical event. Students also recognize that **opinions** vary about matters of taste, such as preferences in food or music, that rely on people's interpretation of facts. Simple examples are easy to spot. **Fact-based passages** include certainty-grounded words like *is, did,* or *saw*. On the other hand, **passages containing opinions** often include words that indicate possibility rather than certainty, such as *would, should,* or *believe*. First-person verbs also indicate opinions, showing that one person is talking about his or her experience. Less clear are examples found in higher-level texts. For example, primary-source accounts of a Civil War battle might include facts ("*x* battle was fought today") and also opinions ("Union soldiers are not as brave as Confederate soldiers") that are not clearly written as such ("I believe Union soldiers..."). At the same time that students learn to interpret sources critically (Was the battle account written by a Southerner?), they should practice sifting fact from these types of opinion. Other examples where fact and opinion blend together are self-authored internet websites.

Review Video: Distinguishing Fact and Opinion
Visit mometrix.com/academy and enter code: 870899

Determining the Adequacy, Relevance, and Consistency of Information

Before information is sought, a list of **guiding questions** should be developed to help determine whether information found is adequate, relevant, and consistent. These questions should be based on the **research goals**, which should be laid out in an outline or concept map. For example, a student writing a report on Navajo social structure might begin with questions concerning the general lifestyle and location of Navajos and follow with questions about how Navajo society was organized. While researching his questions, he or she will come up with pieces of information. This information can be compared to his or her research questions to determine whether it is **relevant** to his or her report. Information from several sources should be compared to determine whether the information is **consistent**. Information that is **adequate** helps answer specific questions that are part of the research goals. Inadequate information for this particular student might be a statement such as "Navajos had a strong societal structure," because the student is probably seeking more specific information.

Drawing Conclusions and Making Generalizations About a Topic

Students reading about a topic will encounter different facts and opinions that contribute to their overall impression of the material. The student can critically examine the material by thinking about what facts have been included, how they have been presented, what they show, what they relate to outside the written material, and what the author's conclusion is. Students may agree or disagree with the author's conclusion, based on the student's interpretation of the facts the author presented. When working on a research project, a student's research questions will help him or her gather details that will enable him or her to **draw a conclusion** about the research material.

Generalizations are blanket statements that apply to a wide number of examples. They are similar to conclusions but do not have to summarize the information as completely as conclusions. Generalizations in reading material may be flagged by words such as *all, most, none, many, several, sometimes, often, never, overall,* or *in general.* Generalizations are often followed by supporting information consisting of a list of facts. Generalizations can refer to facts or the author's opinions, and they provide a valuable summary of the text overall.

EVALUATING AND INTERPRETING MAPS

The **map legend** is an area that provides interpretation information such as the key, the scale, and how to interpret the map. The **key** is the area that defines symbols, abbreviations, and color schemes used on the map. Any feature identified on the map should be defined in the key. The **scale** is a feature of the map legend that tells how distance on the map relates to distance on the ground. It can either be presented mathematically in a ratio or visually with a line segment. For example, it could say that one inch on the map equals one foot on the ground, or it could show a line segment and tell how much distance on the map the line symbolizes. **Latitude** and **longitude** are often shown on maps to relate their area to the world. Latitude shows how far a location is north or south from Earth's equator, and longitude shows how far a location is east or west from Earth's prime meridian. Latitude runs from 90°N (North Pole) to 0° (equator) to 90°S (South Pole), and longitude runs 180°E (International Date Line) to 0° (prime meridian) to 180°W (International Date Line).

Review Video: Elements of a Map
Visit mometrix.com/academy and enter code: 437727

POPULAR MAP PROJECTIONS

- **Globe**: Earth's features are shown on a sphere. No distortion of distances, directions, or areas occurs.
- **Mercator**: Earth's features are projected onto a cylinder wrapped around a globe. This generates a rectangular map that is not distorted at the equator but is greatly distorted near the poles. Lines of latitude and longitude form a square grid.
- **Robinson**: Earth's features are projected onto an oval-looking map. Areas near the poles are truer to size than in the Mercator. Some distortion affects every point.
- **Orthographic**: Earth's features are shown on a circle, which is tangent to the globe at any point chosen by the mapmaker. This generates a circular, 3D-appearing map similar to how Earth is seen from space.
- **Conic maps**: This family of maps is drawn by projecting the globe's features onto a cone set onto the globe. Some distortion affects most points.
- **Polar maps**: The land around the poles has been projected onto a circle. This provides much less distortion of Antarctica and the land around the North Pole than other map types.

CARTOGRAPHIC DISTORTION AND ITS INFLUENCE ON MAP PROJECTIONS

Cartographic distortion is the distortion caused by projecting a three-dimensional structure, in this case, Earth's surface, onto the two-dimensional surface of a map. Numerous map projections have been developed to minimize distortion, but the only way to eliminate distortion completely is to render Earth in three dimensions. Most map projections have minimal distortion in some location, usually the center, and the distortion becomes greater close to the edges of the map. Some map projections try to compromise and distribute the distortion more evenly across the map. Different categories of maps preserve, or do not distort, different features. Maps that preserve directions accurately are **azimuthal**, and maps that preserve shapes properly are **conformal**. Area-preserving maps are called **equal-area maps**, and maps that preserve distance are called **distance-preserving**. Maps that preserve the shortest routes are **gnomonic projections**.

Review Video: Map Projections
Visit mometrix.com/academy and enter code: 327303

Comparing Maps of the Same Place from Different Time Periods

Maps of the same place from different time periods can often be initially aligned by **geographic features**. Political and land-use boundaries are most likely to change between time periods, whereas locations of waterways and geologic features such as mountains are relatively constant. Once geographic features have been used to align maps, they can be compared side-by-side to examine the changing locations of human settlement, smaller waterways, etc. This kind of map interpretation, at the smallest scale, provides information about how small groups of humans **interact with their environment**. For example, such analysis might show that major cities began around ports and then moved inland as modes of transportation, like railroads and cars, became more common. Lands that were initially used for agriculture might become incorporated into a nearby city as the population grows. This kind of map analysis can also show the evolution of the **socio-economics** of an area, providing information about the relative importance of economic activities (manufacturing, agriculture, or trade) and even the commuting behavior of workers.

Natural, Political, and Cultural Features on Maps

Map legends will provide information about the types of natural, political, or cultural features on a map. Some maps show only one of these three features. **Natural features** such as waterways, wetlands, beaches, deserts, mountains, highlands, and plains can be compared between regions by type, number, distribution, or any other physical characteristic. **Political features** such as state and county divisions or roads and railroads can be compared numerically, but examining their geographic distribution may be more informative. This provides information on settlement density and population. In addition, road and railroad density may show regions of intense urbanization, agricultural regions, or industrial centers. **Cultural features** may include roads and railroads, but might also include historic areas, museums, archaeological digs, early settlements, and even campgrounds. Comparing and contrasting the number, distribution, and types of these features may provide information on the history of an area, the duration of settlement of an area, or the current use of the area (for example, many museums are found in current-day cultural centers).

Comparing Maps with Datasets or Texts

Maps can provide a great deal of information about an area by showing specific locations where certain types of settlement, land use, or population growth occurred. **Datasets** and **texts** can provide more specific information about events that might only otherwise be hypothesized from maps. This specific information may provide dates of significant events (for example, the date of a fire that gutted a downtown region, forcing suburban development) or important numerical data (e.g., population growth by year). Written datasets and texts enable map interpretation to become concrete and allow observed trends to be linked with specific causes ("Real estate prices rose in 2004, causing middle-class citizens to move northwest of the city"). Without specific information from additional sources, inferences drawn from maps cannot be put in **context** and interpreted in more than a vague way.

Evaluating and Interpreting Other Graphic Formats

The type of information being conveyed guides the choice of **format**. Textual information and numeric information must be displayed with different techniques. Text-only information may be most easily summarized in a diagram or a timeline. If the text includes numeric information, it may be converted into a chart that shows the size of groups, connects ideas in a table or graphic, or shows information in a hybridized format. Numeric information is often most helpfully presented in tables or graphs. When information will be referred to and looked up again and again, tables are often most helpful for the reader. When the trends in the numeric information are more important than the numbers themselves, graphs are often the best choice. Information that is linked to the land and has a spatial component is best conveyed using maps.

Interpreting Charts and Tables

Charts used in social science are a visual representation of data. They combine graphic and textual elements to convey information in a concise format. Often, **charts** divide the space up in blocks, which are filled with text and/or pictures to convey a point. Charts are often organized in tabular form, where blocks below a heading all have information in common. Charts also divide information into conceptual, non-numeric groups (for example, "favorite color"), which are then plotted against a numerical axis (e.g., "number of students"). Charts should be labeled in such a way that a reader can locate a point on the chart and then consult the surrounding axes or table headings to understand how it compares to other points. **Tables** are a type of chart that divides textual information into rows and columns. Each row and column represent a characteristic of the information. For example, a table might be used to convey demographic information. The first column would provide "year," and the second would provide "population." Reading across the rows, one could see that in the year 1966, the population of Middletown was 53,847. Tracking the columns would show how frequently the population was counted.

Interpret Graphs and Diagrams

Graphs are similar to charts, except that they graphically show numeric information on both axes. For example, a **graph** might show population through the years, with years on the *x* axis and population on the *y* axis. One advantage of graphs is that the population during the time in between censuses can be estimated by locating that point on the graph. Each axis should be labeled to allow the information to be interpreted correctly, and the graph should have an informative title.

Diagrams are usually drawings that show the progression of events. The drawings can be fairly schematic, as in a flow chart, or they can be quite detailed, as in a depiction of scenes from a battle. Diagrams usually have arrows connecting the events or boxes shown. Each event or box should be labeled to show what it represents. Diagrams are interpreted by following the progression along the arrows through all events.

Using Timelines in Social Science

Timelines are used to show the relationships between people, places, and events. They are ordered chronologically and usually are shown left-to-right or top-to-bottom. Each event on the **timeline** is associated with a date, which determines its location on the timeline. On electronic resources, timelines often contain hyperlinks associated with each event. Clicking on the event's hyperlink will open a page with more information about the event. **Cause-and-effect relationships** can be observed on timelines, which often show a key event and then resulting events following in close succession. These can be helpful for showing the order of events in time or the relationships between similar events. They help make the passage of time a concrete concept and show that large periods pass between some events, while other events cluster very closely.

Using Political Cartoons in Social Science Studies

Political cartoons are drawings that memorably convey an opinion. These opinions may be supportive or critical and may summarize a series of events or pose a fictional situation that summarizes an attitude. **Political cartoons** are, therefore, secondary sources of information that provide social and cultural context about events. Political cartoons may have captions that help describe the action or put it in context. They may also have dialogue, labels, or other recognizable cultural symbols. For example, Uncle Sam frequently appears in political cartoons to represent the United States government. Political cartoons frequently employ caricatures to call attention to a situation or a person. The nature of the caricature helps show the cartoonist's attitude toward the issue being portrayed. Every element of the cartoon is included to support the artist's point and should be considered in the cartoon's interpretation. When interpreting political cartoons, students should examine what issue is being discussed, what elements the artist chose to support his or her point, and what the message is. Considering who might agree or disagree with the cartoon is also helpful in determining the message of the cartoon.

Analyzing Artifacts

Artifacts, or everyday objects used by previous cultures, are useful for understanding life in those cultures. Students should first discover, or be provided with, a **description** of the item. This description should depict what time period the **artifact** was used in and what culture used it. From that description and/or from examination of the artifact, students should be able to discuss what the artifact is, what it is made of, its potential uses, and the people who likely used it. They should then be able to draw **conclusions** from all these pieces of evidence about life in that culture. For example, analysis of coins from an early American archaeological site might show that settlers brought coins with them, or that some classes of residents were wealthy, or that trade occurred with many different nations. The interpretation will vary depending on the circumstances surrounding the artifact. Students should consider these circumstances when drawing conclusions.

Chapter Quiz

Ready to see how well you retained what you just read? Scan the QR code to go directly to the chapter quiz interface for this study guide. If you're using a computer, simply visit the online resources page at **mometrix.com/resources719/texessocst4-8** and click the Chapter Quizzes link.

Social Studies Instruction and Assessment

Social Science Classroom Management

Overview of Classroom Management

- **Organization**—the state or manner of being organized
- **Discipline**—training expected to produce a specific character or pattern of behavior, especially training that produces moral or mental improvement
- **Procedures**—a set of established forms or methods for conducting the affairs of an organized body
- **Learner responsibility**—the student must have responsibility for their actions or non-actions
- **Interventions**—interference so as to modify a process or situation

Review Video: Classroom Management - Rhythms of Teaching
Visit mometrix.com/academy and enter code: 809399

Instructional Approaches to Classroom Management and Student Motivation

- Model-based classroom management
- Concise and efficient instructions
- Developmentally and age-appropriate instruction
- Large (whole) group instruction
- Small group instruction

Be able to create and maintain an atmosphere that encourages questions, conjectures, problem-solving, and experimentation.

Reteaching, Enrichment, and Extensions

- **Reteaching**—The act of teaching over again
- **Enrichment**—above and beyond the given
- **Extensions**—small add-ons that help in teaching

Curriculum Components

- **Scope and sequence**—effective instruction focusing on the essential skills and concepts commonly found on standardized tests.
- **Curricular materials**—equipment and materials needed to teach a subject.
- **Learner objectives**—types and levels of objectives of what will be taught.

Prior Knowledge

Prior knowledge is a combination of one's existing attitudes, experiences, and knowledge. Attitudes can range from beliefs about ourselves as learners or being aware of our own strengths and weaknesses. It can also be our level of motivation and responsibility for our own learning. The experiences from our daily activities, especially ones with our friends and families, give us a background from which we derive most of our understanding. Individual events in our lives provide us experiences we can draw from, both bad and good, and influence how we deal with future situations. This knowledge is drawn from a wide variety of things, from knowledge of specific content areas and the concepts within, to the goals that we have for ourselves academically.

Using Computers to Better Manage the Classroom

Computers have revolutionized virtually every area of society, and teaching is no exception. Various forms of digitalization can significantly increase the efficiency of a teacher's ability to manage the classroom. Teachers can use the computer to do traditional paperwork and help free them from a number of tasks that are classified as noninstructional. A computer will not make a classroom a success by itself, and a teacher must know, like a business manager, what programs will do and how they are used. Teachers can use computers to:

- Keep student progress records, tests, and cumulative and average scores.
- Prepare individualized notes and observations for each student.
- Keep thorough records of attendance.
- Keep an inventory of supplies that include what quantities are available and where they are located.
- Generate tests and worksheets, as well as often grade them instantly. Students may also be able to take the test on the computer.
- Produce posters and calendars and generally provide more options for time organization.
- Appreciably increase communication between the teacher, parents, and their children.

Teacher Planning and Preparation

Despite the status of the teacher's knowledge on instructional matters, he or she selects certain curricular content, makes decisions about groupings, and allocates specific time periods for activities. These are the crux of teacher preparation and planning. Teachers must turn curricular goals and related content into a plan that works; the planning may be informal, or it may be formal and explicit. This includes textbook and material selection, content strategies, learning assessments for particular pupils, scheduling lessons, and detailing instruction for particular days. A skillful teacher plans his or her school day before they ever enter into the classroom. Teachers have perceptions of the students' needs in different subject areas, but very little is accomplished if the teacher is hindered in their plans.

Questioning Strategy in Reciprocal Teaching

One of the surest signs of proficiency in a subject is the ability to teach the concepts that have been learned to others. Reciprocal teaching provides students with the opportunity to absorb the information that has been read or taught and begin summarizing, questioning, clarifying, and ultimately predicting the content that they read, as though they might have to teach it to someone else. Students first identify the kind of information significant enough for the substance of a question when those questions are first generated as they read through a text. They then ask this information in the form of a question and test themselves to find out if they might answer their own questions. The generation of questions is a flexible strategy insofar as students can be taught and encouraged to ask questions on a number of different levels. When students know before reading that they need to think of questions about the text, they then read while aware of the important ideas in that text. This helps increase comprehension, process the meaning, and make inferences and connections to prior information before forming a question.

Oral Questioning in Class

One easy way for teachers to conduct a formative assessment in class is to briefly quiz students on the material covered. Whether it is to be done for a grade or not, it is generally useful to give a brief overview of the previous day's lesson at the beginning of class. Oftentimes, this can be best accomplished by allowing students to articulate the material and to critique one another's understanding. Some probing questions from the teacher can ensure that the recent material is understood in the context of the material that has already been learned. It is not always necessary to formally grade students on their participation or performance in an informal question-and-answer session; the main thing is to develop an idea of the students' progress.

Forms of Assessments and Using Students' Work to Guide Instruction

- Identify what students are doing correctly.
- Identify the concepts that your class is developing.
- Point out your students' misconceptions and errors.
- Identify appropriate measures of scoring aptitude.

- Figure out appropriate methods of remediation and acceleration.
- Know the appropriate uses of rubrics.

Review Video: Assessment Reliability and Validity
Visit mometrix.com/academy and enter code: 424680

Hurdles Students Face Studying at Home

The personal difficulties students have and priorities that compete with classwork have drastically changed as the world has become digitally saturated. The presence and ubiquitous nature of social media influences culture and mindsets in ways that society still does not fully comprehend. Students may have difficulties with homework because parents come home tired after a hectic day and are unable to properly monitor the students' assignments, or the parents are less familiar with the more modernized methods of teaching and assignments and become frustrated or apathetic—choosing to simply remain in ignorance rather than confront the unfamiliar territory. Oftentimes, the parents do not actually realize that their child is having a problem until they see that their child's grades are suffering. Students may also be involved in various extracurricular activities that vie for their time or suffer specific personal difficulties such as an unstable home life, a lack of adult role models, or drug problems.

Strategies to Have Students Complete Homework Assignments

Teachers should make known their expectations early in the school year before the first piece of homework is ever assigned. Ensuring that the students clearly understand the rules of the classroom, the types of assignments they are likely to encounter, the methods and means for turning the assignments in, and how those assignments will be graded, can prevent much of students' confusions and frustrations. A written explanation of expectations helps to increase the chances of students successfully completing homework. In elementary school, as well as to a certain extent in junior high and high school, homework can teach students the fundamentals of working independently, as well as encourage self-discipline through time management and meeting deadlines.

Students should know:

- Homework is important and has meaning.
- Doing assignments or not doing them has consequences such as lower grades if the assignments are not done.
- Students need to be held to a high standard. Research has shown that students make better gains academically when teachers set high expectations and tell the students of their expectations. Students also should know how much and when homework will be assigned.

Creating Assignments with Purpose in Completing Homework and Study Skills

Assignments that are given to students to complete outside of class should be given with a purpose rather than to provide busywork. If a student believes that the homework given is meaningful or beneficial to them, they will be more likely to consider it as something worth doing. While students may appreciate understanding an assignment's purpose, the purpose might not become clear until students are midway through the assignment or have completed it. The teacher should not just tell a student to read something or answer questions without knowing why they are doing it. Students should be shown the bigger picture of how their assignments fit in the realm of what they are studying, even though the student may not entirely appreciate the project's significance until it is finished or partially finished.

The following are some of the main purposes of homework:

- To review and practice what the students have learned for implementation in the future
- To prepare for exams

- To improve overall study skills by learning to use resources such as the library, reference material, encyclopedias, or the internet
- To explore subjects more deeply than time allows while in class

Helping Students Better Understand and Study with Focusing Assignments

Assignments that are focused are less difficult for students to complete and understand. Assignments that try to reinforce an overabundant number of ideas are not likely to help a student learn. This is especially the case for students who have not yet developed abstract thinking to the point where they can successfully integrate many of the concepts. Assignments need not be a large, overwhelming dissertation about what it is the teacher expects. The assignment should stick to one issue or concept, and it should ask for maybe four or five examples. A teacher can easily determine if the students are comprehending what is being taught and if not, help can be given in studying for the objective. Focus and the appropriate background information are also important in class discussions of assigned readings because some children can become overwhelmed if asked to read too much at once.

Helping Students Think Through While Studying with Challenging Assignments

Homework can give a student the ability to apply concepts that are beyond the controlled environment of a classroom. It can also help students collect and connect information from a variety of sources, subjects, and places. The best assignments challenge students to expand or break away from how they normally think. Such an assignment might combine two unassociated ideas. Assignments can range from listing what one finds in a desk drawer to writing paragraphs about family members. In those assignments, students can break the punctuation or capitalization rules in order to better learn the rules. Integrating topics also helps the thinking process, such as putting together an art, writing, and science class.

Helping Students Study and Complete Their Work by Varying Assignments

If all assignments are alike, students are very likely to get bored. Mixing approaches and styles is one of the fastest ways to elicit change. All students will not be interested in a given assignment, but mixing it up creates better chances that some of the homework will be enjoyed by the students. Short-term assignments can help students practice and review material already covered in class. Long-term projects allow students to vary the pace of their work, get into subjects of interest to them, and to manage time and deadlines. Variety may also help keep teachers engaged and excited about the schoolyear and convince them to try experimenting with their approaches and styles.

Enhancing Studying by Tying Assignments to the Present

Students may often feel that they cannot relate to assignments about events from long ago. It is hard to teach most types of history unless they are related somehow to the present, so assignments should draw comparisons between what is happening today and events years or centuries ago. For instance, students might approach an assignment on a Civil War battle by contrasting it with more modern battles. They might see the battle through the eyes of a television war correspondent who interviews the principal leaders and ask what they might do differently if they were to "do over" the battle. Students learn the specifics of such battles through these interviews and can appreciate the significance of the events that took place. This is a way of piquing interest in studying.

Helping Students Study a Subject by Matching Skills, Interests, and Needs

The chances are greater that a student will complete his or her homework assignments if they:

- Are not too hard or too easy.
- Match children's preferred learning styles.
- Let students work on material that they really like. Assignments cannot be customized for every student. But teachers can give assignments to a heterogeneous class that varies in content, format and style. This will better the chance that all students will have some elements of the assignments that are of interest.

Teachers can give the students choices. The student may be expected to master all the same material, but it can be done in different ways. This helps the student feel they control parts of their learning, which encourages studying and helps them to enjoy an assignment that they otherwise might not.

Test-Taking Tips Benefiting Intermediate Students

When it is time to take a test, the student should:

- Think positively about doing the best that he or she can do.
- Take some deep breaths and relax. Breathe slowly. Clear the mind of worries and anxious thoughts.
- Push his or her feet down on the floor to the count of five. Push them harder and hold. Relax and then repeat.
- Visualize by closing his or her eyes and picturing his or herself in a happy and peaceful place.
- Bring all materials needed for the test.
- Listen carefully to the directions and ask if they are not understood.
- Reread the directions carefully
- Look over the entire test to see what must be done before beginning.
- Determine how much time there is to spend on each question, allowing more time for essay questions.
- Skip difficult questions and go back later to answer those skipped.

Carefully Reading Entire Test Items and All Answers for Elementary Students

Students should carefully consider each possible option or alternative before selecting an answer on an assignment or exam. It is common for a student to stop reading after determining that one of the answer choices is an acceptable answer rather than ensuring that they have made the best choice. Students should be encouraged to very carefully go over each question and pay particular attention to key terms. This information may be translated by the student into different forms, such as changing the question into their own words or substituting common words. They can use their knowledge to anticipate what an answer might be and to select an answer that appears similar to the one they predicted. These skills may be practiced in regular classroom activities.

Importance of Checking Work When Taking Tests in Elementary Classes

It is worthwhile to instill into students the idea of checking their work after completion. Confirming that they have correctly answered each question to the best of their ability is an excellent use of any extra time a student may have after finishing an assignment or test. When they check their work, they need to ensure that the answers are correctly marked on the answer sheet and that the answers match the number of questions on the answer sheet. Students should have time to check and reconsider their work if time has been efficiently managed, and they should be encouraged to change answers when they think a better answer is appropriate. Students need reinforcement that their work should be checked daily. Teachers can do this by refusing to accept work until it is confirmed the work has been checked.

Helping Achieve Positive Learning Outcomes from High Teacher Expectations

Most, if not all, teachers have high hopes for their students. However, some teachers may be better than others at consciously communicating those expectations. Others might unconsciously expect less of students who show little interest in learning or who have significant barriers to hurdle. But by holding all students to high standards, most teachers believe they can help students achieve their full potential. Studies do show that students tend to internalize beliefs teachers have about their ability. When students are not expected to make a lot of progress, they may tend to take on a defeatist outlook. Some students may think their teachers believe they are not capable of handling demanding assignments. Teachers must see themselves as responsible for finding ways to raise performance despite whatever circumstances the students face.

Home, Cultural, and Parental Involvement

Many of the differences in academic achievement in children can be explained by the quantity and quality of reading materials in the home, the number of pages read for homework, the number of days absent from school, the number of hours in which TV is watched and social media is consumed, and the presence of two parents in the home. There are other environmental factors that impact academic acheivement. For instance, the activities in which children engage outside of school, such as reading storybooks, visiting libraries, or playing word games. Another factor is the potential difference between the home and school cultures. Culture is used in this sense as a broad term to include the behavior and attitudes of parents. If there is a wide gap between the home culture and school culture, children may perceive tasks like reading as unrewarding or devaluing their identity.

Effect of Peer Influence on Learning

Peer influence on children's behavior, as well as on learning, is well recognized in psychological literature. Peer influence can operate both positively and negatively. Teachers will try normally to exploit the positive influence on peers and promote many of the learning experiences the children may have by organizing them into small groups in which they can become involved in learning. The negative aspects of peer influence are obvious when parents of children expect them to show interest in school work and spend time on homework, but many of the children's peers do not have the same goals for themselves. There may be times where it might become necessary to have a child discontinue his or her association with those peers who are negative influences.

Literacy Problems Within the School System

There are various statistics that indicate that the overall literacy rates of students within the US school system are well below desired values. According to the Literacy Project in 2019, almost 65% of fourth graders did not read at a proficient level, and roughly 90% of children who were below average readers at the end of first grade remained that way by the end of fourth grade. There also appears to be at least some correlation between literacy and income, as over 80% of the fourth graders who were reading below the proficient level were from low-income families. While many solutions have been proffered, no major solution has been discovered to significantly reduce or eliminate this issue. To further complicate matters, recent studies have also shown that over 85% of juvenile offenders have difficulty reading. Debates over policy and methodology continue as no one-size-fits-all strategy has been determined to be effective at reducing overall illiteracy rates within the school system.

Ensuring Literacy for Students of Lower Socioeconomic Classes

There are disagreements among scholars as to the nature of the correlation between a child's socioeconomic level and comprehension level in school. Some see a direct correlation, while others say the correlation is more in degrees. Most data shows that children who are from low-income families are significantly more likely to fall behind in reading. This typically compounds as those with poor literacy skills through school tend to maintain them into adulthood often resulting in lower paying jobs, which then continues the cycle of poverty. There are many debated reasons as to why certain children may not be excelling in school, but in order to progress effectively, one needs to have a good foundation, and that foundation is being able to read and to communicate.

Improving School Literacy Levels

If a school performs poorly on assessments, they are sometimes required to adjust their entire curriculum. When such changes take place, there are many aims that are incorporated, much more than just a single program or a single type of instruction. These aims may include helping students' lifelong skills, improving the quality of teaching, and making sure all teachers recognize the role that language plays in learning. Another possible aim might be to include a set time for students to read, such as a literacy hour. The focus might include having staff mark all children's books for spelling and grammar as well as content, that all departments provide a glossary of subject-specific words for pupils, and that all departments would use a writing frame to provide writing structure for children in each subject.

Impact of Family Background on Education

The exact nature of the impact parental education and socioeconomic status has on student achievement is unknown, although it does have an impact. Studies have found that parental education and family socioeconomic status alone are not necessarily predictors of how students will achieve academically. Studies have found that parental education accounts for about a quarter of the variance in student test scores, while socioeconomic status accounts for slightly more than a quarter. Other research indicates that dysfunctional home environments, low expectations from parents, parenting that is ineffective, differences in language, and high mobility levels may account for the low achievement levels among those students that come from lower socioeconomic levels. Other impacts that family culture has on a student's performance might include cultural dispositions that end up isolating a student from his or her peer group. One of the most reliable ways of addressing family or socioeconomic background is by increasing the student's awareness of their future, whether that be in education or a particular career path. Having the student start thinking about his or her future will help to set and achieve short-term goals that will naturally lead to their long-term goals.

Negative Peer Influences of Learning

Students, teenagers specifically, look to each other to learn, and this sometimes brings about problems. Teenagers are growing and learning, and through this development, the students look to each other to acquire what their peers deem to be acceptable. In many instances, this may lead to inaccurate understandings. Teenagers purposely acquire knowledge sometimes that is unmistakably wrong and continue to use it in everyday situations. Some students are so influenced by their culture that, even though they are capable of speaking properly, they will not do so for fear they will not fit in with their peers. These students—who readily acknowledge that they have been taught formal language—choose to continue using slang because their culture has shaped them to do so.

The Hispanic Culture in Reading Lessons for Elementary Students

One of the greatest ways to expand cultural intelligence and remove barriers of ignorance is to simply expose children to various cultures and highlight what makes them unique. The Hispanic population is the fastest growing ethnic population in the United States. In order to better incorporate Hispanic culture into lesson plans, teachers will likely need to intentionally implement new strategies to properly engage and inform students. Assigning students the task of researching and presenting famous Hispanic Americans in history, presenting videos with Hispanic speakers and Spanish vocabulary, or reading about major historical events in the formation of Hispanic nations are all excellent ways to celebrate and better understand Hispanic culture. It is imperative to make sure that classrooms have ample amounts of resources for children to properly explore and engage with various cultures and their traditions. Showing how culture influences society, from foods eaten to the names of cities, children are better able to comprehend and understand one another and the larger world around them.

IEP

Special education teachers help to develop an Individualized Education Program (IEP) for each special education student. The IEP sets personalized goals for each student and is tailored to the student's individual needs and ability. When appropriate, the program includes a transition plan outlining specific steps to prepare students with disabilities for middle school or high school, or, in the case of older students, a job or post-secondary study. Teachers review the IEP with the student's parents, school administrators, and the student's general education teacher. Teachers work closely with parents to inform them of their child's progress and suggest techniques to promote learning at home.

Observations Assessing Prediction Skills

Teachers observing students will at some point hear the language of prediction. Students might say, "I think..." or "I wonder if..." By observing, the teachers can view certain reading behaviors that students show. When observing students making predictions about fiction text, the teacher should look out for these reading behaviors:

- Do students look at the text cover and make predictions that are based on the title or illustration?
- Do students stop prediction-making while they are reading?
- When reading the text, do students make predictions based on clues from the illustration or text?

These behaviors should be observed for nonfiction text reading:

- Do students use headings or subheadings in order to make predictions?
- Do students use charts, graphs, illustrations, or maps to make predictions?
- Do students predict what is likely to be learned based on clues from the illustration or text?

Effectively Using Paraprofessional Skills and Time

Especially with special education, teachers do not have enough time to meet all of the needs of every individual student in each classroom, and paraprofessionals are often sent into classrooms to help students with special needs. Regardless of the use, the roles and routines in which the paraprofessional is used need to be carefully and clearly laid out. Say the paraprofessional is in the classroom for reading a half-hour each day. It is important to consider the routines that could be put into place for that time period. One might discuss the benefits of the paraprofessional helping with readers who struggle. Also, one might plot the progress of students that are being helped by the paraprofessional. Ensuring that the paraprofessional is helpful to both the teacher and students and is not being pushed beyond the limitations of their expertise effectively manages the paraprofessional's skills and time.

Establishing a Successful Learning Center

Effective classrooms have a combination of direct instruction, cooperative learning, independent practice, and learning center activities. Learning centers help play an important part in classroom management and should be established one at a time. Possible centers include a writing center, an alphabet center, a science center, a writing center, or various other centers, but these can always be changed to meet the students' needs. Clear rules and routines for using each center should be understood, and a chart should be posted at each center that indicates how many children should be in the center or what materials and equipment may be used. The center will likely need to be closely supervised at first, as teachers begin determining when children are able to work both independently or cooperatively.

Curriculum Standards

Standards focus on developing coherency across grade levels, teaching for understanding, and relevancy of subject matter, helping courses to build upon each other in age-appropriate ways. This farsighted statement sets an excellent vision for what students should be learning. The standards are broken into ten areas within two broader categories. Process Standards, the first category, defines how students should "do" the content and how they should be able to use their knowledge. The second category, the Content Standards, deals with the content that students should learn.

Controversy Over Teacher Expectations on Learning Outcomes

The original Pygmalion study gave teachers false information about the learning potential of certain students in grades 1-6 in a San Francisco elementary school. Teachers were told that one of their students had been tested and found to be on the edge of a period of rapid intellectual growth, but in actuality, the student had actually been selected at random and the tests were measuring how the expectations of the teacher towards a student can impact their success. At the end of the experimental period, some of the targeted students exhibited superior scores on IQ tests compared to those of similar abilities. The results led researchers to claim that inflated expectations of teachers for target students actually caused accelerated intellectual growth. A number of studies have since taken place, and some found technical defects serious enough to cast doubt on the original findings. Whether one accepts or doubts the Pygmalion study, educators and the public are very interested in the power of expectations affecting the outcomes of students.

Effects of Higher Teacher Expectations Supplemented with Other Measures

High expectations may not be the magic trick needed to close achievement gaps, but raising expectations can make a difference when the effort is accompanied by a relevant and rigorous curriculum, adequate materials,current textbooks, effective teaching strategies, good classroom management, tutoring programs, uncrowded classrooms, and involved parents. It is likely the case that in life, as well as in teaching, there is a need for balance. Teachers should believe and expect that students can learn given time and hard work, and students must be convinced that the reward of an education is worth the effort. When students and teachers mutually understand and believe that success is obtainable and that it can only be obtained through consistent and intentional work, both students and teachers are significantly more likely to achieve their goals.

Chapter Quiz

Ready to see how well you retained what you just read? Scan the QR code to go directly to the chapter quiz interface for this study guide. If you're using a computer, simply visit the online resources page at **mometrix.com/resources719/texessocst4-8** and click the Chapter Quizzes link.

TExES Practice Test

Want to take this practice test in an online interactive format?
Check out the online resources page, which includes interactive practice questions and much more: **mometrix.com/resources719/texessocst4-8**

1. Unlike slaves, who were considered to be the property of their masters, which of the following was true regarding most indentured servants in colonial times?

a. They received wages for their labor
b. They were generally treated kindly by their employers
c. They were highly educated
d. They voluntarily entered into servitude

2. Which of the following systems was NOT in place for indigenous peoples before settlers arrived?

a. Market-based economy
b. Sustainable hunting
c. Oral history and story telling
d. Governing bodies

3. Which of the following accurately reflects acculturation vs. assimilation?

a. A nondominant culture giving up all of its traits in favor of the dominant culture is acculturation.
b. A dominant culture absorbing other cultures is assimilation.
c. Assimilation is when cultures adopt traits from other cultures.
d. When two or more cultures adopt some of each other's traits, this is assimilation.

4. What judicial system did America borrow from England?

a. Due process
b. Federal law
c. Commerce law
d. Common law

5. The civil rights act that outlawed segregation in schools and public places also did which of the following?

a. Gave minorities the right to vote
b. Established women's right to vote
c. Outlawed unequal voter registration
d. Provided protection for children

6. How was the vice president chosen before the 12th Amendment was ratified?

a. The president chose the vice president
b. Congress chose the vice president
c. The vice president came in second in the Electoral College
d. There was no vice president

7. Sociocultural evolution:

a. Describes the inclination of cultures to increase in complexity in the long run
b. Describes the interconnection which exists between people
c. Describes the quantity of cultural elements which are environmentally based
d. Describes a specific method of categorizing societies

8. What is the main reason that the Federal Reserve Board lowers interest rates?

a. To lower prices
b. To stimulate consumer spending
c. To encourage international trade
d. To control inflation

9. Which of the following is a power held only by the federal government?

a. The power to levy taxes, borrow money, and spend money
b. The power to award copyrights and patents to people or groups
c. The power to establish the criteria that qualify a person to vote
d. The power to ratify proposed amendments to the Constitution

10. On which type of map would Nigeria be bigger than Australia?

a. Contour map of elevation
b. Flow-line map of the spice trade
c. Mercator projection
d. Cartogram of population

11. The Trail of Tears was:

a. The forced removal of British soldiers after the American Revolution
b. The forced evacuation of Cherokee peoples into Oklahoma
c. The forced evacuation of freed slaves from the South after the Civil War
d. The tears of Betsy Ross while she sewed the first American flag

12. A teacher is planning a lesson focused on the impact of space exploration in the mid to late 20th century. Which of the following modern technologies should the teacher discuss in the lesson?

a. The internet
b. Modern cars
c. Antibiotics
d. GPS systems

13. During a lesson on personal money management, a student referred to the amount of money an individual makes from working at their job. Which of the following terms should the teacher share with the student to describe this concept?

a. Expenses
b. Income
c. Investments
d. Debt

14. How are members of the Federal Judiciary chosen?

a. They are elected by voters.
b. They are appointed by the president and confirmed by the House of Representatives.
c. They are chosen by a committee.
d. They are appointed by the president and confirmed by the Senate.

15. On a globe, the distance between Buenos Aires and Tokyo is 35 cm. If the globe has a scale of 1 cm for every 516 km, what is the real distance?

a. 18,060 km
b. 35 km
c. 21,080 km
d. 14,740 km

16. Which of the following is NOT a method of representing relief on a physical map?

a. Symbols
b. Color
c. Shading
d. Contour Lines

17. The popularity of hockey in Canada and the northern United States is an example of

a. Expansion diffusion
b. Indirect diffusion
c. Forced diffusion
d. Direct diffusion

18. Inflation has what effects?

a. Harms all members of an economy
b. Helps all members of an economy
c. Harms no members of an economy
d. Harms some members of an economy, helps others

19. The results of increased production of crops and a managed approach to agriculture is called:

a. The industrial revolution
b. The information revolution
c. The agricultural revolution
d. The scientific revolution

20. Which of the following scenarios most accurately portrays the concept of supply and demand?

a. The manufacturer of the newest smart phone made several million units to fulfill expected orders. However, orders were much lower than predicted. The manufacturer was able to fulfill orders with several phones left over.
b. Before sending a new toy into production, a company lets customers preorder to ensure they can access one. This helps the company ensure they will have enough toys to meet the needs of consumers.
c. A popular clothing item is in high demand, but the manufacturer cannot maintain production to meet the needs of consumers. As a result, the cost of the clothing item increases.
d. A snack company produced too many bags of one type of chip. Because they have so many, they increased the price of each bag. If they can sell all of them, they will make a record profit.

21. A teacher is discussing the materials used to build homes and other structures near fault lines. Which of the following is the most likely focus of this conversation?

a. The impact of resources on human settlement
b. The impact of geography on human migration
c. The impact of natural hazards on human adaptation
d. The impact of weather on human survival

22. Students have been asked to use at least one secondary source for a Holocaust research project. Which of the following should they select?

a. *The Diary of Anne Frank*
b. A virtual map of Auschwitz
c. An interview with a Holocaust survivor
d. Documents from a concentration camp

23. On a map of Africa, there is a small box around Nairobi. This city is depicted in greater detail in a box at the bottom of the map. What is the name for this box at the bottom of the map?

a. Inset
b. Legend
c. Compass rose
d. Key

24. When state legislatures pass laws that regulate driving, marriage, and public education, they are exercising which of the following?

a. Implied, or suggested, powers
b. Shared, or concurrent, powers
c. Expressed, or enumerated, powers
d. Reserved powers

25. Among the following, which is correct regarding some essential geography concepts?

a. An example of absolute location is urban vs. rural land prices.
b. Relative location equals the latitude and longitude of a place.
c. Product and land prices are affected by geographical distance.
d. Achievability relates to surface conditions and never changes.

26. Which social science focuses primarily on how a society produces and distributes goods?

a. Sociology
b. Anthropology
c. Psychology
d. Economics

27. The price of fleece blankets goes up from $10 to $11. At the same time, demand goes down from 1,000 blankets to 800 blankets. Which of the following statements is true?

a. Demand is elastic
b. Demand is inelastic
c. The price elasticity quotient, or E_d, is less than 1
d. The price elasticity quotient, or E_d, is equal to 1

28. The best definition of culture is:

a. The actual expression of societal norms
b. The ideal of what should occur in a particular society
c. The universal practices evident in all societies
d. The sum of everything learned by participants in a society

29. A teacher has asked her students to explain the concept of "built environment" in their own terms. Based on the following responses, which student demonstrates an understanding of this concept?

a. Humans have developed intricate systems of transportation to meet the needs of a particular environment.
b. The harsh climate of some regions requires populations to either adapt or migrate to survive.
c. The overuse of natural resources in building practices can have long-term negative impacts on the biodiversity in an area.
d. Populations develop extensive political systems over time to meet the needs of the individuals living there.

30. The social scientists most likely to study the role of kinship relationships within a cultural group are:

a. Economists
b. Political scientists
c. Psychologists
d. Anthropologists

31. During class discussion, a teacher explains that many mountain communities have maintained their own unique cultures, dialects, and ways of life. She further explains that this is due to the fact they have not been subject to outside influences, as mountainous areas are hard to reach. Which of the following concepts are they likely discussing?

a. The impact of migrants on belief systems
b. The impact of landforms on adaptations
c. The impact of distance on culture
d. The impact of geography on human activities

32. Students were given the following prompt:

Provide and explain one cause of European exploration of North America

Which of the following responses indicates a student may need further instruction on the topic?

a. European exploration of North America was driven by religious motives, including spreading Christianity and escaping religious persecution.
b. The European population was growing exponentially. Therefore, it was important to find land in other parts of the world to sustain this growth.
c. Exploration was motivated in part by the accumulation of wealth, as Europe sought out expensive resources from new lands.
d. Establishing a trade route with direct access to Asia was a motivating factor in European exploration.

33. The Erie Canal is 363 miles long and connects which body of water to Lake Erie?

a. The Mississippi River
b. The Hudson River
c. The Susquehanna River
d. The Lehigh River

34. Which of the following best characterizes ethnocentrism?

a. The belief that one's personal culture is superior to others
b. The idea that it is difficult to adapt to a new culture
c. The idea that some cultures pre-date others
d. The belief that matriarchal societies are superior

35. A fifth grade class is studying a country whose economy is described as a "market economy." Which of the following statements would the teacher use to elaborate on this concept?

a. Members in communities across this country work together to meet the needs of their community. They focus on producing what is needed to survive and disregard the modern concept of luxury.
b. Government groups maintain control of the economy. They establish what goods can be produced, the cost of the goods, and who has access to them. This has both negative and positive impacts on citizens.
c. The price of goods in this country is based on supply and demand. Sellers set their prices based on what consumers are willing to spend on their product.
d. This economy is regulated by the government in some respects and by sellers in others. Sellers can produce and price the goods they chose within reason, and the government can intervene when necessary.

36. Students are participating in a role-playing activity to learn about money management. They receive a salary and must create a budget that meets their basic needs before allotting money for any unnecessary expenses. Which of the following concepts are students applying in this lesson?

a. Entrepreneurship
b. Financial literacy
c. Scarcity
d. Goods and services

37. Which of the following was NOT an immediate effect of rapid urban growth in the 1800s?

a. Poor sanitation conditions in the cities
b. Epidemics of diseases in the cities
c. Inadequate police and fire protection
d. Widespread urban political corruption

38. The writers of *The Federalist Papers* published under the pen name "Publius." Who were the authors?

a. James Madison, John Jay, and Alexander Hamilton
b. George Washington, Thomas Jefferson, and James Madison
c. Alexander Hamilton, Benjamin Franklin, and Thomas Jefferson
d. Benjamin Franklin, John Jay, and Thomas Jefferson

39. According to George Murdock, which of the following is NOT a general characteristic of all cultural practices?

a. Religion
b. Folklore
c. Property disputes
d. Laws

40. Tracy needs to determine the shortest route between Lima and Lisbon. Which of the following maps should she use?

a. Azimuthal projection with the North Pole at the center
b. Azimuthal projection with Lisbon at the center
c. Robinson projection of the Eastern Hemisphere
d. Robinson projection of the Western Hemisphere

41. A teacher wants students to understand the impact of geography on human migration through reading primary sources. Which of the following readings should he assign?

a. An article about the Great Migration and the impact it had on those who moved
b. Diary entries of a woman who migrated to an urban area during Industrialization
c. Interview transcripts of individuals forced to seek refuge due to political events
d. A collection of letters written by Dust Bowl survivors who lived in the Great Plains

42. A family moves to America from another country with a very different culture. They discard their native cultural practices and adopt American customs. This is an example of:

a. Accommodation
b. Adaptation
c. Acculturation
d. Assimilation

43. How did the ruling in *Marbury v. Madison* alter the Supreme Court's power in the federal government?

a. It lessened it. The Supreme Court was concerned about the possibility of judges overturning laws enacted by voters through referendums and took away that power.
b. It increased it. The decision in *Marbury v. Madison* gave the Supreme Court its now traditional right to overturn legislation.
c. It increased it. The decision in *Marbury v. Madison* strengthened the Supreme Court's Constitutional right to overturn legislation.
d. There was no change. *Marbury v. Madison* was a case involving a president who was unwilling to obey laws enacted by his predecessor; there was nothing about the case or decision that would have more than a cursory connection to federal powers of government

44. The following response was written by a student after a lesson on westward expansion in the 19th century.

During the 19th century, people moved out west to pursue a better life. This movement was driven by Manifest Destiny, which is the belief that America should spread from coast to coast and share its beliefs. The development of railroads and steamships helped make moving easier, but it was still difficult and stressful for most families. The support many families received from Native American tribe members along the way helped reduce this stress. As a whole, westward expansion improved the economy, increased the size of America, and improved the quality of life for many people.

This response indicates that the students could use another lesson focused on which of the following topics?

a. The concept of Manifest Destiny and how it guided expansion efforts
b. The timeline of railroad and steam ship development
c. The impact westward expansion had on settlers' relations with Native Americans
d. The changes in the economy as the country expanded west

45. Land is typically more expensive in urban areas than in rural areas. Which geography concept does this reflect?

a. Location
b. Distance
c. Pattern
d. Interaction

46. Which of the following contributions should be examined when a student is studying Ancient Rome?

a. Aqueducts and sewage systems
b. Silk and crop rotation methods
c. Geometry and irrigation methods
d. Philosophy and democratic government

47. In the United States, what is the correct term for a settlement with fewer than 100 inhabitants?

a. Village
b. Town
c. Hamlet
d. City

48. When the Senate held an impeachment hearing against Andrew Johnson for overstepping his authority, what did they invoke?

a. Checks and balances
b. Bicameralism
c. Legislative oversight
d. Supremacy

49. Social dialects typically emerge when

a. a particular group is isolated from the rest of society due to class, race, age, or gender differences.
b. a group of new immigrants is assimilated into society.
c. two social groups that share a common language become geographically isolated.
d. specialized jargons develop in certain industries and academic disciplines.

50. The concept of due process in the Fifth Amendment to the U.S. Constitution protects individuals in which of the following ways?

a. Guaranteeing a citizen's right to a trial by jury within a reasonable timeframe
b. Restricting the government's ability to remove basic rights without following the law
c. Guaranteeing a citizen's right to equal protection under the law
d. Restricting the government's ability to remove basic rights without dire cause

51. Which invention had a major role in communication during the Civil War?

a. Morse Code
b. Telephone
c. Radio
d. Computer

52. Which of the following best defines American GDP?

a. The value, in American dollars, of all goods and services produced within American borders during one calendar year
b. The value, in American dollars, of all goods and services produced by American companies during one calendar year
c. The total value, in American dollars, of all American household incomes during one calendar year
d. The value, in American dollars, of a "market basket" of goods and services in one year divided by the value of the same market basket in a previous year multiplied by 100

53. Of the following economists, who advocated government intervention to prevent and remedy recessions and depressions?

a. Adam Smith
b. John Maynard Keynes
c. Friedrich Hayek
d. Milton Friedman

54. Why was US industrialization confined to the Northeast until after the Civil War?

a. Because the Civil War delayed the development of water-powered manufacturing
b. Because the Northeast had faster-running rivers than the rivers found in the South
c. Because Slater's first cotton mill with horse-drawn production lost so much money
d. Because the technical innovations for milling textiles had not as yet been invented

55. Which of the market structures is most efficient?

a. Perfect competition
b. Monopolistic competition
c. Oligopoly
d. Monopoly

56. What was the purpose of Lyndon Johnson's Great Society?

a. To eliminate poverty and racial injustice in America
b. To erase the last vestiges of the Great Depression from the American economic landscape
c. To encourage economic prosperity through trickledown economics
d. To increase educational standards in the United States

57. Which biome is NOT found in the Torrid Zone?

a. Desert
b. Savanna
c. Rainforest
d. Taiga

58. The telephone was a solution to which of the following problems with the telegraph?

a. Telegraph lines were thick and difficult to maintain.
b. Telegraph messages could only be received by people who had specialized equipment.
c. Telegraphs could only relay one message at a time.
d. Telegraphs frequently broke down if subject to extended use.

59. A fifth grade teacher asks his students to list ways humans adapt to survive in a variety of regions. Use this student's list to answer the following question.

4. People in areas that are cold developed insulated housing.
5. People survived in harsh areas while migrating.
6. People in flood-prone areas build homes on stilts.
7. People use irrigation systems to support extensive crop growth.

What information should the student remove to make his list correct?

a. Statement 1
b. Statement 2
c. Statement 3
d. Statement 4

60. A sixth grade teacher wants to challenge her students to apply their understanding of distance. Which of the following enrichment activities should she assign?

a. Draw and label your own version of a compass rose. Ensure it features both cardinal and ordinal directions and label it properly.
b. Use the key on a tourism map to plan a day trip to Niagara Falls that includes at least three stops at major landmarks within city limits.
c. Plot two sets of coordinates on a map. Map out a route from one set of coordinates to the next and determine what major cities the route passes through.
d. Using a ruler and the scale on a map, map out the shortest possible route between two points without using highways.

61. Which of the following is NOT true about democracy and the formation of the United States?

a. The founding fathers stated in the Constitution that the United States would be a democracy.
b. The Declaration of Independence did not dictate democracy but stated its principles.
c. The United States Constitution stipulated that government be elected by the people.
d. The United States Constitution had terms to protect some, but not all, of the people.

62. A popular apple orchard typically sets its price at $1.00 per apple. The weather this season has not been favorable for growing, resulting in a smaller crop yield than usual. To compensate for their loss, they raised their price to $1.50 per apple.

Which of the following concepts can this scenario help demonstrate?

a. Opportunity cost
b. Supply and demand
c. Competition
d. Capital

63. Which of the following BEST describes the significance of the US Supreme Court's decision in the Dred Scott case?

a. The ruling effectively declared slavery to be a violation of the Constitution.
b. The ruling guaranteed full citizenship rights to freed slaves.
c. The ruling turned many Southerners against the Supreme Court.
d. The ruling furthered the gap between North and South and hastened the Civil War.

64. Students were asked to briefly describe a form of government. Which of the following student responses does NOT accurately describe their assigned form of government?

a. A democracy allows citizens to play a role in decision making by participating in elections.
b. A small group of individuals is responsible for controlling the government in an oligarchy.
c. A religious leader holds the highest position of power and rules with religious laws in a theocracy.
d. A dictatorship features an individual king or queen that serves as the head of state.

65. Before the Civil War, to which of the following did Southern states object?

a. An increase in Southern tobacco production
b. An increase in tariffs on Northern manufactured goods
c. An increase in western mining for gold
d. An increase in the voting rights of slaves

66. Students have been given a list of regions with extreme climates and asked to research adaptations made by residents in each region. Use this list written by one of the students to answer the following question.

1. People who live in areas with extreme heat alter their routines to avoid the sun and outdoor areas during the hottest part of the day.
2. Individuals in high altitude regions have high lung capacities to compensate for low oxygen levels.
3. Residents in areas of extreme cold tend to layer clothing for better insulation.
4. Many small tribes cultivate only what they need to survive as a means to protect land.

Which of the following pieces of feedback should be given to the student to help improve the accuracy of their list?

a. Remove statement 1 and replace it with a description of cooling systems to improve the accuracy of the list.
b. Change statement 4 to reflect the type of crops that can grow in these tribal areas based on weather conditions.
c. Add detailed descriptions of the clothing used by residents in colder regions to statement 3.
d. Combine statements 1 and 3 to demonstrate the difference in adaptations based on temperature.

67. Which of the following was NOT a tax levied on the American colonies by the British government in the 1760s and '70s?

a. The Sugar Act of 1764
b. The Stamp Act of 1765
c. The Lead Act of 1772
d. The Tea Act of 1773

68. What is the name for the traditionally Arab district in a North African city?

a. Souk
b. Medina
c. Wadi
d. Bazaar

69. Following a lesson on community, a teacher wants to assign a formative assessment to gauge student understanding before continuing to the next lesson. Which of the following should she assign?

a. A multiple-choice test on the overall concept of community for each student to complete independently
b. A concept map to illustrate the properties of a community for each student to complete independently
c. A community service project that allows students to work collaboratively to contribute to bettering their community
d. A portfolio that demonstrates an understanding of community concepts within small learning groups

70. When the prices farmers receive for their crops decline in a developing country, this typically results in which of the following?

a. Increased urbanization
b. Increased college enrollment
c. Declining literacy rates
d. Higher prices for those crops in developed countries

71. Which of the following statements is false regarding the Puritans?

a. In terms of their theology, the Puritans were considered Calvinists.
b. Many Puritans agreed with radical views that criticized the Swiss Calvinists.
c. Many of those identified as Calvinists opposed the Puritans.
d. The Restoration and the Uniformity Act reunified the Puritan movement and the Church of England.

72. The Seven Years' War, called the French and Indian War by the Colonists:

a. Was the precursor to the American Revolution
b. Was a conflict related to European colonization
c. Primarily took place in Canada
d. Ended European conquests

73. Which of the following statements is accurate about individualistic vs. collectivist orientations of some world cultures?

a. Latin American and African cultures are more often individualistic.
b. Individualism is less common in Canadian and Australian cultures.
c. Native American and Asian cultures are typically more collectivist.
d. European and North American cultures tend to be more collectivist.

74. A country's currency increases in value on foreign currency exchange markets. What will happen as a result?

I. Exports will drop
II. Imports will rise
III. The balance of payments will rise

a. I only
b. II only
c. I and II
d. II and III

75. Thai food has become increasingly popular in the United States, though it is prepared in slightly different ways here. This is an example of:

a. Cultural divergence
b. Assimilation
c. Cultural convergence
d. Acculturation

76. In 1997, he was called the "richest man in America" for his approximate net worth of $37 billion, which he earned in the computer industry. He tries to keep the American Dream alive for others by philanthropically donating money to schools, libraries, and computer labs. Who is this American entrepreneur?

a. Warren Buffett
b. Bill Gates
c. Robert Johnson
d. Sam Walton

77. Which of the following is considered to be the largest cause of death among Native Americans following the arrival of European colonists in North America?

a. Wounds from wars with the European settlers
b. Wounds from wars with the other Native American tribes
c. European diseases
d. Exposure during the wintry, forced marches on which the European settlers forced them

78. Which of the following represents a discretionary expense?

a. Textbook
b. Rent
c. DVD
d. Groceries

79. Which of the following is NOT true regarding the Virginia Companies?

a. One of these companies, the Virginia Company of Plymouth, made its base in North America.
b. One of these companies, the Virginia Company of London, made its base in Massachusetts.
c. One company had a charter to colonize America between the Hudson and Cape Fear rivers.
d. One company had a charter to colonize America from the Potomac River to north Maine.

80. After a lesson on how conflict between American colonies and Great Britain pushed America toward independence, a teacher leads a class discussion. Which of the following phrases will likely come up in this discussion?

a. "Let them eat cake"
b. "No taxation without representation"
c. "I came, I saw, I conquered"
d. "I have a dream"

81. In the Constitution of the United States, which of the following powers is reserved for the states?

a. Taxation
b. Declaring war
c. Regulation of intrastate trade
d. Granting patents and copyrights

82. Which of the following learning targets would NOT be appropriate for a unit on human geography?

a. Students will be able to explain how landforms play a role in creating borders.
b. Students will be able to explain how the economy is impacted by urbanization.
c. Students will be able to explain how migration patterns are impacted by climate.
d. Students will be able to explain how natural disasters impact landscapes.

83. Approximately what percentage of the Earth's surface is land?

a. 50
b. 10
c. 30
d. 85

84. When instructing a lesson on the American Revolution, a teacher refers to both a letter sent home from a soldier and a documentary on The Battle of Saratoga. What are the advantages to using both sources?

a. Students will be able to compare and contrast the documents.
b. Studying both resources will help students better understand primary sources.
c. Using both documents will provide students with multiple points of view.
d. Using as many sources as possible helps students solidify learning.

85. A teacher wants students to display an understanding of the concept of chronology. Which of the following should NOT be assigned?

a. A timeline of the American Revolution and related battles
b. A presentation of US wars in order from earliest to latest
c. A speech on the beginning, middle, and end of the Great Depression
d. A mock diary entry from the point of view of a Confederate soldier

86. A teacher is planning a lesson on the various forms of government. Which of the following instructional tools would best support learning?

a. A video compilation of the coronation ceremonies of multiple British monarchs
b. A role-playing activity in which students act out a mock trial of a government official
c. An infographic on a country's economy before and after authoritarian rule
d. A graphic organizer comparing and contrasting diverse government systems

87. Which of the following prompts would best assess an understanding of the chronology of events?

a. Write a mock diary entry from the perspective of a Colonial American child and parent.
b. Explain the significant events that led up to the outbreak of WWI and their impacts.
c. Construct a diorama of your choice of Civil War battlefield, and be sure to include accurate uniforms.
d. Craft a recreation of ancient trade route maps used by China to obtain goods.

Refer to the following for question 88:

During a report on the Industrial Revolution, Mary uses a poster to illustrate cause and effect relationships in the War of 1812.

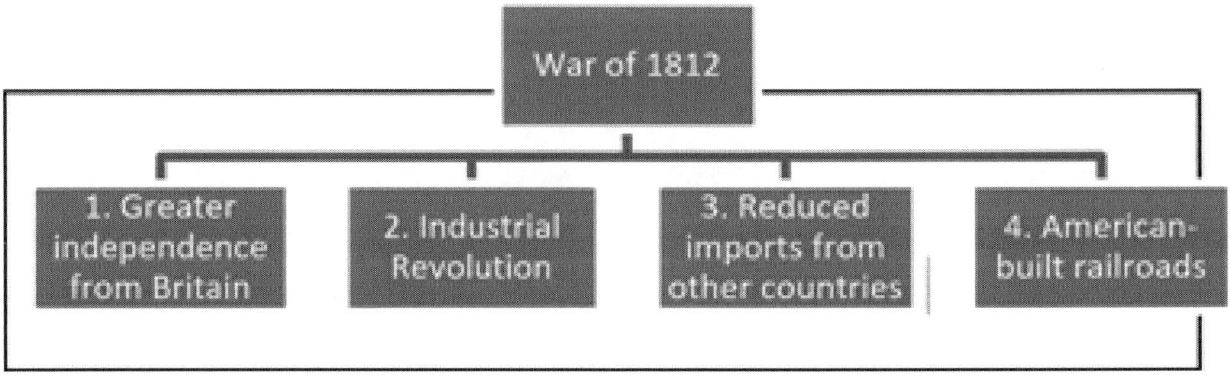

88. Of the following, which should Mary include in her report as more of a cause than an effect of the Industrial Revolution?

a. Emergence of socialism
b. Emergence of capitalism
c. The Romantic movement
d. The Protestant work ethic

89. What does the 10th Amendment establish?

a. Any power not given to the federal government belongs to the states or the people.
b. The president is responsible for executing and enforcing laws created by Congress.
c. Congress has the authority to declare war.
d. The Supreme Court has the authority to interpret the Constitution.

90. What did the Mason-Dixon Line divide?

a. The East from the West before the western states were incorporated
b. The East from the West along the Mississippi River
c. The North from the South before the Civil War
d. The Senate from the House of Representatives

91. Which of the following assignments will best allow a teacher to determine if her students understand the development of the United States government?

a. Having students create a timeline on which they detail important events and documents from the late 18th century
b. Having students participate in a mock debate between colonies and the British government
c. Having students create a map of the United States before and after they gained political independence
d. Having students reenact the signing of The Declaration of Independence at the Second Continental Congress

92. "Self-actualization" is a term associated with the ___________ approach to understanding human behavior.

a. behaviorist
b. humanistic
c. psychodynamic
d. cognitive

93. Which of the following activities can be used to assess student understanding of absolute location?

a. Provide students with a map and list of coordinates. Ask them to find the landmark at each point.
b. Provide students with a blank map of the US. Have them color code regions based on their geography.
c. Provide students with a state map. Ask them to describe the location of towns based on how far they are from the capital.
d. Provide students with a map and game token. Have them move the token a set number of spaces in an assigned cardinal direction and record where they end.

94. On the first day of a new unit, a teacher provides students with a T-chart and a list of sample tasks before the lesson. She asks them to sort each task as either a right or a duty. Which of the following best defines this activity?

a. A preassessment of prior knowledge of responsible citizenship
b. A summative assessment of the new unit
c. A formative assessment of the first lesson in the unit
d. A norm-referenced assessment to compare student knowledge

95. Which of the following are the leading producers of petroleum in Latin America?

a. Argentina and Bolivia
b. Mexico and Guatemala
c. Brazil and Venezuela
d. Colombia and Uruguay

96. Which of the following exemplifies the multiplier effect of large cities?

a. The presence of specialized equipment for an industry attracts even more business.
b. The large population lowers the price of goods.
c. Public transportation means more people can commute to work.
d. A local newspaper can afford to give away the Sunday edition.

97. Which of the following is *not* one of the Baltic states?

a. Moldova
b. Latvia
c. Lithuania
d. Estonia

98. A caste system is BEST described as

a. a primarily social phenomenon that has no economic consequences.
b. a system that discriminates mainly based on race, but permits upward social mobility.
c. a system wherein individuals' social, economic, and political destinies are determined at birth by group membership.
d. equivalent to the modern-day class system.

99. The president serves as commander-in-chief. What are the president's two limitations in that role?

a. The president cannot declare war or make rules governing the military.
b. The president cannot enforce blockades or declare war.
c. The president cannot enforce quarantines or make rules governing the military.
d. The president cannot enforce blockades or quarantines.

100. What do the executive, legislative, and judicial branches of government compose?

a. The federal government
b. The democratic process
c. Bicameralism
d. Rule of law

Answer Key and Explanations

1. D: Indentured servants agreed to work for a set period of time in exchange for transportation to the New World and such basic necessities as food and shelter. They did not receive wages and were generally not highly-educated people. Employers often viewed indentured servants with scorn and treated them as harshly as they treated slaves.

2. A: Prior to the arrival of settlers, indigenous peoples established trade with neighboring tribes. When settlers arrived, these tribes were forced to trade with them, which led to the development of a market-based economy. Indigenous peoples are well known for having had sustainable hunting, fishing, and farming practices. This makes choice B incorrect. Similarly, indigenous peoples engaged in oral history and storytelling long before settlers arrived, making choice C incorrect. Tribes had individual governing and decision-making bodies established well before the arrival of settlers. Most groups had some type of chief or leader and a council. This makes choice D incorrect.

3. B: When a dominant culture absorbs other cultures so that they all adopt all the behaviors of the dominant culture, this is called assimilation. The other options represent the opposite of the truth; answer A is an example of assimilation, answer C is acculturation, and option D is acculturation.

4. D: America is a common law country because English common law was adopted in all states except Louisiana. Common law is based on precedent and changes over time. Each state develops its own common laws.

5. C: The Civil Rights Act of 1964 affected the Jim Crow laws in the Southern states. Many minorities suffered under unfair voting laws and segregation. President Lyndon Johnson signed the Civil Rights Act of 1964 into law after the 1963 assassination of President Kennedy, who championed the reform.

6. C: The 12th Amendment passed in 1804 gave each member of the Electoral College one vote for the president and another for the vice president. Previously, the runner up in the presidential election became vice president.

7. A: The best characterization of sociocultural evolution is that it describes the inclination of organizations to increase in complexity in the long run. Choice B is incorrect because it is the description of society, not of sociocultural evolution. Choice C and Choice D are also wrong because they describe the ecological approach, not sociocultural evolution.

8. B: Lower interest rates allow banks to lend out more money, which serves to stimulate consumer spending. Increased spending tends to raise, not lower, prices. The Federal Reserve Board is not actively involved in international trade. The fear of inflation usually leads to a rise in interest rates.

9. B: Only the federal government has the power to give copyrights and patents to individuals or companies. The power to levy taxes, borrow money, and spend money (A) is a power shared by federal and state governments. The power to set the criteria that qualify individuals to vote (C) is a power given to state governments, though it is subject to federal limits. The power to ratify amendments proposed to the Constitution (D) is a power of only the state governments.

10. D: On a cartogram of population, Nigeria would be bigger than Australia. Even though the area of Australia is several times greater than that of Nigeria, Nigeria has a much larger population. A cartogram is a map on which countries or regions are sized according to a certain variable. So, in a cartogram of population, the country with the most people will be the biggest. The countries would be depicted at their usual size in a contour map of elevation or in a flow-line map. On a Mercator projection, Nigeria would actually be smaller relative to Australia because it is closer to the equator.

11. B: The Trail of Tears was the forcible removal of Native American tribes from their homes in the Southeastern US to Oklahoma. The name came due to the high number of Native Americans who died on the journey.

12. D: GPS systems use satellites to perform their functions. Satellites were first developed for space exploration and were initially launched in the 1950s. This makes discussing modern GPS systems relevant to this lesson. The internet was developed collaboratively by many researchers and developers but not as a result of space exploration, making choice A incorrect. Modern cars could be discussed in the context of internal combustion engines, which were developed in the late 1800s and early 1900s, or other related advancements; however, none of these were associated with space exploration. This makes choice B incorrect. Antibiotics were developed following the discovery of penicillin in the early 1900s, which was unrelated to space exploration. This makes choice C incorrect.

13. B: Money earned through salary, wages, or investments is referred to as income. This term best describes what the student is explaining, making choice B correct. Expenses are the money spent on goods, services, and living necessities. Expenses are often viewed as the opposite of income. As such, choice A is incorrect. Investments occur when money is put toward a project or venture that is expected to make more money for the investor later. This makes choice C incorrect. Choice D is incorrect, as debt is money that is owed to someone else, such as a lender.

14. D: According to Article III of the Constitution, Justices of the Supreme Court, judges of the courts of appeals and district courts, and judges of the Court of International Trade are appointed by the president with the confirmation of the Senate. The judicial branch of the government is the only one not elected by the people.

15. A: The distance between Buenos Aires and Tokyo is approximately 18,060 km. The process of converting a scaled distance to a real distance is fairly simple. In this case, multiply the number of centimeters by the number of kilometers represented by each of these centimeters. The calculation can be expressed as (35 cm)(516 km/1 cm). Because centimeters are in the numerator of the first term and the denominator of the second term, they cancel out, leaving kilometers as the unit.

16. A: Symbols are not used to represent relief on a physical map. A physical map is dedicated to illustrating the landmasses and bodies of water in a specific region, so symbols do not provide enough detail. Color, shading, and contour lines, on the other hand, are able to create a much more complicated picture of changes in elevation, precipitation, etc. Changes in elevation are known in geography as relief.

17. D: The popularity of hockey in Canada and the northern United States is an example of direct diffusion. Direct diffusion is the transfer of cultural practices and ideas between two groups living in close proximity to each other. Expansion diffusion, also known as forced diffusion, is the transfer of cultural practices from a subjugating culture to a subjugated culture. One example of expansion diffusion was the Western imposition of trading practices on China during the nineteenth and early twentieth centuries. Indirect diffusion is the spread of cultural traits over a long distance without there necessarily being any direct contact between the cultures. The popularity in the United States of henna tattoos, which originated in India, is an example of indirect diffusion.

18. D: While rising prices may hurt many members of an economy, those same rising prices may benefit other members of the same economy. For example, rising prices may help those who sell goods and services and are able to keep their costs of production low, increasing their profit margin. Meanwhile, rising prices can hurt consumers because their income is now able to purchase fewer goods and services than before.

19. C: The agricultural revolution. A dependable food supply is essential to all populations. The agricultural revolution, an organized, almost scientific approach to agriculture, increased the food supply necessary for a growing world population.

20. C: Supply, the amount of a good or service that is available, and demand, the number of people willing to purchase the good or service, play a significant role in determining the price of a good or service. When high demand items are in low supply, the price typically rises. In contrast, when low demand items are in high supply, the price drops. This is best demonstrated in choice C. Choice A describes a situation in which a manufacturer has a surplus of new phones. Because the impact that this could have on pricing is not mentioned, it does not describe supply and demand. While the concept of preordering can help ensure there is enough supply to meet demand, the scenario in choice B does not explicitly address the concept overall. Choice D explains a situation that is the opposite of supply and demand. This scenario would reflect the concept of supply and demand if the company lowered the price of each bag of chips. Therefore, choice D is incorrect.

21. C: Homes and structures built near fault lines are at greater risk for damage from seismic activity such as earthquakes. As such, they are typically built with specialized resources and methods. A conversation regarding this would focus on the impact of natural hazards on human adaptation. This makes choice C correct. The availability of resources and how they impact human settlement is not related to fault lines, making choice A incorrect. The conversation is focused on changes in building practices that sustain life, not causes of migration. This makes choice B incorrect. Seismic activity along fault lines is not considered weather, nor is the conversation focused on survival, making choice D incorrect.

22. B: Primary sources are original documents, artifacts, or interviews created or collected during a particular time period. Secondary sources are interpretations, recreations, or edited versions of primary sources. An updated, virtual map of a historical area is a secondary source. Only maps developed during the same time during which World War II occurred would be considered primary sources for this project. *The Diary of Anne Frank* is considered a primary source, as it is a collection of diary entries written by Anne Frank during the time surrounding the Holocaust. This makes choice A incorrect. Interviews given by survivors would be considered primary sources, making choice C incorrect. Documents recorded at a concentration camp are considered primary sources. This makes choice D incorrect.

23. A: A smaller box in which some part of the larger map is depicted in greater detail is known as an inset. Insets provide a closer look at parts of the map that the cartographer deems to be more important (for instance, cities, national parks, or historical sites). Often, traffic maps will include several insets depicting the roads in the most congested area of the city. Legends, also known as keys, are the boxes in which the symbols used in the map are explained. A legend, or key, might indicate how railroads and boundaries are depicted, for example. A compass rose indicates how the map is oriented along the north-south axis. It is common for cartographers to tilt a map for ease of display, such that up may not be due north.

24. D: According to the Tenth Amendment to the Constitution: "The powers not delegated to the United States by the Constitution, nor prohibited by it to the States, are reserved to the States respectively, or to the people." As the regulation of education and marriage are neither delegated to the federal government nor prohibited to the states, they are powers reserved for the states.

25. C: One geographical concept is distance. For example, product prices are affected by the cost of transportation, which in turn is affected by how far away raw materials are from the factories that process them, and prices for land closer to highways are higher than for land farther away from them. Location is another geography concept. Absolute location is determined by a place's latitude and longitude, not land prices (A). Relative location is determined by a region's changing characteristics, which surrounding areas can influence; one example is that land costs more in urban than rural areas. Relative location is not determined by latitude and longitude (B). Achievability is related to the accessibility of a geographical area; for example, villages with surrounding forests or swamps are less accessible than those on beaches. The dependency of an area, and hence its achievability, *does* change (D) as its technology, transportation, and economy change.

26. D: While all social science is concerned to some extent with how societies make use of whatever resources are available to them, the production and distribution of goods is of primary concern to the economist.

27. A: The change in demand is 20% (1,000 − 800 = 200), and the change in price is 10% ($11 − $10 = $1). Because the change in demand is greater than the change in price, the demand is considered elastic. In this case, the price elasticity quotient is greater than 1.

28. D: Culture can best be defined as the sum of everything that is learned by participating in a society. Choice A is incorrect because it is the specific definition of real culture, rather than a general definition of culture itself. Choice B defines ideal culture; again, this is a specific definition of a type of culture, rather than a definition of culture itself. Choice C refers not to culture, but to a cultural universal.

29. A: The built environment is an aspect of human geography that refers to infrastructure built by humans to meet their needs within a particular environment. This includes transportation systems, buildings, and a variety of landmarks. As such, choice A is correct. Choice B is incorrect because it addresses concepts of adaptation, not built environment. Though choice C mentions building practices, it does not address the concept of built environment, making it incorrect. Choice D is incorrect, as it explains the development of political systems, not built environment.

30. D: Anthropology is the study of human social relationships and the analysis of cultural characteristics. Economists study how societies use resources and distribute goods. Political science is the study of government and political institutions. Psychologists focus on mental functions and human behavior.

31. D: This teacher explained the impact of geography on human activities. Because mountainous areas are harder to reach, there is less outside influence on mountain communities. This allows these communities to maintain their own cultures, dialects, and ways of life. The teacher does not explain how individuals who migrate to an area may influence belief systems in that area, making choice A incorrect. The characteristics of the mountainous areas she describes are not adaptations, which makes choice B incorrect. Though the teacher is discussing influences on culture, she does not directly describe distance as a factor in preventing changes. She only discusses mountainous landforms, making choice C incorrect.

32. B: Population growth was not a primary reason for European exploration. This makes the response in choice B incorrect, indicating this student may need further instruction. Religious motivation was a significant driving factor in European exploration. Some individuals wanted to spread Christian beliefs to native populations, while others wanted to avoid religious persecution in Europe. The response in choice A demonstrates a clear understanding of these factors. Exploration was motivated by resources that could be found on newly settled land. The acquisition of new land allowed Europe to acquire additional resources. Examples include animal furs, lumber, agriculture products, and other natural resources. Therefore, the student in choice C is correct. The primary goal in European exploration was to establish a trade route with direct access to Asia to avoid routes controlled by the Ottoman Empire. During this effort, they came across North America. Choice D demonstrates an understanding of this motivation.

33. B: The Erie Canal opened in 1825 and created a water route between the Hudson River and Lake Erie. Water routes have historically been cheaper and easier than overland ones and the Erie Canal was originally proposed in the 1700s as a means of providing a shipping route to assist in settling the areas west of the Appalachian Mountains. The Mississippi River is to the west of the Great Lakes; its source is in Minnesota and it discharges into the Gulf of Mexico approximately 100 miles downstream of New Orleans, Louisiana. The Susquehanna River runs through New York, Pennsylvania, and Maryland and is the home of Three Mile Island, the site of the United States' largest nuclear disaster. The Lehigh River is located in eastern Pennsylvania.

34. A: A major characteristic of ethnocentrism is the conviction that one's personal culture is the superior one.

35. C: Market economies are characterized by the production, distribution, and pricing of goods based on the law of supply and demand. Choice C best explains this concept. Choice A is incorrect because it describes a traditional economy. Choice B is incorrect, as it explains a command economy. The economy described in choice D is incorrect because it is a mixed economy.

36. B: Financial literacy is a term used to describe the knowledge and skills needed to effectively manage one's money. Budgeting to meet one's needs before spending money on unnecessary expenses is a key component of financial literacy. Entrepreneurship would best be explored through an activity in which students create their own business plans, making choice A incorrect. Scarcity explains the concept that resources are limited, while the human need for these resources is not. This concept would best be addressed with a simulation in which students must share limited resources to meet the needs of an entire group. This makes choice C incorrect. Goods and services are the products, activities, or assistance available for purchase in an economy. This is unrelated to the scenario, making choice D incorrect.

37. D: Political corruption was not an immediate effect of the rapid urban growth during this time. The accelerated growth of cities in America did soon result in services being unable to keep up with that growth. The results of this included deficiencies in clean water delivery and garbage collection, causing poor sanitation. That poor sanitation led to outbreaks of cholera and typhus, as well as typhoid fever epidemics. Police and fire fighting services could not keep up with the population increases, and were often inadequate. With people moving to the cities at such a fast rate, there were also deficits in housing and public transportation.

38. A: James Madison, John Jay, and Alexander Hamilton published *The Federalist* in the *Independent Journal* and other publications in New York. It was a response to the Anti-Federalists in New York, who were slow to ratify the Constitution because they feared it gave the central government too much authority.

39. C: According to George Murdock, it is the preponderance of property rights, rather than property disputes, which is a characteristic of all cultural practices. It may be that property disputes arise from the characteristic of property rights, but property disputes are not, in and of themselves, one of Murdock's cultural universals.

40. B: To determine the shortest route between Lima and Lisbon, Tracy should use an azimuthal projection with Lisbon at the center. An azimuthal projection depicts one hemisphere of the globe as a circle. A straight line drawn from the center of the map to any point represents the shortest possible distance between those two points. Tracy could obtain her objective, then, with an azimuthal projection in which either Lisbon or Lima were at the center. If the North Pole were at the center, the map would not include Lima because this city is in the Southern Hemisphere. A Robinson projection approximates the sizes and shapes of landmasses but does distort in some ways, particularly near the poles.

41. D: In the 1930s, severe drought in the Western US led to the "Dust Bowl." These dust storms, along with crop failures caused by a lack of rain, led farmers and their families to move to areas with more desirable weather conditions. As weather is a concept of geography and letters written by survivors of an event are considered primary sources, choice D is correct. Articles are usually considered secondary sources, making choice A incorrect. Though diary entries would be a primary source, the topic of industrialization would focus on the economy rather than geography. This makes choice B incorrect. While seeking refuge is a driving factor of migration, it is not related to geography, which makes choice C incorrect.

42. D: Assimilation is the process whereby members of one cultural group (voluntarily or involuntarily) give up their own traditions to adopt those of another culture, often one which is dominant. Acculturation (C) can mean gradual cultural modifications to a person or group through adopting some elements of another culture, the merging of cultures via long-term interaction, or a person's acquiring a society's culture from birth. Accommodation (A) as a general vocabulary word means providing a service (as in hospitality services) or adjustment (as in schools) to meet a need. As a term used by Piaget, it means forming a new schema (concept) or altering an existing one to include new input. Piaget also used assimilation (D) to mean fitting new input into an existing schema without changing the schema. Adaptation (B) in general vocabulary means adjustment; for Piaget, it meant the learning process of assimilation and accommodation combined.

43. B: *Marbury v. Madison* started with the election of Thomas Jefferson as third President of the United States. The lame-duck Congress responded by issuing a large number of judicial patents, which the incoming president and Secretary of State refused to deliver to their holders. Marbury, who was to receive a patent as

Justice of the Peace, sued to demand delivery. What makes this case important is the decision which declared the judiciary's ability to overturn legislation that conflicted with the Constitution. The case states:

"It is emphatically the province and duty of the judicial department to say what the law is. Those who apply the rule to particular cases must, of necessity, expound and interpret that rule. If two laws conflict with each other, the courts must decide on the operation of each.

"So if a law be in opposition to the Constitution; if both the law and the constitution apply to a particular case, so that the court must either decide that case conformably to the law, disregarding the Constitution; or conformably to the Constitution, disregarding the law; the court must determine which of these conflicting rules governs the case. This is of the very essence of judicial duty.

"If, then, the courts are to regard the Constitution, and the Constitution is superior to any ordinary act of the legislature, the Constitution, and not such ordinary act, must govern the case to which they both apply."

Later, the ruling states: "The judicial power of the United States is extended to all cases arising under the Constitution." It was in this way that the Supreme Court achieved its now traditional ability to strike down laws and to act as the final arbitrator of what is and is not allowed under the US Constitution.

44. C: Westward Expansion created conflict between settlers and Native Americans. This movement violated treaties between the groups, caused competition for resources, and increased tensions due to clashes in cultural beliefs. This is not reflected in this student's summary, as they explain that Native Americans helped families while moving. This is inaccurate, making a lesson focused on the relationship between the two groups necessary to correct this misconception. Choice A is incorrect because the student accurately describes the concept of Manifest Destiny and its role in expansion. Railroads and steam ships are often recognized for their roles in expansion. These quick transportation methods increased accessibility and promoted settlements near tracks and ports, making choice B incorrect. The student correctly stated that the economy improved with westward expansion, making choice D incorrect.

45. A: In geography, location—specifically, relative location—determines things like land prices based on the characteristics of an area, which are affected by nearby regions. An example of distance (B) is that land that is close to major highways is more expensive, while land far from main thoroughfares costs less. One example of pattern (C) in geography is that where rock folds form mountains (fold regions), the rivers accordingly form trellis patterns. Another example of pattern, in geographically oriented human behavior, is that settlements in mountainous areas form mainly spreading patterns. An example of interaction (D) in geography is when an industrial city needs raw materials from a rural village for production, and the village needs the city both as a market to buy its resources and for its industrial products: their mutual interdependence creates interaction between them.

46. A: Rome is well known for the development of aqueducts that were used to efficiently transport water throughout the city. They also developed public toilets connected to underground sewers. Answer B is incorrect because the spread of silk and the development of crop rotation are attributed to Ancient China, not Rome. Choice C is incorrect, as Ancient Egypt is responsible for major contributions to geometry. Ancient Egypt also used irrigation to redirect water from the Nile River to their crops. Choice D is incorrect because Ancient Greece is known for their philosophers and for having the first democratic government in the city of Athens.

47. C: In the United States, geographers typically define a hamlet as a settlement with fewer than 100 inhabitants. A hamlet may have a few businesses, but it is unlikely to have a post office or a government office. A village is slightly larger than a hamlet; it may contain about 500 to 1,000 people. A village is likely to have a grocery store. A town is larger than a village. It usually has about 2,500 inhabitants. A city is larger than a town.

48. A: Checks and balances were established to keep one branch of government from taking too much authority. When Johnson violated the Tenure of Office Act by replacing Secretary of War Edwin Stanton,

Johnson was impeached, but the final vote in the Senate trial came up one vote short of the number needed to convict him.

49. A: Social dialects typically emerge when a particular group is isolated from the rest of society due to class, race, age, or gender differences. Dialects are language variants, and those that result from geographic isolation are called regional dialects. Assimilation of immigrants includes language acquisition, and thus would not typically produce a new dialect. Jargon is simply the development of a specialized vocabulary, and although it may be unintelligible to outsiders, this is the result of a vocabulary gap, not dialect differences.

50. B: Under the Fifth Amendment to the U.S. Constitution, the government may not strip certain basic rights from citizens without following the law. In the language of the Fifth Amendment itself, a person shall not "be deprived of life, liberty, or property without due process of law." Of all the options, option B is the only one that accurately describes the concept of due process as understood in the Fifth Amendment. Because due process does not explicitly guarantee a trial by jury within a reasonable timeframe, nor equal protection under the law (concepts covered elsewhere in the Constitution), options A and C can be rejected. Option D can be rejected because the Constitution restricts the government's ability to take away certain rights without following the law, not without a "dire cause" (such as the threat of imminent attack).

51. A: Samuel Morse invented a code of dots and dashes that became known as Morse Code, and in 1844 the first message was transmitted over a telegraph line. Morse code played an important role in communications during the Civil War.

52. A: GDP (Gross Domestic Product) is restricted to value produced within borders, whereas GNP (Gross National Product) is focused on value produced by companies regardless of borders.

53. B: Keynesian economics is based on the notion that governments can effectively stimulate economic growth through taxation, adjustment of interest rates, and the funding of public projects. His economic philosophy contrasts sharply with the free-market philosophies of Smith, Hayek, and Friedman.

54. B: US industrialization was confined to the Northeast until after the Civil War because the Northeast had faster-running rivers than the South. The earliest American factories used horse-drawn machines. When waterpower was developed and proved superior, the Northeast's faster rivers were more suited to water-powered mills than the South's slower rivers. The war did not delay the development of waterpower. Waterpower was developed before the Civil War in the late 1790s. Steam power, a more efficient alternative to waterpower, was developed after the Civil War and eventually replaced waterpower. With steam-powered engines, industry could spread to the South, since steam engines did not depend on rapidly running water like water-powered engines. While British emigré Samuel Slater's first cotton mill using horse-drawn production did lose a lot of money, this was not a reason for industrial delay. In fact, Slater's Beverly Cotton Manufactory in Massachusetts, the first American cotton mill, in spite of its financial problems, was successful in both its volume of cotton production and in developing the water-powered technology that ultimately would succeed the horse-drawn method. Slater's second cotton mill in Pawtucket, Rhode Island, was water-powered. Industrial delay was not because milling technology had not yet been invented. Slater learned of new textile manufacturing techniques as a youth in England, and he brought this knowledge to America in 1789.

55. A: Perfect competition is a theoretical type of market more so than one actually found in real life. That's because it is the most efficient, operating where P = MR = MC.

56. A: Lyndon Johnson became president following the assassination of John F. Kennedy on November 22, 1963. The Great Society was a series of social programs implemented under the direction of Lyndon Johnson. The Great Society's goal was to eliminate poverty and racial injustice in America. The Great Society began with economic reforms including a tax cut and the creation of the Office of Economic Opportunity. From there, it grew to include the enacting of laws creating the Medicare and Medicaid systems to assist the elderly and poor with their health care costs, respectively. Educational and Housing reforms followed.

57. D: The taiga, or boreal forest, is found only in the North Temperate Zone between the tundra and the steppes. In addition to being the largest biome on land, it is characterized by coniferous forests and stretches across the northern regions of North America and Eurasia. Deserts, savannas, and tropical rainforests are all found at lower latitudes within the Torrid Zone.

58. C: The telegraph was a gigantic leap forward in the realm of communications. Before the telegraph, messages could take days, weeks, or months to reach their intended recipient, based upon the distance that they had to travel. The telegraph allowed people to send messages through use of electric signals transmitted over telegraph wires, allowing for instantaneous communications. The main drawbacks to the telegraph included the need to "translate" the message into and out of the appropriate telegraphic code and that the telegraph could only relay one message at a time. In contrast, the telephone allowed for spoken communication between people at different locations, increasing the efficiency and speed as the people on each end of the conversation could communicate multiple messages quickly and in one telephone conversation.

59. B: Temporary survival in harsh conditions does not typically require adaptations. This makes choice B the best statement to remove from the list. Developing insulated housing is a human adaptation to frigid conditions, making choice A appropriate for the student's list. Building homes on stilts in flood-prone areas demonstrates humans adapting housing to compensate for natural hazards. This makes choice C appropriate for the student's list. The use of irrigation systems demonstrates the adaptation of farming methods to grow additional crops on land that may not typically sustain plant growth, making it appropriate for the student's list.

60. D: A scale is used to illustrate the ratio of the distance on a map to the distance in reality. By measuring the distance between points and converting it according to the scale, students are applying an understanding of the concept of distance, which makes choice D correct. The activity in choice A would assess student understanding of direction, not distance. Choice B is incorrect, as this activity would assess a student's ability to understand and use the map key. Mapping coordinates and determining routes between would assess an understanding of absolute location and using reference maps, not distance. This makes choice C incorrect.

61. A: It is not true that the founding fathers specifically stated in the Constitution that the United States would be a democracy. The founding fathers wanted the new United States to be founded on principles of liberty and equality, but they did not specifically describe these principles with the term *democracy*. Thus, the Declaration of Independence, like the Constitution after it, did not stipulate a democracy, although both did state the principles of equality and freedom. The Constitution also provided for the election of the new government, and for protection of the rights of some, but not all, of the people. Notable exceptions at the time were black people and women. Only later were laws passed to protect their rights over the years.

62. B: The law of supply and demand explains that prices are determined by the relationship between supply, which is the quantity of a good available, and demand, which is the amount of people willing to buy the good. In this scenario, the weather has impacted the supply, but there have been no indicated changes in demand. This resulted in a higher price per apple. This makes choice B, supply and demand, the best fit for this scenario. Opportunity cost is the value of an unselected choice when deciding between two options. This would better portray a scenario in which an individual must choose between purchasing two items, making choice A incorrect. Competition occurs when more than one business sells the same goods and competes for profit. This would be illustrated by a scenario in which multiple businesses continually lowered prices of their similar goods to attract the most buyers. This makes choice C incorrect. Capital is the financial resources a business has access to that can be used to fund operations. This can be in the form of cash or assets. This would be better explained in a scenario in which a business liquidates assets to make a purchase to further expand the business, making choice D incorrect.

63. D: In the Dred Scott decision of 1857, the Court ruled that no slave or descendant of slaves could ever be a United States citizen. It also declared the Missouri Compromise of 1820 to be unconstitutional, clearing the way for the expansion of slavery in new American territories. This ruling pleased Southerners and outraged the North, further dividing the nation and setting the stage for war.

64. D: Choice D inaccurately describes a dictatorship. Dictatorships are characterized by a single leader, called a dictator, with the power to make all decisions related to governance. Dictators are typically supported by a small inner circle of advisers. The "individual king or queen that serves as the head of state" mentioned in this answer best describes a monarchy. Choice A accurately describes a democracy, as it is true that citizens play a role in decision making through participation in elections. Oligarchies are characterized by a small group of leaders serving as the decision-making body of a nation or government, making choice B an accurate description. Religious leaders hold the highest positions of power in theocracies, which makes choice C accurate.

65. B: Southern states provided raw materials that were manufactured into commodities in Northern states. Southerners resented paying taxes to Northern states for these products (textiles, furniture, etc.).

66. B: Statement 4 does not relate to climate-based adaptations. Changing the statement to reflect the types of crops that can grow in the region's weather would reflect a better understanding of climate-based adaptations, making choice B correct. Because statement 1 provides an accurate statement regarding hot climate adaptations, removing it is unnecessary. This makes choice A incorrect. While adding examples to statement 3 may improve the quality of the response, it does not correct the response in statement 4, making choice C incorrect. Choice D is incorrect because combining information would not improve the quality of the response or correct the misunderstanding in statement 4.

67. C: The Sugar Act of 1764 raised import duties on goods which were not of British origin, including sugar, while reducing the import tax on molasses. The Stamp Act of 1765 was a tax of paper and printed products, intended to help the British government recoup some of the costs of the French and Indian War. It was extremely unpopular with the colonists and was repealed in 1766. Lead was one of the goods taxed under the Townshend Acts, enacted in 1767, but it did not receive its own specific tax act. The Tea Act of 1773 was another unpopular tax and led to tea boycotts and was the catalyst for the Boston Tea Party.

68. B: The Arab districts in North African cities are known as medinas. These are typically old neighborhoods surrounding a large mosque. Many Arabs who made their living in trade eventually settled in countries like Algeria, Tunisia, and Libya. There, they influenced culture by bringing Sunni Islam to the indigenous people. A souk, meanwhile, is a market area surrounding the mosque in the medina. A wadi is a dry North African creek bed, which becomes an essential source of water during the sporadic rains. The location of wadis has been a crucial factor in the political and economic history of North Africa. A bazaar, finally, is an open-air market in the Middle East.

69. B: Formative assessments are those used throughout learning to monitor student understanding. These are meant to be short assignments that ensure students have grasped the newly introduced concepts before continuing to the next lesson in a unit of study. Examples of formative assessments include quizzes, exit tickets, homework, class discussion, and worksheets. Of the choices given, only the concept map falls into the category of a formative assessment. The assignment in choice B would be completed quickly by students and assess their understanding of the lesson's topic. Summative assessments are meant to assess cumulative learning from a unit or specified period, such as at the end of a grading term or the end of a school year. Tests, projects, and exams are all examples of summative assignments. The multiple-choice test, community service project, and learning portfolio featured in these answer choices all fall into the category of summative assessments, as they would assess the understanding of an overall unit of learning. This makes choices A, C, and D incorrect.

70. A: When the prices farmers receive for their crops decline in a developing country, this typically results in increased urbanization. When crop prices decline, farmers can no longer make a living from their land. As a result, they often choose to migrate to cities in search of low-wage employment in the manufacturing or service sectors.

71. D: Because the Puritans took on a Reformed theology, they were in this sense Calvinists. However, many Puritans endorsed radical views that criticized such Calvinists as John (Jean) Calvin and Huldrych (Ulrich) Zwingli in Switzerland. Not only were Puritans critical of Calvinists despite their mutual Reformed approaches, reciprocally many Calvinists were opposed to the Puritans as well. The Puritan movement changed less in American colonies than in England during the 1660s. Following the Restoration (1660) and the Uniformity Act (1662) in England, nearly all of the Puritan clergy objected and left the Church of England, thereby creating a dramatic change in the movement in that country. Nevertheless, in America, the Puritans who had emigrated from England continued their original Puritan traditions for a longer time, as they had neither the same Anglican Church as in England nor the legislation restoring earlier church status against which the English Puritans had reacted.

72. B: The Seven Years' War was a global military conflict. In the Americas, the conflict was largely between Western European countries, particularly Great Britain and France.

73. C: Native American and Asian cultures tend to be collectivist; i.e., they value interdependence among people, relationships, and social interactions. Latin American and African cultures also are more likely to embrace collectivism, focusing on the common good more than individual achievement; thus (A) is incorrect. Individualism, however, is *more* common in Canadian and Australian cultures, not less; so (B) is incorrect. European and North American cultures also favor individual expression, self-determination, independence, uniqueness, and self-actualization; hence they are typically considered more individualistic cultures, not more collectivist, so (D) is incorrect.

74. C: If a country's currency increases in value, foreigners will have to give up more of their own currency to get the original country's currency in order to buy the original country's goods and services. This will cause a drop in exports. At the same time, it will be less expensive for people in the original country to exchange their currency for foreign currencies, causing the price of imported goods to drop and the total value of imports to rise.

75. C: The increasing popularity of Thai food in the United States is an example of cultural convergence, or the intersection of traits or customs from two distinct cultures. Thailand's cuisine has been introduced to the United States, but it has undergone subtle changes as a result of the desires and practices of the American consumer. The phenomenon of cultural convergence is credited with much of the innovation in any society. Cultural divergence, on the other hand, is the practice of shielding one culture from the influence of another. France, for instance, seeks to limit the influence of American culture on its citizens. Assimilation is the process by which a minority group gradually adopts the culture of the majority group. For example, many Native Americans assimilated into the European-style culture of the early American settlers. Acculturation is the process of obtaining the practices and ideas of a culture. A child undergoes acculturation, wherein he or she learns to think and act appropriately for his or her setting.

76. B: While all the entrepreneurs listed are also philanthropic donors and have at times been considered one of the richest men in the world, the mention of "computer industry" will be a clue to most students with basic social studies/current events knowledge that Bill Gates is the correct answer.

77. C: While wounds from war most certainly killed more than a few, European disease laid waste to vast swaths of Native American people who had no immunity to the foreign diseases which the Europeans carried. The forced marches took place in the mid-19th century under Andrew Jackson's presidency and are thus removed from the time frame in question.

78. C: Purchasing a DVD is a discretionary expense because it is based on personal desire rather than need. In other words, it is an expense made at the discretion of the consumer. Discretionary expenses are those over which a consumer has the most control. A comprehensive budget must include discretionary expenses as well as fixed and variable expenses. Fixed expenses, such as rent, are the same every month. Variable expenses, including groceries, school supplies, and heating oil, are always present but vary in amount over the course of a year.

79. B: The Virginia Company of London was based in London, not Massachusetts. It had a charter to colonize American land between the Hudson and Cape Fear rivers. The other Virginia Company was the Virginia Company of Plymouth, which was based in the American colony of Plymouth, Massachusetts. It had a charter to colonize North America between the Potomac River and the northern boundary of Maine. Both Virginia Companies were joint-stock companies, which had often been used by England for trading with other countries.

80. B: "No taxation without representation" was a phrase used by colonists to convey the idea that colonies should not be taxed by Britain without having proper representation in the British government. This lack of representation was a factor that contributed to colonial America's desire to be fully independent. The phrase "let them eat cake" is attributed to Marie Antoinette. She is believed to have said this during the French Revolution in response to being told poor individuals had no bread to eat. This makes choice A incorrect. "I came, I saw, I conquered" is attributed to Julius Caesar. It is believed he said this in response to his victory in a battle, making choice C incorrect. Martin Luther King, Jr. stated "I have a dream" during his 1963 speech in Washington, DC, making choice D incorrect.

81. C: Intrastate trade is solely within a state, so the state has jurisdiction over it. Taxation is a right granted to both federal and state authorities. Declaring war is a national decision. Patents and copyrights apply to goods made and/or sold throughout the country; therefore, they are a federal responsibility.

82. D: Human geography is the study of the relationship between humans and their environments. The learning target in choice D does not contain a human influence or impact, making it incorrect. As some landforms are difficult to navigate, they often establish borders that influence human behaviors. Choice A is incorrect because it addresses this concept of human geography. Urbanization, the movement from rural to urban areas, is a key concept of human geography. Choice B is incorrect because it addresses how this impacts the economy. Choice C is incorrect because human migration affected by climate is another key concept in human geography.

83. C: About 30 percent of the surface of the Earth is covered by land.

84. C: Using primary and secondary sources together in instruction provides students with multiple perspectives of an event and helps develop a deeper overall understanding. While students could compare and contrast the documents, this would not be an advantage to using both. This makes choice A incorrect. Choice B is incorrect because a documentary is not a primary source. The quality of sources and the way they are used is more important than the quantity of sources, which makes choice D incorrect.

85. D: The concept of chronology refers to ordering events in time sequence. Therefore, a timeline of the American Revolution would require a firm understanding of the events in chronological order. Presenting all wars with US involvement in the order in which they happened would also reflect an understanding of chronological concepts. Speaking about the beginning, middle, and end of a time period requires events to be ordered chronologically. A mock diary entry would assess a student's understanding of events and the impact they had on those involved, not chronological information. This assignment does not inherently require the ability to understand chronological concepts, which makes choice D correct.

86. D: A graphic organizer that compares diverse government systems would best support learning during a lesson on various forms of government. This tool would provide students with information on multiple forms of government in one document. Though a monarchy is one form of government, a compilation of coronation videos would not support student learning in this scenario nor provide adequate detail about the various forms of government. This makes choice A incorrect. A mock trial would be more useful in a lesson on the judicial system or the Rule of Law, making choice B incorrect. An infographic on a country's economy before and after authoritarian rule would investigate one form of government. Because the lesson is on various forms of government, choice C is incorrect.

87. B: Explaining the series of events that led to WWI and how they impacted one another would require a student to understand the chronology of the events. This makes choice B the best answer. Writing a mock diary entry of a Colonial American child or parent would assess a student's understanding of the events and conditions of that time; however, there would not be events to place in order in a single diary entry. This makes choice A incorrect. Constructing a diorama would not assess an understanding of time. Dioramas best assess an understanding of individual events, making choice C incorrect. Recreating a trade route map does not require an understanding of the order of events. This makes choice D incorrect.

88. D: The Protestant work ethic is considered by many historians to have contributed to the Industrial Revolution. In Britain, where industrialization started, financial stability encouraged investment in industry, and the eventual dominance of Protestantism is believed to have contributed to a class of entrepreneurs who believed in education, technological progress, and hard work. The other choices are considered effects of industrialization. Mass production enabled the privately owned, for-profit enterprises that characterize capitalist economic systems. Socialism developed as a criticism of capitalism; Karl Marx argued that capitalism polarized societies into owners versus workers. Marx also viewed capitalism as a necessary precursor to socialism within the logical progression of economies. Romanticism also developed in reaction against mechanization and involved using art and literature to contrast nature with the dark side of scientific progress.

89. A: The 10th Amendment establishes that any power not given to the federal government in the Constitution belongs to the states or the people. The federal and local governments share many responsibilities.

90. C: The Mason-Dixon Line was the manifestation of a border dispute between the British colonies of Pennsylvania, Maryland, and Delaware. It effectively separated, or illustrated, a cultural divide between North and South before the Civil War.

91. A: For a timeline of the late 18th century, students would list and explain topics pertinent to the formation of the US government. This timeline would feature the following events and documents: The Declaration of Independence, The Articles of Confederation, The Constitutional Convention, and The Bill of Rights. This makes choice A the best assignment for determining an understanding of the development of the US government. A mock debate between the colonies and the British government would not best evaluate an understanding of the formation of the US government, as it would mainly focus on differing perspectives between the colonies and the British, not on the development of the US government. This makes choice B incorrect. A map would best check for an understanding of ownership of land and territories. This makes choice C incorrect. While The Declaration of Independence is a key part of the formation of the US government, it does not encompass the development of the government as a whole. Because this assignment lacks depth, choice D would not best assess understanding.

92. B: The humanistic approach to understanding human behavior is driven by the idea that a person has a need to reach self-actualization, which includes the proclivity to seek after the highest possible growth and development that is attainable. In this approach, each individual has his or her own distinctive needs, desires, talents, skills, etc. According to the humanistic approach, a person who is well adjusted must be free to express his or her own uniqueness.

93. A: Absolute location refers to the exact geographical location of a place or thing using latitude and longitude. Choice A provides students with the coordinates and has them apply this understanding to determine what is found at these points. This makes it the most appropriate activity to assess an understanding of absolute location. Choice B would assess an understanding of US geography and landforms, making it incorrect. Choice C asks students to describe the location of a town based on its relation to the capital. This is assessing an understanding of relative location, making it incorrect. Choice D could be used to assess cardinal direction, as it would require students to understand north, south, east, and west.

94. A: In this scenario, the teacher is checking students' prior understanding of the difference between civic duties and rights before instruction begins. This is a preassessment used to inform instruction and gauge existing knowledge. Summative assessments are administered after a unit of learning to evaluate overall understanding of the content, making choice B incorrect. Formative assessments occur during instruction and are used to monitor student learning and adjust teaching as needed, making choice C incorrect. Norm-referenced assessments are standardized assessments used to compare student performance to that of other students, often for ranking or comparison purposes, making choice D incorrect.

95. C: Brazil is the 10th largest producer of oil in the world and the largest in South America. Venezuela is the second largest producer of oil in South America and has the world's largest oil reserves. Bolivia and Guatemala produce oil but are not major producers in Latin America. Uruguay has no significant petroleum production.

96. A: One example of the multiplier effect of large cities would be if the presence of specialized equipment for an industry attracted even more business. Large cities tend to grow even larger for a number of reasons: they have more skilled workers, they have greater concentrations of specialized equipment, and they have already-functioning markets. These factors all make it easier for a business to begin operations in a large city than elsewhere. Thus, the populations and economic productivity of large cities tend to grow quickly. Some governments have sought to mitigate this trend by clustering groups of similar industries in smaller cities.

97. A: Moldova is not one of the Baltic states. Latvia, Lithuania, and Estonia all border the Baltic Sea, which has enabled them to become major traders. Unfortunately, the smallness and advantageous locations of these nations has made them attractive to invaders. The Soviet Union took over these lands in 1939, and it was not until 1991 that they regained independence. All three of these nations are now struggling to establish themselves as viable economic actors.

98. C: A caste system is a system wherein individuals' social, economic, and political destinies are determined by group membership within the caste. Systems fitting this description have been in place throughout the world and directly impact each individual's economic destiny by circumscribing upward economic and social mobility regardless of ability. Class and caste are distinct in the sense that class is assigned based upon an individual's life path, while caste membership is assigned at birth and is essentially immutable. Also, caste systems have well-defined functions for each group, whereas class distinctions are based solely on wealth (as opposed to social function).

99. A: The president of the United States serves as commander-in-chief, but the writers of the Constitution, who feared how authority was used by monarchs, limited the president's power in this role. The president cannot declare war or make rules governing the military, although presidents have traditionally authorized the use of force without war being declared.

100. A: The federal government has three branches: executive, including the president, the vice president, and the president's cabinet; legislative, including the House of Representatives and the Senate; and judicial, including the Supreme Court and the court system.

Online Resources

Due to our efforts to try to keep this book to a manageable length, we've created a link that will give you access to all of your online resources:

mometrix.com/resources719/texessocst4-8

It's Your Moment, Let's Celebrate It!

Share your story @mometrixtestpreparation